Adobe

User Guide

W9-CPV-023

Adobe® PageMaker® 6.5 version

CONTENTS

INTRODUCTION

Welcome to the Adobe® PageMaker® program—powerful and versatile page layout software. Creative professionals use PageMaker for its exceptional typographic controls, exacting page design capabilities (including layers, frames, and multiple master pages), and numerous customization options.

PageMaker's extensive importing and linking capabilities let you incorporate text, graphics, spreadsheets, charts, and movie frames from most popular programs. Linking makes it easy to track file changes and update imported files.

PageMaker incorporates menu plug-ins that extend the program's features and capabilities. For example, you can apply Adobe Photoshop-compatible plug-in filters directly within PageMaker.

You can also publish files electronically using two improved export features: one that creates Portable Document Format (PDF) files that can be viewed, shared, and printed across any platform; and one that converts pages to the hypertext markup language standard (HTML) used on the Internet. The HTML export feature even preserves multi-column page layouts. Both PDF and HMTL export capabilities are enhanced by the new Hyperlinks palette, which lets you quickly create and manage hyperlinks, or jumps from text and graphics to resources on the Internet (including other text or graphics in the exported file).

PageMaker 6.5 supports advanced color printing technologies, including high-fidelity inks (which you can edit directly in PageMaker), color management support, automatic trapping, built-in imposition tools, and complete separation capabilities for text and graphics.

ABOUT THIS MANUAL

Before using this user guide, you'll need to install the program following the instructions given in the *Adobe PageMaker 6.5 Getting Started* book. This book also provides information on new features in PageMaker 6.5, allocating memory, working efficiently, network installation, and converting publications from earlier versions of PageMaker into PageMaker 6.5.

The *Adobe PageMaker 6.5 User Guide* provides detailed information about PageMaker features and commands, as well as a hands-on tutorial to give you some familiarity with PageMaker features. This book is designed to be a reference tool in your everyday work with PageMaker.

Chapter 1 reviews fundamental techniques you'll use in your work with PageMaker, as well as an orientation to the program's interface.

Chapter 2 is a hands-on tutorial that introduces you to the basic features used to create a letterhead and brochure.

Chapter 3 covers the steps necessary to set up a PageMaker publication, from specifying basic document attributes, such as size and number of pages, to using master pages and layout grids.

Chapter 4 explains how to add, create, and import text; use story editor for word-processing tasks; and create and apply paragraph styles.

Chapter 5 describes features and techniques you can use to produce professional-quality type in your publication.

Chapter 6 describes how to create and edit frames and graphics in PageMaker, manipulate objects with the Control palette, and use features such as layers. It also covers techniques related specifically to imported images, such as varying lightness and contrast, and explains how to use Adobe Photoshop-compatible plug-ins to apply effects.

Chapter 7 discusses features specific to long documents, such as indexing, generating a table of contents, and automatic pagination.

Chapter 8 describes how to define, apply, and trap color in a PageMaker publication.

Chapter 9 explains how to use the color management features in PageMaker 6.5.

Chapter 10 describes how to create and edit full-color tables using Adobe Table 3.0—a stand-alone utility included in PageMaker 6.5.

Chapter 11 discusses PageMaker's versatile importing, linking, and exporting capabilities, which make it a powerful integration tool for all types of publications.

Chapter 12 covers the steps necessary to print a file from PageMaker, including proofs and color separations.

Chapter 13 is an overview of electronic delivery capabilities provided directly from PageMaker using the new Hyperlinks palette feature, and two improved features: Export Adobe PDF and Export HTML.

Chapter 14 explains how to use PageMaker's Scripts palette to automate various tasks, such as setting up pages or importing a standard set of elements.

Appendix A contains tables that list the key combinations you can use to type special characters.

Appendix B explains how to troubleshoot if a font used in the active publication is missing from your system.

Appendix C describes procedures and tips for transferring publications from Windows to Macintosh and vice versa.

Appendix D offers procedures and guidelines for using PageMaker Tags to import and export character- and paragraph-level attributes in text files.

Appendix E provides troubleshooting tips.

BASIC CONCEPTS

Chapter 1: Basic Concepts

This chapter describes fundamental techniques you need to know in order to work with PageMaker once it is installed: tasks like how to open, name, save, and close a publication. It also provides an orientation to the PageMaker interface, so you can adjust the view of a page, select objects, move from page to page, use multiple windows, and so on.

CREATING AND OPENING PUBLICATIONS

Once you start PageMaker, you can either create a new publication from scratch, or open an existing PageMaker publication. You can also begin a new publication based on an existing design by opening a template. See "Starting a Publication From a Template" on page 23 for more information.

Using the Document Setup dialog box • You can enter custom settings in the Document Setup dialog box or click OK to begin laying out your publication using the default, or standard, settings that come with PageMaker.

A When Double-sided is selected, side margins are labelled Inside and Outside. Otherwise, side margins become Left and Right.

B If you know how many pages the publication will have, you can create them now. If you don't know, you can easily add and remove pages later.

C Select this option when you change the page settings of an existing layout and want PageMaker to automatically move and scale text and graphic objects.

D Select this option only if the publication is part of a larger book (a linked set of publications) but will not be numbered sequentially. For example, you may want appendixes numbered separately from the other chapters in a book.

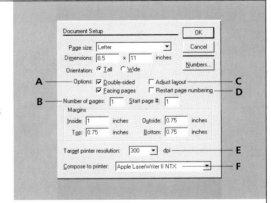

E Select or enter the number of dots per inch (dpi) of your final output device.

F In Windows, specify the printer you will use to print the final version of your publication. Do this as you start your publication, so that PageMaker displays the correct fonts and page sizes available for your printer.

Creating a publication from scratch

When creating a publication from scratch, you make basic design decisions in the Document Setup dialog box, which opens automatically when you choose File > New. For example, you can specify page size, whether the pages are printed on one or both sides (double- or single-sided), and the placement of page margins.

In PageMaker for Windows, you can also specify the printer you will use to print the final version of the publication. See "Setting Print-Related Document Setup Options" on page 66 for more information.

The number of publications you can have open at once is limited by the amount of memory available.

To start a publication from scratch:

1 Start PageMaker, and choose File > New.

2 Specify options in the Document Setup dialog box.

You specify page layout details—number of text columns, page-numbering scheme, and the basic design of the publication—in the publication itself. For more information, see "Setting Up Pages" on page 65.

Opening an existing publication

Use the File > Open command to open the original version or a copy of a PageMaker 6.5 publica-tion or template. PageMaker keeps track of the last eight publications you opened and saved, and lists these when you choose File > Recent Publications.

To open PageMaker 4.0-6.01 publications, you use either the File > Open command (to open one file at a time) or the Utilities > Plug-ins > Publication Converter command (to locate and open all or some of the PageMaker 4.0-6.01 publications on your system). With File > Open, PageMaker 4.0-6.01 files are converted into untitled PageMaker 6.5 publications, and the original publication is preserved. With Utilities > Plug-ins > Publication Converter, you have the option of replacing the earlier files with the converted versions in order to save disk space.

Note: You cannot convert 4.0-6.01 publications at the same time as you translate them from one platform to another. For example, to open a Macintosh PageMaker 5.0 file with the Windows version of PageMaker 6.5, you must open the publication using Windows PageMaker version 5.0, and then convert it to a Windows PageMaker 6.5 file.

To open a publication:

1 Choose File > Open.

2 Select the publication you want to open.

3 Select Original or a Copy.

```
Open:
  ○ Original
  ● Copy
```

When you select a template or a PageMaker 4.0-6.01 publication, PageMaker automatically selects Copy. To open the original of a template instead, click Original. (The Original option is not available for a PageMaker 4.0-6.01 publication.)

4 Click OK.

If you are opening a publication that has links to external text or graphics files, you will see a Cannot Find dialog box if a file cannot be located. Use this dialog box to locate the file or to tell PageMaker to ignore the link. See Chapter 11, "Importing, Linking, and Exporting," for more information.

After you select a publication to open, the fonts used in the publication are matched with those available in your computer. If a font used in the selected publication isn't available, PageMaker displays the PANOSE Font Matching dialog box to allow you to select available fonts to substitute for the missing fonts. For more information about substituting fonts, refer to Appendix B, "Font Substitution."

To quickly open a recently-saved publication:

Choose File > Recent Publications, and select the publication you want to open from the Recent Publications menu.

If you want to open a copy of a recently-saved publication, hold down Option (Macintosh) or Shift (Windows) as you choose File > Recent Publications and select the publication from the Recent Publications menu.

To open PageMaker 4.0-6.01 publications with the Publication Converter plug-in:

1 Close all open publications.

2 Choose Utilities > Plug-ins > Publication Converter.

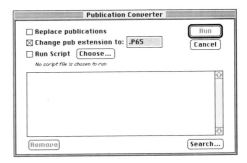

3 Specify conversion options as follows:

• Select the Replace Publications option only if you want to overwrite the file you are converting with the converted publication. We recommend you leave this option deselected, so that you open an untitled copy of the original file; you then have the original file available as a backup.

• Select the Change Publication Extension To option if you want to change the file names of converted publications, and then type in the extension you want to add to the filename.

• Select Run Script if you want to process the converted publications with a PageMaker script. Select the script by clicking Browse and double-clicking the script file stored on your hard drive.

4 Click Search in the Publication Converter dialog box.

5 Specify the kind of files you want to open, and the drive or mounted volume on which they are stored, and then click Search.

PageMaker then lists the files available for converting on the specified drive or volume. To remove a file from the list, select the file name in the list box, and click Remove.

6 Click Run to convert each file listed in the dialog box.

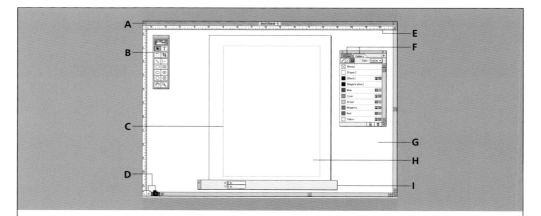

The default PageMaker window

A The publication window contains a single publication.

B The toolbox displays tools you can select to create or edit objects and view a publication.

C Margins appear as dotted or pink lines.

D Page icons show the master pages (L for left, and R for Right) and the regular pages in the publication. The open page is highlighted. Scroll arrows appear if there are more page icons to view than can be displayed at one time.

E Rulers help you align objects on the page.

F The Colors and Styles palettes are used to add, delete, and edit colors and styles.

G The pasteboard stores items for later use. Items on the pasteboard are visible from any page but do not print.

H The publication page is at the center of the pasteboard.

I The Control palette lets you make precise changes to text and graphics without switching to the toolbox or choosing menu commands.

WORKING IN THE PAGEMAKER WINDOW

When you create a publication, PageMaker opens a publication window, which contains an empty page centered on the pasteboard. The page and pasteboard, where you lay out text and graphics, are similar to the work space used in traditional paste-up.

USING THE TOOLBOX

The icons in the toolbox represent the tools you use in PageMaker. To select a tool, click it. If the toolbox restricts your view of your work, drag its title bar to move it or choose Window > Hide Tools to close the toolbox.

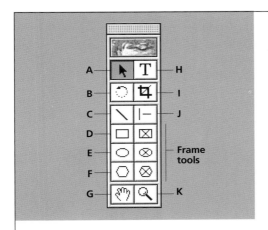

The toolbox

A Use the pointer tool to select, move, and resize text objects and graphics.

B Use the rotating tool to select and rotate objects.

C Use the line tool to draw straight lines in any direction.

D Use the rectangle tool to draw squares and rectangles. Use the rectangle frame tool to create a rectangular placeholder for text and graphics.

E Use the ellipse tool to draw circles and ellipses. Use the ellipse frame tool to create a circular or oval placeholder for text and graphics.

F Use the polygon tool to draw polygons. Use the polygon frame tool to create a polygonal place-holder for text and graphics.

G Use the hand tool to scroll the page, or to pre-view and test hyperlinks.

H Use the text tool to type, select, and edit text.

I Use the cropping tool to trim imported graphics.

J Use the constrained line tool to draw vertical or horizontal lines

K Use the zoom tool to magnify or reduce an area of the page.

WORKING WITH PALETTES

Adobe PageMaker includes several palettes: the Colors palette, the Control palette, the Hyperlinks palette, the Layers palette, the Master Pages palette, the Styles palette, and the Tools palette. Additionally, two plug-in palettes—the Scripts palette and the Library palette—are installed automatically and are listed separately on the Window menu.

The following techniques can help you save time when you are working with palettes:

• Choose the appropriate Show or Hide command from the Window menu to control the display of the palette or group of palettes. (Use the Window > Plug-in Palettes command to show or hide palettes for installed plug-ins.)

You can open and close most palettes by using keyboard shortcuts. You can also show or hide all palettes by pressing the Tab key (make sure an insertion point is not selected in your text).

• To hide all palettes except for the Tools palette, press Shift + Tab.

• To rearrange, separate, or reorganize palettes, drag a palette's tab. You can drag a palette outside of an existing group to create a separate palette or drag it over an existing group to add the

palette to that group. (The Control palette, Library palette, Scripts palette and Tools palette cannot be grouped with other palettes.) By default the Colors and Styles palettes are grouped together so that they appear as panels within a larger palette; the Layers and Master Pages palettes are also grouped together in this way.

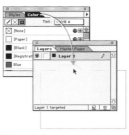

Drag a palette over an existing group…   *…to add the palette to that group.*

Drag a palette tab outside group…   *…to create a separate palette.*

• Click a palette's tab to make it appear at the front of the group.

• Drag the palette to a convenient place on your desktop and leave it open while you work.

• To move an entire palette group, drag its title bar.

• To display a palette's menu commands, click the triangle in the upper right corner of the palette.

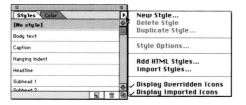

• To change the height or width of a palette, drag the size box at the lower right corner of the palette.

• To increase your work space, click the zoom box in the far right corner of the title bar to collapse the palette group (or, to preserve the width of a palette when you collapse it, double-click a palette's tab). (If you resized the palette, the first click of the zoom box returns the group to the default size and the second click collapses it.) Submenus are still available when palettes are collapsed.

• To hide a palette group, choose the appropriate Hide command from the Window menu or click the group's close box. Choosing a Hide command for any palette in a group hides the entire group.

Each palette is described later in this manual.

VIEWING PAGES

PageMaker lets you view your pages at several preset magnifications. Alternatively, you can use the zoom tool to specify an area of the page to view, and increase or decrease its magnification at the same time. To change the part of the page or pasteboard that displays at the current view or magnification level, you can scroll within the window using the scroll bars or using the hand tool.

Choosing preset page views

Use commands on the View menu to display the page or pasteboard at preset views. A page retains its view until you change the view again.

View settings serve various purposes. Use Fit in Window when you need to check the overall composition of a page or a two-page spread; use Actual Size to see text and graphics as they will appear when printed; and choose View > Zoom To > 200% Size or 400% Size when precision is imperative. To find or view objects on the pasteboard, use Entire Pasteboard.

The following techniques provide useful shortcuts:

• To toggle between Fit in Window and Actual Size, press Command + Option and click (Macintosh) or press Shift and press the right mouse button (Windows). The place you click becomes centered in the publication window. To toggle between Actual Size and 200% Size, press Command + Option + Shift and click (Macintosh only).

• Windows only: To quickly display a menu listing preset page view choices, click the right mouse button on an empty part of the page.

You can then choose a view from the menu. The place on the page where you click becomes centered in the publication window at the view you select.

• To set all pages in the active publication to the same view, press Option (Macintosh) or Alt (Windows) as you choose the view you want from the View menu or View > Zoom To submenu.

• To move to the next greater or lesser preset view of a page, choose View > Zoom In or View > Zoom Out.

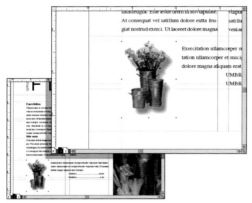

Choosing a preset view option with an object selected centers the object in the publication window at that view.

Check the overall composition in Fit in Window, or zoom in to 200% view or greater for detail work.

Magnifying and reducing with the zoom tool

The zoom tool lets you magnify or reduce the display of any area in your publication. You can also double-click the tool to jump to Actual Size, or press Option (Macintosh) or Alt (Windows) as you double-click the tool to go to Fit in Window view.

To magnify or reduce with the zoom tool:

1 Select the zoom tool.

The pointer becomes a magnifying glass with a plus sign in its center, indicating that the zoom tool will magnify your view of the image. (The magnifying glass shows a minus sign in its center when in reduction mode.) To toggle between magnification and reduction, press the Option key (Macintosh) or the Ctrl key (Windows).

2 Position the magnifying glass at the center of the area you want to magnify or reduce, and then click to zoom in or out.

 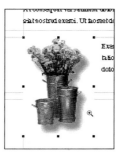

Continue clicking until the publication is at the magnification level you want. When the publication has reached its maximum magnification or reduction level, the center of the magnifying glass appears blank.

To magnify part of a page by dragging:

1 Select the zoom tool.

2 Drag to draw a marquee around the area you want to magnify.

To zoom in or out while using another tool:

1 Press Command + Spacebar (Macintosh) or Ctrl + Spacebar (Windows) to zoom in. Press Command + Option + Spacebar (Macintosh) or Ctrl + Alt + Spacebar (Windows) to zoom out.

2 Click to zoom in or out, or drag to select an area you want to zoom in on.

Scrolling within a window

You can use the scroll bars along the bottom and right sides of the active window to control what displays in the publication window. You can show or hide the scroll bars at any time.

In addition, PageMaker lets you reposition the page quickly by dragging the mouse. This technique works in layout view only.

To display or hide the scroll bars:

Choose View > Show/Hide Scroll Bars.

To reposition the page by dragging:

1 Do one of the following:

• Press Option (Macintosh) or Alt (Windows).

• Select the hand tool in the toolbox.

2 Drag to display the part of the page or pasteboard you want to view.

If you press Option or Alt in step 1, the hand icon changes back to the tool you were using before you dragged the page.

Drag with the hand tool . . .   to reposition a page.

WORKING WITH TEXT AND GRAPHICS

In PageMaker, graphics that you draw or import and text (which can be contained either in text blocks or in text frames), are called objects. An object can be on a page or on the pasteboard. The following sections describe the basic ways you work with text and graphics.

Selecting objects

You use the pointer tool to select objects. You can select a single object, or you can select multiple objects and modify them all at once. When objects overlap, you can select them through the stack of objects.

Typing text

This section provides a basic understanding of how PageMaker handles text. For complete information on working with text, see Chapter 4, "Text Formatting and Word Processing."

You can type text directly in PageMaker or import it from another program. Once text is in PageMaker, you can work with it in two ways: by editing and formatting characters and paragraphs, and by manipulating text objects on the page.

Note: *Text can occupy either a text frame or a text block. For the purposes of this overview, these two kinds of text objects work the same. See "Comparing Text Frames and Text Blocks" on page 108 for more information.*

The options available when you work with text depend on the tool you use. When you use the text tool, you can type, edit, and format text. When you use the pointer tool, you can manipulate a text block as an object—for example, select, move, and resize it.

You insert text in PageMaker like you would in a word-processing program: click the insertion point where you want to begin, and then type. When you type text, it may appear as greeked text (which displays as gray bars rather than individual characters), depending on the size of the text and the view magnification of your page.

To type text:

1 Select the text tool from the toolbox.

The text tool turns into an I-beam ($\mathcal{I}$) when you move it onto the page.

2 Click the I-beam where you want to insert text on the page, and then begin typing.

Selecting objects • Use the following techniques to select objects. To select all objects on the current page or spread, choose Edit > Select All. Click an empty part of the page or choose Edit > Deselect All to deselect.

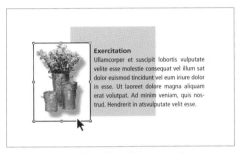

To select a single object, click the object with the pointer tool.

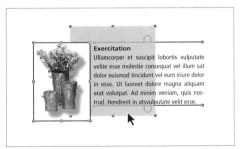

To add objects to a selection, hold down Shift as you click other objects.

To select several objects at once, drag the pointer tool around multiple objects. Be sure to include each object's bounding box (as indicated by its selection handles) within the selection area, not just the visible portion of the object.

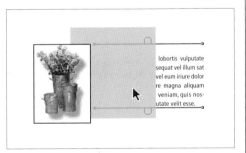

To select an object underneath another object on the same layer, press Command (Macintosh) or Ctrl (Windows) and click the object you want to select. Each time you click, PageMaker selects an object one level deeper in the stack of objects.

TIP: IN LAYOUT VIEW, YOU CAN TRIPLE-CLICK ON A TEXT OBJECT WITH THE POINTER TOOL TO OPEN STORY EDITOR.

If you click outside of an existing text object, you create a new text block automatically.

Text you create becomes part of a PageMaker story. A story is a collection of text that PageMaker recognizes as a single unit for editing purposes. A story can comprise numerous text objects, or it can be just one text object. When a story is comprised of more than one text object, the text is threaded between them.

3 To view the boundaries of the text block you just created, select the pointer tool and click anywhere in the text.

Understanding text objects

All text in PageMaker is contained either in text blocks or in text frames. When you click text with the pointer tool, the text object's border is displayed. A text object, like a graphic, is an object that you can move, resize and otherwise manipulate. You can connect a text object to other text objects or separate it from other text objects while keeping the flow of text (the story) intact from text object to text object.

For more information, see "Adjusting Text Objects" on page 114.

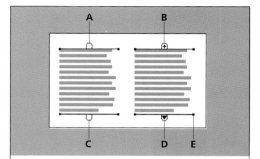

Identifying a text object • The borders of a text object are defined across the top and bottom by lines with loops, called windowshade handles, and by solid square handles at the four corners of the text block. (A text frame has a handle on each side of the object, as well as at the corners, and a non-printing cyan border.)

A An empty windowshade handle at the top of a text object indicates the beginning of a story.

B A plus sign in the windowshade handle indicates that text from the same story is contained in another text object.

C An empty windowshade handle at the bottom of a text object indicates the end of a story.

D A down arrow in the windowshade handle indicates that there is more text to be placed onto the page.

E A handle indicates the point where you drag to resize a text object.

Selecting text with the text tool

To edit or format text, you must first select the range of characters you want to affect. To deselect text, click another insertion point, or select any tool in the toolbox.

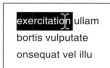

Double-click to select a word.

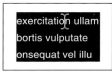

Triple-click to select an entire paragraph.

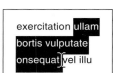

Drag the I-beam to select a range of text.

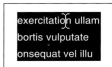

Click in a text block and choose Edit > Select All to select all the text in that story.

Editing text

You can edit text in PageMaker in two ways: on the page in layout view, or in story editor, PageMaker's built-in word processor. You switch between the two with the Edit Story and Edit Layout commands.

In layout view, you select and edit text with the text tool. This is useful when you need to see how the revisions look on the page, or when you are making only a few changes to the text.

In story editor, you work only on the text, not the layout, so revising text is fast and easy. Working in story editor is a convenient way to type or edit lengthy blocks of text. You can apply formatting to text in story editor, but you won't see most of the formatting until you return to layout view. You can also use story editor to find and change text.

You can edit text in story editor or in layout view.

To work in story editor:

1 Click in a story with the text tool or the pointer tool.

2 Choose Edit > Edit Story.

3 When you are finished working in the story editor, choose Edit > Edit Layout to return to layout view.

For more information on editing text and using story editor, see Chapter 4, "Text Formatting and Word Processing."

MOVING BETWEEN PAGES

You can easily move from one page to another when you are working on a publication with multiple pages. You can go directly to a specific page or thumb through pages in sequential order. You can also view master pages.

To move between publication pages:

Use the technique that suits your needs:

• Click a page icon along the bottom of the layout window. (Click the left or right arrows to view lower- or higher-numbered page icons.)

• Choose Layout > Go to Page, and type the page number you want.

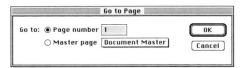

• To go to the previous page, press the Page Up key; to go to the next page, press the Page Down key

• To go to the first page, press the Home key; to go to the final page, press the End key.

• To move sequentially through the publication as in a slide show, press Shift and choose Layout > Go to Page. To stop the slide show, click the mouse, or press any key on the keyboard.

For information on viewing master pages, see "Displaying Master Pages and Master Page Items" on page 75.

ADDING AND DELETING PAGES

You can add or delete pages as follows:

• If you choose File > Document Setup to alter the number of pages, PageMaker adds or deletes pages from the end of the publication

Shortcut: *To add a page to the end of the publication, press Command + Option + Shift + G (Macintosh) or Ctrl + Alt + Shift + G (Windows).*

• If you choose Layout > Insert Pages or Layout > Remove Pages, you can add or remove pages anywhere in the publication, and also specify which master to apply to new pages you insert.

You can also add or remove master pages. See "Using Master Pages" on page 68 for more information.

To preserve text or graphics on the pages you remove, first drag them to the pasteboard—a storage place that is independent of any page.

If you remove a page from the middle of the publication, PageMaker automatically rethreads text on the pages before and after the deleted page (provided the text is in the same story), and renumbers all subsequent pages.

In a double-sided publication with different inside and outside margins, adding or removing an odd number of pages causes PageMaker to shift the margins and numbering of the subsequent pages and to reposition the page's contents accordingly to fall within the margins.

You can rearrange pages at any point in your work. See "Rearranging Pages" on page 94 for more information.

To add pages anywhere in the publication:

1 Go to the place where you want to insert pages.

2 Choose Layout > Insert Pages.

3 Type the number of pages you want to add, and select a location for the new pages.

4 Specify the master pages you want to apply, and then click Insert.

See "Applying Master Pages" on page 71 for more information on specifying a master page for the new pages.

To remove pages:

1 Choose Layout > Remove Pages

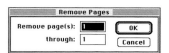

2 Type the range of pages you want to remove, and then click OK.

WORKING WITH MULTIPLE OPEN PUBLICATIONS AND MULTIPLE WINDOWS

You can have several publications open at the same time in PageMaker 6.5, so it's easy to move or copy graphics and text from one publication to another. This feature also lets you compare page designs, search for and replace text and formatting, and check the spelling in all open publications at once. (The number of publications you can open simultaneously is limited by the amount of memory, or RAM, available on your computer.)

Each publication opens in its own window. To activate a window (bring it to the front), click any visible part of its window or choose an open publication from the list in the Window menu. The Window menu lists each open publication and any open story windows associated with the publication.

On the Macintosh only, you can send a window from the front to the back of all open windows by pressing Option (Macintosh) and clicking the title bar.

Managing story windows

PageMaker also lets you open each story in its own window. See "Moving Between Story Editor and Layout View" on page 119.

In story view, choose Story > Close Story to close the story window when you finish working on a story. To close all open story windows in a publication, hold down Option (Macintosh) or Shift (Windows) as you choose Story > Close All Stories.

What happens when you choose Close Story depends on the status of the story:

• When the story is new and not yet placed, PageMaker displays an alert message in which you choose to discard the story, place it on the page, or continue editing. If you choose to place the story, PageMaker returns to layout view with a loaded text icon (click the icon to begin placing the story text).

• When the story has already been placed, Close Story closes the story window and, if no other story windows are open, returns to layout view. PageMaker automatically re-flows the story within existing text objects. If other story windows are open, PageMaker displays the next story window.

Tiling and cascading windows

Two commands on the Window menu, Tile and Cascade, help you arrange windows on the screen so you can see them easily. In layout view, the commands act only on the layout window of the publication, not on the open story windows. In story editor, the commands act only on the story windows, not on the layout windows.

Use the following techniques to rearrange open layout or story windows:

• To place all layout windows (or all open story windows in the active publication) in rows and columns, choose Window > Tile. The number of open windows determines how PageMaker arranges them.

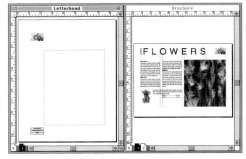

Tiled windows in layout view

• To place all open story windows from all open publications side-by-side, go to story editor, press Option (Macintosh) or Shift (Windows) and choose Window > Tile All. The number of open story windows determines how PageMaker arranges them.

• To stack and overlap all layout windows (or all open story windows in the active publication) so that you can view their title bars, choose Window > Cascade.

Cascading windows

• To stack and overlap all open story windows from all open publications so that you can view their title bars, go to story editor, press Option (Macintosh) or Shift (Windows) and choose Window > Cascade All.

SETTING DEFAULTS AND PREFERENCES

PageMaker ships with preset specifications, called defaults, for all aspects of publishing, but you can change these to suit your particular needs either for a specific job or for all your work until you change the specifications. A subset of defaults are preferences, or settings that modify PageMaker's performance, interface, and overall behavior.

This section describes general ways to change custom settings. For information on changing specific kinds of preference settings, see the chapter that covers the feature area. For example, for color management defaults, see Chapter 9, "Color Management."

Setting defaults

PageMaker has two kinds of defaults:

• Application defaults are remembered even after you quit and restart PageMaker. You set application defaults by changing menu and dialog box settings while no publication is open. The settings you specify will apply to every new PageMaker publication you create from scratch.

• Publication defaults apply to the current publication only. You set publication defaults by changing menu and dialog box settings while the publication is active and no object is selected. PageMaker saves the new settings with the publication so that you don't have to reset them the next time you open the publication.

Shortcut: *You can double-click text and drawing tools in the toolbox to set text and drawing-tool defaults for the publication. Double-click the pointer tool to open the General Preferences dialog box.*

USING THE RIGHT MOUSE BUTTON (WINDOWS ONLY)

Many of the PageMaker commands available from menus or palettes are also available from a special context-sensitive pop-up menu that appears when you click with the right mouse button. The contents of the menu depend on whether you click an object, or rather the page or pasteboard; the kind of object you click; the tool selected when you click, and so on. This menu also appears if you press the application key on a Windows 95 compatible keyboard.

Note: You can press Shift and click the right mouse button to zoom to Actual size view; the point you click becomes centered in the window.

Once you become familiar with PageMaker, you might find that using the right mouse button provides a more convenient method for making changes to your publication. For example, rather than use the left mouse button to select an object, and then open a menu and choose a command from that menu in order to modify the object, you might prefer to select the object with the right mouse button: this simultaneously selects the object and displays a pop-up menu of many applicable commands for that kind of object.

CORRECTING MISTAKES

PageMaker provides two ways to correct mistakes or to reverse actions you've taken: Choose Edit > Undo or File > Revert.

Undoing changes and reverting publications

PageMaker remembers your last action and lets you reverse it by choosing Edit > Undo. You must, however, choose this command before performing any other action, as this command only reverses your most recent action. If you accidentally click anywhere on the pasteboard, you won't be able to undo your last action as intended.

Note: The Undo command cannot reverse all actions. For example, it cannot reverse changes made using the Styles and Colors palettes, using most commands on the File menu, or using commands on the Type menu. The Undo command can, however, reverse text edits, applying masters, moving or resizing of objects, certain commands from the Edit and Layout menus, and more.

To abandon all changes and display the most recently saved version of your publication:

1 Choose the File > Revert command.

2 Click OK in the Alert that appears.

The Revert command can also restore your last mini-saved version, a version of the file that PageMaker saves automatically whenever you move to a different page, insert or delete a page, change the document setup, or print.

Other operations that cause a mini-save include switching between layout view and story editor, using the Clipboard, and clicking the active page icon.

To restore a mini-saved version of your publication:

1 Hold down Shift.

2 Choose File > Revert.

Whenever you revert to either the last-saved or last mini-saved version, you will also lose any links updated since the last time you saved the publication. If you are working in story editor on a story that has not yet been placed and you choose Revert, you will lose the story.

If your computer malfunctions or loses power, opening the publication file as usual will open the last mini-saved version. On Windows only, if the publication was untitled when the problem occurred, PageMaker creates a temporary file, named with a TMP extension (for example, PM6331F.TMP), and placed in the Windows default temporary folder. If you rename this file with the .P65 filename extension, you can open the publication, as long as one of the mini-save operations was carried out in that file. In the PageMaker Open Publication dialog box, select the temporary folder, select All Files from the List Files of Type menu, and double-click the temporary file. See Microsoft Windows documentation for more information about creating a temporary folder.

STARTING A PUBLICATION FROM A TEMPLATE

A template is a publication with a prebuilt page design that you can use as is or as the starting point to design your own publication. PageMaker provides several professionally-designed templates stored as scripts. You can install and then open these script templates, but you can also save any publication as a template.

When you open a template, an untitled copy appears. You can work in a template created in this way just as you work in any other publication. You can add and remove pages, manipulate text and graphics, and perform any other function as you would in a publication you created from scratch.

This section describes how to work with the prebuilt templates installed with PageMaker. For information on saving a publication as a PageMaker template, see "Naming and Saving a Publication" on page 26.

PageMaker comes with a variety of templates. We recommend that you experiment with the templates, and modify them to suit your own needs. The templates are designed with fonts that are installed automatically when the templates are installed.

Note: You do not need to open a PageMaker template when creating your own template from scratch. See "Building Your Own Template" on page 25 for more information.

To open a PageMaker script template:

1 Choose Window > Plug-in Palettes > Show Scripts.

2 Click the Templates section within the Scripts palette.

If the folder is not present, it probably means templates were not installed with the copy of PageMaker you are using. See the *Adobe PageMaker 6.5 Getting Started* manual for details on installing PageMaker and its component files.

3 Double-click the name of the template you want to open.

If you don't have the proper fonts installed, you are prompted to specify substitute fonts; see Appendix B for step-by-step instructions.

Name and save the untitled publication, if necessary, either as a template or as a publication. See "Naming and Saving a Publication" on page 26 for more information.

Adding text and graphics to templates

Many of the templates provided with PageMaker contain text and graphics placeholders. In most cases, all you need to do is replace the placeholders with your own text and graphics to complete your publication. If you create your own template, you will probably use existing text and graphics as placeholders.

Use text placeholders to reserve space on template pages for text, including headlines, captions, and body text. Use graphics placeholders to show suggested positions and sizes for graphics, such as logos and other illustrations. (Some of the templates provided don't have text or graphics placeholders, but are layout grids, which you can use as a basis for designing any publication.)

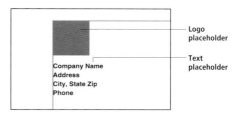

To replace a placeholder with imported text or graphics:

1 Use the pointer tool to select the graphic placeholder, or use the text tool to click in the text you want to replace.

2 Choose File > Place, and select the text or graphic file you want to add to the publication.

3 Select Replacing Entire Graphic or Replacing Entire Story.

4 Click OK.

You may need to adjust the proportions of the graphic or the length of the text object when you replace a placeholder. For information about placing text and graphics in PageMaker, see Chapter 11, "Importing, Linking, and Exporting."

To replace a placeholder with text you type in PageMaker:

1 Use the pointer tool to select the text placeholder you want to replace.

2 Choose Edit > Edit Story to open story editor.

3 Choose Edit > Select All.

4 Type your own text.

5 When you finish entering text, choose Edit > Edit Layout to return to layout view.

Building your own template

If none of the prebuilt templates in the Scripts palette meet your needs, you can create a new template much as you create an original publication. The difference between a template and a publication lies in how you save it. Saving a publication as a template ensures that PageMaker opens a copy of the publication, rather than the original, when you open it by choosing File > Open. In the Open Publication dialog box, templates can be identified by their unique icons. (In Windows, PageMaker templates have a t65 filename extension. Refer to your Windows documentation for information on showing and hiding filename extensions.)

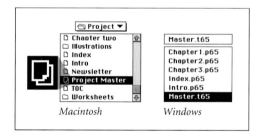

Macintosh   *Windows*

To save a publication as a template:

1 Choose File > Save As.

2 Type a name for the template.

3 Select Template for the Save As option, and click OK.

Editing a template

You may find it quicker to edit an existing template than to build a completely new one; the changes you make will be reflected in all future publications you create using that template.

To edit an existing template:

1 Choose File > Open.

2 Select a template.

3 Click Original, and then click OK.

If you don't click Original, PageMaker opens a copy of the template, leaving the original intact.

4 After you edit the template, choose File > Save As.

5 Select Template for the Save As option, and then click OK.

NAMING AND SAVING A PUBLICATION

One of the most practical habits you can develop is to save your PageMaker publication often. When you save a publication, you ensure that it remains stored in your computer even if there

is a power failure or system crash. To avoid the frustration of rebuilding a lost publication, save your work regularly.

To name and save a publication for the first time:

1 Choose File > Save or File > Save As.

2 Select a folder in which to store the saved file.

3 Type a name for the publication, and then click OK (Macintosh) or Save (Windows).

PageMaker saves your publication in the current location unless you specify a different folder.

To save all open publications:

Press Option (Macintosh) or Shift (Windows) and choose File > Save All.

After you name and save a publication once, the Save and Save As commands function differently: by default, choosing Save causes PageMaker to perform a *fast save*. In saving a file quickly, PageMaker does not compact the publication file to its smallest size, and the

TIP: IF YOU NEED TO DISTRIBUTE YOUR PUBLICATION SO THAT IT CAN BE READ AND PRINTED ON COMPUTERS THAT MIGHT NOT HAVE PAGEMAKER 6.5 INSTALLED, YOU CAN CREATE A PORTABLE DOCUMENT FORMAT (PDF) VERSION OF YOUR PUBLICATION. SEE CHAPTER 13, "DISTRIBUTING A PUBLICATION ELECTRONICALLY."

file takes up more disk space than necessary. However, when you choose Save As, PageMaker compacts the publication so that it takes up the smallest possible amount of disk space, but the process takes more time than a fast save. Saving a smaller version of a publication also makes it a cleaner file, less susceptible to file problems.

You can set a preference to determine how PageMaker saves files—faster or smaller—when you choose the Save command.

To specify a Save Option preference:

1 Choose File > Preferences > General.

2 Select Smaller or Faster for the Save Option.

3 Click OK.

If you select Smaller, PageMaker will save your publication at the smallest size possible each time you select File > Save or use the keyboard shortcut.

To save a publication with a new name or in a different location:

1 Choose File > Save As.

2 Type a new name or specify a new location.

3 Click OK (Macintosh) or Save (Windows).

Changing a publication's name or location using Save As creates a new copy of the publication, so two versions of the publication exist: one with the old name or location and one with the new. The versions are completely separate, and the work you do on one publication has no effect on the other.

To provide a safety net, PageMaker saves intermediate versions of the publication you're working on. For information on these mini-saved versions and a list of functions that cause PageMaker to create them, see "Correcting Mistakes" on page 22. Remember, though, the best way to guard against losing your work is to create backup copies of your publication. A backup copy saves you from recreating the entire publication if the file develops problems or is deleted by mistake.

Saving linked and associated files with a publication

Several options in the Save Publication As dialog box let you control the kinds of externally-stored files that are saved with the publication:

• No Additional Files, the default setting, lets you save the current publication only. If you are saving in a new folder, the files linked to your publication remain where they are and are not copied to the new location.

• Files for Remote Printing copies all the files needed to print the publication to one location. This includes linked files and special files (such as the tracking values file) that contain instructions for composing and printing the publication. Once the files are saved in one location, you can copy them quickly and easily to portable disks. For more information on printing remotely, see "Using the Save for Service Provider Plug-in" on page 411.

• All Linked Files copies all externally located files to the folder in which your publication is being saved.

If there is not enough room in the currently selected location for both your publication and its linked files, PageMaker displays an alert to this effect and no linked files are copied. In this situation, you can try making more space available, or saving to a different drive.

Saving a preview (Macintosh only)

Select the Save Preview option in the Save Publication As dialog box if you plan to catalog the publication in Adobe Fetch® When you catalog the publication in Fetch after selecting this option, a thumbnail of the publication's first page appears in the Fetch catalog.

Saving a file to open in an earlier version of PageMaker

If you need to open a PageMaker 6.5 publication in PageMaker 6.0, you must first save it as a PageMaker 6.0 file using the File > Save As command. Select the A Copy in 6.0 Format option in the Save Publication dialog box.

PageMaker 6.0 does not recognize some of the features added to PageMaker in version 6.5. Note the following PageMaker 6.5 features that do not convert to PageMaker 6.0 or are modified in the process:

• Irregular polygons (those you create by clicking vertices rather than by dragging the polygon tool) are retained but you cannot reshape them.

• Hyperlinked text and graphics lose their hyperlink attributes; anchor information is deleted.

• Text frames are converted to text blocks (if they contain text).

• Layers are merged into a single visible layer.

• Kodak CMS profiles are mapped to the closest corresponding profiles included with PageMaker 6.0

• Imported native Illustrator files are deleted. You can save an EPS from the original Illustrator file and import the EPS into the PageMaker 6.0 publication.

CLOSING A PUBLICATION

To close the active publication without exiting PageMaker, choose File > Close. To close all open publications without exiting PageMaker, hold down Option (Macintosh) or Shift (Windows) and then choose File > Close All.

If you have made changes since you saved the publication, PageMaker asks if you want to save those changes. (If you are closing more than one publication, PageMaker prompts you to save any publication containing unsaved changes.) You can save changes, ignore them, or cancel the Close command.

If you want to save changes but have not yet named the publication, PageMaker responds with the Save Publication As dialog box.

GETTING HELP

Online Help is available by choosing PageMaker Help Topics from the Balloon menu (Macintosh) or by choosing commands from the Help menu (Windows).

For context-sensitive online Help, which brings up a Help screen with information about the active item, do the following:

• On the Macintosh, press Command + / (slash) or press the Help key on an extended keyboard. When the pointer turns into a ? (question mark), choose a menu command.

• In Windows, press Shift + F1 and when the pointer turns into a ? (question mark), choose a menu command. You can also get help from within a dialog box. While any PageMaker dialog box is open, hold down Shift and click the right mouse button in the background of the dialog box.

Chapter

2

Chapter 2: Tutorial

The best way to learn PageMaker is to try it yourself. This chapter is a tutorial that guides you through some basic PageMaker skills as you create and print a letterhead and brochure for the fictitious company Earth & Ware, a garden center.

You'll learn how to:

• Set up page and printer options and position ruler guides.

• Create a template.

• Type and format text, and define text styles.

• Set indents and tabs.

• Work with threaded text blocks.

• Resize, move, and rotate objects.

• Place text and graphics from other applications.

• Print a PageMaker publication.

How you can best put this tutorial to use depends on your past experience with desktop publishing and with PageMaker. If you are new to desktop publishing and to PageMaker, you might want to read Chapter 1, "Basic Concepts," and then follow the directions in this tutorial to create your first publications. If you've used earlier versions of PageMaker, you might want to review the Adobe PageMaker 6.5 Getting Started book to see what's new in this version, and then complete the tutorial to review some basic skills.

This tutorial assumes that you have a working knowledge of your computer hardware and operating system—Windows 95, Windows NT, or Macintosh System 7.1 or later—and that you have successfully installed PageMaker 6.5.

For complete information about PageMaker's tools and features, refer to the remaining chapters of this user guide. Tutorial movies on the PageMaker CD-ROM help you discover several powerful features not covered in this chapter.

If your screen doesn't match our samples

The fonts in our sample illustrations may differ slightly from those that appear on your screen. This means that the fonts and printers we used to create this book differ from yours. In most cases, the differences are insignificant. Your results depend on several factors:

• The screen and printer fonts you have installed.

• Whether or not you use a type-management program.

• The printer you choose.

The practice publications in this book are designed for either US letter-size paper or international A-4 paper. Instructions apply to both document sizes. We have provided approximate metric equivalents for inch measurements.

STARTING A NEW PUBLICATION

When you start a new publication, you first establish the characteristics of the publication pages (size, orientation, and margins), whether it will be printed on one side or two, and the printer you'll use for the final version of your publication.

1 Launch PageMaker 6.5. When the PageMaker opening screen disappears, you'll see an empty application window.

2 Choose New from the File menu (File > New).

The Document Setup dialog box appears with PageMaker's default settings, which you will change in the next few steps.

3 Deselect the Double-sided option.

4 Click in the margin text boxes and set these margins:

• Left: 2.25 inches (57mm)

• Right: 1 inch (25mm)

• Top: 2.75 inches (70mm)

• Bottom: 1.5 inches (38mm)

5 In Windows, use the Compose to Printer option to select the printer you plan to use for the final version of your publication. (This may not be the desktop printer you'll use to print drafts or proofs.)

6 Set the Target Printer Resolution to match the printer you'll use to print the final copy of your publication. PageMaker uses this resolution to correctly scale bitmap images when you resize them using magic stretch. See "Resizing 1-Bit Bitmap Images" on page 199 for more information.

7 Click OK.

You will see an untitled publication window containing the pasteboard and a letter-size, vertical page.

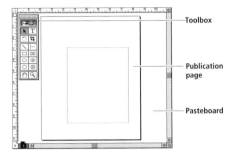

POSITIONING RULER GUIDES

PageMaker provides nonprinting guides to help you align and position objects on the page. The page already has margin guides—a dotted or colored rectangle that represents the page margins you specified in the Document Setup dialog box. Now you'll add ruler guides to help position the logo and company address for the letterhead.

1 Make sure a checkmark appears beside the Snap to Rulers command on the View menu.

When Snap to Rulers is selected, PageMaker pulls the pointer into line with each tick mark on the ruler when you create your guides. This ensures exact placement of the ruler guides.

2 Press Command + Option and click in the upper left corner of the page (Macintosh), or press Shift and click using the right mouse button in the upper left corner of the page (Windows).

This action centers your view in the upper left corner of the page and changes the page display to the actual size of the page, so you can place the ruler guides precisely.

Magnified view of the upper left corner of the page.

3 Position the pointer on the horizontal ruler (which extends across the top of the publication window) and drag down to the 1¼-inch (3.2cm) mark on the vertical ruler. A horizontal ruler guide appears.

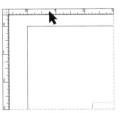
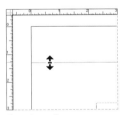

When you click and drag from here…

the pointer changes to a two-way arrow until you release the mouse button.

4 Use the scroll bars or the hand tool to move the view to the lower left corner of the page.

5 Create three more ruler guides as follows:

• Drag a vertical guide to the 1 1/8-inch mark on the horizontal ruler.

• Drag a vertical guide to the 2 1/4-inch mark on the horizontal ruler.

• Drag a horizontal guide to the 9 3/4-inch mark on the vertical ruler.

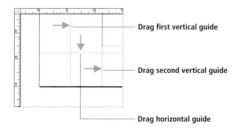

Drag first vertical guide

Drag second vertical guide

Drag horizontal guide

6 Choose Lock Guides from the View menu (View > Lock Guides).

When Lock Guides is selected, PageMaker locks the ruler guides in place, so you can't accidentally reposition them.

SAVING YOUR WORK

Now that you've completed the layout grid, you'll want to save your work. It's a good idea to save your work often to avoid losing it in a power failure or other disruption. PageMaker gives you two ways to save your work: as a publication or as a template. A template is a predesigned model for other publications.

In this exercise, we'll show you how to save the letterhead you create as a template, so you can use a copy of it to produce an actual letter.

1 Choose Save from the File menu to save your work (File > Save).

The Save Publication As dialog box appears.

2 On the Macintosh, choose Template for the Save As option. In Windows, choose Template from the Save as Type pop-up menu.

Note: *If you modify a template and want to save it as a template under a different name, choose Save As from the File menu and specify Template again. That's because PageMaker defaults to Publication when you save a file under a new name.*

3 In the PageMaker 6.5 folder on your hard drive, open the Lesson1 folder of the Tutorial folder and type the filename **Letter** into the text box.

4 Click OK (Macintosh) or Save (Windows).

On the Macintosh, PageMaker automatically uses a template icon for your file, which you can view using the Finder. In Windows, PageMaker automatically adds a .T65 extension to the filename, which specifies that the file is a template.

The Letter file contains a blank page with the layout grid you created. In the next exercise, you add text and graphics.

TYPING TEXT

For the letterhead you create here, you'll type the address of a fictitious garden center called Earth & Ware. First, you'll set the text defaults—the formatting that PageMaker applies to every new text block you create.

If the master page icon (in the lower left corner of the publication window) is black, you are working on the master page, which contains basic design elements, such as page numbers, that are common to most or all pages in your publication. Click the page 1 icon to turn to page 1.

1 Choose Character from the Type menu (Type > Character) and change only what is indicated in the illustration on this page. Then click OK.

When no text is selected and you change the type specifications, you reset the default formatting for all new text you type in the active publication. Everything you type now appears in your chosen font and size. You can override these new defaults by selecting the text and changing it, or you can set new defaults by choosing formatting options with no text selected.

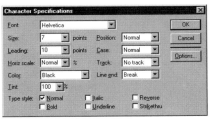

The font Helvetica is used in our sample illustrations. If you're working in Windows, you can substitute Arial, which is similar to Helvetica.

2 Choose 200% Size from the Zoom To submenu on the View menu (View > Zoom To > 200% Size).

3 Use the scroll bars or the hand tool to move to the lower left corner of the page.

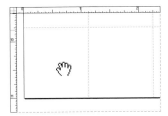

T

4 Select the text tool from the toolbox. The pointer tool turns into an I-beam. You are now ready to create a text block for the text you'll type.

5 Position the tiny horizontal tick mark on the I-beam at the intersection of the leftmost vertical guide and the horizontal guide at the bottom of the page.

6 Drag the I-beam down and to the right until you intersect the next vertical ruler guide, as shown below, and then release the mouse button.

This creates a text block that controls the width of the text.

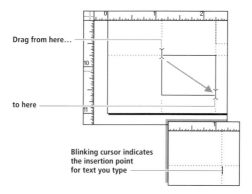

Drag from here...

to here

Blinking cursor indicates the insertion point for text you type

7 Type the street address shown in the illustration on this page for the Earth & Ware garden center, pressing Return (Macintosh) or Enter (Windows) after each line to create a new line.

If text wraps to the next line, select the pointer tool, click on the text block, and then drag a right corner handle to the right until the text fits on the line.

8 If your text block is not positioned as shown, select the pointer tool, and click inside the text block to select it. Drag the block as necessary to align the text within the margins as shown.

If a down arrow appears in the lower window-shade handle, drag it down to reveal all the text in the block. When the handle is empty, there is no additional text to reveal.

The top edge aligns with the horizontal guide

The right edge aligns with the vertical guide

FORMATTING TEXT CHARACTERS

The text you've typed so far is 7-point Helvetica with 10-point leading (the vertical spacing between two lines of text). That's because you previously selected 7-point Helvetica as the default size and font and 10-point as the default leading.

You can select any text in a publication and use commands on the Type menu to apply formatting that is different from the defaults. In this exercise, you'll practice formatting text.

1 Select the text tool and click anywhere in the text.

2 Choose Select All from the Edit menu to select all the text you typed so far (Edit > Select All).

3 Choose 14 from the Leading submenu on the Type menu (Type > Leading > 14). If 14 is not available, choose Other from the Leading menu, and type 14 in the dialog box that appears.

Text with 10-point leading   *Text with 14-point leading*

FORMATTING PARAGRAPHS

Certain formatting decisions, such as alignment (centered or justified, for example), indents, and tab positions, apply to an entire paragraph. To format a paragraph, you must use the text tool. You can format a single paragraph by either clicking three times anywhere in the paragraph to select the paragraph or clicking an insertion point anywhere in the paragraph. PageMaker begins a new paragraph each time you press Return (Macintosh) or Enter (Windows).

1 If the address is not already selected, select a portion of all three paragraphs in the address by dragging the text tool from the first line to the last line.

2 Choose Align Center from the Alignment submenu on the Type menu (Type > Alignment > Align Center).

Align Left   *Align Center*

3 Choose Save from the File menu (File > Save) before proceeding.

If you like, you can spend a few minutes experimenting with the text formatting commands on the Type menu. For example, change the font and the size, or try different type styles. When you're done, choose Revert from the File menu (File > Revert) to discard all the changes you've made since you last saved your work.

DRAWING A BOX

Now you'll draw a black box around the address to add visual appeal.

 1 Select the rectangle tool from the toolbox.

When you move the pointer onto the page, it becomes a crossbar.

2 Choose 1 pt from the Stroke submenu on the Element menu (Element > Stroke > 1 pt).

A stroke is the thickness (or weight) of the border of shapes you create—in this case, for the box you're about to draw.

By choosing formatting options from the Element menu before you begin drawing, and with nothing selected, you set the default formatting for all new objects you add to your publication or template. You can override the default formatting by selecting an object and changing its formatting, or you can set new defaults by choosing formatting options with no object selected.

3 To draw the box, click the crossbar on the intersection of the ruler guides at the upper left corner of the text block, and then drag to the lower right corner of the text block, as shown below.

If you align the box precisely with the ruler guides, it may be difficult to distinguish the top and sides of the box from the ruler guides. Choose Show Guides from the View menu (View > Show Guides) to display the ruler guides; choose View > Hide Guides to make them invisible.

DRAWING LINES

Now you'll draw two horizontal lines in the box you created to separate the lines of the address.

 1 Select the constrained-line tool in the toolbox.

2 Click the crossbar on the left side of the box beneath the first line of the address, and then drag it to the right side of the box, as shown below. Repeat to draw a line under the second line of the address.

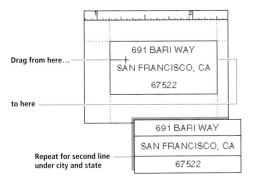

Drag from here...

to here

691 BARI WAY
SAN FRANCISCO, CA
67522

Repeat for second line under city and state

3 Choose Save from the File menu to save your work (File > Save).

PLACING A GRAPHIC

PageMaker offers a variety of ways to manage graphics in your publication. In this exercise, you'll place a graphic from another application into your publication to use as a company logo.

In this exercise, you'll place a company logo at the top of the letterhead.

1 Select the pointer tool from the toolbox.

2 Choose Actual Size from the View menu (View > Actual Size).

3 Use the scroll bars or the hand tool to move to the upper left corner of the page.

Note: *If ruler guides are hidden, choose Show Guides from the View menu to display the ruler guides.*

4 Choose Place from the File menu (File > Place). Select the Logo.tif file from the Lesson1 folder of the Tutorial folder (in the PageMaker 6.5 folder), and then click OK (Macintosh) or Open (Windows).

5 Click near the top of the page to place the logo.

6 While the logo is still selected, position the pointer tool over the center of the logo, click, and drag it into alignment with the top and leftmost ruler guides.

When you move an object, the cursor turns into an arrow.

For more information on placing and modifying a graphic, see Chapter 11, "Importing, Linking, and Exporting."

RESIZING A GRAPHIC

In this exercise, you'll resize the graphic you just placed, maintaining its original proportions so that it fits neatly between the two vertical ruler guides you created earlier.

1 Using the pointer tool, select the graphic if it is not already selected.

2 Hold down the Shift key, click the lower right handle of the graphic, and drag it to the rightmost vertical ruler guide.

Note: Pressing the Shift key while you drag ensures that PageMaker maintains the proportions of the original graphic as you resize it. You must release the mouse button before you release the Shift key for this to work.

 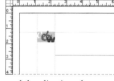

While pressing the Shift key, size the graphic…   *and then line it up between the two vertical rulers.*

3 Choose Save from the File menu to save your work (File > Save).

Congratulations on completing your first PageMaker template! You have combined text and graphics to create a simple letterhead for Earth & Ware, a fictitious garden center. Now we'll show you an easy way to use the template. You'll place a letter on the page and turn a copy of your template into a PageMaker publication.

PLACING A LETTER ON THE LETTERHEAD

Keep your template open as you get ready to place a text file on the letterhead page. Placing text is similar to placing a graphic.

1 Choose Fit in Window from the View menu (View > Fit in Window).

2 Select the pointer tool from the toolbox.

3 Choose Place from the File menu (File > Place).

4 In the Place Document dialog box, select the Text file from the Lesson1 folder of the Tutorial folder (in the PageMaker 6.5 folder), and then click OK (Macintosh) or Open (Windows).

In Windows, click Open in the Import Filter dialog box.

5 Position the loaded text icon as shown below and click.

After the text flows onto the letterhead, it has windowshade handles indicating that it is selected. If a down arrow appears in the lower windowshade handle, drag it down to reveal all the text in the block. When the handle is empty, the text block contains no additional text.

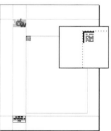 

When you click the loaded text icon here…   *the story flows onto the page.*

6 Choose Save As from the File menu, and then choose Publication as the Save As option (Macintosh) or choose Publication from the Save As Type pop-up menu (Windows).

7 Open the Lesson1 folder, type the file name **Letter1** into the dialog box, and then click OK (Macintosh) or Save (Windows).

PRINTING THE LETTERHEAD

You are now ready to print the letterhead you created.

Macintosh Note: *Be sure you select the PSPrinter 8.3.1 (or later) driver in the Chooser when printing to a PostScript printer. See Chapter 12, "Printing Publications," for more information.*

To print:

1 Choose Print from the File menu (File > Print) to open the Print Document dialog box.

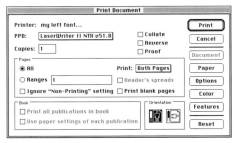

Settings for a PostScript printer

2 If you're printing to a PostScript printer, select a PPD option.

For more information see "PostScript Printer Description Files" on page 394.

3 Click Print.

4 After the file has printed, choose Close from the File menu (File > Close).

CREATING A BROCHURE

Now that you've learned some PageMaker fundamentals, we'll guide you through additional techniques that are essential to creating distinctive publications. You'll create a brochure for the fictitious garden center, Earth & Ware, as you learn how to:

• Work with master pages to provide a consistent look for a publication.

• Create, import, rotate, and resize objects.

• Overlap text and graphics.

• Work with text in story editor.

• Work with multiple open publications.

• Print a publication.

OPENING A TEMPLATE

PageMaker comes with several prebuilt templates that include a page design, text styles, and text and graphics placeholders to simplify your work.

Template for brochure

PageMaker templates offer two major benefits: they provide a fast, easy way to create professionally designed documents, and you can use them repeatedly to establish a consistent design theme for publications. You can focus on the content of publications, because the design decisions have already been made.

We've provided a template for the brochure you'll create. From the template, you'll create a new brochure, adding text, a logo, and graphics.

The template has two pages. You will work only on page 1 to create the brochure in this tutorial. After you've finished, you can use page 2 to create your own version of the brochure.

For more information on creating and using templates, see "Starting a Publication from a Template" on page 23.

To open a template:

1 Choose Open from the File menu (File > Open).

2 In the Open Publication dialog box, select the BrochUS file from the Lesson2 folder of the Tutorial folder (in the PageMaker 6.5 folder). If you will be printing on A4-size paper, select the BrochINT file.

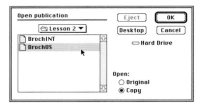

3 Click OK to open a copy of the file and begin.

An untitled publication window opens. Some of the work has already been done for you: the margins are set and several guides are positioned to create a design grid. Having a prebuilt grid is one advantage of using a template.

CREATING COLUMNS

Everything you see on the page is actually on the master page. The master page contains design elements common to every page in a publication. Master pages provide a foundation for

TIP: PRESS COMMAND +; (MACINTOSH) OR CTRL +; (WINDOWS) TO HIDE OR DISPLAY GUIDES, INCLUDING COLUMN GUIDES. HIDE THEM WHEN YOU WANT TO SEE APPROXIMATELY HOW THE PRINTED PAGE WILL LOOK. DISPLAY THEM WHEN YOU NEED TO POSITION AN ELEMENT.

most publications that you create in PageMaker. They help establish a consistent look within and between publications, and save you time.

For more information on using master pages, see Chapter 3, "Constructing a Publication."

You'll modify this master page by adding column guides, which you'll use to position text.

Master page

Design elements on the master page appear on every page in the publication, but you can omit them from specific pages if needed.

Column guides are nonprinting vertical lines that let you align text and graphics within the publication. Creating column guides on the master page ensures that the columns are identical throughout the publication. For this brochure, you'll create four columns.

To create columns:

1 Click the master page icon to move to the master page.

2 Choose Column Guides from the Layout menu (Layout > Column Guides).

3 Type 4 for Number of Columns, and then press Tab or click in the Space Between Columns text box and type .25 (.64cm).

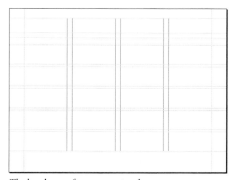

4 Click OK to close the dialog box.

Column guides appear, dividing your page into four equal columns.

The brochure, after you create columns.

5 Click the page 1 icon to return to page 1, where you'll be doing your work in this tutorial.

6 If you don't see the column guides on page 1, choose Copy Master Guides from the Layout menu (Layout > Copy Master Guides).

For more information on using column guides, see Chapter 3, "Constructing a Publication."

SAVING YOUR WORK

It's a good idea to save your work now, before you go any further.

1 Choose Save from the File menu (File > Save).

2 Open the Lesson2 folder of the Tutorial folder, click in the text box, and type **Brochure** for the file name.

3 Select Publication as the Save As option, and then click OK (Macintosh) or Save (Windows).

PLACING GRAPHICS

PageMaker lets you import graphics in a variety of formats, including WMF (Windows metafile), EMF (enhanced metafile), BMP (Windows bitmap), GIF, PICT, TIFF, and EPS (encapsulated PostScript). EPS and TIFF are often your best choices on both the Macintosh and in Windows, although you should avoid EPS if you're printing to a non-PostScript printer.

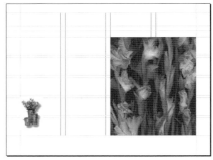

The brochure, after you place the graphics

The next step is to place one TIFF graphic on the right side of the page and a smaller TIFF graphic on the left side of the page.

1 Make sure Snap to Guides on the View menu is selected (View > Snap to Guides).

The Snap to Guides option helps you align objects with the guides and rulers. When you create, place, or move an object, PageMaker pulls it into line with the nearest guide.

2 Choose Place from the File menu (File > Place), select the Flowers.tif file from the Lesson2 folder of the Tutorial folder, and then click OK (Macintosh) or Open (Windows).

3 Position the loaded icon as shown on the next page, and then click at the intersection of the 1⅞-inch (4.5cm) horizontal guide and the left edge of the third column to place the graphic.

If the upper left corner of the graphic is not positioned as shown here, click the pointer on the graphic and drag the graphic into position.

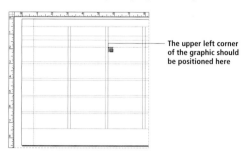

The upper left corner of the graphic should be positioned here

4 Choose Place from the File menu (File > Place), select the Bouquet.tif file from the Lesson2 folder in the Tutorial folder, and then click OK (Macintosh) or Open (Windows).

5 Position the loaded icon as shown, and then click at the intersection of the 5¼-inch (13.3cm) horizontal guide and the left margin.

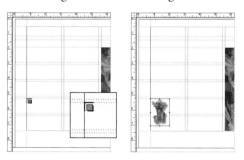

CREATING AND STYLING A HEADING

Now you'll create a text block in which you'll type the heading for the brochure. You'll position the heading to span the first three columns.

The brochure, after you add a heading

1 Select the text tool and position the I-beam at the intersection of the top and left margin guides.

2 Drag the I-beam diagonally to define the text block. Drag from the 1-inch (2.5cm) mark on the horizontal ruler over to the right edge of the third column and down to the 1¼ inch (3.2cm) mark on the vertical ruler.

When you release the mouse button, you will see a blinking cursor at your starting position.

3 Type **FLOWERS**.

Note: *You might want to change the view by choosing 75% Size from the Zoom To submenu on the View menu.*

4 If FLOWERS is not already highlighted, select the text tool and double-click the word FLOWERS to select it.

5 Choose Force Justify from the Alignment submenu on the Type menu (Type > Alignment > Force Justify).

This distributes the characters evenly over the width of the text block.

6 Choose Character from the Type menu (Type > Character), and set type attributes to match those in the Character Specifications dialog box shown here.

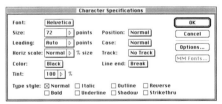

If Helvetica is not available, choose Arial (Windows) or another font.

7 Click OK to close the dialog box.

You may need to adjust the position of the heading or the width of the text block to match the illustration below. Use the pointer tool to select the text block and position it. Leave ¼ inch (.6cm) between the letter F and the left page margin, and position the baseline of the letters (the imaginary line on which the letters rest) on the horizontal guide at the 1¼-inch (3.2cm) mark on the vertical ruler.

CHANGING TYPE STYLE AND ALIGNMENT

You can use the commands on the Type menu to format text. Some of these commands (Font, Size, and Type Style, for example) apply to characters. Other commands (such as Paragraph, Indents/Tabs, and Alignment), apply to entire paragraphs. To make a change to a specific character or paragraph, the text tool must be selected and the characters must be highlighted, or an insertion point must be clicked in the paragraph. If you select more than one paragraph, the changes will apply to all the selected paragraphs.

Note: *If you choose commands from the Type menu without any characters or paragraphs selected, you'll reset the default attributes, which will apply to all new text you type.*

For more information about formatting text, see Chapter 4, "Text Formatting and Word Processing."

> Lorem ipsum dolor sit amet, consectet etuer adipiscing elit sed diam nonum nibh euismod tinci dunt ut laoreet do magna aliquam era volutpat. Ut wisi ad enim minum quis.

> Lorem ipsum dolor sit amet, consectet etuer adipiscing elit sed diam nonum nibh euismod tinci dunt ut *laoreet* do magna aliquam era volutpat. Ut wisi ad enim minum quis.

Some formatting commands apply to characters (for example, type style, tracking, font, type size, and leading). Here we used the Type Style command to italicize a word.

> Lorem ipsum dolor sit amet, con sectet etuer adip iscing elit sed diam nonum nibh euis euismod tinci dunt ut laoreet do magna aliquam era volutpat quis.

> Lorem ipsum dolor sit amet, con sectet etuer adip iscing elit sed diam nonum nibh euis euismod tinci dunt ut laoreet do magna aliquam era volutpat quis.

Some formatting commands apply to paragraphs (for example, paragraph spacing, indents, tabs, and alignment). Here we used the Alignment command to center the paragraph.

USING THE CONTROL PALETTE

The Control palette is an alternative to moving, resizing, and rotating an element manually. Using the Control palette, you have precise control over text and graphics and can make several changes without changing tools or choosing commands.

The settings and options available in the Control palette change according to what you select in the PageMaker window.

When you select graphics and text objects with the pointer tool, you can enter precise numeric values in the Control palette to move, resize, rotate, scale, and crop the objects. When you click in a text object with the text tool, you can apply formatting to text and paragraphs.

In this tutorial, you'll use the Control palette to precisely rotate a text block in the brochure.

For more information on how to use the Control palette to format text, see Chapter 4, "Text Formatting and Word Processing." For more information on how to use the Control palette to move, resize, and transform graphics, see Chapter 6, "Graphics and Text Objects."

Control palette with objects selected

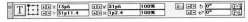

Control palette with text selected

ROTATING AND MOVING A TEXT BLOCK

PageMaker provides extensive control over the objects in your publication. You can position graphics and text blocks precisely, rotate them in .01-degree increments, and resize them to exact specifications.

You can rotate an object (text or graphics) by using the rotating tool in the toolbox, the Rotate option on the Control palette, or both. For this exercise, you'll use the rotating tool to rotate an object, while viewing the angle of rotation on the Control palette. When you finish rotating the object, you'll set the angle of rotation precisely with the Control palette before dragging the object into position on the brochure.

First, create the text block you will rotate.

1 Select the text tool, move to the pasteboard (as shown), and then drag to create a text block approximately 1-inch (2.5cm) wide and ½-inch (1.3cm) long.

2 Type **SPRING**.

3 With the text selected, format it in 14-point Helvetica using the Size command on the Type menu (Type > Size).

Now you'll rotate and move the text block.

1 Use the zoom tool to magnify the area around the word SPRING and the letter F in FLOWERS, or press Command + Spacebar (Macintosh) or Ctrl + Spacebar (Windows) and drag diagonally over the area.

2 Choose Show Control Palette from the Window menu to open the Control palette (Window > Show Control Palette).

3 Select the pointer tool, and click the SPRING text block. (You can also use the rotating tool to select objects you wish to rotate.)

The text block has windowshade handles at the top and bottom, indicating that it is selected.

 4 Select the rotating tool, and position the starburst over the center of the text block.

The location on the text block where you click the starburst is called the fixed point. Rotating an object moves it around its fixed point.

The pointer changes to a starburst.

5 Drag the starburst counterclockwise to rotate the text block. Continue rotating until the base-line of SPRING is parallel to the left edge of the F in FLOWERS and the angle of rotation shown on the Control palette is approximately 90 degrees.

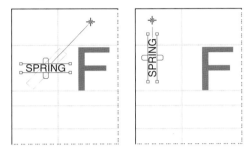

You may need to move SPRING closer to FLOWERS to view and align both text blocks. Select the pointer tool and drag the SPRING text block closer to the F in FLOWERS.

6 To ensure that the angle of rotation is exactly 90 degrees, be sure that the number displayed in the Rotate option on the Control palette is 90. If not, type 90, and then press Return (Macintosh) or Enter (Windows).

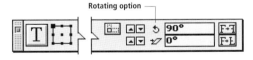

7 Select the pointer tool, and click the SPRING text block again.

8 Drag the rotated text block into position next to the F in FLOWERS, as shown below. The bottom of the letter S in SPRING should rest on the baseline of FLOWERS.

9 Choose Save from the File menu to save your work before proceeding to the next exercise (File > Save).

PLACING A TEXT FILE

Placing text in PageMaker is similar to placing a graphic. In this step, you'll place a text file in the brochure. To view the entire brochure, choose Fit in Window from the View submenu on the Layout menu. (Layout > View > Fit in Window)

The brochure, after you place the first column of the text file

1 Make sure there is not a checkmark next to the Autoflow command on the Layout menu (Layout > Autoflow). If there is, choose Autoflow to deselect it.

Autoflow is useful for flowing all the text in a file into a publication. In this case, however, you want to place the text column-by-column.

2 Choose Place from the File menu (File > Place).

3 In the Place Document dialog box, select the E&WText file from the Lesson2 folder of the Tutorial folder, and then click OK (Macintosh) or Open (Windows).

4 Position the loaded text icon at the intersection of the left margin and the horizontal guide at the 2-inch (5cm) mark on the ruler, and then click to place the text.

A down arrow in the bottom windowshade handle indicates there is more text to be placed.

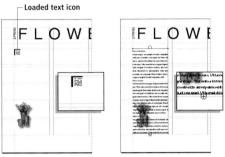

When you click the loaded text icon, text flows from the point where you clicked to the bottom of the column.

CREATING THREADED TEXT BLOCKS

One of the strongest features in PageMaker is the flexibility of text objects. You can move them, break them apart, and change their shapes as the page layout and graphic images in your publication dictate, while keeping the flow of the story intact.

The brochure, after you place the second text block

In PageMaker, you can create separate text blocks in the same story to accommodate any page design. These threaded text blocks can be on the same page or on different pages. In this exercise, you'll flow a second text block from the same story into the second column of your brochure.

For more information on working with threaded text objects, see Chapter 4, "Text Formatting and Word Processing."

1 Using the pointer tool, drag the bottom windowshade of the text block up to the 5⅛-inch (13cm) mark on the vertical ruler.

When you move the windowshade up, the text block shortens. This is called "rolling up the windowshade."

2 Click the down arrow in the bottom windowshade handle.

The loaded text icon appears.

3 Position the loaded text icon at the left edge of the second column at the 2-inch (5cm) horizontal guide, and click to place the text.

The text flows into the second column.

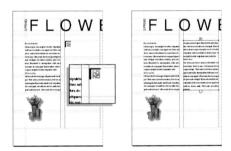

4 Roll up the bottom windowshade of the second text block until both columns of text are equal in length.

DRAGGING TO PLACE TEXT

Now you'll create the final text block. The process you'll use—called drag-placing—lets you place text in any area you define, even across multiple columns.

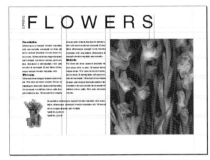

The brochure, after you place the third text block

1 Click the down arrow in the bottom window-shade handle of the second text block.

The loaded text icon appears.

2 Position the loaded text icon at the intersection of the 5¼-inch (13.3cm) horizontal guide and the right edge of the bouquet graphic.

3 Drag diagonally to the intersection of two guides shown below, and then release the mouse button.

Drag from here…

to here

4 If necessary, move or resize the text block with the pointer tool.

The top of the text in the block should be even with the top edge of the bouquet graphic you placed earlier. You can resize a text block by dragging one of its handles, just as you resize a graphic.

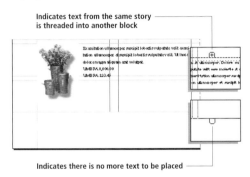

Indicates text from the same story is threaded into another block

Indicates there is no more text to be placed

5 Choose Save from the File menu to save your work before going on to the next exercise (File > Save).

USING PARAGRAPH STYLES

A paragraph style is a set of attributes that define the look of a paragraph: its font, type style and size, alignment, and so on. The most efficient way to use PageMaker is to create and apply paragraph styles. A style might include the following attributes:

Font: Helvetica… Type size: 24 points…
Leading: 28 points… Type style: Bold…
Color: Blue… Alignment: Left…
Tab settings: 1 inch from the left margin

CHANGING A PARAGRAPH STYLE

Styles let you change the formatting of many paragraphs at once by simply changing the definition of the style that has been applied to those paragraphs. In this exercise, you'll edit the paragraph headings in the publication to make them stand out from the body text. One change to the Headline style changes all paragraphs in the brochure that have the Headline style applied.

For more information on using and defining styles, see Chapter 4, "Text Formatting and Word Processing."

1 Choose Show Styles from the Window menu to open the Styles palette (Window > Show Styles).

2 Double-click Headline in the list of styles.

This opens the Style Options dialog box. The formatting attributes of the Headline style appear at the bottom of the dialog box.

You can change formatting by clicking the buttons at the right side of the dialog box. In this exercise, you'll enlarge the typeface and make it bold.

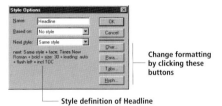

Change formatting by clicking these buttons

Style definition of Headline

Styles palette • When you choose Windows > Show Styles, the Styles palette appears, which lists the styles defined for the publication. Use the Styles palette to apply a style to a paragraph; just click in the paragraph with the text tool and then click a style name.

A Click the close box to close the Styles palette.

B The highlighted style indicates the style of paragraph containing the text tool.

C A plus icon (+) indicates that the formatting of the selected paragraph has been modified since the style was applied.

D Click to open the Styles palette menu.

E A disk icon indicates that a style was imported from a document that was created in a word-processing application.

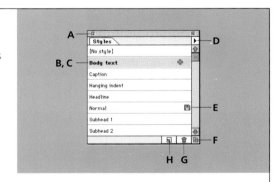

F Resize the Styles palette by dragging the Resize box.

G Click the trash button to delete a style.

H Click the new style button to quickly create a new style.

3 Click the Char… button to open the Character Specifications dialog box.

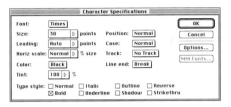

4 Select 10 for Size, and then click Bold for Type Style.

5 Click OK to return to the Style Options dialog box.

The style definition now includes the changes you made to the Headline style.

6 Click OK to close the dialog box.

When you click OK in the Style Options dialog box, all the headings change to the new style. To view these changes, select 75% Size from the Zoom To submenu in the View menu (View > Zoom To > 75% Size).

The headings in the brochure now stand out from the rest of the text.

SETTING INDENTS, TABS, AND LEADERS

In desktop publishing, indents and tabs are used to precisely position text within tables, columns, and paragraphs. Indents move text from the left and right edges of a text block. Tabs position text at specific locations relative to the left and right edges of a text block.

The brochure, after you set an indent and a tab.

In this exercise, you'll indent the price at the bottom of the brochure and format the price to make it stand out more clearly. When you're done, you'll add another price and apply the same indents and formatting in two quick steps.

For more information on setting and using tabs, see Chapter 4, "Text Formatting and Word Processing."

1 Use the zoom tool to magnify the bottom of the third text block, or press Command + Spacebar (Macintosh) or Ctrl + Spacebar (Windows) and drag diagonally over the area.

2 Using the text tool, click after the word UMBRA, and then press Tab.

Pressing Tab creates the space for the leader dots you're about to add. A leader is a repeated pattern, such as a series of dots or dashes, placed in a row between items in a table.

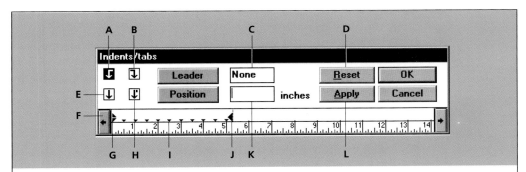

Indents and Tabs

A Left tab icon sets a tab stop inward from the left margin of the text block.

B Right tab icon sets a tab stop inward from the right margin of the text block.

C Leader box specifies a leader style for a tab stop.

D Reset abandons tab settings and returns to the default tabs.

E Center tab icon sets a tab stop that centers text in the text block.

F First-line indent marker sets the indentation of the first line of a paragraph.

G Left indent marker sets the indentation of text from the left margin of the text block.

H Decimal tab icon lines up numbers at their decimal point.

I Default tab marker indicates preset tab stops.

J Right indent marker sets the indentation of text from the right margin of the text block.

K Position box displays the amount of indentation for tabs and indents.

L Apply shows the effects of the tab and indent changes you have made while the dialog box is displayed.

TIP: YOU'LL FIND
THE DECIMAL TAB
USEFUL FOR ALIGNING
NUMBERS BY THEIR
DECIMAL POINTS.

3 Choose Indents/Tabs from the Type menu (Type > Indents/Tabs).

4 Drag the first-line indent marker to the right until you see 1 inch (25mm) in the Position edit box.

Positioning the first-line indent marker moves the line 1 inch from the left margin.

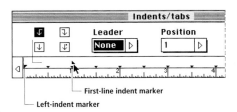

First-line indent marker

Left-indent marker

5 Select the right tab icon, position the pointer anywhere on the ruler, click, and drag the right tab marker to the 3-inch (76mm) position. The Position edit box reflects the placement of the tab marker.

Positioning the right tab aligns the price 3 inches from the left margin.

The tab marker you just positioned is selected (highlighted). All the default tab markers to the left of the new tab disappear.

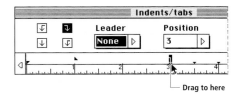

Drag to here

6 With the tab selected, click the Leader list box, and select the leader dots (. . .) from the pop-up menu.

In the publication, leader dots will fill the tab space between the item description and the price.

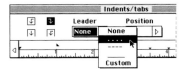

7 Click Apply and compare your results with the illustration below.

The Apply button displays your formatting changes before you exit the dialog box, so you can modify them quickly. If you're satisfied, click OK.

8 Using the text tool, click after the last number in the price, and then press Return (Macintosh) or Enter (Windows).

9 Enter a second price by typing UMBRA, pressing the Tab key, and then typing 3.45.

COPYING A GRAPHIC BETWEEN PUBLICATIONS

PageMaker lets you open several publications at once, and then copy any object in a publication into another open publication. You'll now open the letterhead you created earlier, and copy the logo from the letterhead into the brochure.

1 Choose Fit in Window from the View menu for this exercise (View > Fit in Window).

2 Choose Open from the File menu (File > Open), select the Letter1 file from the Lesson1 folder of the Tutorial folder (in the PageMaker 6.5 folder), and then click OK.

3 Choose Tile from the Window menu (Window > Tile) to view the two publications side by side.

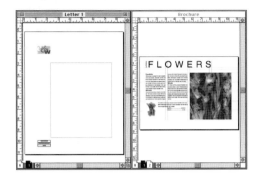

4 Using the pointer tool, drag the E&W logo from the letterhead into the layout window for the brochure, and release the logo anywhere on the page or pasteboard.

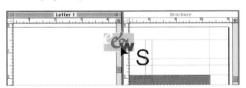

5 Close the Letter1 window by clicking its Close box.

— Close box

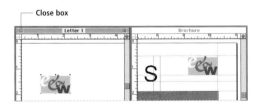

6 Enlarge the Brochure window to fill the entire application window by clicking its Zoom box.

Zoom box

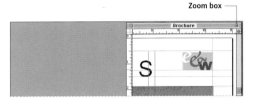

MANAGING WINDOWS IN PAGEMAKER

Each PageMaker publication opens in its own window. You can click any visible window to activate it (bring it to the front), or you can activate any open PageMaker publication from the Window menu. When you choose the name of a publication from the menu, a submenu appears listing the layout window for the publication as well as each of the stories currently open in story editor. You can bring any window in any open publication to the front of your screen by choosing its name from the submenu.

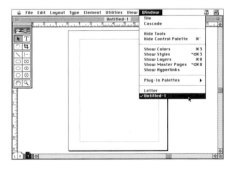

POSITIONING AND RESIZING THE LOGO

Now that you have a copy of the E&W logo in your Brochure window, you can position and resize it to fit the brochure.

The brochure, after you position and resize the logo.

1 Use the pointer tool to drag the logo into the upper right corner of the page, aligned with the top and right page margins as shown.

2 To resize the logo and retain its original proportions, hold down the Shift key as you drag the lower left handle of the logo to measure exactly 1-inch (25mm) wide. (You must release the mouse button before you release the Shift key for this to work.)

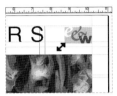

Press the Shift key while you resize a graphic to retains its original proportions.

3 Choose Save from the File menu to save your work (File > Save).

It's a good idea to save your work now, before you print the brochure in the next exercise.

PRINTING THE PUBLICATION

After you look over the brochure on the screen, you're ready to print a proof copy for a final review on paper. A proof copy does not show graphics. Since graphics can take a long time to print, printing a proof copy can save time when you only want to proofread text. After you've reviewed the proof copy and made any necessary changes to the publication, you'll print a final copy that includes the graphics.

Note: For best results, if the final output will be printed to a PostScript printer, the proof should also be printed to a PostScript printer.

Macintosh Note: Select the PSPrinter 8.3.1 driver in the Chooser when printing to a PostScript printer. See Chapter 12, "Printing Publications," for more information.

To print a proof version:

1 Choose Print from the File menu to open the Print Document dialog box (File > Print).

Settings for a PostScript printer

2 Windows only: Select the name of an available printer for the Printer option.

This printer can be the one you specified in the Page Setup dialog box for the final printout of your publication, or it can be a desktop printer for a proof copy.

3 If you're printing to a PostScript printer, select a printer file for the PPD option.

For more information on printer files, see "PostScript Printer Description Files" on page 394.

4 Select the Proof option.

5 Click Ranges in the Pages option and type 1 so that PageMaker will print only the page you've completed.

6 Click Print.

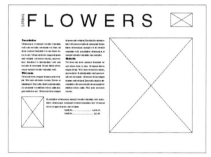

Proof of the brochure

7 Check your proof copy to see that it matches ours, make any changes, and then choose Save from the File menu (File > Save).

Now you can print the final copy of the brochure, including the graphics.

To print the final version:

1 Choose Print from the File menu (File > Print).

2 If the printer you'll use to print the final version differs from the one you used for your proof copy, change it now in the Print To (Windows only) and PPD options (PostScript printers only).

3 Click the Proof option to deselect it.

4 Click Print.

Final copy of the brochure

THE PROJECT IS COMPLETE

Congratulations! You've created and printed a brochure and letterhead with PageMaker. Now that you've learned the basics of PageMaker, remember to read about or explore the other powerful features available to you. These include:

• Multiple master pages to provide control and flexibility in page design.

• Multiple layers for structuring complex documents and making the design and editing process easier and faster.

• Frames for laying out pages before content (final text and graphics) is available.

• Hyperlinks palette to let you jump from specified text or graphics to other pages or to other documents on the World Wide Web.

• Color Management for consistent and reliable color output.

• Expert kerning and tracking controls for high-quality typography.

CHAPTER 3: CONSTRUCTING A PUBLICATION

This chapter explains the important steps in setting up a PageMaker publication, from specifying basic document attributes such as size and number of pages to using master pages and layout grids. By setting up an effective design framework for your publication, you will have an easier time creating and formatting its content.

The following sections describe options for setting up new publications, as well as for making revisions to existing publications.

SETTING UP PAGES

When you choose File > New to begin a new publication, the Document Setup dialog box appears. You can define the basic parameters of the publication, such as page size, orientation, margins, and the number of sides on which you print.

To set up a new publication:

1 Start PageMaker, and then choose File > New.

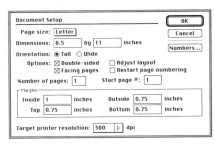

2 Specify page size and page attributes in the Document Setup dialog box as follows:

• Select a standard page size from the Page Size pop-up menu. When you select a page size, its dimensions appear in the Dimensions text boxes.

• Use the Dimensions text boxes to specify a custom page size up to 42 by 42 inches (1065 by 1065 mm). (You can also choose Page > Custom to set your own page size.)

• For Orientation, select Tall for a page that is taller than it is wide (Portrait orientation), or select Wide for a page that is wider than it is tall (Landscape orientation).

• Click Double-sided to set Inside and Outside margins to accommodate binding on pages that will be printed on two sides and to make the Facing Pages option available. Deselect Double-sided if you intend to print your publication on one side of the paper (single-sided) and don't want to turn on Facing Pages.

• Click Facing Pages if you want left and right pages displayed together (as a two-page spread) and you have selected Double-sided.

3 Enter the Number of Pages you initially plan for the publication. (You can add or delete pages later if necessary.)

For information about adding and formatting page numbers, see "Numbering Pages" on page 93. Also note that several pagination options are designed to help you work with a single long document divided into two or more booked publications (publications linked together with the Utilities > Book command). See "Numbering Pages in a Multiple-Publication Document" on page 237 for more information.

Setting margins

The margins you specify in the Document Setup dialog box are applied to the Document Master (the default master page initially applied to all pages in a new publication). When you create additional masters, you can specify margins different from those of the Document Master. See "Using Master Pages" on page 68 for more information.

When Double-sided is selected, margins are set as Inside and Outside. The inside margin is on the right side of even-numbered (left) pages and on the left side of odd-numbered (right) pages; the outside margins are correspondingly reversed. When Double-sided is deselected, PageMaker changes Inside and Outside to Left and Right margins.

When Double-sided is unchecked, margins appear as Left and Right rather than Outside and Inside.

The margins will display on pages as pink (horizontal) and blue (vertical), nonprinting lines.

Setting print-related Document Setup options

To avoid printing problems, specify the following options in the Document Setup dialog box:

• For Compose to Printer (Windows), choose the name of the printer you will use to print the final copy of your publication. Font choices and sizes, resolution of text and graphics, and the print area depend on the printer you select here.

• For Target Printer Resolution, select the number of dots per inch (dpi) your printer will use for the final printing of the publication. PageMaker uses this information to make 1-bit bitmap images conform to the printer resolution when you resize them. For more information on resizing bitmap images, see "Resizing 1-bit Bitmap Images" on page 199.

CHANGING DOCUMENT SETUP OPTIONS IN EXISTING PUBLICATIONS

Although the Document Setup dialog appears when you choose File > New to create a publication from scratch, you can modify a publication's Document Setup at any point in your work by choosing File > Document Setup while the publication is active.

Be sure to check the Adjust Layout option in the Document Setup dialog box if you change margins, page size, or orientation, and you want PageMaker to accordingly reposition (and in some cases resize) text, graphics, and nonprinting guides. Otherwise, objects on pages might not align with the modified page layout, and might even fall outside the margins or spill onto the pasteboard.

How PageMaker repositions or resizes objects and guides when you change the document setup depends on several factors, including the settings you specify in the Layout Adjustment Preferences dialog box (File > Preferences > Layout Adjustment), the kind of changes you make, and the position of objects and guides on each page. See "Adjusting a Layout Automatically" on page 85 for more information.

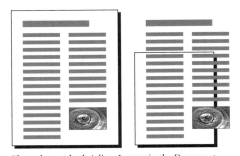

If you do not check Adjust Layout in the Document Setup dialog box, PageMaker does not reposition or resize objects and guides when you change margins, page size, or orientation.

Other changes you make in the Document Setup dialog box may not require layout adjustment, but can lead to conditions you need to consider:

• When you increase or decrease the starting number or number of pages in a publication by an odd number (1, 3, 5, and so on), left-hand, even-numbered pages become right-hand, odd-numbered pages, and vice versa. In a double-sided publication, text and graphics that bleed across the pages stay with the new right-hand, odd-numbered pages and spill onto the pasteboard. For more information, see "Adding and Deleting Pages" on page 18.

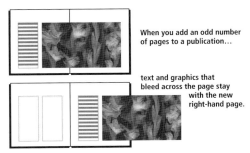

When you add an odd number of pages to a publication...

text and graphics that bleed across the page stay with the new right-hand page.

• If you change from a double-sided to a single-sided page, or vice versa, elements on left-hand pages may be repositioned relative to the new margins. When text flows onto the pasteboard or onto pages where you don't want it, you must reposition it manually on each page.

• If you change the Target Printer Resolution value, you should also resize existing 1-bit bitmap images to match the new printer resolution. See "Resizing 1-bit bitmap images" on page 199.

USING MASTER PAGES

In multi-page publications, your design will be more cohesive if each page is built on a common foundation, or master page. A master page typically contains basic design elements, such as

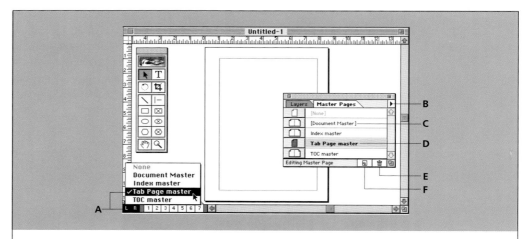

Master page basics • Typically you'll use the Master Pages palette to create and apply masters, and use the master page icons at the bottom of the window when you want to go to a master page for editing.

A Click to go to the master applied to the current page, or click and hold down the mouse button (Macintosh) or click the right mouse button (Windows) to display masters from which to choose.

B Click to open the Master Pages palette menu.

C Each new publication includes a Document Master, which is applied to your initial pages. The options specified in Document Setup determine the margins and orientation of the Document Master.

D Click a name or an icon to apply a master to the current page.

E Click the trash button to delete a selected master page.

F Click the new master button to quickly create a new master.

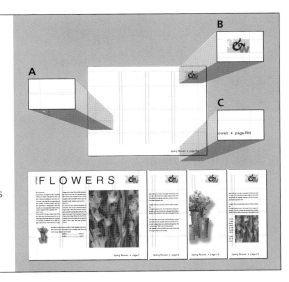

Formatting publications with master pages •
Master pages can save time and ensure consistency across pages and publications.

A Position nonprinting guides on the master pages to help you place text and graphics accurately and consistently throughout your publication.

B Create basic design elements on the master pages, including graphics or text that you want to appear on each page in your publication.

C Add headers or footers (such as page numbers and the book or chapter title) to master pages.

headers, footers, and page numbers, that are common to most or all pages in your publication. Master pages also contain nonprinting layout guides, such as column guides, ruler guides, and margin guides. Each publication can have a virtually unlimited number of master pages.

You can create, modify, and delete objects on master pages just like any other objects, but you must do so from the master pages themselves.

Each publication you open contains a Document-Master page or (if the publication includes facing pages) a Document-Master page spread. The Document Master applies to all pages in the publication until you specify otherwise, and cannot be renamed or removed from the publication.

An icon representing the master pages appears at the lower left corner of a publication window in layout view. The letters *L* and *R* (for left and right) mark the master page icon for facing pages; a single-sided publication icon is marked by an *R* alone. Click the icon to turn to the master applied to the current publication page.

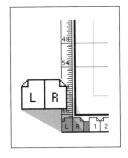
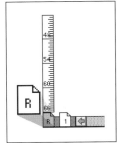

To create additional master pages, you use commands on the Master Pages palette menu. To create publication pages without basing them on master pages, apply the master None. (You can also choose to apply a master, but hide the master page items on particular pages. See "Displaying Master Pages and Master Page Items" on page 75 for more information.)

Creating master pages

In addition to using the default Document Master in your publication, you can create a master page from scratch, or create a master based on an existing master or publication page. If you plan to have several master pages that share one or more design attributes (such as position and formatting of page numbers), you can save time by designing the Document Master page or spread (for example), and then basing additional masters on the Document Master, rather than creating each new master from scratch.

To make a new master from scratch:

1 Choose Window > Show Master Pages.

2 Choose New Master from the Master Pages palette menu, or click the new master button (⌷) at the bottom of the palette.

3 Type a name for the master, and specify whether you want a single page or a two-page spread.

If your publication is single-sided, you do not have the option of creating a spread. See "Setting Up Pages" on page 65 for more information on creating single-sided or double-sided pages.

4 Specify the margins, number of columns, and space between the columns.

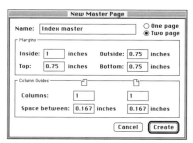

If you are creating a two-page master spread, be sure to specify columns and distance between them for both Left and Right pages in the spread.

5 Click Create.

PageMaker displays the newly created master page in the publication window, and adds its name to the Master Pages palette.

To make a new master from an existing master page:

1 Choose Window > Show Master Pages.

2 Do one of the following:

• Drag the name of the master you want to duplicate to the new master button (). In the dialog box that appears, type a name for the new master, and then click Duplicate.

• Choose Duplicate from the Master Pages palette menu, and, in the dialog box that appears select a master to duplicate. Then specify a name for the new master, and click Duplicate.

The new master page becomes active and its name appears on the Master Pages palette.

To make a new master from an existing page:

1 Turn to the publication page on which you want to base a new master.

2 Choose Window > Show Master Pages.

3 Choose Save Page As from the Master Pages palette menu.

4 Specify a name, and then click Save.

Objects and guides are copied to the new master, as well as master elements from the master page applied to the selected publication page. The new master page then becomes active and its name appears on the Master Pages palette.

APPLYING MASTER PAGES

When you create a master page, remember that it has no effect until you apply it to specific pages. This section describes the options you have for applying masters.

About the Adjust Layout option

By default, applying a master does not affect existing objects on the page. So, if you apply a master with margins or column setups that differ from the page's original master, you might need to reflow text or reposition objects on the page to fit them within the new master's page design. However, you can choose the Adjust Layout option on the Master Pages palette menu to have PageMaker automatically reposition (and even resize) text, graphics, and ruler guides on the pages to which the new master is applied, based on the margins and column setup of the new master. (Always check your pages to verify that the layout adjustments meet your needs, and to make corrections and manual adjustments as required.)

How PageMaker repositions or resizes objects and guides when you apply a master depends on several factors, including the settings you specify in the Layout Adjustment Preferences dialog box, the differences between the newly-applied master and the previous master applied to the page, and the position of objects and guides on the affected page. See "Adjusting a Layout" on page 85 for more information.

When you apply a master page...

objects on the page are repositioned only if Adjust Layout is selected on the Master Pages palette menu.

Applying a different master to existing pages

The Document Master is applied to all pages in your initial publication. You can use a variety of methods to apply a different master to a page.

To change one page or spread at a time:

1 Turn to the page you want to change.

2 Choose Window > Show Master Pages.

3 Select Adjust Layout on the Master Pages palette menu if you want objects and guides on the page or spread to be repositioned or resized as appropriate for the margins and columns of the master you are about to apply.

4 Click the master name or icon on the Master Pages palette.

Note: *If you apply a master to a page and PageMaker asks you to confirm that you want to apply the master, click Apply in the dialog box that appears. To prevent this message from appearing subsequently, deselect the Prompt on Apply command on the Master Pages palette menu.*

To quickly apply the same master to several pages throughout a publication:

1 Choose Window > Show Master Pages.

2 Choose Apply from the Master Pages palette menu.

3 Specify a range of pages to change.

If appropriate, use the Page Range text boxes to type a contiguous range (use a hyphen to separate the first and last page numbers in the range—as in 3-6) or a discontiguous range (use commas to separate the numbers—as in 2, 4, 8) or a combination of both. For example, typing "1, 3-6, 10-" applies the specified master to pages 1, 3, 4, 5, 6, 10, and all subsequent pages in that publication.

4 Do one of the following:

• To apply a single master, select its name from the Master Page pop-up menu.

• If the publication is double-sided, and you want to apply one master to the left-hand pages in the range and another master to the right-hand pages in the range, select the Set Left and Right Pages Separately option, and then select the masters you want to apply.

5 Select Adjust Layout if you want objects and guides on the specified pages to be repositioned or resized as appropriate for the margins and columns of the master you are about to apply.

6 Click Apply.

Applying masters to new pages as you create them

Master pages are automatically applied to newly created pages, but how this happens is determined by the command you use to add the new pages:

• The Layout > Insert Pages command adds pages before or after the currently selected page (or, optionally, between the pages of the selected spread). In the Insert Pages dialog box, you select a master to apply the new pages. If the publication is double-sided, and you want to apply one master to the new left-hand pages and another master to the new right-hand pages, select the Set Left and Right Pages Separately option, and then select the masters you want to apply.

• The File > Document Setup command lets you increase the number of pages in the publication. When you click OK, PageMaker inserts the new pages at the end of the publication, and applies the Document Master to them.

Shortcut: *Press Command + Opt + Shift + G (Macintosh) or Ctrl + Alt + Shift + G (Windows) to insert a new page at the end of a publication.*

Applying spreads versus single pages

When you apply a master page spread to a page or pair of facing pages, the publication pages are not associated with the left- or right-hand master page specifically, but with the spread itself. That is, when repagination causes a left-hand publication page to change to a right-hand page, the right-hand page of the master spread is automatically applied to the page. (This is consistent with earlier versions of PageMaker.)

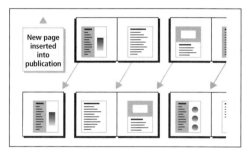

Left-hand masters are applied to former right-hand page elements, and vice-versa.

Note: *If you want to ensure that a page doesn't switch masters when the pages are rearranged, you can create and apply a single-sided master page.*

In a publication that is double-sided with facing pages, you can take advantage of two special techniques:

• Apply one page from a master page spread to any page, including either the left or the right publication page in a spread. (You can only apply the left side of a master page spread to a left-hand page, and the right side of master page spread to a right-hand page.) The palette will highlight both master page names in the palette list, but only highlight the left or right side of the page icon in the palette.

• Apply a single-sided master (or the empty None master) to either side of a spread. The palette will highlight the single-page master, but display an L or an R to indicate the side of the spread to which it is applied.

Note: *Objects that straddle both sides of a master page spread are associated with the left-hand master page. Therefore, if a left-hand page's master includes an object that straddles both sides of the master-spread, then that object will appear on the right-hand publication page, regardless of that page's master.*

To change the master on only one side of a two-page spread:

1 Go to the spread you want change.

2 Choose Window > Show Master Pages.

3 Select Adjust Layout on the Master Pages palette menu if you want objects and guides on the affected page to be repositioned or resized as appropriate for the margins and columns of the master you are about to apply.

4 Press Option (Macintosh) or Alt (Windows) and do one of the following:

• To assign a master page spread to a left-hand page, click the left-hand side of the master page icon on the palette. (If the master is a single page, click the left edge of the icon.)

• To apply a master page spread to a right-hand page, click the right side of the master page icon on the palette. (If the master is a single page, click the right edge of the icon.)

DISPLAYING MASTER PAGES AND MASTER PAGE ITEMS

You must turn to a master page if you want to add or modify guides and objects on the master. (If you simply want to edit the name of the master or change margins or column setup, you can use the Setup command on the Master Pages palette menu. See "Revising, Deleting, and Renaming Masters" on page 76.)

To turn to a master page, use any of the following techniques:

• Click the master page icon at the bottom of the publication window to display the master page applied to the current page. If you are working on a spread with two different masters applied, PageMaker turns to the master applied to the right-hand page.

• Click the master page icon and hold down the mouse button (Macintosh) or click the right mouse button (Windows) until the list of masters appears. Then select the master you want to view.

• Choose Layout > Go to Page, and then select the name of the master you want.

Note: *When the master page icon is highlighted, clicking a master name or icon on the Master Pages palette displays the master you selected. But when a publication-page icon is selected, clicking a master name or icon on the Master Pages palette applies the master.*

The guides and objects on the master page appear on the pages to which the master is applied; however, you can specify that a page not display or output the items from its associated master page.

To display or hide master page objects on specific publication pages:

1 Go to the publication page you want to change.

2 Choose View > Display Master Items.

When the menu option is checked, master page items are visible on the page.

REVISING, DELETING, AND RENAMING MASTERS

When you revise master pages, the changes appear instantly on associated publication pages. You can add or manipulate text and graphics, and change guides or rulers on masters just as you can on any publication page. To change a master page's margins, however, you use the Setup command on the Master Pages palette menu, not the File > Document Setup command. Document Setup controls margins for the Document Master (and all pages to which that master is applied).

Note: *To change column setup, turn to the master page and use either the Layout > Column Guides command or the Master Page Options command from the Master Pages palette menu.*

To revise or rename a master page:

1 Turn to the master page you want to revise. (If you are changing the master's name or its margins or columns only, you can skip this step and go to step 3.)

See "Displaying Masters and Master Page Items" on page 75 for more information.

2 Add or modify text, graphics, or nonprinting guides on the page.

If you use the mouse or the control palette to reposition guides on a master, the changes appear on associated publications, but the objects on those pages do not change position or size.

3 To change the master's name, margins, or column guides, either click the name of the master you want to modify and choose Master Page Options from the Master Pages palette menu, or press Command (Macintosh) or Ctrl (Windows) and click the name of the master you want to modify.

4 Type the new name and the new values you want for margins or columns.

5 Select Adjust Layout if you want objects and guides on the associated pages to be repositioned or resized as appropriate for changes to margins and columns of the master you are editing.

6 Click OK.

Shortcut: *To quickly open the Master Page Options dialog box, press Command (Macintosh) or Ctrl (Windows) and click the name of the Master Page you want to edit.*

To delete a master page and all the objects on it:

1 Choose Window > Show Master Pages.

2 Select the master page or spread to delete, and either choose Delete ["Master name"] from the Master Pages palette menu, or click the trash button on the bottom of the palette.

When prompted, click OK or Delete.

Note: To bypass the prompt message when deleting a master page, press Option (Macintosh) or Alt (Windows) as you drag.

PageMaker deletes the master, and applies the None master to all pages that had the deleted master applied.

Removing master page formatting

You can quickly clear one or more publication pages of the current master page's formatting (with the exception of margins) by applying the None master, which is available from every publication. By default, applying the None master removes only the objects, not the column and ruler guides, that had been on the previously-assigned master page, but by using keyboard modifiers as you apply the None master, you can specify that column guides and rulers are also removed from the pages.

To remove master page formatting from several publication pages at a time, choose the Apply command from the Master Pages palette menu and select None as the master. The following procedure explains how to quickly apply None to the active page.

To remove master page formats from a page:

1 Turn to the page you want to change.

2 Use one of the following options:

Note: To apply any of the following changes to only one page in a pair of facing pages, press Option (Macintosh) or Alt (Windows) and click on the side of the None master icon that corresponds to the side of the spread you want to change as you follow the step.

• To remove the master page objects but retain column and ruler guides from the page, click None in the Master Pages palette.

• To remove the master page objects, column guides, and ruler guides from the page, click Shift + None in the Master Pages palette.

• To remove the master page objects and column guides but retain ruler guides, press Option (Macintosh) or Alt (Windows) + Shift, and then click None in the Master Pages palette.

• To remove the master page objects and ruler guides but retain column guides, press Command (Macintosh) or Ctrl (Windows) + Shift, and then click None in the Master Pages palette. (You can only apply this change to both pages in a pair of facing pages.)

CHOOSING A MEASUREMENT SYSTEM AND SETTING UP RULERS

Each publication window can include horizontal and vertical rulers that extend along the top and left borders of the window. You can display rulers when you need them and hide them when you want more room on the screen to view a publication. The rulers must be visible in order to manually create ruler guides, which are nonprinting extensions of the ruler.

When you need to position text objects and graphics precisely on a page, you can use the ruler increments. The increments shown on the rulers depend on the size and resolution of your screen, the unit of measure you specify, and the display size you choose. You can make any item you place, resize, or move align to the nearest intersection of tick marks on the invisible grid defined by the rulers.

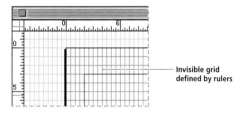

Invisible grid
defined by rulers

Because you use the rulers to set up your layout grid, it's a good idea to choose a measurement system before you begin laying out pages. You can set the unit of measure separately for each ruler. For example, you may want to measure lines of text vertically in points, but prefer millimeters for margins, tabs, and other horizontal measurements.

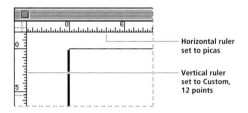

Horizontal ruler
set to picas

Vertical ruler
set to Custom,
12 points

The horizontal ruler reflects the unit of measure used for most measurements in the publication. You specify tabs, margins, indents, and other measurements according to the measurement system reflected on the horizontal ruler.

You usually work with one unit of measure throughout a publication, but you can change to another unit of measure at any time. Guides and objects already positioned using the original measurement system will stay in place and may not align with the altered ruler tick marks.

To hide or display rulers:

Choose View > Show/Hide Rulers.

To select a measurement system and set the vertical ruler:

1 Choose File > Preferences > General.

2 Select the Measurement System option you want to use.

The horizontal ruler reflects the measurement system you select.

3 Select a Vertical Ruler option, and then click OK.

To use points as the vertical measurement, select Custom, and then type the number of points you want between tick marks on the ruler—typically this will match the leading for body text in your publication.

Note: PageMaker uses PostScript points, which do not correspond exactly to traditional printer points. (There are 72.27 traditional printer points in an inch, as opposed to 72 PostScript points.) Because a point is such a small unit, if you set the vertical ruler to Custom, the ruler actually shows picas, not points. For more information on using the vertical ruler to create a leading grid, see "Aligning Elements to a Leading Grid" on page 167.

Temporarily overriding the measurement system • To override the unit of measure in a particular place, type a one-character abbreviation after the value you enter in any text box.

To change to...	Type...
Inches	i after the number (as in 5.25i for 5¼ inches).
Millimeters	m after the number (as in 25m for 25 millimeters).
Picas	p after the number (as in 18p for 18 picas).
Points	p before the number (as in p6 for 6 points).
Picas and points	p between the numbers (as in 18p6 for 18 picas and 6 points).
Ciceros	c after the number (as in 5c for 5 ciceros).

Overriding the unit of measure

You can temporarily override the current unit of measure when you enter a value in any dialog box. For example, if you have specified inches as your publication measurement system, but you want the top margin of your page to be six picas, enter **6p** for the top margin in the Document Setup dialog box. PageMaker converts the measurement for you.

Using the zero point

The zero point is the position at which the zeros on the vertical and horizontal rulers intersect.

When you start a new, single-sided publication, PageMaker puts the zero point at the intersection of the top, left edge of the page. When you work with facing pages, the default zero point is at the intersection of the top, inside edges of the facing pages.

You can move the zero point easily to measure distances from a specific part of your page or to customize the way oversized pages print. To avoid moving the zero point accidentally after you set it, you can lock it in place.

To move the zero point:

1 Position the pointer tool on the crosshair in the zero point window.

2 Drag to the new location.

3 Release the mouse button; the zero point is reset.

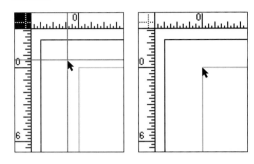

To lock the zero point:

Choose View > Zero Lock.

To reset the zero point:

Double-click the zero point window to reset it to the default location.

WORKING WITH NONPRINTING GUIDES

Nonprinting guides are lines that help you position objects on pages but do not appear in print. These lines form the framework of the layout grid. There are three kinds of nonprinting guides: margin guides, column guides, and ruler guides.

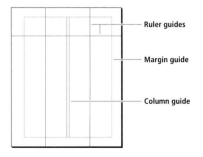

Ruler guides

Margin guide

Column guide

• Margins are defined in the Document Setup dialog box when you first create a publication, and are applied to the Document Master page. Margin guides appear automatically on the pages to which the Document Master is applied. Master pages you create in addition to the Document Master can have different margins. You can change the Document Master margins using the File > Document Setup command or by choosing Master Page Options from the Master Pages palette menu with the Document Master selected. You change the margins on other master pages only by using the Master Page Options command on the Master Pages palette menu.

• Column guides serve as boundaries for text you place within them. Every page has at least one column, which is the area between the margins. When you specify multiple columns (with the Layout > Column Guides command, or when creating or editing a master page), PageMaker automatically creates columns of equal size that fit between the margins. To create unequally-sized columns, use the pointer tool to drag the column guides to the positions you want. (Or use the Grid Manager plug-in described later in this chapter.)

• Ruler guides, like column guides, are non-printing lines that help you align items on a page. Unlike column guides, ruler guides don't control the flow of text; they help you align objects precisely.

You can define and revise each kind of guide separately, or you can use the Grid Manager plug-in to define and save a collection of margin, column, and ruler guides as layout grids. You can apply a grid to any range of pages in the publication, and reuse grids in other publications.

To display or hide the column, ruler, and margin guides on the page:
Choose View > Show/Hide Guides.

If you try to select an object but instead select a guide that overlaps it, you can press Command (Macintosh) or Ctrl (Windows) to select the object through the guide. Or, you can set guides to display in back of page elements throughout the current publication by choosing View > Send Guides to Back. (To set the option for all new publications you create, choose the command with no publication open.)

To force objects you move or resize to align with the nearest guide:
Choose View > Snap to Guides.

All margin, column, and ruler guides exert a magnetic-like pull on any tool, text, or graphic within three pixels of the guide. (A pixel, or picture element, is one dot in an array of dots that together create an image on the screen.) This option makes it easy to align text and graphics precisely to a guide, regardless of whether or not the guide rests on ruler increments.

Setting up column guides

You create columns to control the flow of text in text blocks that you place automatically and to help position text and graphics. How you specify columns is determined by the command you use:

Before column guides are applied

Reformatted, after column guides are applied

• The Layout > Column Guides command creates a specified number of columns of identical widths, fitting them within the margins of the page. If there is text or graphics already on the page, PageMaker can reposition them to align with the revised column setup if you select Adjust Layout in the Column Guides dialog box. See "Adjusting a Layout" on page 85 for details.

• The Utilities > Plug-ins > Grid Manager command provides the additional capability of fitting columns within any area you specify, or creating columns of a specified width. For more information, see "Creating and Applying Layout Grids" on page 90.

You can create up to 20 columns on a page. (PageMaker's default setting is one column per page, which is the entire area between the margins.) To save time and ensure consistency, add column guides to master pages rather than to specific publication pages. For more information about setting up columns on master pages, see "About Guides and Master Pages" on page 84.

To set up columns on a page:

1 Turn to the publication page or master page where you want the columns.

2 Choose Layout > Column Guides.

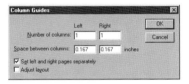

When facing pages appear in the publication window and you choose Column Guides, the Set Left and Right Pages Separately option appears so you can set columns differently for each page.

3 Enter the number of columns you want on the page and the space you want between columns, called the gutter.

If you are setting left and right pages separately, enter values for both pages.

4 Select Adjust Layout if you want existing text and graphics on the page to adjust to the revised column setup.

5 Click OK.

PageMaker creates the specified number of columns, equally spaced and equally sized.

Moving and locking columns

To adjust column widths, you can move the column guides by dragging them. The two lines forming the gutter between columns move together. Text and graphics already on the page are not changed in any way when you drag column guides.

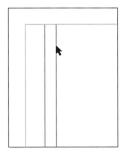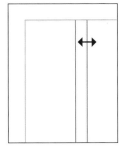

The leftmost and rightmost column guides, which overlap the margin guides, move individually. (Moving these column guides does not affect the margin guides.) All other column guides move in pairs, so that the space between columns remains consistent.

Note: *If you choose the Column Guides command after moving column guides manually, the word Custom appears for the Number of Columns option. The space between columns remains as originally specified.*

Once you have set up your columns, you can lock them in place to prevent accidental moving.

To lock or unlock column and ruler guides:

Choose View > Lock Guides.

Creating a page with different numbers of columns

You can vary the number of columns on different parts of the same page. For example, you may want two columns on the top half of the page and three columns on the bottom. You can mix columns in almost any combination within the limit of 20 columns per page.

Completed layout with different numbers of columns

To create different column setups on the same page:

1 Choose Layout > Column Guides, enter the number of columns you want in the top part of your page, and then click OK.

2 Position a ruler guide where you want the two-column format to end.

3 Position text within the first column down to the ruler guide. Then, click on the bottom of the windowshade handle.

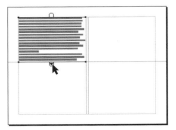

4 Position text within the second column down to the ruler guide.

5 Repeat step 1, only this time enter the number of columns you want in the bottom part of your page, and make sure the Adjust Layout option is not selected in the dialog box. Then pull a ruler guide down and position it where you want the top of the columns to begin.

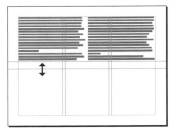

6 Place the rest of the text within the newly defined columns, or select another document to place.

ABOUT GUIDES AND MASTER PAGES

You can use the Layout > Column Guides command to add or change columns on master pages and publications. Alternatively, you can set up columns when you first create a new master or revise one using the Master Page Options command on the Master Page palette menu. The column setup options in the New Master dialog box and in the Master Page Options dialog box provide the same capabilities as the Layout > Column Guides command—that is, they let you define the number of columns, and the space between them. Both dialog boxes let you specify whether or not you want text or graphics to be repositioned or resized to align with the revised column setup.

Any guides (including column guides) that you create on a master page are automatically displayed on the publication pages to which the master is applied. Unlike text and graphics on a master page, you can select and move master page guides from a publication page. If you adjust master page guides on a publication page, or add new ruler guides to them, PageMaker considers those guides to be customized.

You can restore the master page guides and delete the custom guides by choosing Layout > Copy Master Guides. This command does not affect master page items that print, such as page numbers, and is available only if you have customized the guides on the current page by moving them from their original positions defined on a master page. The command also has no effect on text and graphics already on the page.

Setting up ruler guides

A publication page can have up to 120 ruler guides, in any combination of horizontal and vertical. If a page contains ruler guides from a master page, those guides count toward the total of 120.

To place a ruler guide:

Move the pointer over a ruler, and then drag a ruler guide from the ruler.

If the rulers aren't visible, choose View > Show Rulers.

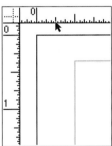 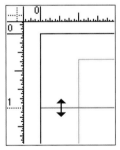

Move the pointer over a ruler, hold down the mouse button...   *and then drag a guide from the ruler.*

To remove a ruler guide:

Select the guide you want to remove and drag it off the publication page.

To remove all ruler guides at once:

Choose View > Clear Ruler Guides. (This command is unavailable if the Lock Guides command is checked.)

To lock or unlock ruler guides:

Choose View > Lock Guides.

If you later change publication-layout attributes such as margins or page size, locking guides can interfere with PageMaker's ability to adjust objects on the page.

To make objects align to the ruler increments:

Choose View > Snap to Rulers.

ADJUSTING A LAYOUT AUTOMATICALLY

The Adjust Layout feature can save you considerable time and effort when you need to revise the layout framework of a page or a whole document—margins or page size, number of columns, orientation, and so on. For example, you can quickly refashion a four-column publication designed for a US Letter-size page, to a two-column format on a US Legal-size page. PageMaker then revises the text and graphics on each page to match the new parameters. This feature also saves you time when you apply a new master to previously-formatted pages.

You can best take advantage of this capability if you understand the specific ways in which PageMaker determines how to reposition or resize objects and guides in response to layout framework changes. Then you can arrange objects on your pages accordingly, preparing for the time when your layout framework may need to change, and ensuring the most predictable and appropriate results if it does.

Since a software program can only make a limited set of decisions about page design, you'll want to double-check your pages after adjusting layout. The more structured and straightforward your initial design and the more directly it maps to the new framework, the more likely the results of layout changes will be acceptable to you. The more your pages deviate from standard placement of text and graphics, and the more the layout revisions deviate from the original layout, the more time you will have to devote to manually touching-up your newly arranged pages.

Setting layout adjustment preferences

When you select the Adjust Layout option in dialog boxes that let you control page, margin, and column setups, or select the Adjust Layout option on the Master Pages palette menu, PageMaker makes layout revisions based on settings in the Layout Adjustment Preferences dialog box.

To set layout adjustment preferences:

1 Choose File > Preferences > Layout Adjustment.

2 For Snap to Zone, specify the area surrounding page edges and nonprinting guides within which objects are considered to be aligned to the page edge or guide. The wider the snap to zone, the more likely an object is associated with (and therefore moved with) a page edge or guide.

3 In the Adjust Page Elements section of the dialog box, select from the following options:

• Select OK to Resize Groups and Imported Graphics if you want changes to page size and column widths to influence the size of those graphics proportionately. The aspect ratio of graphics is maintained if and when they do resize.

• Select Ignore Object and Layer Locks if you want layout framework changes to affect objects you've locked either with the Element > Lock Position command or by locking layers.

• Select Ignore Ruler Guide Alignments if you want to base all layout arrangements on each object's relationship to columns and margins only.

4 In the Adjust Ruler Guides section of the dialog box, select from the following options:

• Select Allow Ruler Guides to Move if you want to reposition ruler guides based on changes to the layout framework. With this option selected, even locked guides will move as required by the revised layout.

• Select Keep Column and Margin Alignments if you've positioned ruler guides over column and margin guides, and want to maintain that relationship in the revised layout framework.

Using automatic layout adjustment • To understand how objects on pages move or resize when the layout framework changes, it's important to understand, first, what kind of changes affect margin, column, and ruler guides. Then, understand how objects aligned to one or more of those guides maintain their guide alignments when the guides change. How objects and guides behave is determined in part by settings in the Layout Adjustment Preferences dialog box. The example on this page shows *what* happens when page orientation changes (with default preference settings).

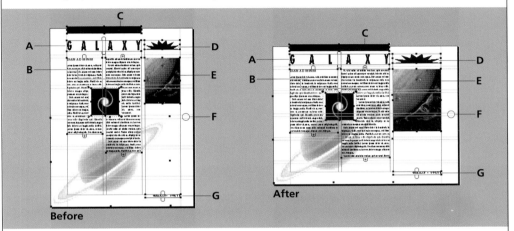

Before

After

Before layout adjustment

A Unthreaded text object spans columns.

B Threaded text objects occupy columns.

C Bleed object extends 2 picas beyond page edge.

D PageMaker-drawn graphic aligns to column guide and margins.

E Imported graphic aligns to column guide and margins.

F Rule falls halfway down the page.

G Footer aligned to margin.

After layout adjustment

A Text object widens to maintain alignment to original two columns.

B Text reflows to fill resized columns.

C Bleed object moves but still extends 2 picas beyond page edge.

D PageMaker-drawn graphic resizes disproportionally and maintains all alignments.

E Imported graphic moves, and resizes proportionally, maintaining alignments to guides on top and left of object.

F Rule moves to new halfway point, while rules aligned to columns move with column guides.

G Footer moves with margin.

How guides change when layout is revised

When this attribute changes...	These guides change, moving any object aligned to them*
Page size / orientation Before After	Margins are repositioned but their widths are maintained. Columns change width and height to fill the new page size. By default, ruler guides move to maintain relative position on the page (a ruler halfway down the original page moves to the halfway point on the new page). See "Setting Layout Adjustment Preferences" on page 86 for details on controlling how rulers move.
Margins Before After	Columns change width and height to adjust to new margins. By default, rulers move with the column or margin guides they overlay.
Column width or space between columns 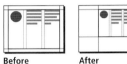 Before After	All column widths change. Layout adjustments only occur when column setup values are changed in the Column Guides or Master Page Option dialog boxes, or if a master with a different column setup is applied. Layout adjusment does not occur when you drag column guides. By default, rulers move with the column or margin guides they overlay.
Number of columns 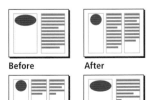 Before After Before After	Columns are added or removed from the right side of the page. All column widths are resized. **When adding a column:** Text flows into new columns if the previous rightmost column was occupied by a text block (not a text frame). Other objects aligned to the previous rightmost column stay aligned to that column in its new position. **When deleting a column:** If the previous rightmost column was occupied by a text block (not a text frame), the text block is closed (provided there's another text block on the page in which to flow the story). Other objects aligned to the previous rightmost column maintain relative position to page edges.

* Settings in the Layout Adjustment Preferences dialog box specify whether objects move with rulers.

How objects change when layout is revised

Relationship to guide	Change
Aligned on one side Before After	The object moves vertically or horizontally with the guide.
Aligned on neighboring sides Before After	The object moves vertically and/or horizontally to maintain both alignments.
Aligned on opposing sides Before After	PageMaker-drawn text and graphics move and resize to maintain both alignments. Groups and imported graphics resize proportionally, but only if specified in the Layout Adjustment Preferences dialog box.
Aligned on 3 or 4 sides Before After	PageMaker-drawn text and graphics move and resize to maintain all alignments. Groups and imported graphics resize proportionally to maintain alignment with guides on left and right sides, but only if specified in the Layout Adjustment Preferences dialog box.
Not aligned to guides	The object moves only if page size changes, maintaining position relative to page edges

CREATING AND APPLYING LAYOUT GRIDS

Once you understand the basics of margins, column guides, and ruler guides, you can use the Grid Manager plug-in to define, apply, and save collections of guides, which you can store in layout grid files to use later on different pages or in different publications.

You can also use the Grid Manager plug-in to create an evenly proportioned grid within an area of the page you specify, to create rows and columns of any height and width, and to automatically position guides to match your leading grid.

Creating a grid

Creating a grid with the Grid Manager plug-in is similar in many ways to creating a grid manually in the PageMaker layout window. The main difference is that you use the Grid Manager dialog box to type values specifying the number of guides and width of gutters, and use the preview window within the dialog box to position guides exactly as you want them on the page.

If you want to start off a new grid by using one or more of the guides from an existing page, you can copy the guides. See "Copying Grids" on page 92 for more information.

As you type values or make changes in the Grid Manager dialog box, the preview within the dialog box shows how the layout grid appears.

To set up a grid:

1 Choose Utilities > Plug-ins > Grid Manager.

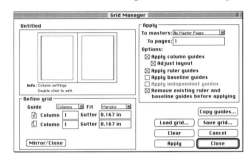

2 In the Define Grid area, specify the kind of guide you want from the Guide pop-up menu, as follows:

• Columns lets you divide the page or pages vertically using column guides.

• Rulers lets you divide the page or pages vertically and horizontally using ruler guides. If you are defining a two-page spread, the horizontal rulers span both pages, while the vertical columns can be set differently on each of the pages. Note that the columns are created with ruler guides, not column guides.

• Baseline lets you insert horizontal ruler guides at intervals matching the leading of your body text. This is a useful effect if you work with a leading grid. For information on creating a baseline grid, see "Aligning Elements to a Leading Grid" on page 167.

3 Type the number of rows you want (available only if you chose Rulers for Guide type), or the number of columns you want per page. The plug-in sets the width of the rows and columns you create, based on the number of columns you want and the space available. To create columns of varying sizes, see "Customizing Guides" on page 91.

• In the Gutter text boxes, specify the space between the rows and between the columns. If you later change this setting, the size of the rows and columns is adjusted so that the overall width or height of the rows and columns is preserved.

• For Fit, specify whether you want to fit column and ruler guides between margins, or within the dimensions of the entire page (changing this setting changes the size of rows and columns).

4 Apply the guides to specific pages. See "Applying Grids" on page 91 for more information.

Note: *You can create guides of one type (for example, columns), and then, for the same grid, add additional guides of any other type (for example, rulers).*

Customizing guides

With the preview section of the Grid Manager dialog box, you can change the width of columns, rows, or gutters.

To create columns or rows of varying widths:

1 Choose Columns or Rulers from the Guide option depending on the item you want to resize.

2 Double-click within the column or row you want to change.

3 Select Column Width or Row Height as appropriate, and type the new height and/or width value you want in the appropriate section of the Set Width or Height dialog box.

4 Select an option to specify how to apply the new width or height—changing both sides of the row or column equally, or changing just one side—and then click OK.

Applying grids

Once a grid setup is defined, you can apply it to any range of pages in the active publication, including master pages.

To apply a grid:

1 In the Grid Manager dialog box, define or load the grid you want to apply.

2 In the Apply To section, type the publication page numbers in the text box or, from the pop-up menu, choose the master page to which you want to apply the grid.

You can specify a contiguous range (type a hyphen to separate the lowest and highest pages in the range, as in 3-6), or a discontiguous range (type commas between the numbers, as in 1,2,7,9) or both. For example "1, 3-6, 10-" applies the grid to pages 1, 3, 4, 5, 6,10, and all subsequent pages.

3 In the Options section, select options to indicate which kinds of guides you want to apply. You can also select to remove existing guides on the pages you selected in step 2.

Note: If you choose to apply column guides, you can also select Adjust Layout to have text and graphic objects adjust to the new layout. See "Adjusting a layout automatically" on page 85 for more information.

4 Click Apply.

Mirroring and cloning grids

As you define a grid you can work on one page and then mirror or clone the grid so that it applies to both sides of a two-page spread. Mirroring means you reflect or flip the grid; cloning means you simply copy the grid from one page to the other without flipping it.

To mirror or clone a grid:

1 Define or load the grid in the Grid Manager dialog box.

2 Click Mirror/Clone.

3 In the Mirror and Clone dialog box, select the option corresponding to the way you want to reuse the current grid.

4 Click OK.

Copying grids

You can make use of the guides you've defined manually on a master page or publication page by importing them into the Grid Manager dialog box.

To copy one or more guides from a page:

1 Open the publication and turn to the page that has the guides you want to copy.

2 Choose Utilities > Plug-ins > Grid Manager.

3 Click Copy Guides.

4 Specify whether you want the guides from the left-hand or from the right-hand page, or both (if you turned to a spread in step 1).

5 Click Copy.

Note: Copied ruler guides are treated as custom (independent) ruler guides in the Grid Manager dialog box. See "Customizing Guides" on page 91 for more information.

Managing grids

You can save grids you've defined, and load any grid you've saved so that you can freely apply grids to other pages or within other publications.

To save a grid:

1 Set up the grid in the Grid Manager dialog box.

2 Click Save Grid.

3 Type a name for the grid, specify a location in which to store it, and then click OK.

To load a grid:

1 Click Load Grid in the Grid Manager dialog box.

2 Locate the grid you want, and then click OK.

To clear a grid:

Click Clear in the Grid Manager dialog box.

NUMBERING PAGES

To print page numbers in a publication, you must tell PageMaker where to put the numbers and how you want them to look. For example, you may want page numbers to include some text, such as the word *Page* before the number, or you may want to number your introduction with Roman numerals. In PageMaker you do this by adding a page-number marker, a special character that keeps track of the page order in the publication and ensures that each page is numbered correctly at all times.

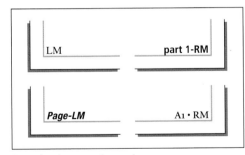

Examples of page number markers

Pages are numbered starting from 1, unless you specify a different starting point in the Document Setup dialog box, or unless the publication is part of a booked publication (a series of individual publications forming a single large document) that is being numbered sequentially. PageMaker provides several options for numbering pages across two or more publications; see "Numbering Pages in a Multiple-Publication Document" on page 237 for more information.

PageMaker won't allow more than 999 pages per single publication, but page numbers can be as large as 9999 (for example, you can start a 50-page chapter with page 9949).

Although you can add a page number to any publication page, it is best to add the page numbers to master pages. This saves time and ensures the numbers appear at the same place on each page. Be sure to add a page number marker to all master pages applied in your publication (assuming you want all pages to appear with a page number).

To add page numbers to a publication:

1 Turn to a master page or to a publication page.

2 Use the text tool to click an insertion point on the page where you want the page number to appear, or click in a text frame you've placed on the page for the page number.

3 Press Command + Option + P (Macintosh) or Ctrl + Alt + P (Windows).

4 Use the text tool to select and format the text as desired.

On the master pages, a page-number marker (LM for a left master page, RM for a right master page or single page master) indicates where page numbers will appear.

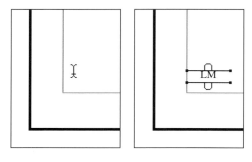

To specify the starting page number:

1 Choose File > Document Setup.

2 Depending on whether or not the publication is part of a book being numbered sequentially, specify options as follows:

• To start pagination at a certain number, type the starting page number in Start Page #. If the publication is part of a book, click Restart Page Numbering.

• To let PageMaker calculate the starting page number based on the publication's location in a book, deselect Restart Page Numbering.

To change the numbering system:

1 Choose File > Document Setup.

2 Click Numbers.

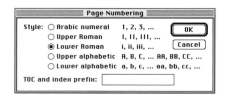

3 Select the numbering system you want to use, and then click OK.

You can select Arabic numerals, Roman numerals, or letters of the alphabet to number your pages. For information on the TOC and Index Prefix option, see "Specifying a Page-Number Format" on page 241.

REARRANGING PAGES

You can move pages from one position to another in the active publication simply by arranging thumbnail representations of your pages in the page order you want. PageMaker then reorders and renumbers your pages based on the changes you make.

Changing the order of pages does not alter the text in a story. The story remains intact even though text objects may have moved to different pages.

To move pages:

1 Choose Layout > Sort Pages.

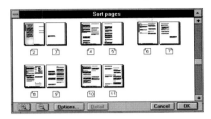

2 Select the page or pages you want to move, as follows:

• To select either a single-sided page or a pair of facing pages, click the page icon.

• To select one page in a pair of facing pages, press Command (Macintosh) or Ctrl (Windows) and click the page.

3 Drag the selection to the location you want. To insert a selection between a pair of facing pages, press Command (Macintosh) or Ctrl (Windows) and drag the selection over the facing pages.

A black bar indicates where the selected pages will be inserted. When you release the mouse button, the pages are dropped into the new position and are renumbered accordingly.

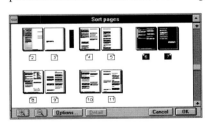

Once a page is moved within the window (or affected by the repositioning of another page), the original page icon is dimmed and another page icon appears beside the thumbnail to indicate its new page number and its left- or right-page status. In this way, the page icons provide a visual reminder of the original page order and a clear representation of the new page order.

4 Click OK to change the page order.

Resizing the Sort Page thumbnails

While rearranging pages you can view more or fewer thumbnails at a time by resizing the dialog box, and also by changing the size of thumbnails in the Sort Pages window. In addition, you can view pages at the current size in greater or lesser detail.

• To reduce or enlarge the size of the pages, click the magnifying icon or the reduction icon.

Shortcut: *You can press Alt +. (Windows) or Command + Shift + . (Macintosh) to magnify pages, or press Alt +, (Windows) or Command + Shift + , (Macintosh) to reduce them.*

• To display detailed thumbnails of all pages, click Options, and then click Show Detailed Thumbnails.

• To display detailed thumbnails for selected pages only, click Detail in the Sort Pages dialog box.

Changing Document Setup

While rearranging pages you can make the publication double-sided, single-sided, or facing pages. In the Sort Page dialog box, click Options, and select the option you want.

When double-sided pages become single-sided, the inside margin becomes the left margin and the outside margin becomes the right margin. In this case you can have PageMaker move all elements to fit within new inside and outside margins by deselecting Don't Move Elements.

CREATING RUNNING HEADERS AND FOOTERS

Some publications, such as dictionaries or directories, require headers or footers that indicate the content of each page. If you've used text blocks to contain a story, you can use the Running Headers/Footers plug-in to generate these headers or footers automatically. PageMaker searches a story and locates the text you specify

(for example, the first word in the first occurrence of a specific paragraph style) and then inserts the text into the text block defined for the header or footer. The Running Headers and Footers plug-in works on one story at a time, in one publication at a time.

Positioning and formatting running headers and footers

In PageMaker you create and define the size, position, and style of the running header text block—which maintains a consistent look and position from page to page—at the same time as you define its content, which changes from page to page.

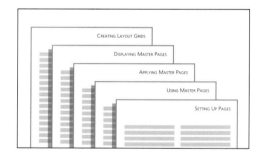

To position and format the header or footer's text block:

1 Use the pointer to select a text block in the story for which you want a header or footer.

2 Choose Utilities > Plug-ins > Running Headers/Footers.

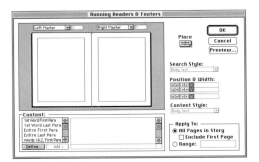

3 At the top of the sample page, select the master or publication pages whose guides you want to use for positioning purposes.

4 Click or drag the Place icon to create a text block placeholder, and position it where you want the header or footer to appear.

Text block placeholder — Place icon —

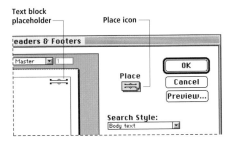

To remove a placeholder, drag it off the page.

5 Use the nudge buttons or the Position and Width text boxes to finalize the placement and width of the selected placeholder.

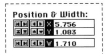

The position is calculated relative to the publication's zero point, which is indicated in the page preview.

The leftmost nudge buttons snap the placeholder to the nearest guide.

6 From the Content Style menu, select a paragraph style with which to format the text that will appear in the selected header or footer text block.

7 For Apply To, select a page range for the selected text block or select Each Page in Story.

This determines which pages the selected running header will appear on.

You can use the Range text box to specify a contiguous range (type a hyphen to separate the lowest and highest pages in the range, e.g. 3-6), or a discontiguous range (type commas between the numbers, e.g., 1,2,7,9) or both. For example "1, 3-6, 10-" applies the header or footer to pages 1, 3, 4, 5, 6, 10, and all subsequent pages.

8 Repeat steps 4-7 for each running header or footer text block you want to appear.

Defining header and footer content

The first step in defining the content of a running header or footer is to specify the paragraphs from which you want to draw the content. In an employee directory, for example, you might want the header on each page to indicate the first employee name listed on the page; in this case you'd want PageMaker to ignore the paragraphs describing each employee, but search only for the first instance of text with the paragraph style applied to each employee name.

Then, you describe how much of the text in the specified paragraphs to restate in the header, or how to reuse and rearrange the text. For example, you might want to include in an employee directory's running header only the last name of the first employee listed on each page.

To specify content:

1 Select the text block placeholder for the header or footer you are defining.

2 Choose a defined paragraph style from the Search Style menu, or choose Any Style if paragraph style doesn't matter.

3 In the Content section of the dialog box, specify the content for the selected placeholder. Your options are:

• Select a predefined header/footer from the Content list box, and click Add.

• Select a predefined header/footer and add text before or after it. In the Content text area, you can type text or special characters (such as tabs or spaces) outside the brackets that enclose each predefined header/footer. Text you type outside the opening and closing brackets that enclose each predefined header/footer is "static"—that is, added to the each instance of the running header/footer text block. For example, you might want to preface the running header/footer with the text "Section 3."

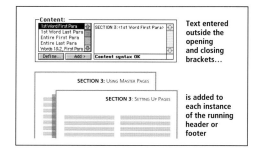

• String one or more predefined headers/footers together. After you add the first predefined header/footer to the Content text box, click an insertion point in the Content text box where you want the next one to appear, select the predefined content in the list, and then click Add. For example, if you want a running header to list the first *and* last employee listed on that page, you could select the option "First word, First Para" and then "First word, Last Para."

By typing the word "to" between them ("<First Word, First Para> to <First Word, Last Para>") the header on page one would state, for example, "Adams to Barrett."

• Click Define to create your own headers/footers (which then appear in the list of predefined headers/footers to choose from), or to edit existing ones. This lets you customize to suit the needs of a particular publication. For example, if you wanted your headers to list the first word of company names in a directory, but, for foreign companies, omit articles such as "Le" or "La," you could define your own header that excluded all the foreign language articles you wanted.

4 Repeat steps 1-3 for each header or footer you need.

5 Click Preview to confirm that the running header/footer is defined correctly, or click Apply to close the dialog box and begin generating the running header/footer you defined.

Previewing is a good idea since it lets you detect problems ahead of time. See "Previewing the Running Header/Footer" on page 100 for more information.

Defining and editing customized content

When the list of predefined running headers/footers does not provide the particular information or arrangement of text that you need to display in the running header/footer, you can click

Define to describe the kind of running header/footer you need, or to describe just one part of a header/footer (called a "selector") that forms, with other selectors, a complete header/footer. PageMaker then makes the header/footer (or selector) you define available in the list of predefined headers/footers. Custom definitions are stored in the HDR2.ini file in the Plug-ins folder.

To define or edit a custom header/footer:

1 In the Running Headers dialog box, click Define.

2 Do one of the following:

• To base the custom content on an existing running header/footer option, select the option from the list, and then click New Selector.

• To revise an existing custom running header/footer, select it and then click Edit Selector.

3 If necessary, type a name for the new content.

4 Define or change the content by completing options in the Selector Definition section of the dialog box.

By choosing options from menus, you construct a sentence describing the effect you want. If you select Range from any menu, you must then type in the range of words, lines, or characters you want PageMaker to work with. To define exceptions or limitations (for example, to leave out vowels from the header/footer) you can type the words or characters you want to omit or include at the appropriate place in the sentence.

5 Click OK in the Edit Selector and Define dialog boxes.

Previewing the running header/footer

You can quickly preview publications with the running header/footer you have defined without closing the dialog box.

To preview the headers/footers:

1 Click Preview to display a representation of the pages selected for Apply To.

2 Use the following techniques to view pages:

• To center the header or footer text block, click the view next button. Repeat for each header or footer you want to preview.

• To change pages, click a page tab at the bottom of the preview window.

• To change the page view, click the magnify icon and choose the preset size you want, or click the up or down arrow to go to the next lower or higher view.

• To scroll, move the cursor within the preview window and drag the hand icon.

3 Click OK to return to the Running Header/Footer dialog box.

Updating or removing running headers and footers

Remember that the Running Headers and Footers plug-in does not automatically update headers/footers if the story or publication subsequently changes. If, for example, you add or remove text from a story with headers/footers, or if your publication repaginates, you'll need to rerun the plug-in so that the headers/footers accurately reflect the content of each page.

• To update the running headers/footers due to a change in the associated story (or simply to change the format, position, or content of the running headers/footers), choose Utilities > Plug-ins > Running Headers/Footers, make any changes (if desired) to any aspect of the headers/footers, and then click OK.

- To delete running headers and footers associated with an existing story, select any text blocks in the story, choose Utilities > Plug-ins > Running Headers/Footers, drag the placeholder for the appropriate header/footer off the page, and click OK.

- To delete running headers and footers after their associated story has been deleted, select any running header or footer text block and choose Utilities > Running Header/Footer.

Chapter

4

CHAPTER 4: TEXT FORMATTING AND WORD PROCESSING

PageMaker gives you complete control over text in your publication. You can type and format text directly in layout view, or take advantage of PageMaker's story editor, a built-in word processor that makes it easy to create and edit text. This chapter describes how to add, create, and import text; arrange text on a page; use story editor to perform word-processing tasks; and create and apply paragraph styles.

In layout view, text is contained in text objects— either a text block (which is created with the text tool or by flowing text into columns) or a text frame (which is created with a frame tool or by choosing the Element > Frame > Change to Frame command with a PageMaker-drawn shape selected). The smallest text object can contain a single character in a tiny point size, and the largest text object can be 21 inches by 21 inches (53cm by 53cm). When you edit text, you work with letters and words, but you can manipulate text objects in the same way you manipulate graphics: as movable objects. Most of the changes you make to text as an object (for example, rotating or duplicating) are discussed in Chapter 6, "Graphics and Text Objects."

The way you work with text depends on the tool you use. The text tool lets you type, edit, format, and fine-tune characters and paragraphs. The pointer tool lets you work with text objects themselves.

CREATING TEXT OBJECTS

You use very different methods for creating the two kinds of PageMaker text objects—text frames and text blocks. But once the objects are created you work with one in much the same way as with the other.

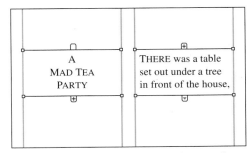

A text block must be rectangular; it cannot have a stroke or fill, and it cannot be empty.

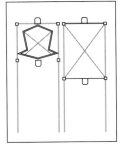
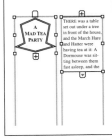

A text frame can be any shape; it can have a stroke or fill, and it can be empty, serving as a placeholder for text to come.

About text frames

You can turn any object you've created with the PageMaker drawing tools (with the exception of a line) into a frame, or you can draw a frame with a frame tool.

A frame becomes a text frame or a graphics frame depending on the content you add. Remember that once you add a graphic to a new frame, that graphic frame cannot include text (unless you first delete or detach the graphic from the frame).

Text frames do not change height or width as you add or remove text.

To create a text frame:

Either draw a new frame with a frame tool, or select a PageMaker-drawn shape and choose Element > Frame > Change to Frame.

See "Drawing and Editing Lines and Shapes" on page 179 for more information on drawing with PageMaker tools.

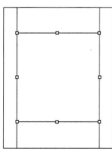 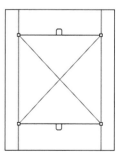

PageMaker-drawn rectangle   Rectangle changed to frame

The shape is ready to receive content. An empty frame displays with a nonprinting cyan marker, but otherwise behaves and prints like any other PageMaker-drawn shape.

Note: You can apply space, called an inset, between the text and the boundary of the frame; you can also align text vertically between a text frame's top and bottom boundaries. See"Positioning Content Within a Frame" on page 187 for details on these options.

To add text to a frame:

Do one of the following:

• Click the text tool, click in the frame, and then type or paste text directly into the frame.

• Choose File > Place, double-click a text file, and, when the cursor becomes a loaded icon, click on the frame you want to fill with text.

• Attach a text block to a frame, effectively deleting the text block and adding its text to the frame.

To attach a text block to a frame:

1 Select a text block, hold down Shift, and then select an empty frame.

2 Choose Element > Frame > Attach Content.

The text flows into the frame and the text block disappears.

About text blocks

A text block is similar to a text frame in that it contains text you type, paste, or import. You cannot see the borders of a text block until you select it with the pointer tool.

You create text blocks in two ways:

• Click or drag the text tool outside an existing text object on the page or pasteboard, and then type. (Unlike text frames, text blocks must contain text.)

• Click a loaded text icon in an empty column or page. This creates as many new text blocks (the exact size of the page columns) as needed to contain the text in the loaded text icon. For information on loading a text icon with text, see "Placing Text on the Page" on page 110.

To create a text block with the text tool:

 1 Select the text tool from the toolbox. The pointer turns into an I-beam.

2 On an empty area of the page or pasteboard, do one of the following:

• Click the I-beam where you want to insert text. This creates a text block the width of the column or page. By default, the insertion point jumps to the left side of the text block.

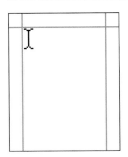

• Drag a rectangular area to define the width you want the text to occupy. This creates a custom-size text block that may or may not fall within column or page margins. The insertion point jumps to the left side of the text block.

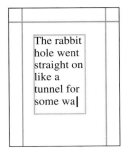

3 Type the text you want.

Unlike with a text frame, you do not see the borders of a text block until you click the text with the pointer tool.

SELECTING TEXT OR TEXT OBJECTS

Whether you are using text frames or text blocks, you must use the text tool to edit or format text. To modify the text object itself (for example, to rotate it) you select with the pointer tool.

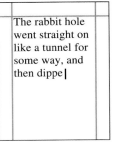 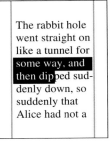

Select a text object with the pointer tool.   *Select text within a text object with the text tool.*

Comparing text frames and text blocks • Whether you use text frames or text blocks (or both), you'll be able to create the same kinds of publications and enjoy the same high-quality typographic and word-processing features in PageMaker. You can work most efficiently, however, if you understand the particular strengths of each kind of text object, and then select the approach that best matches the needs of your project. The following list, intended as a starting point only, highlights the differences between text frames and text blocks, and offers a basic summary of their strengths.

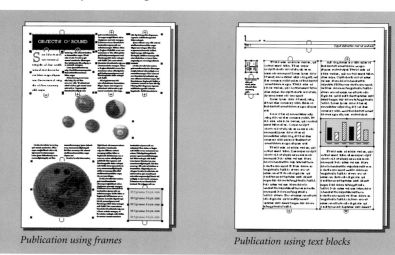

Publication using frames   *Publication using text blocks*

Text frames, unlike text blocks…

• Can be created and threaded before content is added, preserving a layout for text to come.

• Maintain their initial height as you add, delete, and reformat text.

• Support vertical alignment of text (so text can align to the bottom of a column and flow upwards).

• Can be any shape—rectangle, oval, or polygon—and can have strokes and fills applied.

In summary: *Text frames*, with their ability to act as threaded placeholders, generally work best for highly-structured and layout-intensive documents (such as newsletters or magazines) where the design is determined before the text is ready to flow.

Text blocks, unlike text frames…

• Can be created quickly by dragging the text tool and immediately typing or pasting.

• Can be created and threaded automatically throughout a publication by flowing text into columns.

• Work with all text-related PageMaker plug-ins.

In summary: *Text blocks*, which can be created and threaded together almost instantly with the Autoflow feature, are most suitable for long document work, such as technical manuals and other books.

To select text within a text object:

1 Select the text tool from the toolbox.

2 Do one of the following:

• Drag the I-beam to select characters.

• Click an insertion point at the start of the range of characters you want, hold down Shift, and then click again at the end of the range. Alternatively, hold down Shift as you press the arrow keys to extend the selection either one character at a time (right or left arrow keys) or one line at a time (up or down arrow keys).

• Double-click to select a word, or triple-click to select a paragraph.

• Click an insertion point and choose Edit > Select All to select all the text in the story. (If you choose Select All while the pointer tool is selected, PageMaker selects all objects on the visible pages and pasteboard.)

IMPORTING TEXT

You can import text generated in another application. PageMaker supports a wide-variety of word-processing applications (and has special capabilities for the most popular ones) and text file formats (including RTF or Rich Text Format) and can even import text from other PageMaker publications. You can install import filters to handle the kinds of files you want to bring into PageMaker. See the *Adobe PageMaker 6.5 Getting Started* book for information on installing filters.

Once text is in PageMaker you can treat it exactly like text you typed directly into the publication. Alternatively, you can choose to update the source document with the application that created the text, and have PageMaker automatically incorporate the changes into the version of the text file that resides in PageMaker. There are several ways to import and update text and graphic files, and these are described in Chapter 11, "Importing, Linking, and Exporting."

UNDERSTANDING TEXT OBJECTS AND STORIES

Once text is in PageMaker, it is part of a story. A story is text that PageMaker recognizes as a single unit. A story can be one letter or several hundred pages of text, and can be contained in a single text object or *threaded* through many different ones.

A PageMaker story is similar to an article in a newspaper. The front page of a newspaper may contain several independent articles, some of which continue on other pages. Likewise in PageMaker, several stories may appear on the same publication page and continue elsewhere in the publication, but each story is a separate unit with its own story window in story editor.

Normally, text that you edit as a unit should be contained in a single story. When you edit one article in a newsletter, for example, you don't want other, unrelated articles to change.

These captions are threaded as one story, so adding text to the upper text object affects text in the lower text object.

These captions are separate stories, so adding text to the upper text object does not affect the lower text object.

When you add or remove text in a story or adjust the size or shape of text objects that contain part of a threaded story, the text flows through existing text objects until it gets to the end of the story. If you add text to a threaded story, you may need to resize the last text object or create a new text object so that all of the text is visible.

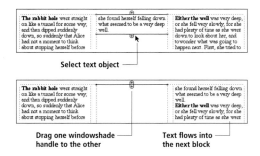

PLACING TEXT ON THE PAGE

When you have text to place on a page, PageMaker displays a loaded text icon. Click the icon to flow text into the frame or column you click on (or drag to define a new custom-size text block). You can load a text icon in several ways:

• Use the File > Place command to import a word-processed document or another PageMaker story into layout view. After PageMaker imports the file, the pointer becomes a loaded text icon. See "Placing and Linking" on page 335 for more information.

• Create or import a new story in story editor, and then choose Story > Close Story to return to layout view. PageMaker displays an alert message that says, "The story has not been placed." You can then click a button to place the story or to discard it from the publication.

• Use the pointer tool to select a text block. If there is unplaced text at the end of the block, an arrow appears in the bottom windowshade handle. If the text is part of a threaded story, you'll see a plus sign. Click the arrow or plus sign to turn the pointer tool into a loaded text icon. (Threaded text frames also display an arrow or plus sign, but you cannot load the text into an icon.)

THREADING TEXT BLOCKS

Once you have a loaded text icon, you can use one of three text-flow options to place text in text blocks, or you can drag the mouse to define a text block into which the text flows. To flow text into text frames as opposed to text blocks see "Threading Text Frames" on page 113.

Flow text in PageMaker one of three ways: automatically, where PageMaker adds pages until all text is placed; into one column at a time (manually or semiautomatically); or into a space that you define on the page.

To flow an entire story automatically:

1 If the automatic text-flow icon does not display as your loaded text icon, choose Layout > Autoflow to turn on automatic text flow.

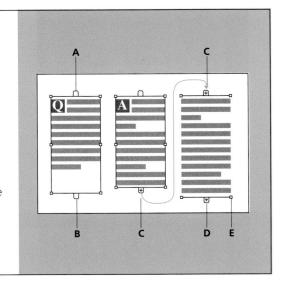

Working with windowshades • Windowshades stretch horizontally across the top and bottom borders of a selected text object.

A An empty windowshade handle at the top of a text object indicates the beginning of a story.

B An empty windowshade handle at the bottom of a text object indicates the end of a story.

C A + (plus sign) in a windowshade handle indicates that the text object is threaded to another text object containing the same story.

D A down arrow in a bottom windowshade handle indicates that there is more text in the story to be placed but no remaining text objects in which to place it.

E Drag a handle to resize a text object.

2 Position the loaded text icon where you want the top of the first text block to be, and then click to begin flowing the text.

Text fills the column to the bottom margin and then moves to the top of the next column (or the next page). PageMaker continues flowing text, adding pages as necessary until the entire story is placed.

Shortcut: *To temporarily switch between manual and automatic text flow, hold down Command (Macintosh) or Ctrl (Windows) as you click to place text.*

To flow one column of text at a time:

1 If you don't see the manual text flow icon on the screen, choose Layout > Autoflow to turn off automatic text flow.

2 Position the text icon at the point where you want the top of the text block, and then click.

Text flows to the bottom of the column or page, and the text icon becomes the pointer tool. If there is more text to be placed, an arrow appears in the bottom windowshade handle.

3 If there is more text to place, click the arrow in the bottom windowshade handle to reload the text icon.

4 Repeat Steps 2 and 3 until the entire story is placed or, to flow text semiautomatically, hold down the Shift key while the loaded text icon is displayed. PageMaker flows text one column at a time, as in manual flow, but the text icon automatically reloads after each column is placed.

The bottom windowshade handle is empty when there is no more text to place.

To define an area in which to place text:

1 Position the loaded text icon at a corner of the area where you want to place text, hold down the mouse button, and drag to define the text block. Release the mouse button.

Text flows into the defined area. If there is more text than fits in the text block you defined, an arrow appears in the bottom windowshade handle.

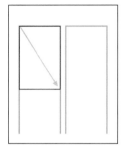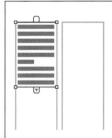

2 If there is more text to place, click the arrow in the bottom windowshade handle.

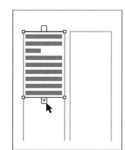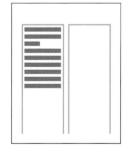

3 Repeat steps 1 and 2 until the entire story is placed.

The bottom windowshade handle is empty when there is no more text to place.

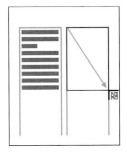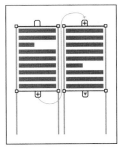

THREADING TEXT FRAMES

Whereas text blocks are threaded together somewhat automatically as you flow text, text frames must be threaded together manually. Once text frames are threaded, however, you can more easily redirect the flow of text through them than you can with text blocks. (Threaded frames also differ from threaded text blocks in that, when you delete a threaded frame, the text in the frame moves to the next frame in the thread.)

You can begin threading text frames whether or not they contain text.

To thread one text frame to another:

1 With the pointer tool, select a text frame or an empty frame.

2 Click the bottom windowshade handle.

Even if the windowshade handle indicates there is more text to flow, the cursor does not change to a loaded text icon after you click the handle (as it would with a text block). The cursor changes to the thread icon.

3 Click the text frame you want to thread to.

The frames are threaded together. Plus signs appear in the text frame handles to indicate that the frames are threaded. If the frame you selected in step 1 had more text to flow, the text now appears in the frame you selected in step 3.

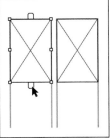

To thread text frames, click the bottom windowshade handle on one frame…

and then click a different frame.

Traversing text frames

You can follow the flow of text from one frame to the next by using commands on the Element > Frame menu.

To go to the next frame:

Select a threaded text frame, and choose Element > Frame > Next Frame.

TIP: WHEN REDIRECTING
TEXT IN THREADED
FRAMES, HOLD COM-
MAND + SHIFT + CON-
TROL (MACINTOSH) OR
CONTROL + SHIFT + ALT
(WINDOWS) TO BREAK A
LINK AND AUTOMATI-
CALLY TURN THE CURSOR
INTO THE THREAD ICON.

To go to the previous frame:

Select a threaded text frame, and choose Element > Frame > Previous Frame.

Redirecting text flow in threaded text frames

Just as you establish the original order of threaded text frames by clicking windowshade handles, so you can revise the order (or add new frames into the thread) by clicking windowshade handles.

If you want to revise the threading order in the middle of a set of threaded frames, you must first break the thread at the point where you want to change the threading order. For example, say your text threads from frame 1 to 2, frame 2 to 3, and frame 3 to 4. To thread the text from frame 2 to a new frame on the page, you must first break the connection between frame 2 and 3; when you do this, frames 3 and 4 remain threaded together, but become empty (since the text thread will now end at frame 2).

You use the Element > Frame > Remove From Thread command to omit a selected frame from the flow entirely. PageMaker automatically threads together the frames before and after the one you removed from the thread.

To redirect text flow through frames:

1 Using the pointer tool, select the frame you want to thread to a different frame.

You can skip to step 3 if the selected frame is not threaded to a subsequent frame.

2 Press Command + Shift (Macintosh) or Ctrl + Shift (Windows), and click the selected frame's top or bottom windowshade handle. Clicking the top handle breaks the thread to the previous frame; clicking the bottom handle breaks the thread to the next frame. The text rolls up to the frame that immediately precedes the break.

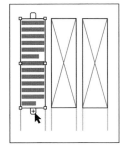

3 With the frame still selected, click in the bottom windowshade handle.

The cursor turns into the thread icon.

4 Click the frame you want to be next in the thread.

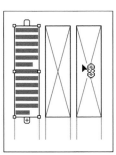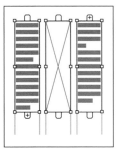

To disconnect a frame from a thread:

1 Using the pointer tool, select the frame you want to unthread.

2 Choose Element > Frame > Remove From Thread.

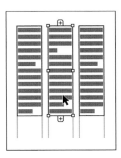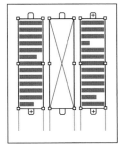

ADJUSTING TEXT OBJECTS

After you add text, you can adjust the size, shape, or location of text objects without affecting the order of text in the story or its formatting. In addition, you can combine text objects from different stories or break threaded text into separate text objects and stories.

To move a text object:

1 Position the pointer tool anywhere inside the text object and hold down the mouse button.

2 When the pointer changes, drag the text object to a new position.

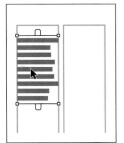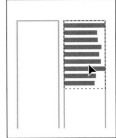

If you click a text object and then pause slightly before dragging, you'll see the text as you move it, making it easy to position accurately. Otherwise, you'll see the outline of the text object as you drag.

To resize a text object:

With the text object selected, click the pointer tool on a corner handle (for a text block) or any selection handle (for a text frame) and drag to resize the text object.

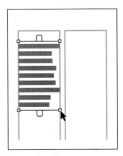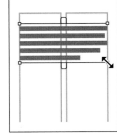

Drag a handle…   *to resize a text object.*

To break threaded text into a separate, unthreaded story:

1 Use the text tool to select the text to be separated from the story, and choose Edit > Cut.

2 Click an insertion point outside an existing text object to create a new text block, or click in an empty unthreaded frame, and choose Edit > Paste. The pasted text appears, but it is no longer threaded to the original story.

If the text you want to separate is in its own text frame with no other text, select the frame and choose Element > Frame > Break Threads. This does not break the flow in the remaining text frames in that thread.

To combine two text blocks from different stories into one story:

1 Use the pointer tool to select the text block you want to remove, and choose Edit > Cut.

2 Click an insertion point in the text block where you want to insert the text, and choose Edit > Paste.

> **Deleting threaded text objects •** One important difference between deleting threaded text frames and deleting threaded text blocks is what happens to the text. When you delete a text block, the text is deleted from the story, and other text blocks in the thread are unchanged. However, when you delete a threaded text frame, the text moves to the next frame in the thread. (If you delete the last frame in the thread, the previous frame in the thread indicates that there is unplaced text—the text previously contained in the frame you deleted.)

You may need to extend the last text object in the story or add pages to see all the text.

You can also use this procedure to change the order in which text is threaded within a single story.

BALANCING COLUMNS (TEXT BLOCKS ONLY)

Sometimes you want the columns on a page to be of equal size, so that their top and bottom edges align. If you've used text blocks to contain the text, PageMaker can automatically calculate the average length of selected columns and then resize them to that length.

 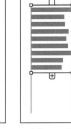

PageMaker calculates the average length of selected columns…

and then resizes all the columns to that length.

To make two or more columns align:

1 Use the pointer tool to select two or more columns (or text blocks) within the same story.

2 Choose Utilities > Plug-ins > Balance Columns.

3 Select an alignment option and specify where you want leftover lines added when text cannot be divided evenly among the selected columns.

4 Click OK.

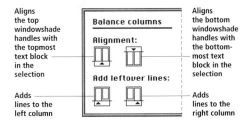

Aligns the top windowshade handles with the topmost text block in the selection

Aligns the bottom windowshade handles with the bottom-most text block in the selection

Adds lines to the left column

Adds lines to the right column

CONTROLLING PAGE AND COLUMN BREAKS

Certain paragraphs, such as headings, belong at the top of a column or page. You can use paragraph-level formatting to ensure that certain paragraphs are positioned correctly no matter where they land in the publication, regardless of editing or reformatting elsewhere in the story.

Note: PageMaker also lets you prevent a paragraph from breaking at the end of a column or page under certain conditions. See "Controlling Widows, Orphans, and Other Paragraph Breaks" on page 169.

To start a paragraph at the top of a page or column:

1 Select a paragraph or paragraph style.

2 Choose Type > Paragraph.

3 Select one of these options:

• The Column Break Before option forces the paragraph to start at the top of the next available column.

• The Page Break Before option forces the paragraph to start at the top of the next available page.

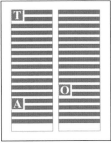

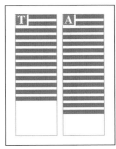

Without column breaks   With column breaks

ADDING JUMP LINES (TEXT BLOCKS ONLY)

Many publications use jump lines–"Continued on…" and "Continued from…"–to tell the reader where to find the next or previous section of a story. If you've created your columns with text blocks, PageMaker can automate this process by adding a one-line text block after the last text block on a page ("Continued on…") and before the first text block on a page ("Continued from…").

A jump-line is added to a text block, shortened by one line.

PageMaker shortens the selected text block by one line and places a jump-line story with the correct page number. To make it easy to format jump lines, two new styles are added to your style sheet: Cont. From and Cont. On.

Note: *Perform this step when layout and pagination are finalized; although PageMaker supplies the correct page number, the number is not updated when changes in pagination occur.*

To add and format jump lines:

1 Use the pointer tool to select the first or last text block on a page.

2 Choose Utilities > Plug-ins > Add Cont'd Line.

3 Specify whether you want to add the jump line to the top or bottom of the text block.

4 After adding all the required jump lines, edit the paragraph styles Cont. From and Cont. On to format the jump lines.

COUNTING STORIES, WORDS, AND OTHER ITEMS

You can use the Utilities > Plug-ins > Word Counter command to keep track of the number of stories, text objects, characters, words, sentences, and paragraphs in the current publication. If you have text selected with the text tool when you run the plug-in, PageMaker counts only the characters, words, and paragraphs in the selection.

MOVING BETWEEN STORY EDITOR AND LAYOUT VIEW

You can edit text in PageMaker either on the page in layout view or as a story in story editor, a word-processing environment.

Layout view   *Story editor*

Major text revisions are quicker and easier to make in story editor, where the focus is on the text, not its appearance. Screen redraw is faster in story editor because only a limited amount of formatting is visible, and navigating through stories is easier because you don't have to change pages or views to see all of the text in a story. Spelling, Find, Find Next, and Change commands are available only in story editor.

See "Managing Story Windows in PageMaker" on page 19 for more information about working with several publication and story windows open at the same time.

To open a new story editor window:

With nothing selected in layout view, choose Edit > Edit Story.

To open an existing story in story editor:

1 Select the text object with the pointer tool, or click an insertion point in the text object.

2 Choose Edit > Edit Story.

The existing story opens in story editor with the insertion point positioned at the top of the text object or where you clicked within the text object.

Shortcuts: *With the pointer tool, triple-click on a text object to open its story window, or press Command (Macintosh) or Ctrl (Windows) + E while text or the text object is selected.*

To return to layout view:

In story editor, do one of the following:

• Choose Story > Close Story. You return to your previous position in layout view and close the story window.

• Choose Edit > Edit Layout. You return to your previous position in layout view without closing the story window.

• Click in the layout window. The story window remains open but moves behind the layout window.

Shortcut: *If you have multiple stories open, close all stories by pressing Option (Macintosh) or Shift (Windows) as you choose Story > Close All Stories.*

BASIC EDITING IN STORY EDITOR

You can edit text character by character at the insertion point, or you can select a range of text to edit.

To cut, copy, or clear text:

1 Select the text you want to edit.

2 Choose Edit > Copy (to keep the text where it is) or Edit > Cut (to remove it for use elsewhere) or choose Edit > Clear to preserve the current contents of the Clipboard and not save the text.

3 Click an insertion point where you want to insert the text (or select text you want to replace), and then choose Edit > Paste.

Setting text preferences • By setting preferences, you can control how text appears in layout view and story editor. Story editor settings do not affect text in layout view or in the printed publication. These settings apply to every story in the current publication. (Choose File > Preferences > General, and then click More to set these text preferences.)

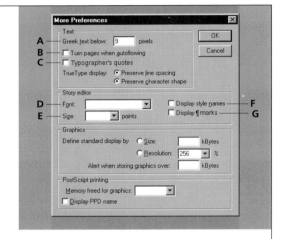

A Specify the size below which PageMaker displays text as gray lines in layout view. Screen redraw improves when greeked text displays instead of actual characters.

B Click to display all pages while autoflowing.

C Click to have PageMaker substitute typographer's quotation marks or apostrophes whenever you type normal quotation marks or apostrophes.

D Select a font that is easy to read if you will be working in story editor for a long time.

E Select a small text size to view more of a story on the screen or a large size to read text more easily.

F Click to view the style name of each paragraph. Paragraphs with no style attached are identified with a bullet. (Choose Story > Display Style Names to override this setting for the current story.)

G Click to view the nonprinting characters in a story, such as tabs and spaces. (Choose Story > Display ¶ Markers to override the setting.)

ABOUT FORMATTING TEXT

PageMaker provides several ways to apply character-level formatting, such as font and size, and paragraph-level formatting, such as alignment and indentation.

How PageMaker applies formatting depends on what is selected when you choose options:

• Pointer tool selected: Sets the publication's default type and paragraph specifications. If no publication is open, the changes apply to text you type in all new publications you open.

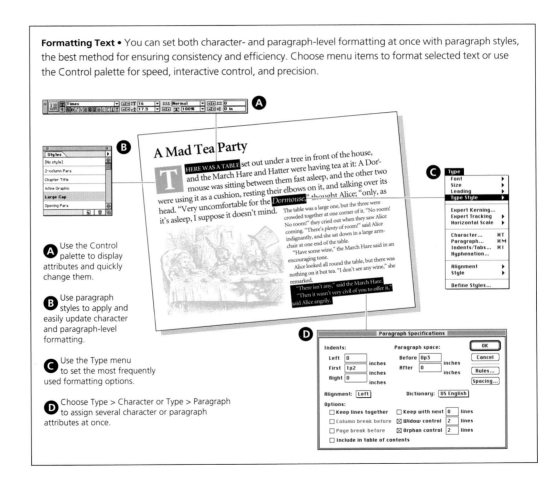

Formatting Text • You can set both character- and paragraph-level formatting at once with paragraph styles, the best method for ensuring consistency and efficiency. Choose menu items to format selected text or use the Control palette for speed, interactive control, and precision.

A Use the Control palette to display attributes and quickly change them.

B Use paragraph styles to apply and easily update character and paragraph-level formatting.

C Use the Type menu to set the most frequently used formatting options.

D Choose Type > Character or Type > Paragraph to assign several character or paragraph attributes at once.

• Text selected with text tool: Changes just the selected text or, for paragraph-level attributes, just the paragraphs selected.

• Insertion point selected: Applies character-level formatting to new text you type at that point, and paragraph-level formatting to the paragraph containing the insertion point.

USING THE CONTROL PALETTE TO FORMAT TEXT

When you are in story editor or use the text tool in layout view, the Control palette displays options that let you assign attributes to text. To open or close the Control palette, choose Window > Show Control Palette. The Control palette appears in front of the publication and story windows. You can move it by dragging the bar at the left edge of the palette.

Click an option to activate it or move from option to option by pressing Tab or, to return to a previous option, press Shift + Tab.

The contents of the Control palette vary depending on whether you select character or paragraph view:

T • In character view, you can apply character attributes, such as font, size, or leading, to selected text.

¶ • In paragraph view, you can apply paragraph styles, select alignment options, and set other paragraph attributes.

When you click the Control palette to select an option, PageMaker immediately applies the option to the selected text. If you type a numeric value for an option, apply the new setting in any of these ways:

• Press Tab to apply the change and move to the next Control palette option.

• Press Return (Macintosh) or Enter (Windows) to apply the change and make the layout or story window active. (If you hold down the Shift key while pressing Return or Enter, the change is applied but the Control palette remains active.)

• Click the Apply button on the left end of the Control palette.

• Click any other option on the Control palette.

When you press a nudge button, you adjust attributes in predefined increments. If you press Command (Macintosh) or Ctrl (Windows) while nudging, you multiply the nudge amount increment by ten.

Shortcut: *You can change the font, tracking, and paragraph-style Control palette options by typing a font, track, or style name. As you type, PageMaker compares the available options with the characters you're typing and displays the closest option in the text box. For example, when you type a **T** in the Font option, PageMaker might display "Tekton," but when you type **Ti** PageMaker would jump ahead to "Times."*

For more information on using the Control palette, see "Manipulating an Object Using the Control Palette" on page 191. Keyboard shortcuts for the Control palette are in online Help.

FORMATTING CHARACTERS

Character attributes determine how text looks on the page. Size, typeface, and character width (or horizontal scale) are a few of the attributes that you can set in PageMaker.

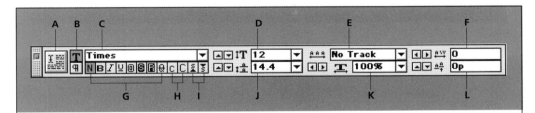

Control palette in character view

A Apply button: Click to apply formatting to selected text.

B Character-view and paragraph-view buttons: Toggle between two kinds of type settings.

C Font: Type or choose a typeface.

D Type-size option: Specify type size in points. Nudge amount: 0.1 point.

E Expert Tracking option: Type or select the amount of space between letters and words.

F Kerning option: Increase, decrease, or view kerning increments, accurate to 0.001 of an em space. Nudge amount: 0.01 em.

G Type-Style buttons: Apply Normal, Bold, Italic, Underline, Outline (Macintosh only), Shadow (Macintosh only), Reverse, or Strikethru.

H Case buttons: Specify small caps or all caps, or deselect both buttons for normal case.

I Position buttons: Specify Superscript or Subscript type, or deselect both buttons for normal position.

J Leading option: Specify the vertical space between lines of type in a paragraph. Auto turns on automatic leading at 120% of type size. Nudge amount: 0.1 point.

K Horizontal Scale option: Type values from 5% to 250% in increments of a tenth of 1% (Normal equals 100%, or the character width in the original font design). Nudge amount: 1%.

L Baseline-Shift option: Specify the vertical position of text relative to the baseline. Nudge amount: 0.01 point.

Most character-formatting options can be applied in several different ways. Horizontal Scale, for example, appears on the Type menu, in the Character Specifications dialog box, on the Control palette, and in dialog boxes for finding or changing type attributes.

To format text:

1 Using the text tool, select the text you want to format.

2 Choose the formatting attribute you want from the Type menu or use the Control palette.

To format several text attributes at once:

1 With the text tool, select the text you want to format.

2 Choose Type > Character, or click the Control palette to activate it.

3 Change settings in the Character Specifications dialog box or on the Control palette.

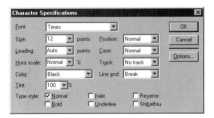

To format characters by editing paragraph styles:

1 Choose Window > Show Styles.

2 Press Command (Macintosh) or Ctrl (Windows) and click the paragraph style you want to revise.

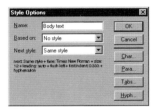

3 Click Char to open the Character Specifications dialog box.

4 Select the formatting options you want.

5 Click OK in each dialog box to apply the changes.

The changes appear automatically in all paragraphs formatted with that paragraph style. See "Using Paragraph Styles" on page 136 for more information.

Applying a font

Times ▼ A font is a set of characters in a single typeface, such as Helvetica, Times New RomanPS, or Palatino. Most sets consist of uppercase and lowercase letters, numerals, punctuation marks, and extended characters.

Wherever you set character-level formatting, PageMaker displays a list of fonts available, as well as any additional fonts that may have been used in your publication. PageMaker can notify you when a font applied in your publication is not available to PageMaker, and propose a substitute for it. See Appendix B, "Font Substitution" for more information on this feature.

ABCDEFGHIJKLMNOPQRSTU
VWXYZßabcdefghijklmnopqrstu
vwxyz1234567890~!¡@#$£¢%^&
?¿()[]{}.,;:<>'"""*°`\|/§¶†¥øπ©çµ
Σüéùîñç ÆŒÅØfifl=≠±- – —

Example of a font set

Using Multiple Master or TrueType fonts

PageMaker supports Adobe's Multiple Master font technology, as well as TrueType fonts, and provides special options for working with those fonts. See "Font Printing Basics" on page 391 for more information on printing TrueType fonts.

To modify a Multiple Master font from within PageMaker (Macintosh only):

1 Select the text that has a Multiple Master font applied.

2 Choose Type > Character.

3 Click MM Fonts.

4 Edit the font, as described in the documentation included with your Multiple Master font.

To control leading or character shape of TrueType fonts:

1 Choose File > Preferences > General.

2 Click More.

3 Click one of the following TrueType Display options:

• The Preserve Line Spacing option preserves the body clearance of TrueType fonts by adjusting character height as necessary. For example, if you type a capital letter with an accent above it, PageMaker reduces the height of the character so it doesn't print above the height of the line.

• The Preserve Character Shape option adjusts leading rather than character shape. This allows, for example, a capital letter with an accent above it to print above the height of the line.

4 Click OK.

Applying a type size

Type size refers to the point size of the text. Point size is the height of the font from the bottom of the descenders (such as lower stem in *p*) to the top of the ascenders (such as the upper stem in *h*), but does not indicate the exact height of each letter. For example, a lowercase *a* set in 12-point type is not 12-points high. Type samples can help you determine what font size you need.

In PageMaker, you can set type from 4 to 650 points, in one-tenth of a point increments. The Size submenu lists standard sizes. You can also choose Other from the Type > Size menu to apply any point size, or type a size in the Control palette or in the Character Specifications dialog box.

Applying leading

⬆⬇ ↕ 14.4 ▾ Leading sets the vertical space in which text is placed (the slug). Like type size, leading is measured in points. Unlike type size, leading is an exact measurement: 12-point leading is always exactly 12-points high. You can also choose from three different leading methods to determine how the type sits within the leading space.

There was a table set out under a tree in front of the house, and the March Hare and the Hatter were having tea at it: a Dormouse was	There was a table set out under a tree in front of the house, and the March Hare and the Hatter were having tea at it: a Dormouse was

12 on 12 leading   *12 on 14 leading*

You can specify leading as follows:

• Choose the Auto option from the Leading submenu to have PageMaker calculate the leading based on the size of the type. By default, the autoleading value is 120% of the type size.

• Choose any of the standard amounts of leading listed on the Leading submenu.

• Type a custom leading value (in one-tenth of a point increments) in the Control palette or Character Specifications dialog box, or choose Type > Leading > Other to specify a specific leading amount.

See "Selecting a Leading Value" on page 144 for details on all these options.

Applying horizontal scale

◀▶ T 100% ▾ Use Horizontal Scale to adjust the width of characters. You can specify a scaling percentage between 5 and 250% (in increments of a tenth of 1%) or choose from commonly used character-width percentages on the Horizontal Scale submenu.

If the typeface you are using has a condensed or expanded font (for example Helvetica Condensed), favor using that variant over the Horizontal Scale command. Horizontal Scale is valuable for special type effects, not for copyfitting, and not in place of condensed or expanded typefaces already available to you.

When you apply Horizontal Scale, you specify the width of printed characters. The results you see on the screen and in your printed output depend on the kind of printer and screen fonts you use, and whether or not you use a type-management program, such as Adobe Type Manager®. Print a proof to see if the results are acceptable.

Applying a type style

⬚ Use type styles to change the look of text. For example, to show text while indicating that it has been deleted from the paragraph, as in a legal contract, use Strikethru to draw a line through the text. Or, to create paper-colored text on a contrasting black, tinted, or colored background, use Reverse, which applies the default paper color.

Changing case

⬚ PageMaker provides three type-case attributes. Normal leaves uppercase and lowercase letters as typed; All Caps displays letters as full-sized capitals; and Small Caps displays lowercase letters as small capitals, based on the size you specify with Type > Character. For details on changing the default size of small caps, see "Changing Case and Position" on page 172.

To quickly change capitalization of a selected range of text, choose Utilities > Plug-ins > Change Case. Your options include capitalizing the first letter of each word or the first letter of each sentence in the selection.

Note: You cannot use the Case type attribute on the Control palette or in the Character Specifications dialog box to change the case of characters typed while the Caps Lock key is down.

Specifying the position of text

⬚ You can set the position of text relative to its normal position in the slug, making the text superscript or subscript. Apply superscript and subscript settings for text that you want to position consistently throughout a publication (for example, numbers in mathematical formulas). Additionally, you can modify the size and position of text based on the values you specify in the Type Options dialog box. For more information on changing the default size and position of superscript or subscript characters, see "Changing Case and Position" on page 172.

Applying tracking

⬚ **No Track** ▼ Tracking determines the amount of space between letters and words. Tracking is particularly useful for darkening or lightening a page (type with tight tracking darkens the page; type with loose tracking lightens a page) and for changing the spacing of selected lines of very large or very small type (headlines and captions). You can also use track settings to make text fit in a defined space on the page.

March Hare —— Very tight

March Hare —— Normal

March Hare – Very loose

When you choose Type > Expert Tracking, PageMaker displays a submenu of six tracks:

• No Track (the default setting) means that PageMaker applies no tracking and the letters and words are spaced as the original font dictates.

• Normal tracking improves letter spacing by reducing it for large point sizes and increasing it for small point sizes, but adjusting it very little for medium point sizes.

• Very Loose, Loose, Tight, and Very Tight are used under special conditions.

For details on applying and editing tracks, see "Tracking Type" on page 150.

Note: When you use Horizontal Scale to scale type, PageMaker applies tracking based on that setting. For example, 12-point type set at 150% character width is tracked as if it were 18-point type.

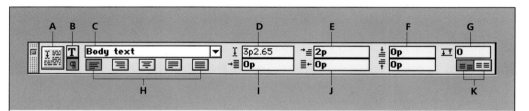

Control palette in paragraph view

A Apply button: Click to apply formatting to selected paragraphs.

B Character-view and paragraph-view buttons: Toggle between two kinds of type settings.

C Paragraph-style option: Type or choose a defined style.

D Cursor-position indicator: Tracks the position of the cursor on the publication page.

E First indent: Specify the amount of indent for the first sentence in a paragraph.

F Space-before and space-after options: Specify the amount of space to insert above or below the selected paragraphs.

G Grid-size option: Specify the point size of the text grid to use when Align to Grid option is on.

H Alignment buttons: left align, right align, center align, justify, and force justify.

I Left-indent option: Specify the amount of indent for the left side of the paragraph.

J Right-indent option: Specify the amount of indent for the right side of the paragraph.

K Align-to-grid option: Click the rightmost icon to align columns vertically, according to the point size set in the Grid-size option. (See "Aligning Paragraphs to the Grid" on pages 167.)

FORMATTING PARAGRAPHS

Paragraph attributes specify how your paragraphs appear on the page, including alignment, position of indents and tabs, and the amount of space before and after the paragraph. In PageMaker, a paragraph is any contiguous text followed by a paragraph return. You can apply attributes to selected paragraphs, or you can change the attributes of all paragraphs of a particular paragraph style.

PageMaker provides several ways to apply paragraph attributes, including the Styles palette, which lists a predefined group of character and paragraph attributes applied to selected paragraphs, and the Control palette.

To format paragraphs:

1 Using the text tool, click an insertion point in a single paragraph or select a range of paragraphs.

2 Choose Type > Paragraph.

Indents and tabs

A Left tab: Sets a tab stop inward from the left margin of the text object.

B Right tab: Sets a tab stop inward from the right margin of the text object.

C Leader box: Specifies a leader style for a tab stop.

D Position box: Displays the amount of indentation for tabs and indents.

E Reset: Abandons tab settings and returns to the default tabs.

F Center tab: Sets a tab stop that centers text in the text object.

G Decimal tab: Lines up numbers at their decimal point.

H Left indent: Sets the indentation of text from the left margin of the text object. (Press Shift to move independently of the first-line indent marker.)

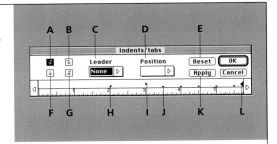

I First-line indent: Sets the indentation of the first line of a paragraph.

J Default tab: Indicates preset tab stops.

K Apply: Shows the effects of the tab and indent changes made while the dialog box is displayed.

L Right indent: Sets the indentation of text from the right margin of the text object.

The Paragraph Specifications dialog box lets you apply formatting not available on the Control palette.

3 Select formatting options.

To format paragraphs by editing paragraph styles:

1 Choose Window > Show Styles.

2 Press Command (Macintosh) or Ctrl (Windows) and click a paragraph style to edit.

This opens the Style Options dialog box.

3 Click Char, Para, Tabs, or Hyph to select paragraph-level formatting options. The changes affect all paragraphs with that style.

See "Creating and editing paragraph styles" on page 137 for more information.

SETTING INDENTS AND TABS

Indents and tabs are powerful tools for positioning text. Indents move text inward from the right and left edges of a text object, and tabs position text at specific locations in a text object. You can create left- and right-aligned tabs; center tabs, which center text around the tab; and decimal tabs, which align characters at a decimal point. You can also apply a leader of any style to any tab. A leader is a repeated pattern, such as a series of dots or dashes, between the tab and the preceding text.

You can set indents in several ways:

• Move indent markers in the Indents/Tabs dialog box (layout view only).

• Type indent values in the Paragraph Specifications dialog box.

• Type indent values on the Control palette in paragraph view.

You can also define indents using any of these methods as part of a paragraph style. See "Using Paragraph Styles" on page 136.

Note: *Text frames, unlike text blocks, can have an inset between the text and the frame border; indents are set relative to this inset.*

The first-line indent applies only to the first line of a paragraph and is positioned relative to the left indent. For example, if a paragraph's left indent is one pica, setting the first-line indent to one pica indents the first line of the paragraph two picas from the left edge of the text object. To create hanging indents, enter a negative value for the first-line indent. To move the left indent marker in the Indents/Tabs ruler independently of the first-line indent marker, press Shift as you drag the left indent marker.

To set tabs with the Indents/Tabs ruler:

1 In layout view, click an insertion point in a paragraph or select a group of paragraphs.

2 Choose Type > Indents/Tabs.

3 Click a tab-alignment icon (left, right, center, or decimal) for the first tab you want to set.

4 Click a tab location on the ruler to position the new tab, or move an existing tab by dragging its marker along the ruler.

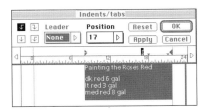

The first tab you set deletes all default tabs (the small triangles regularly spaced along the ruler) to its left. Subsequent tabs delete all default tabs between the tabs you set.

5 If you want the tab leadered, select the tab and choose an option from the Leader menu. To create a custom leader style, choose Custom from the Leader menu and then type a one- or two-character leader.

6 Click Apply to preview the changes to your text, and then click OK to accept the changes.

To move, delete, or repeat a tab for an evenly-spaced series:

1 In layout view, click an insertion point in a paragraph or select a group of paragraphs.

2 Choose Type > Indents/Tabs.

3 In the Indents/Tabs dialog box, select the tab you want to move, delete, or repeat, and then choose an option as follows:

• To move the tab, drag it, or type the new location in the Position text box, and then choose Move Tab from the Position submenu.

• To delete the tab, drag it off the ruler or choose Delete Tab from the Position submenu.

• To create a series of tabs the same distance the selected tab is from the preceding tab (or from the tab ruler's zero point), choose Repeat Tab from the Position submenu for each new tab to add to the series.

Note: *Click Reset to clear all tabs in the selected text and restore the default tabs for the publication.*

To set an indent using the Indents/Tabs ruler:

1 In layout view, click an insertion point in a paragraph or group of paragraphs.

2 Choose Type > Indents/Tabs.

3 Drag the indent markers on the ruler to where you want left, right, and first-line indents. When you release a marker, the indentation is displayed in the Position text box.

4 Click OK to set the indents.

To set an indent using the Paragraph command:

1 Click an insertion point in a paragraph or select a group of paragraphs.

2 Choose Type > Paragraph.

3 Type values for the Indents options, and then click OK.

To set an indent using the Control palette:

1 Click an insertion point in a paragraph or select a group of paragraphs.

2 Choose Window > Show Control Palette or click the Control palette to activate it. If the palette is in character view, click the paragraph-view button to display the paragraph options.

3 Type values for the Indents options, and then click Apply.

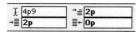

Control palette indent options

Creating a hanging indent

To align text in numbered and bulleted paragraphs, the first line must extend farther left than the rest of the paragraph. You can create this effect, called a hanging indent, by using the Hanging Indent style in PageMaker's default style sheet, or by following the procedure in this section.

A hanging indent in a table of contents

To create a hanging indent:

1 Using the text tool, click an insertion point in a paragraph or select a group of paragraphs to be indented.

2 Choose Type > Indents/Tabs.

3 In the ruler, click to create a tab setting where you want the lines to be indented.

4 Hold down Shift as you drag the left-indent marker (the bottom triangle) to the right until it's aligned with the tab, and then click OK.

5 Click an insertion point in the text where you want a tab (for example after a number or bullet), and then press Tab.

Note: To create a bullet, press Option + 8 (Macintosh) or Alt + 8 (Windows).

Adding bullets and numbers in front of paragraphs

Once you've formatted a hanging indent, you can use the following technique to quickly add bullets or consecutive numbers (each followed by a tab) to a set of consecutive paragraphs, to every paragraph of a certain style, or to every paragraph in the selected story. Make sure your numbering scheme is final before using this technique; if the paragraphs change, the numbers are not updated automatically.

To add bullets and numbers automatically:

1 Click an insertion point in the first paragraph you want to change or select the range of paragraphs.

2 Choose Utilities > Plug-ins > Bullets and Numbering.

3 If you are numbering paragraphs, click Numbers, otherwise go to step 5.

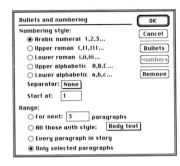

4 Specify the following options:

• Numbering Style

• Separator (the character inserted between the number and the tab that follows it)

• Start at Number

5 Select a Range.

6 If you are adding bullets or other special characters to the paragraphs, click Bullets and do one of the following:

• Click one of the bullet characters supplied.

• Click one of the bullet characters supplied, and then click Edit to change its font or size.

• Click Edit to specify another character of any font or size to use as a bullet.

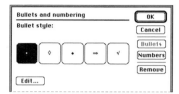

7 Click OK.

Tips for formatting indents and tabs

The following pointers can help you set tabs and indents more accurately and efficiently:

• Tab leaders assume the formatting characteristics of the preceding character. To change the formatting of a leader, insert a thin space before the tab: press Command (Macintosh) or Ctrl (Windows) + Shift + T. Select and format the thin space to define the look of the leader.

• The ruler increments in the Indents/Tabs dialog box match the current layout view's rulers.

• When text is selected and your current view allows, the Indents/Tabs dialog box automatically aligns with the left edge of the selected text, making it easy to see where indents and tabs fall within the text.

• The last tab in a paragraph assumes that paragraph's alignment. You can create a paragraph with both left- and right-justified text without manually positioning tabs: Type the left justified text, a tab, and then the text you want to right justify. Using the Control palette in paragraph view or the Type > Alignment command, select right alignment for the paragraph. The text following the tab is automatically aligned right.

• Use indents instead of tabs to specify first-line indents and spacing between the text and the edges of the text object. If you must use a tab to indent a line in the middle of a paragraph, type a line break immediately before the tab character: press Shift + Return (Macintosh) or Shift + Enter (Windows).

ADDING RULES ABOVE OR BELOW PARAGRAPHS

You can specify rules as a paragraph attribute so that the rules move and resize with the paragraph on the page. Attach a rule above or below the selected paragraphs, or make the rule part of a paragraph-style definition.

See "Changing Strokes and Fills" on page 180 for more information on lines and line attributes.

 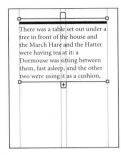

Rules flow and resize with text

To apply a paragraph rule:

1 Select the paragraph you want to edit.

2 Choose Type > Paragraph, and click Rules.

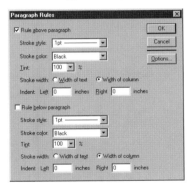

3 Click Rule Above Paragraph or Rule Below Paragraph.

4 Define stroke attributes as follows:

• Choose a stroke pattern and weight from the Stroke Style pop-up menu. To specify a weight not listed on the menu, choose Custom and then type a weight from 0 to 800 points.

• Choose a defined color or tint from the Stroke Color pop-up menu.

• To tint the color applied to the rule, choose a tint percentage from the Tint pop-up menu or type a percentage from 1 to 100%.

• Choose the stroke width you want, either Width of Text (from the left indent to the line end or right indent) or Width of Column (from the left side of the text object to the right side of the text object, regardless of left or right indents or where lines end). For text frames with insets, the stroke width setting is calculated from the text inset, not the frame border.

• Set left or right indents for the rule (not for text) by typing values in the Left and Right text boxes.

5 Click Options to set the space between the paragraph and the rules.

TIP: WHEN YOU BASE A
NEW STYLE ON ANOTHER
STYLE, CHANGES YOU
MAKE TO SHARED
ATTRIBUTES ARE AUTO-
MATICALLY COPIED TO
THE NEW STYLE.

• Enter values in the Top (for rule above) and Bottom (rule below) text boxes. (Choose Auto to align the top of the rule above along the top of the slug of the first line in the paragraph, and the bottom of the rule below along the bottom of the slug of the last line in the paragraph.)

• Click Align to Grid to align the baselines of columns in multi-column text, so that paragraph rules will also align vertically. Set Grid Size to match the leading of your body text.

For rules above a paragraph, PageMaker measures from the baseline of the first line in the paragraph to the top of the rule, adding extra space before the paragraph as necessary. For rules below a paragraph, PageMaker measures from the baseline of the last line in the paragraph to the bottom of the rule below, adding space below as necessary.

ADDING SPACE ABOVE OR BELOW PARAGRAPHS

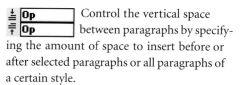 Control the vertical space between paragraphs by specifying the amount of space to insert before or after selected paragraphs or all paragraphs of a certain style.

Note: PageMaker never inserts space before a paragraph set to begin at the top of a column or page (using the Page Break Before or Column Break Before attribute). For those cases you must add the extra space manually by typing one or more paragraph returns.

To increase or decrease space before or after a paragraph:

1 Select the paragraph you want to edit.

2 Choose Type > Paragraph.

3 In the Paragraph Space options, specify the values you want in the Before and After text boxes.

USING PARAGRAPH STYLES

A paragraph style is a collection of character and paragraph formatting attributes that you can apply to a paragraph in one step. You can specify every aspect of a paragraph, including typeface and type size, line spacing, alignment, and indents within the style. Paragraph styles can save considerable time when you apply and revise text formatting, and they provide a consistent look to your publication.

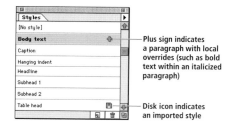

Plus sign indicates a paragraph with local overrides (such as bold text within an italicized paragraph)

Disk icon indicates an imported style

Collectively, a publication's styles are called a style sheet and are listed in the Styles palette, in the Define Styles dialog box, and on the Control palette (in paragraph view). You can copy style sheets to other PageMaker publications and import them from word-processing applications, so you don't have to re-create styles each time you create a publication.

Creating and editing paragraph styles

PageMaker makes it easy to create and edit styles for your publication. If the styles you want already exist, either in another PageMaker publication or in a file created in a word-processing application, you can import those styles for use in your current publication.

Create new styles and edit existing ones using the Style Options dialog box, which you can open in the following ways:

• Choose Window > Show Styles, and either choose New Style from the Styles palette menu or click the new style button (▣) at the bottom of the palette.

• Press Command (Macintosh) or Ctrl (Windows) and either click a style in the Styles palette or a select a style in the Control palette in paragraph view.

• Choose Type > Define Styles, and either click New or double-click an existing style listed in the dialog box to edit that style.

To define a new style based on existing formatting:

1 Select a paragraph with the attributes you want to use for the new style.

2 Press Command (Macintosh) or Ctrl (Windows), and click No Style in the Styles palette.

3 Type a new style name in the Style Options dialog box, and click OK.

To define a new style from scratch:

1 Choose Window > Show Styles.

2 Choose New Style from the Styles palette menu or click the new style button (▣) at the bottom of the palette.

3 Select No Style for Based On and type a name.

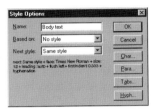

4 Specify formatting as follows:

• Click Char to open the Character Specifications dialog box, and then choose the attributes you want.

• Click Para to open the Paragraph Specifications dialog box, and then choose the attributes you want.

• Click Tabs to open the Indents/Tabs dialog box, and then set up the tabs and indents you want.

• Click Hyph to open the Hyphenation dialog box, and then define how the paragraphs should hyphenate.

5 Click OK.

TIP: YOU CAN VIEW
THE ATTRIBUTES
OF ANY PARAGRAPH
STYLE IN THE CURRENT
PUBLICATION BY
CHOOSING TYPE >
DEFINE STYLES, AND
SELECTING A STYLE NAME
IN THE LIST BOX

To define a new style based on an existing style:

1 Position an insertion point in a paragraph with the existing style applied and adjust the formatting as necessary.

2 On the Control palette in paragraph view, type a new style name for the paragraph-style option and then press Tab. Click OK when the alert message appears.

To edit a previously defined style:

1 Press Command (Macintosh) or Ctrl (Windows) and then either click a style in the Styles palette or click the style name in the Control palette in paragraph view.

2 Click the appropriate buttons in the Style Options dialog box to modify the style attributes, and then click OK.

To copy all styles from another PageMaker 6.5 publication:

1 Choose Import Styles from the Styles palette menu.

2 Double-click the publication you want to copy styles from.

Note: If a style you copy has the same name as a style in the current publication, the copied style definition overwrites the existing style.

To import styles from a word-processed document:

1 Choose File > Place, and then select the name of the document.

2 Click Retain Format.

3 Select other import options as appropriate, and then click OK.

A disk icon beside a style name in the Styles palette (or an asterisk in the Control palette and Define Styles dialog box) indicates an imported style. For more information on importing styles, see "Importing Text Features" on page 341.

Applying a style to a paragraph

Once you set up a style sheet for a publication you are ready to apply styles to your paragraphs.

To apply a style:

Using the text tool, click an insertion point in a paragraph or select a range of paragraphs. Then use one of the following methods to apply a style:

• On the Styles palette, click the name of the style you want to apply.

• On the Control palette (in paragraph view), type or select the name of the style you want to apply, and then click Apply.

Shortcut: On the Macintosh, you can press Command with a paragraph selected, and then press F1 to apply the first style in the Styles palette, press F2 to apply the second style in the palette, and so on.

To view the name of the style applied to each paragraph in story editor, choose Story > Display Style Names. (You can set Display Style Names as the publication default using the File > Preferences command.)

To set a style that will apply to the next paragraph you type:

1 Create or edit a paragraph style that always precedes another paragraph style; for example: Artframe.

Part of this style's definition will be the next style to apply when you type a paragraph return.

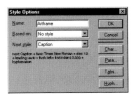

2 In the Style Options dialog box, from the Next Style menu choose the name of the style you want to follow this paragraph style; for example: Caption.

3 Click OK.

FINDING AND CHANGING TEXT AND TEXT ATTRIBUTES

In story editor, you can search for specific occurrences of a word or group of words. Once you find what you're looking for, you can have PageMaker automatically change it to something else.

You can also restrict find-and-change actions to text of a specific format or combination of formats. Selecting among a set of paragraph styles and text attributes, you can specify the formatting of the text you are searching for and replacing. For instance, you can restrict your search to italicized versions of a word and change them to Normal or Bold.

You can search for words that have letters in common by using a wild card—a caret (^) and a question mark (?)—for every letter that might vary. For example, to search a publication for *geese* and *goose*, enter **g^?^?se** for the Find What option in either the Find or Change dialog box. To search for tabs, spaces, and other special characters, enter the character as described in Appendix A, "Special Characters."

To find or change text and formatting:

1 Click an insertion point in a story, or select a range of text if you want to limit your changes to that section.

2 Choose Edit > Edit Story.

3 Choose the Utilities > Find command or the Utilities > Change command.

4 In the Find What text box, type or paste the text you want to find. To change the text, type the new text in the Change To text box. To search for formatting only, leave the text boxes blank.

5 Select Match Case and Whole Word as appropriate:

• Match Case searches for only the word or words that exactly match the capitalization of the text in the Find What text box. For example, a search for "PrePress" will not find "Prepress" or "PREPRESS."

• Whole Word disregards the search text if it is embedded within a larger word. For example, if you are searching for "any" as a whole word, PageMaker disregards "many."

6 To search for text formatting, click Char Attributes or Para Attributes depending on the formatting you want to find.

7 In the dialog box, specify the formatting to search for and, if appropriate, how you want to change it, and click OK.

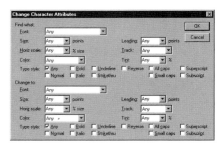

Note: *If you leave all text or paragraph attributes set to Any, you must also type ^?* *in the Find What text box.*

8 Select options to determine the scope of the search (all open publications or only the current one). If you search the current publication only, select a Search Story option.

9 Click Find to begin the search.

PageMaker finds the first instance of the text and formatting you specified, and the Utilities > Find Next command becomes available.

10 Click the button that reflects what you want to do next.

• Change replaces the found text or text format with the revised text or text format. To repeat the search, select Find Next.

• Change & Find replaces the found text or text format with the revised text or text format and then searches for the next occurrence.

• Change All searches for and replaces all occurrences of the found text or text format. If there are no substitutions, PageMaker displays an alert.

If Find What or Change To is underlined in either the Find or Change dialog box, one or more text attributes have been specified for the search. To find or change text regardless of its attributes, set each option in the Find/Change Char Attributes or Find/Change Paragraph Attributes dialog box to Any.

Shortcut: *To quickly reset all Character or all Paragraph attributes to Any, press Option (Mac) or Alt (Windows) and click the Char or Paragraph attribute button. If you press Shift as you perform this shortcut, you reset both Character and Paragraph attributes to Any.*

CHECKING SPELLING

You can use PageMaker to check the spelling in a selected range of text, in all text in the active story, in all stories in a publication, or in all stories in all open publications. PageMaker highlights misspelled or unknown words, words typed twice (such as *the the*), and words with possible capitalization errors.

By default, PageMaker 6.5 uses Proximity 6.0 dictionaries to verify spelling (and to hyphenate words). However, you can install hyphenation and spelling dictionaries from other vendors as they become available.

At least one dictionary is installed automatically with PageMaker. Depending on the language version of PageMaker, more than one dictionary may be available to install. You can use custom installation options to choose from up to 17 language dictionaries to work with.

About user dictionaries

Each language dictionary comes with a user dictionary—a separate file you can customize to supplement the base-language dictionary. For example, you can store a company's product and employee names in a user dictionary to make sure each company publication refers to them correctly. The user dictionary contains all of the words you add to the dictionary during spelling checks, when controlling hyphenation, or while using the Dictionary Editor, a stand-alone utility included with PageMaker. If you are using the Proximity dictionaries installed by PageMaker, you can recognize the user dictionary file for each language by its .udc filename extension.

To check spelling and to hyphenate words with a user dictionary, make sure that the user dictionary file is in the corresponding language folder.

You can install only one user dictionary at one time for each language. To create or use a second user dictionary for a particular language, you must first quit PageMaker, and then move the existing user dictionary to another folder in order to use the new one.

To check spelling in one or more publications:

1 Click an insertion point in a particular story or select a range of text.

2 In story editor, choose Utilities > Spelling.

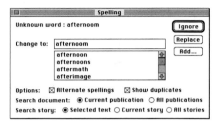

3 Specify options:

• Alternate Spellings lets you see suggested replacements for misspelled words.

• Show Duplicates lets you detect duplicate words, such as *the the.*

Deselect these options to speed-up the spell check.

4 Specify the scope of the search:

• In selected text

• In the current story only

• In all stories in the publication

If you are checking all open publications, PageMaker automatically searches all stories in those publications.

5 Click Start to begin checking the spelling.

6 As PageMaker finds unfamiliar words and other possible errors, choose from the following options:

• Click Ignore to continue checking spelling without changing text. (The word will be ignored for the rest of the PageMaker work session.)

• Select a word from the Change To list, and then click Replace.

• Type the correct text in the Change To text box, and then click Replace.

• Click Add to have PageMaker store the unrecognized word in the user dictionary, so that subsequent occurrences are not flagged as misspellings. See the next section for information on adding words to user dictionaries.

Note: Make sure each person in your workgroup has the same customized user dictionary installed, so that a publication uses the same spelling and hyphenation rules regardless of which workstation it's on.

Assigning dictionaries to paragraphs

By default, paragraphs are assigned the default language dictionary for the language version of PageMaker you installed. But if you use more than one language in a publication, you can tell PageMaker which language dictionary to use for spell-checking paragraphs in a particular language.

If you have three paragraphs, each in a different language, you can set the dictionary for each paragraph to the appropriate language.

To assign a dictionary to a paragraph:

1 Select one or more paragraphs you want to assign a dictionary to or choose Window > Show Styles and double-click a paragraph style to edit.

2 Depending on your selection, do the following:

• If you have one or more paragraphs selected, choose Type > Paragraph.

• If you are editing a paragraph style, click Para in the Style Options dialog box.

3 From the Dictionary menu, choose the dictionary you want to apply.

CUSTOMIZING THE DICTIONARY

You can make minor spelling and hyphenation changes to the current user dictionary from within PageMaker (for example, while checking spelling you can add words that the standard dictionary doesn't recognize). For more extensive changes you can use the Dictionary Editor utility to create new user dictionaries, import word lists, and revise spelling and hyphenation.

As you modify or create user dictionaries, remember that the settings in the PageMaker Hyphenation dialog box determine the way text in your publication will be hyphenated. For example, you can specify that hyphenation be turned on or off, and which type of hyphenation you will allow (manual, dictionary, or algorithm). See "Customizing Hyphenation for Specific Words" on page 161 and "Customizing Hyphenation for Paragraphs" on page 162.

Adding words to a user dictionary from within PageMaker

There are two ways to add words to user dictionaries in PageMaker: while checking spelling (in which case you use the Utilities > Spelling command), and while examining how words are being hyphenated in a publication (in which case you use the Type > Hyphenation command).

To add a word:

1 Select the word in layout view and choose Type > Hyphenation or, if you are checking spelling, type the word in the Change To text box.

2 Click Add.

3 Double-check the spelling and capitalization of the word and insert hyphenation breaks by typing tildes (~). One tilde indicates the most preferable place for a line break, two indicate the next preferable, and three indicate a poor but acceptable place for hyphenation to occur.

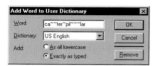

4 From the Dictionary menu, select the dictionary to which you want to add the word.

5 Choose options as follows:

• Click the As All Lowercase option if you want to add the word to the dictionary in its generic form, so that, for example, PageMaker accepts capitalization at the beginning of a sentence.

• Click Exactly As Typed so that the word is acceptable only when capitalized as you typed.

Using the Dictionary Editor

Dictionary Editor is a separate application useful for making extensive changes for spelling and hyphenation purposes. (For example, you can quickly add a long list of employee names to a user dictionary, a process that would take a good deal of time in PageMaker.) The application is installed in the Typography folder within the Extras folder within the PageMaker folder.

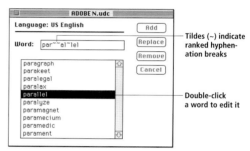

Dictionary Editor displays a separate window for each new or existing dictionary you open.

To create or edit a user dictionary:

1 Double-click the Dictionary Editor icon in the Typography folder .

2 Choose File > New to create a new dictionary or File > Open to edit an existing dictionary.

3 Type a filename for your new dictionary or choose an existing dictionary, and then click OK.

4 Click in the Word text box to type a new word or double-click the word you want to edit.

5 Control how the word hyphenates as follows:

• Choose Edit > Hyphenate to use the built-in algorithm.

• To define your own hyphenation breaks, type a tilde (~) at each point where you would permit hyphenation. To rank hyphenation breaks, type one tilde to indicate the most preferable break, two tildes to indicate the next best break, and type three tildes to indicate the least preferable break.

• To prevent a word from being hyphenated, leave the word unhyphenated.

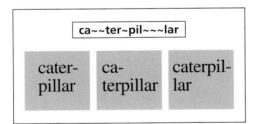

Hyphenation breaks are ranked by tildes (~).

6 Click Add (if you typed a new word) or Replace (if you changed a word) to add the word to the dictionary. Click Cancel to leave the new word or word revisions out of the dictionary.

7 Choose File > Save As to save the file to a location you want. The filename extension .udc is added automatically.

To import a word list:

1 Create a word list in PageMaker or in any application that creates or saves text-only files. Separate each word in the list by a carriage return, space, or tab.

2 In Dictionary Editor, choose File > Import.

3 Select the following options if desired:

• Hyphenate On Import Using Algorithm hyphenates the words according to the built-in algorithm. (Dictionary Editor does not apply the algorithm to words for which you've already added tildes.)

• Import Words Already In Dictionary overwrites words that are already in the user dictionary with words that have the same spelling. If this option is deselected, any words in your list that are already in the user dictionary will not be overwritten.

To export or print a user dictionary:

1 In Dictionary Editor, open the dictionary you want to export or print.

2 Choose File > Export or File > Print.

3 Select the standard export or print options you want.

4 Click OK.

Chapter

5

Chapter 5: Composition and Typography

T his chapter describes the features and techniques you can use to produce professional-quality type in your publication.

The appearance of text on the page depends on a complex interaction of processes called composition. During composition, PageMaker determines where on the page to place each character.

To compose text on the page • PageMaker first adds up the widths of all the characters, including any modifications created by kerning, tracking, or changes to the set width (condensing or expanding characters). Then PageMaker decides where to break lines, based on the line length (the width of the text), the alignment (justified or ragged), and the limits you've set for word spacing, letter spacing, and hyphenation.

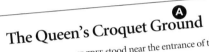

The Queen's Croquet Ground Ⓐ

Ⓑ A LARGE ROSE-TREE stood near the entrance of the garden: the roses growing on it were white, but there were gardeners at it, busily painting them red. Alice thought this a very curious thing, and she went nearer to watch them, and just as she came up to them she heard one of them say, "Look now, Five! Don't go splashing paint over me like that!"

I couldn't help it," said Five in a sulky tone; "Seven jogged my elbow."

On which Seven looked up and said, "That's right, Five! Always lay blame on the others!"

"You'd better not talk!" said Five. "I heard the Queen say only yesterday you deserved to be beheaded!"

"What for?" said the one who had spoken first.

"That's none of your business, Two!" said Seven.

"Yes, it is his business!" said Five, "and I'll tell him—it was for bringing the cook t Ⓓ ts instead of on-ions."

Seven flung down his brush, and had just begun, "Well, of all the unjust things—" when his eye chanced to fall upon Alice as she stood watching them, and he checked himself suddenly: the others looked round also, and all of them bowed low.

"Would you tell me please," said Alice, a little timidly, "why are you painting those roses?"

Five and Seven said nothing, but looked at Two. Two began, in a low voice, "Why, the fact is, you see, Miss, this here ought to have been a *red* rose-tree, and we put a white one in by mistake, and if the Queen was to

 Ⓒ

Ⓐ

You can control tracking and kerning, including adjustments to word and letter spacing.

Ⓑ
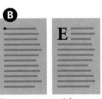

You can create special typographic effects, such as drop caps.

Ⓒ

You can change the way a word is hyphenated in specific instances or as a global change.

Ⓓ

You can eliminate widows, orphans and other undesirable paragraph breaks.

UNDERSTANDING TRACKING AND KERNING

Traditionally, typographers have used tracking to change the visual denseness or openness of type on the page, and kerning to fix particular pairs of letters that draw attention to themselves by being too close or too far apart. In PageMaker, think of tracking and kerning along those lines: the built-in track settings usually apply globally to fonts and change with point sizes, and kerning is typically performed on pairs or on a short range of text to fine-tune the character spacing.

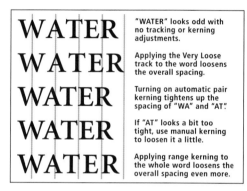

"WATER" looks odd with no tracking or kerning adjustments.

Applying the Very Loose track to the word loosens the overall spacing.

Turning on automatic pair kerning tightens up the spacing of "WA" and "AT."

If "AT" looks a bit too tight, use manual kerning to loosen it a little.

Applying range kerning to the whole word loosens the overall spacing even more.

Tracking and kerning are both measured in relative units—that is, units that are based on the point size of the type. Tracking adjusts the relative space between characters so that it gets slightly tighter at large sizes and slightly looser at small sizes. Kerning is strictly proportional, since the em—the unit that kerning is based on—gets bigger or smaller at the same rate as the characters. The proportions between them are always the same.

TRACKING TYPE

PageMaker includes five built-in tracks which decrease or increase the space between characters to varying degrees, from Very Loose to Very Tight. Tracking in PageMaker is font and point-size dependent; each track is a collection of values that correlates the size of a font with a specific amount of change in letter spacing. You can even edit tracks for specific fonts at specific sizes.

You can apply a track to any range of text. Because tracking in PageMaker is a character-level attribute, you can apply one track to a range of text, then apply a different track to text that's in the same font, even the same size, somewhere else. In a paragraph that's tracked at Loose, for example, you might apply the Very Loose track to a word set in small caps in the middle of the paragraph. A track can also be applied as part of a paragraph style.

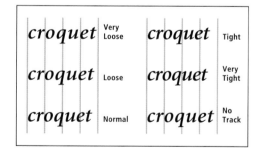

To apply a track:

1 Using the text tool, select the text you want to track.

2 Choose Type > Expert Tracking.

3 Choose one of the five built-in tracks from the menu, or choose No Track to use letter-spacing defined by the font manufacturer.

Editing tracks

You can customize tracking for specific fonts at specific sizes using the track editing feature, which works with any kind of font technology, including bitmap fonts, PostScript Type1 and Type3, and TrueType, as long as the selected font is installed.

Important: *Editing a track permanently modifies PageMaker's tracking values table, to which all of your publications refer by default. If you want to edit the tracking values for a single publication, drag a copy of the Tracking Values file (Macintosh) or the TRAKVALS.BIN file (Windows) from the PageMaker RSRC folder to your publication folder before editing the tracks. See "About the Tracking Values File" on page 153.*

The Edit Tracks dialog box displays tracking values as lines plotted on a grid, with each line representing one track.

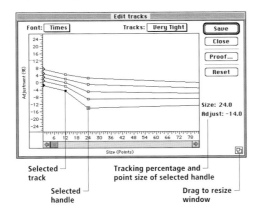

Selected track

Selected handle

Tracking percentage and point size of selected handle

Drag to resize window

Tracking lines can cross one another, but normally appear in order, with Very Loose as the top line and Very Tight as the bottom line. The height of the line indicates how tight or loose the track becomes at specific point sizes. Adjusting in the positive direction loosens the track, and adjusting in the negative direction tightens the track. As a general rule, the larger the point size, the tighter the tracking should be.

Existing tracking values for a particular point size appear as solid squares that act as handles so you can modify the point size or tracking values. The values of the selected handle appear in the dialog box. Adjust the tracking for font sizes from 4 points to 650 points.

If you set your font to a size for which no tracking value has been defined, PageMaker calculates a new value based on the line connecting existing defined values.

To edit a track:

1 Choose Type > Expert Tracking > Edit Tracks.

2 From the Font menu, choose the font you want to edit.

3 Click on a track line to select it, or choose a track from the Track menu.

4 Edit tracks (moving, adding, or deleting handles as necessary) as follows:

• To adjust the tracking percentage value in 1/10% increments, select a handle and press the up- or down-arrow keys. (You can also adjust the tracking percentage by dragging a handle to a new location.)

• To adjust the point size in 1/10-point increments, select a handle and press the left- or right-arrow keys. (You can also adjust the point size by dragging a handle to a new location.)

• To add a track handle, hold down Option (Macintosh) or Alt (Windows) and click a track line.

• To delete a track handle, hold down Option (Macintosh) or Alt (Windows) and click a handle.

5 To save the changes, either click Save to save changes and close the window, or choose a new font to edit, and then click OK when prompted to save changes to the previously selected font.

Copying tracks to another font

Once you have adjusted tracks to your liking, you can copy the tracking information to a different font. For example, you can edit Minion as desired, and then copy the settings to Minion Bold, Minion Italic, and so on. (All five tracks are copied in unison; you cannot copy just one track within a font.)

To copy a track:

1 Choose Type > Expert Tracking > Edit Tracks.

2 From the Font menu, choose the font with the tracks you want to reuse.

3 Press Command + C (Macintosh) or Ctrl + C (Windows) to copy the font information.

4 Select the font to receive the information, and then press Command + V (Macintosh) or Ctrl + V (Windows) to paste the information. All five tracks are copied or pasted as a group.

Proofing tracked text

While editing tracks, PageMaker can create a new, untitled publication with a paragraph style for each track at each point size in a particular font. You can then apply the styles to sample text and print the publication to proof your work.

To proof tracking changes:

1 Select a font in the Edit Tracks dialog box.

2 Click Proof.

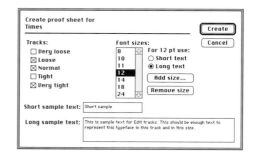

3 Select the tracks you want to include in the sample.

4 Specify what point sizes to include and whether to display a short or long text sample for each displayed point size.

You can change the sample text by typing the text you want in the appropriate text box.

5 Click Create.

The untitled publication opens with sample paragraphs showing each track at each point size.

About the tracking values file

PageMaker stores tracking information in a specific file, which must be available when you edit tracks, and when you compose and print the publication (assuming you want to print with modified tracks). On the Macintosh, the filename is "Tracking Values." In Windows, the filename is "TRAKVALS.BIN." Do not change the name of this file; PageMaker will fail to locate it if you do.

Whether you're editing tracks or printing with modified track settings, PageMaker first looks for the tracking values file in the same folder as the active publication. If the file is not present, PageMaker then looks for it in the Adobe PageMaker folder, and then, lastly, in the RSRC folder within the Adobe PageMaker folder. In a workgroup setting, make sure the customized tracking values file is present on each computer you use to view or modify the publication.

You can use multiple customized tracking values files for different publications. For example, if your work for one client always requires special tracking values, make a copy of PageMaker's default tracking values file and store it in the folder containing that client's publications. When you open a publication in that folder and use Edit Tracks, PageMaker will make changes to the copy you created.

If you send the publication to a service provider for final output, remember to include the modified tracking values file with other files needed for remote printing (for example, by selecting Files Required for Remote Printing in the Save As dialog box).

Note: *If you make copies of the tracking values file, you risk overwriting one copy with another of the same name. You can temporarily change the name of a tracking values file, but before printing or editing tracks remember to change the name back to "Tracking Values" (Macintosh) or "TRAKVALS.BIN" (Windows).*

KERNING TYPE

PageMaker provides several different kinds of kerning:

• Automatic pair kerning adjusts the space between certain character pairs, based on the kerning information that's built into the font. You can turn automatic pair kerning on or off at the paragraph level.

• Manual kerning lets you kern any range of text, from one character pair to a whole story, using cursor keys in increments of either 0.04 or 0.01 of an em. Alternatively, you can use the Control palette to kern in increments of 0.1 or 0.01 of an em, or by entering a numeric value accurate to 0.001 of an em.

TIP: TO KERN THE FIRST
CHARACTER ON A LINE
INTO THE LEFT MARGIN,
INSERT A NON-BREAKING
WORD SPACE BEFORE THE
LETTER, AND THEN KERN
BACK OVER THAT SPACE.

• Expert kerning, a feature best used for headlines and display type, calculates a manual kerning value for every character pair in a selected range of text, based on the character shape and on the kern strength you specify.

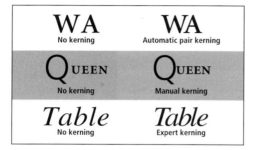

Kerning affects the space after a character. If you want to alter the kerning of a word but don't want to affect the width of the space after the word, select all but the last letter of the word.

You can apply kerning to word spaces as well as to letters and other characters, since the space-band is a character defined in the font. (The spaceband is the character produced when you press the spacebar.)

Note: PageMaker for the Macintosh includes a separate kerning editor, KernEdit (Agfa/Miles Inc.) that you can use to alter the font file. Changes are stored in the screen-font file (the FOND resource of the font). For more information, see the online Help system within KernEdit.

Automatic pair kerning

When you apply automatic pair kerning to text, PageMaker applies the kerning pairs specified in a font design. For example, most fonts kern the following pairs of characters: LA, P., To, Tr, Ta, Tu, Te, Ty, Wa, WA, We, we, Wo, Ya, Yo, and yo. Because kerning is sometimes discernible only at larger point sizes, PageMaker lets you set a size threshold above which all kerning pairs are used.

You can apply automatic pair kerning to a single paragraph, to selected paragraphs, or to all paragraphs of a particular style, but you cannot apply it to some characters in a paragraph and not to others.

To automatically kern character pairs:

1 Use the text tool to select the text.

2 Choose Type > Paragraph.

3 Click Spacing.

4 Select Auto Above, and specify a point size above which you want PageMaker to kern character pairs.

5 Click OK.

TIP: WHEN YOU KERN MANUALLY, A KERNING VALUE APPEARS ON THE CONTROL PALETTE IN CHARACTER VIEW. NOTE THE KERNING AMOUNT ON THE CONTROL PALETTE AND ENTER IT WHEREVER YOU WANT TO DUPLICATE THAT KERNING.

Manual kerning

You can manually kern a specific character pair or selected range of text, either by adjusting the space between characters incrementally or by specifying a value by which you want to alter the original spacing. PageMaker's finest kerning increment is 0.001 of an em (an em is a unit of measure equal to the width of a lowercase *m* of the same size and font).

To kern by entering a value:

1 Use the text tool to select the text to kern.

2 Enter a value for the Kerning option on the Control palette (in character view), and then click the Apply button.

PageMaker accepts kerning values between -1 and 1 (1 equals 1 em space): negative values move characters closer together, and positive values move them farther apart. For example, to move letters apart half an em, type **0.5** in the text box.

To kern in increments (layout view only):

1 Click an insertion point between two characters or select a range of text.

2 Click a nudge button for the Kerning option on the Control palette (in character view) or type one of the kerning key combinations from the following table:

Applying manual kerning

To manually...	Press these keys...
Increase spacing $\frac{1}{25}$ (.04) em	Macintosh: Command + Shift + Delete or Option + Right arrow Windows: Ctrl + Shift + Backspace or Alt + Right arrow
Increase spacing $\frac{1}{100}$ (.01) em	Macintosh: Option + Shift + Delete or Command + Option + Right arrow Windows: Ctrl + Alt + Right arrow
Decrease spacing $\frac{1}{25}$ (.04) em	Macintosh: Command + Delete or Option + Left arrow Windows: Ctrl + Backspace or Alt + Left arrow
Decrease spacing $\frac{1}{100}$ (.01) em	Macintosh: Option + Delete or Command + Option + Left arrow Windows: Ctrl + Alt + Left arrow
Clear all manual kerning from selected text	Macintosh: Command + Option + K Windows: Ctrl + Alt + K

To remove manual kerning:

1 Use the text tool to select the kerned text.

2 Enter **0** for the Kerning option in the Control palette (in character view), and then click the Apply button. Alternatively, select a range of text and press Command + Option + K (Macintosh) or Ctrl+ Alt + K (Windows).

Expert kerning

The Type > Expert Kerning command auto-mates kerning to give you tight control over letter spacing for headlines, poster type, and other display type at large sizes. You can use expert kerning to determine fine kerning values even if you've mixed fonts and sizes in the same line. (This feature requires PostScript Type1 fonts; the corresponding printer fonts—also called outline fonts—must be installed on your computer.)

Expert kerning evaluates every character pair in the selected text, removes all manual kerning, and inserts kern-pair values into the text as manual kerning. Since automatic kerning in-cludes pair kerning and tracking, you should turn off PageMaker's automatic pair kerning when using expert kerning. You can still manu-ally adjust letter spacing after you have kerned type with expert kerning.

Kern Strength set at 0.00	*croquet*
Kern Strength set at 0.75	*croquet*
Kern Strength set at 2.00	*croquet*

You can adjust kerning tightness by specifying a kern strength. Values for kern strength range from 0.00 to 1.00; the higher the value, the tighter the spacing. (The default value is 0.50.)

We recommend that you use expert kerning only for small blocks of type. It can be time-consuming and impractical to kern every character pair in a long document.

To use Expert Kerning:

1 Use the text tool to select the text to be kerned.

2 Choose Type > Expert Kerning.

3 Type the Kern Strength (from 0.00 to 1.00) you want PageMaker to use when creating kerning pairs. Alternatively, use the slider bar to set the value.

4 For Design Class, specify the source of the original master design of the font, if you know it.

You can choose Text, Display, or Poster, or you can choose Other and then type the font size of the master. (The source describes the font designer's expectation of the font's use or the font size from which the designer created the font.) If you don't know the source of the master design of the font, choose Text.

5 Click OK.

UNDERSTANDING HYPHENATION AND JUSTIFICATION

The way PageMaker horizontally spaces words and characters on a line is a complex process. The design of the font, paragraph alignment, word and letter spacing, and hyphenation settings all affect the horizontal spacing of lines and the aesthetic appeal of text on a page. This section discusses options for spacing, aligning, and hyphenating text in PageMaker.

How PageMaker breaks words • If you want to use spacing and hyphenation controls knowledgeably to achieve a particular texture in blocks of justified type, it's useful to understand the choices that PageMaker makes during composition.

PageMaker has to place characters in a line so that they fill the whole line, from one side of the text block to the other; the only variable is how much space to put between words and letters. PageMaker tries each of several options in turn:

> arge rose-tree stood near the entrance of the garden: roses on it were white, but there were gardeners at

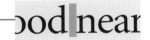

1   Space between words is compressed to fit the last whole word onto the line.

> arge rose-tree stood near the entrance of the den: the roses on it were white, but there were

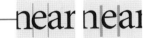

2   If the word can't fit without compressing word spaces beyond the minimum, word spaces are expanded to push the word down to the next line.

> arge rose-tree stood near the entrance of the gar-
> t: the roses on it were white, but there were

3   If word space expands beyond the maximum, PageMaker looks for allowable hyphenation options for the word, to keep it within the spacing limits.

> arge rose-tree stood near the entrance of the garden: roses on it were white, but there were gardeners at

4   If none of the options work, PageMaker adjusts letter spacing in the same way it did word spacing; first compressing the space between letters, then expanding it.

5   If all these options fail, PageMaker uses the maximum letter spacing and expands the word beyond the maximum as much as necessary.

SETTING WORD AND LETTER SPACING

The space between words, created by pressing the spacebar, is called the spaceband and is part of the font design. Default word spacing in PageMaker is 100% of the spaceband of the associated font. You can change the desired spacing to any percentage between 0% and 500%.

Each character in a font is surrounded by a specific amount of space (called the side-bearing), built in by the font designer. A character's width includes not just the character itself but the side-bearing. You can modify the width of characters with the Type > Horizontal Scale command and modify letter spacing with the Type > Paragraph command. Kerning and tracking also modify characters widths. See "Understanding Tracking and Kerning" on page 150.

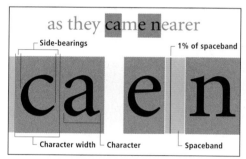

The unit of measure for word and letter spacing is 1% of the spaceband. A character's width includes the character itself plus the side-bearings.

Using the Minimum, Desired, and Maximum options

The Type > Paragraph command includes options for setting Minimum, Desired, and Maximum word and letter spacing. The Minimum and Maximum values only come into play when setting justified text (in which the text is evenly spaced so that it is flush with the left and right sides of the text block or text frame inset).

Using these options, you can set the degree to which you will allow PageMaker to deviate from normal font spacing to justify a line. The more the percentages for Minimum and Maximum options differ from the Desired percentage, the more PageMaker will stretch or compress spacing to justify the line.

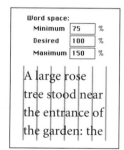 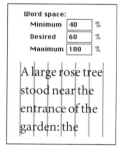

Default settings   Adjusted settings

Note: When specifying word spacing, Minimum must be less than or equal to the percentage set for Desired, and Maximum must be greater than or equal to the percentage set for Desired.

To set word or letter spacing:

1 Select one or more paragraphs, or edit a paragraph style.

To edit a paragraph style, choose Window > Show Styles, press Command (Macintosh) or Ctrl (Windows) and click a paragraph style.

2 Do one of the following:

• If you have one or more paragraphs selected, choose Type > Paragraph.

• If you are editing a paragraph style, click Para in the Style Options dialog box, and click Spacing.

3 In the Word Space or Letter Space text box, type new values as follows:

• For unjustified and justified text, increase or decrease the percentage for Desired. (Word spacing can range from 0% to 500%. Letter spacing can range from -200% to 200%.)

• For justified text only, enter values in the Minimum and Maximum text boxes to define a range of acceptable spacing. (Word spacing values can range from 0% to 500%. Letter spacing can range from -200% to 200%.)

4 Click OK.

Identifying loose or tight lines

Because composing a line of type involves many factors in addition to word and letter spacing (hyphenation preferences for example), PageMaker cannot always honor the word and letter spacing parameters you specified with the Type > Paragraph command. However, in layout view PageMaker can highlight lines of text that have too much (loose) or too little (tight) letter or word spacing.

How PageMaker spaces letters • When you specify more than one letter-spacing attribute, PageMaker applies the attributes in a specific order as it composes lines of text on the page. Kerning, tracking, and desired letter- and word-spacing settings are applied in the following order:

the roses on it were white, but there were gar

1 Text is arranged on a line according to each character's specified character width.

the roses on it were white, but there were gar

2 If automatic pair kerning is turned on, the kerning specified in the font design is adjusted.

the roses on it were white, but there were gar

3 Manual kerning is applied.

the roses on it were white, but there were gard

4 Range kerning is applied.

the roses on it were white, but there were garde

5 PageMaker adds any tracking.

To identify lines that are too tight or too loose:

1 Choose File > Preferences > General.

2 Select Show Loose/Tight Lines.

3 Click OK.

About hyphenation and justified text

The tradeoff between hyphenation and spacing in justified text is that the closer you come to ideal spacing between letters and words, the more likely it is that words will need to be hyphenated.

In a justified paragraph, PageMaker must decide how to justify each line: increase word and letter spacing to push a word to the next line; decrease word or letter spacing to fit a word onto the current line; or hyphenate a word. If hyphenation occurs more often than you like, you can limit the number of consecutive hyphens. For more information, see "Customizing Hyphenation for Paragraphs" on page 162.

Justified text without hyphenation

Justified text with hyphenation

ALIGNING PARAGRAPHS

You can align text with the left or right edges of a text block (or with the inset of a text frame), and you can center or justify it. (Justified text is aligned with both the left and right edges of a text block or with the left and right inset of a text frame.) You can also force-justify text so that the last line of a paragraph, even if it contains only a few characters, is spaced to fit exactly between the left and right edges of the text block or text frame inset.

> *The table was a large one, but the three were all crowded to-gether at the corner of it.*   Justified paragraph
>
> *The table was a large one, but the three were all crowded to-gether at the corner of it.*   Force-justified paragraph

To align a paragraph:

1 Select one or more paragraphs, or edit a paragraph style.

To edit a paragraph style, choose Window > Show Styles, press Command (Macintosh) or Ctrl (Windows) and click a paragraph style.

2 Do one of the following:

• Click an alignment button on the Control palette in paragraph view.

• Choose Type > Alignment or Type > Paragraph, and then choose an alignment option.

TIP: TYPE A NON-BREAKING HYPHEN TO PREVENT A HYPHEN-ATED WORD (SUCH AS "NITTY-GRITTY") FROM BREAKING ON THE MACINTOSH, TYPE COMMAND + OPTION + HYPHEN. IN WINDOWS, CTRL + ALT + HYPHEN.

• If you are editing a paragraph style, click Para in the Style Options dialog box, then select an alignment option, and then click OK.

CUSTOMIZING HYPHENATION FOR SPECIFIC WORDS

PageMaker lets you change the way a word is hyphenated in a specific instance or every time the word occurs. The controls described in this section can be overridden or supplemented with paragraph-level hyphenation settings. See "Customizing Hyphenation for Paragraphs" on page 162.

Adding a discretionary hyphen

In PageMaker you use a discretionary hyphen to indicate hyphenation preferences for a particular occurrence of a word. A discretionary hyphen is different from a hyphen that you insert with the hyphen key. When you type a regular hyphen in a word, that hyphen appears even when the word does not fall at the end of a line. A discretionary hyphen appears only when it falls at the end of a line, and PageMaker determines that a line wrap is necessary.

Discretionary hyphens are preferable to regular hyphens in many cases, because they disappear when edits cause a previously hyphenated word to move from the end of a line. A discretionary hyphen overrides any hyphenation breaks defined in the dictionary.

To change hyphenation for one occurrence of a word:

1 Click an insertion point where you want to insert a discretionary hyphen.

2 Press Command + Shift + - (hyphen) (Macintosh) or Ctrl + Shift + - (hyphen) (Windows).

To prevent hyphenation in one occurrence of a word:

1 Click an insertion point before the first letter of a word.

2 Press Command + Shift + - (hyphen) (Macintosh) or Ctrl + Shift + - (hyphen) (Windows).

To change or eliminate hyphenation for every occurrence of a word:

1 Using the text tool, select a word.

2 Choose Type > Hyphenation, and then click Add.

The selected word appears in the Add Word to User Dictionary dialog box, with the hyphenation breaks suggested by PageMaker.

3 Edit the entry to indicate your preferred hyphenation for the word:

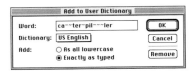

• Type one tilde (~) to indicate the best possible breaking point in the word.

• Type two tildes to indicate the next-best choice.

• Type three tildes to indicate a poor but acceptable break point.

If there is only one acceptable breaking point for a word, type only one tilde. If you have no hyphenation preference, type the same number of tildes between each syllable. If you never want the word to be hyphenated, type a tilde before the first letter of the word.

For more information on editing spelling and hyphenation dictionaries, see "Customizing the Dictionary" on page 143.

Note: If you are in a workgroup setting, make sure the user dictionary containing the correct hyphenation preferences is copied to the computer of each person working on the publication.

CUSTOMIZING HYPHENATION FOR PARAGRAPHS

With the Type > Hyphenation command, you can control several aspects of hyphenation at a paragraph and paragraph-style level, including turning off hyphenation completely. You can determine what methods PageMaker uses to hyphenate individual words, specify how far from the right side of a column you will allow Page-Maker to hyphenate (not applicable in justified text), and specify how many consecutive lines of text can end with a hyphen.

To specify a hyphenation method:

1 Select one or more paragraphs, or edit a paragraph style.

To edit a paragraph style, choose Window > Show Styles, press Command (Macintosh) or Ctrl (Windows) and click a paragraph style.

2 Do one of the following:

• If you have one or more paragraphs selected, choose Type > Hyphenation.

• If you are editing a paragraph style, click Hyph in the Style Options dialog box.

3 Click On for the Hyphenation setting.

If you click Off, PageMaker ignores discretionary hyphens, although it will still break words that have ordinary hyphens in them.

4 Select one of the following options, and then click OK:

• Manual Only hyphenates only those words containing a discretionary hyphen.

• Manual Plus Dictionary hyphenates words containing discretionary hyphens, as well as words in the dictionary assigned to the paragraph.

• Manual Plus Algorithm combines both Manual Only and Manual Plus Dictionary and, if a hyphenation point is not found, an algorithm is used to determine hyphenation. The algorithm is a set of rules for hyphenation, based on the words in the main dictionary; it permits hyphenation breaks in words not found in the PageMaker dictionary or the user dictionary.

Note: *In the case of a conflict between the placement of a discretionary hyphen and where the dictionary would hyphenate the word, the discretionary hyphen prevails.*

Limiting consecutive hyphens

By some typographical standards, it is undesirable to have two or more consecutive lines of type end in hyphens. PageMaker can ensure that the number of consecutive lines ending with a hyphen does not exceed a specified number.

To limit consecutive hyphens:

1 Select one or more paragraphs, or edit a paragraph style.

To edit a paragraph style, choose Window > Show Styles, press Command (Macintosh) or Ctrl (Windows) and click a paragraph style.

2 Do one of the following:

• If you have one or more paragraphs selected, choose Type > Hyphenation.

• If you are editing a paragraph style, click Hyph in the Style Options dialog box.

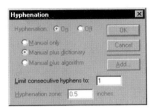

3 For Limit Consecutive Hyphens To, type the maximum number of consecutive lines in a paragraph that can end with hyphens or dashes. You can enter numbers from 1 to 255.

4 Click OK.

Setting the hyphenation zone

PageMaker uses a hyphenation zone, measured from the right side of the text object, to help determine the amount of space in which hyphenation can occur at the end of each line of unjustified text. First, PageMaker applies the desired word and letter spacing for the line. Then, if the last word in the line doesn't fit, and that word starts to the left of the hyphenation zone, PageMaker tries to hyphenate that word. If the word doesn't fit, and starts to the right of the hyphenation zone, PageMaker sends the word to the next line.

In general, the larger the hyphenation zone, the more ragged the right margin of text will be. The smaller the zone, the more hyphenation will occur. This option has no effect on justified text.

To specify a hyphenation zone:

1 Select one or more paragraphs, or edit a paragraph style.

To edit a paragraph style, choose Window > Show Styles, press Command (Macintosh) or Ctrl (Windows) and click a paragraph style.

2 Do one of the following:

• If you have one or more paragraphs selected, choose Type > Hyphenation.

• If you are editing a paragraph style, click Hyph in the Style Options dialog box.

3 Type the width of the hyphenation zone in the Hyphenation Zone text box.

4 Click OK.

LEADING: ADJUSTING THE SPACE BETWEEN LINES OF TEXT

Leading is the vertical space between lines of text. Like letter and word spacing, the right amount of leading makes text easier to read.

Leading settings have two parts: leading value, which measures the entire vertical space allotted for a line of text, and the leading method, which defines where the text is positioned in the slug.

A large rose tree stood near the entrance of the garden: the roses growing on it were white, but there were gardeners at it, busily painting them red. Alice thought this a very curious thing.

PageMaker places each line of text inside a horizontal bar called a slug, which appears as a black rectangle when you highlight characters. The height of the slug indicates the amount of leading you have chosen for the text.

Selecting a leading value

What constitutes reasonable leading varies with the requirements of each publication and font. As a general guideline, set leading approximately

20% greater than the specified font size. For example, use 12-point leading for 10-point type. PageMaker permits fine incremental adjustments in leading—as small as a tenth of a point ($\frac{1}{720}$ of an inch or .0353mm). You can specify leading yourself or let PageMaker determine it automatically.

Note: Leading is a character attribute, which means that you can apply more than one leading amount within the same paragraph. However, if different leading amounts occur within a single line of text, PageMaker uses the largest leading amount for the entire line.

A large rose tree stood near the entrance to the garden: the roses growing on it were white, but there were

10-point type on 10-point leading

A large rose tree stood near the entrance to the garden: the roses growing on it were white, but there were

10-point type on 12-point leading

To specify leading:

1 Select text, or choose Window > Show Styles, press Command (Macintosh) or Ctrl (Windows) and click a paragraph style to edit.

2 Depending on your selection, do the following:

• If you have text selected, choose Type > Leading, or Type > Character, or Window > Show Control palette.

• If you are editing a paragraph style, click Type in the Style Options dialog box.

3 Specify leading in any of these ways:

• Choose a leading value from the Leading menu.

• Choose Auto to apply automatic leading.

• Enter a custom leading value. (If using the Type > Leading command, first choose the Other option from the Leading menu.)

By default, PageMaker sets leading to 120% of the font size when you select Auto for the leading value. You can change that percentage for the current paragraph or for all paragraphs of a particular style.

To change automatic leading:

1 Select one or more paragraphs, or edit a paragraph style.

To edit a paragraph style, choose Window > Show Styles, press Command (Macintosh) or Ctrl (Windows) and click a paragraph style.

2 Do one of the following:

• If you have text selected, choose Type > Paragraph.

• If you are editing a paragraph style, click Para in the Style Options dialog box.

3 Click Spacing, and then enter a percentage for Autoleading.

4 Click OK.

Positioning text within its leading

How PageMaker positions a line of text inside a slug depends on which of three leading methods you select: Proportional, Top of Caps, or Baseline. The leading method is applied uniformly to all characters in a paragraph, even if the leading amounts differ.

A large rose tree stood near the entrance of the garden	A large rose tree stood near the entrance of the garden	A large rose tree stood near the entrance of the garden
Proportional leading	Top of Caps leading	Baseline leading

To change the leading method:

1 Select one or more paragraphs, or edit a paragraph style.

To edit a paragraph style, choose Window > Show Styles, press Command (Macintosh) or Ctrl (Windows) and click a paragraph style.

2 Do one of the following:

• If you have text selected, choose Type > Paragraph.

• If you are editing a paragraph style, click Para in the Style Options dialog box.

3 Click Spacing.

4 Select the leading method you want:

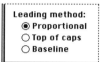

• Proportional positions the baseline of a line of text two-thirds of the way down from the top of the slug. Proportional leading is the default leading method.

• Top of Caps measures the leading (or slug) from the highest point on any character (whether that character appears in the line or not) of the largest font in the line.

• Baseline aligns the bottom of the slug with the baseline of a line of text. This is the method used in traditional typography.

5 Click OK.

Note: *You can raise or lower the baseline of one or more characters. See "Shifting Baselines"* *on page 171 for more information.*

ALIGNING ELEMENTS TO A LEADING GRID

Most publication designs are based on a leading grid to ensure accuracy and consistency. The leading grid refers to the leading of body text in the publication; if your leading is 12 points, you'll want most of your vertically-measured type and page design elements—such as margins, graphics, and paragraph spacing—to be set in multiples of 12. (For example, subheads might have 18 points of leading and 6 points of space before the paragraph to amount to 24 points.)

On a 12-point leading grid, all graphic elements and text baselines snap to the grid in multiples of 12.

PageMaker provides features such as the vertical ruler, baseline grids, and the Align to Grid text attribute for automating grid-based design.

Setting the vertical ruler or guides to match the leading grid

You can set the vertical ruler in layout view to match your leading grid. That way, you can quickly position elements on the page in alignment with the leading grid.

If your publication consists of uniform pages using a single leading grid, you can simply set the vertical ruler once for the publication. But if your publication contains different page designs with two or more leading grids, you can use the Grid Manager plug-in to define baseline grid guides that match your different leading increments, and then apply the grids to the specific pages or to the master pages that organize each page design.

For more information, see "Creating and Applying Layout Grids" on page 90.

To change the vertical ruler:

1 Choose File > Preferences > General.

2 For Vertical Ruler, choose Custom.

3 In the Vertical Ruler text box, type the leading of your body text.

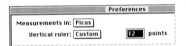

4 Click OK.

5 To ensure that objects align with the leading increments on the ruler, choose View > Snap to Rulers.

To create and apply a set of horizontal guides based on the leading grid:

1 Choose Utilities > Plug-ins > Grid Manager.

2 For Guide, select Baseline.

3 Type the body text leading for the page you are designing, and make a selection for Fit.

4 For Apply, type a range of pages or select the name of the master pages on which you want to display the baseline grid.

5 Click Apply in the Grid Manager dialog box.

Aligning paragraphs to the grid

You can apply Align Next Paragraph to Grid to paragraphs or paragraph styles that are likely to throw succeeding paragraphs off the grid. For example, it's common for multiple-line headings to fall off the leading grid, but the body text that follows should still align with the grid. PageMaker adjusts the spacing between the unaligned paragraph (provided it has the paragraph attribute Align Next Paragraph to Grid) and the next paragraph (provided the next paragraph's leading matches that of the grid size), so that the top of the subsequent paragraph falls on the grid.

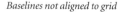
Baselines not aligned to grid   Baselines aligned to grid

Align Next Paragraph to Grid is a paragraph-level attribute, so it can be part of a paragraph style definition. Remember, though, that the attribute actually affects the paragraph after the one to which Align Next Paragraph to Grid is applied: that is, subsequent paragraphs are adjusted so that they fall on the leading grid.

To apply Align Next Paragraph to Grid:

1 Select the paragraph that is likely to throw subsequent paragraphs off the grid. Or, choose Window > Show Styles, press Command (Macintosh) or Ctrl (Windows) and click a paragraph style to edit.

2 Do one of the following:

• If you have a paragraph selected, choose Type > Paragraph.

• If you are editing a paragraph style, click Para in the Style Options dialog box.

3 In the Paragraph Specs dialog box, click Rules, and then click Options.

4 Select Align Next Paragraph to Grid, and type the body text leading increment.

5 Click OK.

The leading grid is measured from the top of the text block or from the top inset in a text frame, based on the increment you specify.

Shortcut: *Use the Control palette in paragraph view to apply Align Next Paragraph to Grid and specify grid size.*

CONTROLLING WIDOWS, ORPHANS, AND OTHER PARAGRAPH BREAKS

The Type > Paragraph command gives you control over how paragraphs break across columns and pages. Use this command to eliminate widows and orphans—words or short lines of text that become separated from the other lines in a paragraph at either the top or bottom of a column or page.

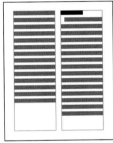

A widow falls at the bottom of a column or page.

An orphan falls at the top of a column or page.

You can also specify that a paragraph not break at the end of a column or page, or when it flows into a graphic that forces text to the next column or page. (If an entire paragraph won't fit in a column, PageMaker moves it to the next column or page that has room for it.) Similarly, you can keep the last line of a paragraph together with a certain number of lines of the next paragraph.

Under some conditions, PageMaker will not be able to honor one or more of these settings. However, PageMaker can highlight on screen the paragraphs that break in violation of the parameters you set.

Note: To control how words break, and where line endings occur within paragraphs, see "Controlling Line Breaks Within Paragraphs" on page 170 and "Understanding Hyphenation and Justification" on page 157.

To control widows and orphans and other breaks:

1 Select one or more paragraphs, or edit a paragraph style.

To edit a paragraph style, choose Window > Show Styles, press Command (Macintosh) or Ctrl (Windows) and click a paragraph style.

2 Do one of the following:

• If you have one or more paragraphs selected, choose Type > Paragraph.

• If you are editing a paragraph style, click Para in the Style Options dialog box.

3 Select any of these options:

• For the Widow Control and Orphan Control options, specify how many lines (up to three) constitute a widow or orphan. When PageMaker finds a widow or orphan with that number of lines, the number of lines specified move to the next column or page.

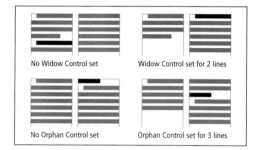

• Select the Keep Lines Together option to prevent the paragraph from breaking.

• Select the Keep With Next _ Lines option to ensure that the last line of the paragraph stays with the top one, two, or three lines of the subsequent paragraphs.

4 Click OK.

To highlight violations of widow, orphan, and other paragraph-break controls:

1 Choose File > Preferences > General.

2 Select Show "Keeps" Violations.

3 Click OK.

CONTROLLING LINE BREAKS WITHIN PARAGRAPHS

When you want a line of text to break in a particular place—or want to avoid line breaks within a selected range of text—you can use a variety of methods to override other spacing and hyphenation considerations. To control how words hyphenate at the end of a line, see "Controlling Hyphenation for Specific Words" on page 161. To understand how PageMaker spaces words and characters on a line, see "Understanding Hyphenation and Justification" on page 157.

Improper use of paragraph returns in address *Proper use of line returns in the same address*

To force a line to break:

1 Click an insertion point where you want to break the line.

2 Press Shift + Return (Macintosh) or Shift + Enter (Windows).

To prevent selected text from breaking:

1 Using the text tool, select the words that you want to keep on one line.

2 Choose Type > Character.

3 For Line Break, select No Break.

4 Click OK.

Using nonbreaking characters

Another method for keeping certain words or phrases intact within a line is to type non-breaking hyphens, spaces, or slashes instead of the normal versions of those characters. For example, by typing a nonbreaking hyphen you prevent a hyphenated proper name such as "Toulouse-Lautrec" from breaking at the hyphen, and thus avoid confusion about the actual spelling of the name.

• To type a nonbreaking hyphen, type Command + Option + - (Macintosh) or Ctrl + Alt + -.

• To type a nonbreaking space, type Option + spacebar (Macintosh) or Ctrl + Alt + spacebar (Windows).

• To type a nonbreaking slash, type Command + Option + / (Macintosh) or Ctrl + Alt + / (Windows).

Note: In PageMaker, em, en, and thin spaces are also nonbreaking characters. See "Typing Relative Spaces" on page 173 and "Typing Em and En Dashes" on page 174 for more information on using those spaces in place of normal spaces.

For a complete list of special characters and how to work with them, see Appendix A, "Special Characters."

FINE-TUNING CHARACTERS

This section describes several typographic enhancements you can make, such as shifting baselines, altering position and case, using correct spaces and dashes, and creating enlarged initial capitals.

Shifting baselines

You can move the baseline of selected characters up or down within a paragraph, which preserves the leading and type size of the character but lets you raise or lower it in relation to the rest of the word or line.

Text with an unchanged baseline has the value of 0. You can specify baseline shift in increments as small as a tenth of a point, and then specify whether you want the baseline to shift up or down.

the rabbit hopped
Before baseline shift is applied

the rabbit *hopped*
After baseline shift has been applied

To shift a baseline:

1 Select the characters you want to shift.

2 Use one of the following methods:

• Choose Window > Show Control Palette and, in the Baseline Shift option, either click a nudge button to adjust the character height or type a value in the text box. Negative values lower the text; positive values raise the text.

• Choose Type > Character, and click Options. For Baseline Shift, click Up or Down and type the value by which you want to adjust the height.

3 Click OK.

Changing case and position

The previous chapter described how to quickly change text from normal case to all caps or small caps, and make text superscript or subscript. This section describes how to control the default size of small caps, and the default size and position of superscript and subscript characters. Since these defaults typically apply to whole publications, you can make the change to the default with no text selected (or with no publication open, to change the setting for all future publications). If the defaults need to vary for a particular kind of paragraph (a numeric or scientific expression for example) you should reset the default for the specific paragraph styles.

To change the default size of small caps:

1 Choose Type > Character.

2 Click Options.

3 In the Small Caps Size text box, specify the size of small caps as a percentage of the current point size, using increments as small as a tenth of 1%.

4 Click OK.

To apply and format superscript or subscript characters:

1 Select the text you want to change.

2 Choose Type > Character or Window > Show Control Palette.

3 Select the Position option you want.

4 Click OK or, in the Control Palette, click the Apply button.

To modify the size or position of superscript or subscript text:

1 Choose Type > Character.

2 Click the Options button.

3 Specify values as follows:

• In the Super/Subscript Size text box, specify the size of superscript and subscript characters as a percentage of the current point size, using increments as small as a tenth of 1%.

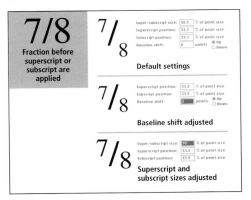

Fraction before superscript or subscript are applied

Default settings

Baseline shift adjusted

Superscript and subscript sizes adjusted

• In the Superscript Position and Subscript Position text boxes, specify Superscript Position as a percentage of an em space shifted up from the baseline (an em space is equal to the width of the uppercase letter *m* in the point size of the selected font), and Subscript Position as a percentage of an em space shifted down from the baseline.

4 Click OK.

Typing relative spaces—en, em, and thin spaces

Unlike regular spaces (the spaceband defined in the font) and nonbreaking spaces, both of which change width in justified text, relative spaces such as the en, em, and thin spaces change width only in relation to point size and font (and are otherwise fixed). The widths of these characters are based on the em width defined in the current font at the current point size. These three spaces are all nonbreaking—that is, a line of type will not wrap to the next line at one of these spaces, but will break at the next most logical point.

The em space is substantially wider than the regular space. It is best to type an em space instead of two regular spaces to separate words.

To type an em space, press Command + Shift + M (Macintosh) or Ctrl + Shift + M (Windows).

The en space (half of an em in width) matches the width of number characters in most fonts, and so is useful to use when aligning single- and double-digit numbers, as in a numbered list.

To type an en space, press Command + Shift + N (Macintosh) or Ctrl + Shift + N (Windows).

The thin space (one quarter of an em in width) is useful for spacing repetitive characters, such as in tab leaders or in manually-typed ellipses (". . . "). Traditionally, the thin space has been used to keep exclamation points and question marks away from the preceding letter.

To type a thin space, press Command + Shift + T (Macintosh) or Ctrl + Shift + T (Windows).

Typing em and en dashes

You use a normal dash (the hyphen) in compound words and names, but in most other cases an em or en dash is the correct character to use. (When you don't want a compound word to break across a line at the hyphen, use a non-breaking hyphen. See "Using Nonbreaking Characters" on page 171.)

• Always use an em dash rather than double hyphens when punctuating sentences. Note that an em dash may butt up against the characters on either side of it; you can increase the kerning in those cases so the characters do not touch.

To type an em dash, press Option + Shift + - (Macintosh) or Alt + Shift + - (Windows).

• The en dash (half of an em dash in width) should be used in place of the word *to* or *through* in phrases such as 9–5, and A–Z. As with em dashes, en dashes may butt up against the characters on either side of it; you can increase the kerning in those cases so the characters do not touch.

To type an en dash, press Option + - (Macintosh) or Alt + - (Windows).

For a complete list of special characters and how to work with them, see Appendix A, "Special Characters."

Enlarging initial capitals

PageMaker lets you quickly add a drop cap—a large initial character—to one or more paragraphs at a time. The drop cap's baseline falls one or more lines below the baseline of the first line of a paragraph.

To create the drop-cap effect, PageMaker resizes and subscripts the initial character in the paragraph, and shifts the baseline of the subscript character. To wrap paragraph lines around the character, PageMaker also inserts tabs and inserts line breaks at the end of each line that wraps around the drop-cap character. (Line breaks prevent the tab at the start of each line from flowing back to the previous line.)

There was a table set out under a tree in front of the house, and the March Hare and the Hatter were having tea at it: a Dormouse was sitting between them, fast asleep, and the

Paragraph before drop cap is applied

There was a table set out under a tree in front of the house, and the March Hare and the Hatter were having tea at it: a Dormouse was sitting between them,

Paragraph after drop cap is applied

To create a drop cap:

1 Click an insertion point anywhere in the paragraph you want to begin with a drop cap.

2 Choose Utilities > Plug-ins > Drop Cap.

3 Specify the number of lines to wrap around the drop cap.

4 Click Apply to view the drop cap without leaving the dialog box.

5 Move to other paragraphs by pressing Prev or Next.

6 Click OK.

To remove a drop cap:

1 Select the paragraphs with the drop caps you want to remove.

2 Choose Utilities > Plug-ins > Drop Cap.

3 Click Remove to reset the type attributes of the initial character and remove the inserted tabs and line breaks.

To edit the drop-cap word:

1 Select the drop-cap character and type a new character.

2 Select the rest of the word and type the new characters. (If you select the entire word and retype it, each character in the word takes on the drop-cap attributes.)

If you edit the lines around the drop cap, you may have to delete the original tabs and line breaks and insert new ones. It is therefore wise to create drop caps after your text is complete.

Note: *You cannot create a drop cap in a paragraph formatted with Top of Caps leading, or when the first character is a graphic, tab, space, bullet, or similar character. Also, if the first character has a descender, you might need to manually adjust the drop cap to achieve the desired effect.*

CHAPTER 6: GRAPHICS AND TEXT OBJECTS

This chapter describes how to create and edit graphics in PageMaker, manipulate objects with the Control palette, and use features to enhance the design process. It also covers techniques related specifically to imported images, such as applying effects with Adobe Photoshop-compatible plug-ins.

DRAWING AND EDITING LINES AND SHAPES

PageMaker drawing tools let you create simple graphics (or frames to hold text or imported graphics) to which you can apply a stroke and fill. (If necessary, choose Window > Show Tools to display the toolbox.)

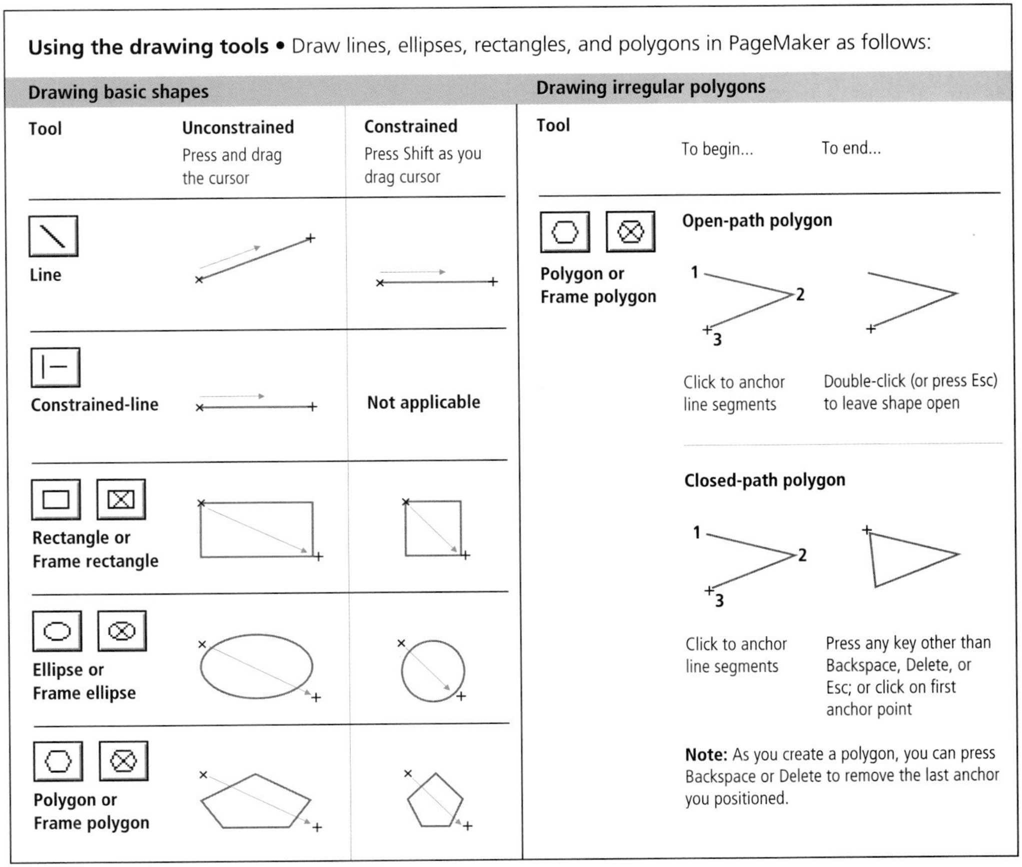

Using the drawing tools • Draw lines, ellipses, rectangles, and polygons in PageMaker as follows:

Drawing basic shapes

Tool	Unconstrained Press and drag the cursor	Constrained Press Shift as you drag cursor
Line		
Constrained-line		Not applicable
Rectangle or Frame rectangle		
Ellipse or Frame ellipse		
Polygon or Frame polygon		

Drawing irregular polygons

Tool	To begin...	To end...
Polygon or Frame polygon	**Open-path polygon** Click to anchor line segments	Double-click (or press Esc) to leave shape open
	Closed-path polygon Click to anchor line segments	Press any key other than Backspace, Delete, or Esc; or click on first anchor point

Note: As you create a polygon, you can press Backspace or Delete to remove the last anchor you positioned.

Changing strokes and fills

You can modify objects a number of ways in PageMaker. For example, you can resize, rotate, and add color to objects. For objects drawn with PageMaker drawing tools, you can also change stroke (the width of lines drawn with the drawing tools, and the width of borders around rectangles, ellipses, and polygons), as well as stroke and fill patterns.

Note: *Changes you make to color attributes do not affect an object if Reverse is selected from the Stroke menu, or if Paper is selected from the Fill menu.*

If you select stroke or fill attributes when no object is selected, those attributes become the new default settings. Objects you subsequently draw adopt those attributes until you change them.

Shortcut: *You can double-click on the drawing tools to change default drawing attributes for the active publication.*

By default, the objects you draw are colored black and knock out underlying objects on color separations. You can prevent an object's stroke, fill, or both from knocking out underlying objects in three ways:

• Define a color as overprinting, and apply the color to the stroke or fill.

• With the object selected, choose Element > Fill and Stroke, and select Overprint for both Fill and Stroke.

• For objects colored black, choose File > Preferences > Trapping, and specify that Fills or Strokes (or both) overprint.

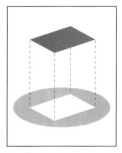 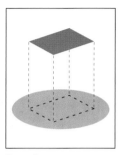

Knockout *Overprint*

For more information about applying and overprinting colors, see "Applying Colors" on page 271, and "Overprinting Colors" on page 277.

To apply or change fill and stroke attributes:

1 Using the pointer tool, select an object.

2 Use one of the following methods:

• To set both the fill pattern and stroke attributes for the selection, choose Element > Fill and Stroke, and select attributes from the Fill and Stroke pop-up menus.

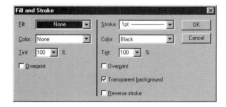

• To change only the fill pattern or stroke attributes, choose Element > Fill or Element > Stroke and select attributes.

If the stroke size you want is not listed on the Stroke menus, choose Element > Stroke > Custom to specify a weight from 0 to 800 points in 0.1 increments.

3 Choose any additional attributes for strokes:

• Click the Transparent Background option if you want objects placed behind a patterned stroke to show through the spaces in the pattern (otherwise, the spaces in the pattern are opaque).

• Click the Reverse Stroke option to draw a paper-colored stroke or outline of a shape on a contrasting black, shaded, or colored background.

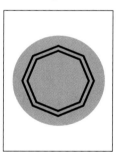 

Transparent option   *Reverse option*

Changing the shape of rectangles and polygons

After you create a rectangle, you can change the shape of its corners. After you create a polygon, you can add, move, or delete its vertices and line segments. For regular polygons only (created by dragging the polygon tool), you can also use the Element > Polygon Settings command to change the number of sides it has, and its inset value (the angle at which the sides point toward the center of the shape).

Note: If you save your publication as a PageMaker 6.0 publication, any irregular polygon you create with the polygon tool is retained in the 6.0 publication, but you cannot edit its shape (other than to resize it).

To round rectangle corners:

1 Select a rectangle you want to change or, to set the default, double-click the rectangle tool.

2 Choose Element > Rounded Corners.

3 Select the corner style you want, and click OK.

To reshape a polygon:

1 Double-click the polygon you want to reshape.

PageMaker displays the vertices.

Polygon in layout mode   *Polygon in edit mode*

2 Do any of the following:

• Add a new vertex by clicking on the line where you want the vertex to appear.

• Reshape the polygon by dragging a vertex.

• Delete a vertex by clicking it.

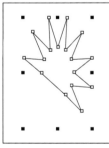

After deleting vertices   *After dragging vertex*

To set the number of sides or inset value for a shape created by dragging the polygon tool:

1 Select a polygon you want to change or, to set the default, double-click the polygon tool.

2 Choose Element > Polygon Settings.

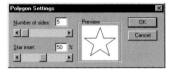

3 Specify the number of sides you want, from 3 to 100.

4 To create a star, enter a value for Star Inset.

A value of 0% represents no star and a value of 100% represents a star whose vertices occupy the same point in the middle of the polygon.

5 Click OK.

Note: *If you reshape a regular polygon by modifying vertices, the Polygon Settings command is no longer available for that object.*

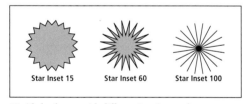

20-sided polygons with different Star Inset values

USING FRAMES

PageMaker 6.5 includes a special kind of object called a *frame*. While a frame behaves in many ways like any other PageMaker graphic object (for example, a frame can have stroke and fill attributes), a frame differs in two important ways:

• A frame can hold content—either text or graphics —or serve as a placeholder for content.

• One text frame can be threaded to other text frames so that a single story can flow through multiple frames.

In general, you'll want to use frames as placeholders for content in structured documents such as newspapers or newsletters.

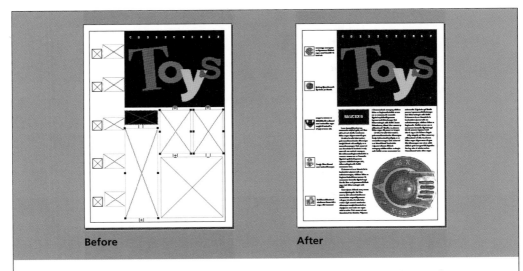

Before　　　　**After**

Taking advantage of frames • By drawing empty frames as placeholders and threading text frames together, you create a template in which the layout and structure of the publication is set and content is easily poured into assigned spaces.

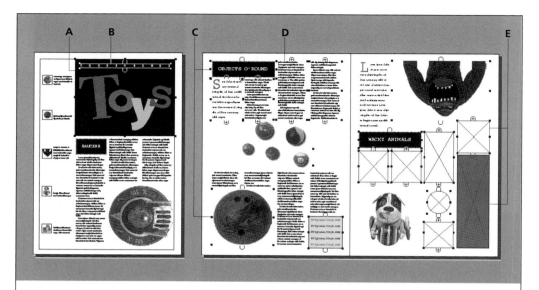

Comparing frames, text blocks, and drawn objects • Frames, text blocks, and drawn objects are alike in that you can select them with the pointer tool and make modifications—move, resize, duplicate, rotate, and more—using the exact same features or techniques. However, each type of object has unique capabilities and purposes.

A PageMaker-drawn elements can have a fill and stroke, have eight selection handles, and cannot contain content other than fill colors or patterns.

B Text blocks have no fill or stroke attributes, must be rectangular, and have four selection handles. A story can flow to the previous or next text block.

C Frames—like any PageMaker-drawn element—can be any shape, can have fill and stroke attributes,

and have eight selection handles. Unlike PageMaker-drawn elements, however, frames can contain content—either text or graphics.

D A story can flow to the previous or next frame.

E Frames act as placeholders for content and are marked with a non-printing "X" if empty.

An empty frame displays with a non-printing "X" but otherwise behaves and prints like any other PageMaker-drawn shape.

Creating a frame

To create a frame you use the frame tools in the toolbox. See "Drawing and Editing Lines and Shapes" on page 179 for more information. You can also turn any object you've created with the PageMaker drawing tools (with the exception of straight lines) into a frame.

If you add a frame to a master page, its border and content appears on each publication page to which the master is applied: you cannot, from a publication page, add content to a frame placed on a master page.

To turn a basic shape into a frame:

1 Create or select a PageMaker-drawn shape.

2 Choose Element > Change to Frame.

The shape preserves its fill, line weight, and other object attributes.

Note: If you don't want the frame border to appear, select the frame and choose Element > Stroke > None. A non-printing light-gray border appears around the frame. If you want to hide the non-printing border, choose View > Hide Guides.

Adding content to a frame

You can fill frames with text or imported images already added to the publication, or with text and graphic files that have not yet been placed. You can also type directly into a frame to start a new story or to edit an existing one.

A frame becomes a text frame or a graphics frame depending on the content you add. Remember that once you add a graphic to a new frame, that graphic frame cannot include text (unless you first delete or detach the graphic from the frame). The only way that a frame can include both text and graphics is if you've filled a frame with text (making it a text frame) and the story includes an inline graphic that flows with the text. For more information on inline graphics, see "Attaching a Graphic to Text" on page 211.

To attach existing text or graphics to a frame:

1 Use the pointer tool to select the frame.

2 Press Shift and select the text block or imported graphic you want to add to the frame.

3 Choose Element > Frame > Attach Content.

To import text or graphics into a frame:

1 Select the frame.

2 Choose File > Place.

3 Select the file you want to place, select the Place Within Frame option along with other place options, and then click OK.

Note: If you choose the Place command without having selected a frame, or if you do not select the Place Within Frame option, you can still add the imported file to a frame after you click OK in the Place dialog box: simply click the loaded text or graphic cursor on the frame you want the imported content to occupy.

To type into a frame:

1 Click the text tool.

2 Click in an empty frame or in a frame containing text and start typing.

To detach content from a frame:

1 Select a graphic frame or an unthreaded text frame.

2 Choose Element > Frame > Separate Content.

The frame becomes empty, and an independent graphic or text block is added to the page. (The command is unavailable for threaded text frames. For more information on threading and unthreading text, see "Understanding Text Objects and Stories" on page 109.)

To delete content from a frame:

1 Select a frame.

2 Choose Element > Frame > Delete Content.

The frame becomes empty. If the selected frame contained text, the entire story is deleted, even if the text was threaded into other frames.

For more information on threading and unthreading text, see "Understanding Text Objects and Stories" on page 109.

Selecting frames and their content

Once a frame contains content, you cannot rotate, skew, or flip the content independently of the frame it is in; text and graphics added to a frame take on the same transformation applied to the frame. You can, however, modify an image within a frame with commands such as Image Control, or Photoshop Effects. To select an image in a graphics frame (so you can modify it, or get link information on it, for example), press Command (Macintosh) or Ctrl (Windows) and click within the frame.

To resize a graphic within a frame, you must first select the frame and then choose Element > Frame > Separate Content. Next, resize the graphic, and then choose Element > Frame > Attach Content with both the graphic and the frame selected.

To select text for editing in a text frame, use the text tool to select the text. To select an inline graphic within a text frame, select the pointer tool, and click the inline graphic.

Positioning content within a frame

You have a variety of options for specifying how the content of a frame is positioned within a frame:

• For graphics larger or smaller than the frames that contain them, you can specify that graphics are clipped to fit within the existing frame borders (applies only to graphics larger than the frame), or scaled to fit the existing frame borders. Alternatively, you can specify that the frame resizes to fit the size of the graphic.

• You can specify an inset value between text and the frame border. You can set a separate inset value for each side of a rectangular text frame, or set a single inset value for oval or polygonal text frames.

• You can change how the content aligns vertically and horizontally within the frame. For example, you might want some graphics to be positioned in the center of a frame; in other frames you might want the graphics to align along the top and left borders of the available space. (For text frames, changes are limited to vertical alignment of rectangular frames.)

To control how content is positioned within frames:

1 Do one of the following:

• Use the pointer tool to select one or more frames to change.

• Deselect all frames to change the default for all new frames in the active publication.

• Close all open publications to change the default for all new publications.

2 Choose Element > Frame > Frame Options. Alternatively, to change the default, double-click a frame tool.

3 Select one of the options for the Content Position area of the dialog box. If you want the graphic to be scaled to the frame, you can select Maintain Aspect Ratio so the scaling is proportional. Otherwise, graphics are scaled only in the direction necessary.

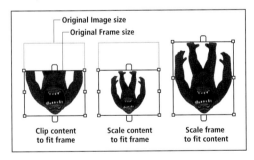

Original Image size
Original Frame size

Clip content to fit frame   Scale content to fit frame   Scale frame to fit content

4 Choose a vertical and a horizontal alignment from the two Alignment pop-up menus.

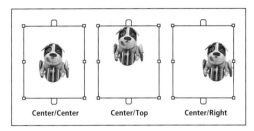

Center/Center   Center/Top   Center/Right

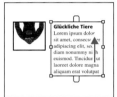

When you apply bottom alignment to a text frame…   *text moves up as new text is added.*

5 In the Frame Inset section of the dialog box, type values to specify the inset on four sides of rectangular frames, or a single value for an inset within oval or polygonal frames.

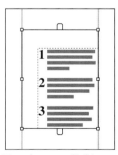

Indented text in frame before inset is applied.   *Text after top and left inset is applied.*

6 Click OK.

To move an image within the borders of a frame:

 1 Select the cropping tool from the toolbox.

2 Click in the frame you want to modify, and drag the image to a new position.

Use the cropping tool to move the image within the frame and reveal different parts of the picture.

DUPLICATING AN OBJECT

Duplicate an object within a publication either by copying and pasting it, using drag-and-drop, or by using the more powerful multiple-paste feature.

To copy and paste an object:

1 Select one or more objects.

2 Choose Edit > Copy.

3 Use any of the following techniques:

• To offset the pasted copy, choose Edit > Paste.

• To paste the copy directly over the original object, press Option + Command + V (Macintosh) or Ctrl + Alt + V (Windows).

• To quickly paste copies of an object at a specific offset, press Command + Option + V (Macintosh) or Ctrl + Alt + V (Windows), drag the copy in the direction and to the distance you want subsequent copies to be offset, and repeat this step as needed to create the effect you want.

If the text insertion point is in a text object and a graphic is on the Clipboard, the graphic is pasted as an inline graphic, and it moves with the text. If text is on the Clipboard, the text is pasted into the text object at the insertion point. (If any other tool is selected, the graphic or text is pasted as an independent object.)

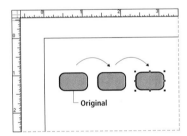

Original

To paste several copies of an object:

1 Select the object you want to duplicate.

2 Choose Edit > Copy.

3 Choose Edit > Paste Multiple.

4 Specify the number of copies to paste and the offset distance between each.

Positive values move the copies to the right and down, respectively. Negative values move copies to the left and up.

Note: Because you cannot use the Undo command to reverse multiple-paste actions, save your work before choosing Paste Multiple. Then, if necessary, you can choose File > Revert to revert to the last-saved version of the publication.

To copy an object from one publication to another:

1 Open both publication windows.

2 Choose Window > Tile to make both windows fully visible.

3 Select the object from one publication window and drag it into position in the second window.

4 Release the mouse button. The object is copied to the second publication, without affecting the contents of the Clipboard.

To copy an object by dragging-and-dropping:

1 With the pointer tool, select the objects you want to copy.

2 Press Control + Option (Macintosh) or Ctrl + Alt (Windows) and drag the selection to the new position.

Note: If you do not press the modifier keys before you begin dragging, PageMaker moves the selection rather than copying it.

3 Release the mouse button to drop a copy of the selection into the new position.

CHANGING THE STACKING ORDER OF OBJECTS

As you draw, type, or import objects, PageMaker assigns each object a position in a stacking order (the order in which objects overlap one another on the same layer within a page). You can change the order at any time. To learn more about creating and working with layers, see "Using Layers" on page 224.

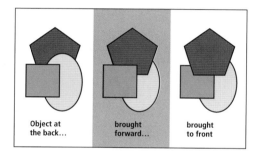

Object at the back...   brought forward...   brought to front

Note: Hold down Command (Macintosh) or Ctrl (Windows) as you click to select an object that is behind another object. Each time you click on overlapping objects, you select the next object down in the stacking order, or through to the topmost object in the next layer in the stack of layers.

To change the stacking order of objects:

1 Select an object.

2 Choose one of the following options:

• To move the object in front of all other objects, choose Element > Arrange > Bring to Front.

• To move the object one position toward the top of the stacking order, choose Element > Arrange > Bring Forward.

• To move the object behind all other objects, choose Element > Arrange > Send to Back.

• To move the object one position toward the bottom of the stacking order, choose Element > Arrange > Send Backward.

DELETING AN OBJECT

When you delete an object, you break all links between your publication and the original object. You can delete inline graphics either in layout view or in story editor.

If you delete a text object that is threaded to other text objects in the same story, the text object that preceded the deleted text object is automatically threaded to the text object that followed the deleted text object. See "Adjusting Text Objects" on page 114 for more information.

To delete an object:

1 Select the object.

2 Choose Edit > Clear, or press Backspace or Delete.

MANIPULATING AN OBJECT USING THE CONTROL PALETTE

The Control palette offers an alternative to manipulating an object manually. Because you can enter exact values, the Control palette lets you work with graphics and text objects precisely, and you can make several changes without switching to the toolbox or choosing commands.

If you prefer to manipulate an object manually, the Control palette can still help you work precisely: when visible, it provides immediate feedback about the object you are modifying, such as the exact position, size, or rotation angle.

Note: Two options, skewing and reflecting, are available only on the Control palette.

Control palette basics

To open or close the Control palette, choose Window > Show Control Palette. The Control palette appears in front of the publication and story windows. You can move it by dragging the bar at the left edge of the palette.

Click an option to activate it. (A selected value or a highlighted bar above or below an option indicates that the option is active.) Alternatively, move from option to option by pressing Tab, or, to return to a previous option, press Shift + Tab.

When you select the text tool, the Control palette displays options for manipulating text within text objects. For more information, see "Using the Control Palette to Format Text" on page 122.

The Apply button changes to indicate the type of object or tool selected. If no objects are selected, the Apply button indicates the tool currently selected in the toolbox. If an object is selected, the Apply button indicates the currently selected object or tool, appears three dimensional, and can be clicked to apply modifications to the object. Alternatively, you can press Return (Macintosh) or Enter (Windows).

Using the reference-point Proxy

Changes you make to objects with the Control palette are affected by the reference point you set. The reference point can be an edge, a corner, or the center of a selected object.

Selected reference point

The Proxy

Control palette with an object selected

A Apply button: Applies changes to objects using numeric values you enter.

B Proxy: Represents the selected object. Click to set a reference point, or the point you are manipulating on the object.

C Position option: Displays the X and Y coordinate values of the reference point or pointer, relative to the current rulers.

D Sizing option: Specifies the width and height of the selected object or cropping rectangle. Nudge amount: 0.01 inches.

E Percent-scaling option: Specifies the percentage changed from the original size. When the reference point on the Proxy is a square, the specified values resize the object from the reference point outward. When the reference point on the Proxy is an arrow, specified values resize the object by repositioning the reference point.

F Scaling option: Click to use scaling to resize an imported graphic.

G Proportional-scaling option: Specifies whether you change an object's height and width independently, or maintain its original proportions.

H Rotating option: Rotates the object around the reference point (if the Proxy shows a square for the reference point) or rotates the reference point by the desired increment (if the Proxy shows an arrow for the reference point). Nudge amount: 0.1 degree.

I Horizontal-reflecting button: Reflects the object vertically, and then rotates the object 180 degrees so it appears reflected horizontally.

J Nudge buttons: Click to move, resize or transform an object incrementally. Press Command (Macintosh) or Ctrl (Windows) while nudging to multiply the nudge increment by ten.

K Cropping option: Click to use the cropping tool to crop an imported graphic (by changing values for X and Y or for H and W).

L Printer-resolution-scaling option: Constrains scaling of imported 1-bit bitmap graphics so that they are compatible with the target printer resolution specified in the Document Setup dialog box.

M Skewing option: Skews objects horizontally -85 to 85 degrees in relation to the selected reference point. Nudge amount: 0.1 degree.

N Vertical-reflecting button: Reflects the object vertically.

The Control palette displays information about an object based on the reference point setting on the Proxy. For example, if the reference point setting for a rectangle is its upper left corner (the default), the X and Y options on the Control palette display the position of the upper left corner of the rectangle relative to the rulers' zero point.

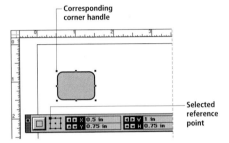

To set the reference point, either select an object and click one of its handles, or click the Proxy itself. Select a corner, a side, the top, the bottom, or the center of the Proxy. That point becomes the reference point for all objects you subsequently select, until you select a new reference point.

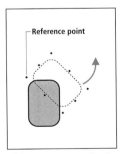

Object rotates around or from the selected reference point

The reference point can work in two ways:

• Click the reference point once, and it displays as a box. The corresponding point on the object remains stationary as you modify the object. (Modifications are measured from the reference point.)

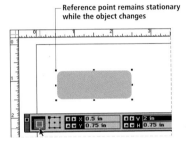

• Double-click the reference point and it becomes a two-way arrow (or a four-way arrow if you click the center point). The corresponding point on the object changes position as you modify the object. (Modifications are applied to the reference point.)

If you select the center point, the reference point works the same way whether it displays as a box or an arrow.

Modifying objects by adjusting values

The values that you can change appear in bold on the palette. The reference point you select determines which values can be changed.

The apply button changes to represent the object or tool selected, or the current task

Pointer tool selected, no objects selected	▸				
A drawing tool selected	╲	├	├	○	⬠
Placing text	🕮				
Placing a graphic	🗅	🖼	🖼	📄	
Graphic selected	🗅	🖼	🖼	📄	
Text object selected	T				
Multiple objects selected	🗇				
Rotating tool selected	↺				
Cropping tool selected	🄰				
Dragging a ruler guide	↔				
Dragging a column guide	↔				
Dragging the rulers' zero point	⬚				
Group selected	▣				

If you make a mistake when changing a value or if the value you enter causes an error message, you can always restore the previous value for that option. Press Esc before tabbing to or clicking another option.

PageMaker is accurate to $\frac{1}{20}$ of a point, or $\frac{1}{1440}$ of an inch (.018mm.) When specifying percentages, PageMaker is accurate to $\frac{1}{10}$ of a percent.

To change values on the Control palette:

1 Select an object.

2 Click or double-click to select the reference point on the Proxy.

3 Adjust values one of the following ways:

• To type a new value, select the value you want to change in the Control palette, and then type the new value.

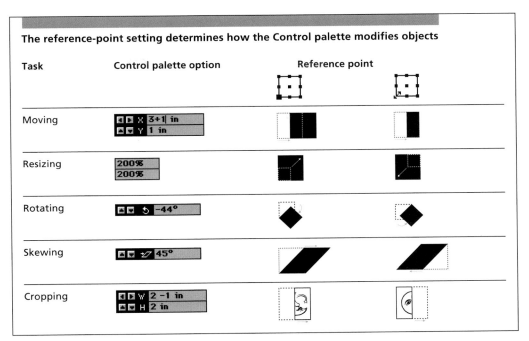

The reference-point setting determines how the Control palette modifies objects

Task	Control palette option	Reference point	
Moving	X 3+1 in / Y 1 in		
Resizing	200% / 200%		
Rotating	-44°		
Skewing	45°		
Cropping	W 2 -1 in / H 2 in		

• To adjust the value using arithmetic, type a + (plus), - (minus), * (times), or / (divided by) sign after the current value and then type a number on the right side of the expression to produce the desired result.

• To adjust the value incrementally, click a nudge button next to the option. The value changes .01 inch (.25mm) (or 0.1 degrees for rotating and skewing). Press Command (Macintosh) or Ctrl (Windows) and click a nudge button to change the value 0.1 inch (2.5mm) (or 1 degree for rotating and skewing).

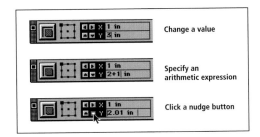

Change a value

Specify an arithmetic expression

Click a nudge button

4 If you typed a new value or used arithmetic, click the apply button or press Return (Macintosh) or Enter (Windows). (Pressing a nudge button applies the changes automatically.)

Setting measurement and nudge preferences

PageMaker lets you specify the measurement system and the distance a selected object moves each time you click a nudge button or move an object using an arrow key on the keyboard. The values on the Control palette appear according to the measurement system selected in the Preferences dialog box. If you specify a different measurement system for the vertical ruler, the vertical values (Y and H) on the Control palette display in the vertical ruler's measurement system.

Note: Nudge preferences do not affect rotating and skewing, for which clicking a nudge button changes the value $^1/_{10}$ of a degree and pressing Command (Macintosh) or Ctrl (Windows) as you click a nudge button changes the value by 1 degree.

To specify unit of measure and nudge distance:

1 Choose File > Preferences > General .

2 Select a measurement system.

3 Enter values and units of measure for both Horizontal Nudge and Vertical Nudge.

4 Click the Use "Snap to" Constraints option if you want nudge movements to snap to guides or rulers.

5 Click OK.

To override the measurement system:

1 Select the X, Y, W, or H option on the Control palette.

2 Press Command + Option + M (Macintosh) or Shift + F12 (Windows) to cycle the units of measure through inches, millimeters, ciceros, and picas. The setting is preserved for that option until you change it again.

MOVING AND RESIZING AN OBJECT

Move and resize any unlocked object either by dragging with the mouse or by using the Control palette. You can also move an object by pressing arrow keys on the keyboard. Although you can move two or more objects simultaneously, you can resize only one object at a time unless you first group the items you want to resize. See "Grouping and Ungrouping Objects" on page 200. For information about resizing text objects, see "Adjusting Text Objects" on page 114.

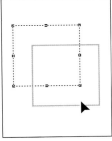 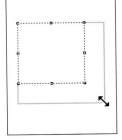

Move an object by dragging it   *Resize an object by dragging a handle*

When you drag to move an object, you have two options:

• If you drag immediately after pressing the mouse button, you see the outline of the graphic or text object in its original position as you drag.

• If you pause after pressing the mouse button, but before dragging, you see the graphic or text object as you drag.

Note: Resize 1-bit bitmap images to match the resolution of your target printer. See "Resizing 1-Bit Bitmap Images" on page 199.

To move or resize an object by dragging:

1 Select the object.

2 Press Shift if you want to constrain movement to vertical or horizontal, to constrain the shape of an object as you resize it, or to resize an imported graphic proportionally.

3 Drag the object to move it or drag a handle to resize it. The pointer changes to an arrowhead (for moving), a two-way arrow (for resizing most objects), or a crossbar (for resizing lines).

Dragging a side handle changes the width or height only; dragging a corner handle changes the width and height simultaneously.

Note: To move an unfilled shape, position the pointer on its outline (but not on a handle).

Constraining the shape of an object

Object	Resized with Shift key
Line	Line angled at 45-degree increments
Ellipse	Circle
Rectangle	Square
Regular polygon	Even-sided shape
Imported	Aspect ratio preserved
Group	Aspect ratio of the group is preserved

To move an object using the Control palette:

1 Select the object.

2 Choose Window > Show Control Palette.

3 Select a reference point in the Proxy to specify the part of a selected graphic that moves.

If the reference point is a box, the object will move; if it is an arrow, the object will change size. Click the reference point to toggle from one mode to the other.

4 To move the object, adjust values for X and Y.

To move an object using the arrow keys:

1 Select the object.

2 Use either of the following methods:

• To move the object incrementally by .01 inch (.25mm), press an arrow key.

• To move the object incrementally by 0.1 inch (2.5mm), hold down Shift as you press an arrow key.

You can change the default nudge distance and measurement system; see "Setting Measurement and Nudge Preferences" on page 196.

To resize an object using the Control palette:

1 Select the object.

2 Choose Window > Show Control Palette.

3 Click or double-click to select the reference point on the Proxy.

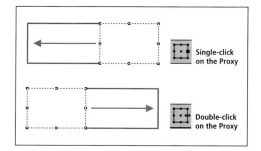

• If you click to select a reference point, it appears as a small rectangle on the Proxy, and the equivalent location on the selected object remains stationary as you resize the object.

• If you double-click to select a reference point, it appears as a two- or four-way arrow, and the equivalent location on the selected object moves as you resize the object.

4 Optionally, turn on the following settings to constrain the resizing:

• Click the Proportional-scaling option on the Control palette to maintain the original aspect ratio of the object. You can then change either the X and W values or the Y and H values, depending on the selected reference point. The related value changes proportionally.

• Click the Printer-resolution-scaling option to resize 1-bit bitmap images based on the resolution of your printer. This option has the same effect as magic stretch. See the following topic, "Resizing 1-bit Bitmap Images."

5 Specify a size in one of the following ways:

• If the reference point is a box or a four-way arrow, resize the object from the reference point outward by adjusting W and H or L options. (L appears only if a line is selected.)

• If the reference point is a two-way arrow, move the reference point to stretch or shrink the object by adjusting values for W, H, and L, or for X and Y. (L appears only if a line is selected.)

• If you want to resize an object to a percentage of its original size, change the percentage values next to W and H.

6 Click the Apply button.

Resizing 1-bit bitmap images

Because the resolution of your printer is different from the resolution of your screen, a resized, 1-bit bitmap image that looks fine on your screen may look mottled when it is printed. PageMaker provides reduction and enlargement sizes for 1-bit bitmap images to ensure that the images print at optimum resolution. Sizes are based on the printer resolution you specify in the Document Setup dialog box and on the resolution of the bitmap.

To resize a 1-bit bitmap image:

1 Choose File > Document Setup.

2 In the Target Printer Resolution text box, specify the printer resolution at which you'll print the final copy of your publication. (In Windows, you must first select a target printer for Compose to Printer.)

3 Select the 1-bit bitmap image and press Command (Macintosh) or Ctrl (Windows) as you resize the object. To preserve the original proportions of the image, press Command + Shift (Macintosh) or Ctrl + Shift (Windows) as you resize it.

Object resized with magic stretch *Object resized without magic stretch*

This technique, called magic stretch, causes the image to snap to sizes that are exact multiples of the resolution of your target printer. After resizing using magic stretch, the image may appear distorted on the screen or when printed at a different resolution than your target printer resolution (for proofing the publication, for example), but your final artwork will print clearly.

Magic stretch neither improves nor harms color or grayscale TIFF, EPS (encapsulated PostScript), or draw-type graphics, and it does not benefit 1-bit bitmap images contained in EPS or draw-type graphics.

You can also use nudge buttons in the Control palette to apply magic stretch: just turn on the Printer-resolution-scaling option before resizing the image. (When the option is off, it appears as a printer with an "X" on it.)

Note: *If you change the target printer resolution after resizing 1-bit bitmap images, use the magic-stretch technique to resize them for the new printer resolution before you print.*

GROUPING AND UNGROUPING OBJECTS

You can combine several objects into a group so that the objects are treated as a unit. This allows you to move or transform a number of objects together. For example, you might group the objects in a logo design so that you can move and resize the logo as one unit.

Note: *When you mask selected objects, PageMaker can automatically group them. For more information, see "Masking Objects" on page 202.*

A group, when selected, appears with four handles at the corners that define the bounding box of all objects in the group. Individual objects

within a group can be selected and modified. For example, you can reformat text within a text object that is grouped with an image.

Before grouping   After grouping

To group objects:

1 Using the pointer tool, press Shift and select the objects to be grouped.

One or more of the objects you select can be a group, but if you select two or more groups note that all selected objects (including those within groups) form a single, unnested group.

2 Choose Element > Group.

To select text or an individual object within a group:

1 Select the pointer tool (to select graphics or text objects), or the text tool (to edit text).

2 If selecting an object within the group, press Command (Macintosh) or Ctrl (Windows) and select the object. To select text, click an insertion point in the text.

To ungroup objects:

1 Select the group.

2 Choose Element > Ungroup.

The objects retain the changes you made while the objects were grouped.

Guidelines for grouping objects

The following rules apply to groups:

• A frame can be grouped with other objects, but you cannot attach a group to a frame.

• Text objects can be resized as part of a group, but text maintains its type and paragraph specifications. For example, type size does not change when the text block is resized.

• Groups cannot be nested—that is, a group can be grouped with other objects (including another group) but if you ungroup, the original group is also ungrouped.

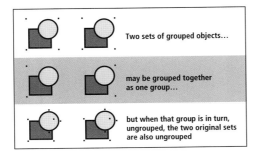

Two sets of grouped objects...

may be grouped together as one group...

but when that group is in turn, ungrouped, the two original sets are also ungrouped

• Groups cannot be pasted as inline graphics. You can group a text object that contains inline graphics, but you cannot group an inline graphic with another object.

• The aspect ratio of all objects in the group is retained if you press Shift while resizing a group (or if you use the proportional resizing option in the Control palette).

• A newly-created group moves to the front of the stacking order. Objects in a group retain their stacking order in relation to each other until you change their stacking order with commands from the Arrange menu. If the objects were grouped from different layers, the group is assigned to the layer of the topmost object in the selection.

• If you created groups in a PageMaker 5.0 publication (using the PS Group It addition), we suggest you ungroup them before converting the publication (using PS Ungroup It). You can then recreate the group in PageMaker 6.5.

LOCKING OBJECTS

You can lock individual objects in place in order to help preserve the design of your pages through all stages of production. You can change the attributes of a locked object, provided the change does not affect the object's size or position. For example, you can change a color or fill applied to a locked object, but not its degree of rotation or its skewing angle. You cannot cut or delete a locked object without unlocking it first, but you can copy a locked object; it will be pasted as an unlocked object.

Although the position of a locked text block is fixed, the bottom windowshade handle expands downward or retracts upward if text is added, deleted, or resized. Text continues to flow through locked text objects, moving inline graphics that are in that text object: only the size and baseline shift of an inline graphic is locked.

The Apply button in the Control Palette appears gray when the selected object is locked. The cursor changes to a lock icon when you try to move a locked item.

Locked   *Unlocked*

To lock or unlock an object:

1 Select the object.

2 Choose Element > Lock Position or Unlock.

MASKING OBJECTS

Masking is a way of covering part of an object so that only a portion of it appears through a shape drawn with the rectangle, ellipse, or polygon tool. In PageMaker, you mask objects by positioning the mask, or masking object, on the objects you want to mask, selecting both objects, and choosing the Element > Mask command. PageMaker simultaneously groups the selected objects if you press Option (Macintosh) or Shift (Windows) and then choose Element > Mask and Group.

The masking object can be behind the object being masked. In that case, if the masking object has a fill, the fill will show through the transparent areas of the object being masked.

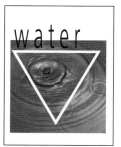 

Masking: masking object placed on top of image   *Result: image appears only through mask*

To mask objects:

1 Draw or select the object you want to use as a masking object.

2 Position the masking object you drew in Step 1 over the objects you want to mask.

Note: *you cannot mask a frame, nor use a frame as a masking object.*

3 Select the mask and the objects you want to be masked.

4 Choose Element > Mask. Alternatively, press Option (Macintosh) or Shift (Windows) and then choose Element > Mask and Group, so that the objects involved in the mask can be treated as a single unit.

You must click within the masking object to select a masked object. To select the masking or the masked object once the objects are grouped, press Command (Macintosh) or Ctrl (Windows) and click the object you want to select. If the masked object is text, you can simply click the text tool in the visible area of the masked text object.

To undo the effects of a mask:

1 Select the masking object or the masked object.

2 Choose Element > Unmask.

Alternatively, press Option (Macintosh) or Shift (Windows) and then choose Element > Unmask and Ungroup.

ALIGNING AND DISTRIBUTING OBJECTS

You can align objects in relation to one another, and then evenly distribute the spaces between the objects. Align or distribute objects based on a common edge or based on the centers of objects. For example, select the align-right icon to move objects horizontally so that their right edges line up with the right edge of the rightmost object. (To align objects to a grid, use rulers and guides.)

When you distribute objects, you can add an even amount of space between their facing edges.

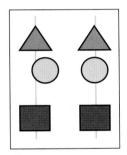 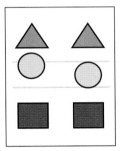

Align *Distribute*

To align and distribute objects:

1 Select the objects you want to align and distribute.

2 Choose Element > Align.

3 Select one icon for each direction (horizontal or vertical) in which you want to align or distribute objects. Select the icon for no alignment if you don't want to align the objects along one of the axes.

4 If you are distributing objects, select one of the following methods for each direction (vertical and horizontal):

• Select Distribute Within Bounds to distribute objects within the bounds of the current selection. In horizontal distribution, for example, objects are evenly spaced between the leftmost and rightmost selected objects, which remain stationary.

• Select Distribute Fixed Amount to insert a specified amount of space between the objects (or between the specified edge), and then type the increment in the Space text box. (Type a negative value to make the objects overlap.) For example, in horizontal distribution, all objects are evenly spaced by the specified amount, and the leftmost and rightmost objects are repositioned accordingly.

5 Click the Do Mini-Save option if you want the option of undoing the changes you are about to make with this command. (That way, you can press Shift and choose File > Revert to restore the publication if the changes are undesirable.)

6 Click OK.

ROTATING, SKEWING, AND REFLECTING AN OBJECT

In PageMaker, rotating, reflecting, and skewing are referred to collectively as transformations. You can transform any unlocked object on the page or pasteboard, including an inline graphic (which you can transform independently of the text object it is in, or with the text object) and an item selected within a group (which you can transform independently of the group it is in, or with the group). Fill patterns and PostScript screen angles are not transformed.

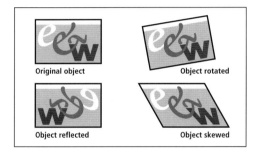

All PostScript and some non-PostScript printers support transformed text. If you have a non-PostScript printer that does not support transformed text, PageMaker uses a low-resolution screen font to simulate the text. You can prevent this problem by using a type-management utility, such as Adobe Type Manager.

Rotating an object

You can rotate any unlocked object ±360 degrees at .01-degree increments. Use the rotating tool in the toolbox to rotate an object manually around any fixed point, or use the Rotating option on the Control palette to rotate relative to the reference point selected on the Proxy.

Whether or not you use the Control palette's Rotate option, the Control palette displays the total degrees of rotation (even if you rotate the object more than once). Rotating an object counter-clockwise increases the angle, and rotating it clockwise decreases the angle. (Zero degrees is at the three o'clock position when using the rotating tool.)

As you rotate a single object, the Proxy on the Control palette also rotates (in 45-degree increments) to approximate the new position of the reference point.

If you select multiple objects before rotating, the Control palette displays the degrees of rotation for the group of selected objects, which is always 0 degrees. PageMaker rotates all selected objects by the same incremental amount, even if some objects are already rotated. For example, if you rotate two objects by 30 degrees, and one has already been rotated, PageMaker rotates both objects an additional 30 degrees. See "Using the Reference-Point Proxy" on page 191 for more information on using the Control palette Proxy.

Note: A metafile or PICT file may appear transparent on the screen when rotated, even if it is opaque when unrotated. When you print to a PostScript printer, the metafile or PICT file will print opaque. When you print to a non-PostScript printer, the metafile or PICT file will print as it appears on the screen.

To rotate an object with the rotating tool:

1 Select the object.

2 Select the rotating tool from the toolbox.

3 Position the starburst at a fixed point—the location around which you want to rotate the selected object. If you are rotating around the center point, press Command (Macintosh) or Ctrl (Windows).

If two or more objects are selected, the center point is based on the bounding box of the entire selection.

4 Drag the starburst away from the fixed point, in the direction you want to rotate the object. To constrain rotation to 45-degree increments from the starting position, press Shift as you drag.

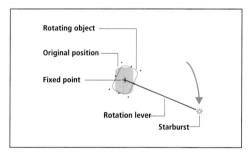

Rotating object
Original position
Fixed point
Rotation lever
Starburst

The rotation lever helps you control the amount of rotation. The farther you drag the starburst away from the fixed point, the more control you'll have when you rotate the object.

5 When the object is in position, release the mouse button.

To rotate an object with the Control palette:

1 Select the object.

2 Choose Window > Show Control Palette.

3 Click or double-click to select a reference point on the Proxy:

• If you click to select a reference point, it appears as a small rectangle on the Proxy, and the equivalent location on the selected object remains stationary as you rotate the object.

• If you double-click to select a reference point, it appears as a two- or four-way arrow, and the equivalent location on the selected object moves as you rotate the object.

4 Adjust values in the Rotating option, and click the Apply button.

Reflecting an object

Use the Control palette to horizontally or vertically reflect any unlocked object, including a text object or a bitmap image.

When you reflect an object horizontally, it is equivalent to reflecting it vertically and then rotating it 180 degrees. Because of this, PageMaker adds 180 degrees to the existing rotation value on the Control palette.

To reflect an object:

1 Select the object.

2 Choose Window > Show Control Palette.

3 Click or double-click to select a reference point on the Proxy:

• If you click to select a reference point, it appears as a small rectangle on the Proxy, and the equivalent location on the selected object remains stationary as you reflect the object.

• If you double-click to select a reference point, it appears as a two- or four-way arrow, and the equivalent location on the selected object moves as you reflect the object.

4 Click the Horizontal-reflecting button or the Vertical-reflecting button on the Control palette.

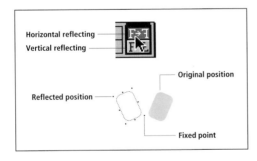

Horizontal reflecting
Vertical reflecting
Original position
Reflected position
Fixed point

Skewing an object

Use the Control palette to skew an object horizontally by ±85 degrees at .01-degree increments. You can skew any unlocked object, including a text block or a grouped item.

To skew an object:

1 Select the object.

2 Choose Window > Show Control Palette.

3 Click or double-click to select a reference point on the Proxy:

• If you click to select a reference point, it appears as a small rectangle on the Proxy, and the equivalent location on the selected object remains stationary as you skew the object.

• If you double-click to select a reference point, it appears as a two- or four-way arrow, and the equivalent location on the selected object moves as you skew the object.

4 Specify a skew angle for the Skewing option on the Control palette.

Positive angles move the top edge of the object to the right, and negative values move the top edge to the left, regardless of the selected reference point.

5 Click the Apply button or press Return (Macintosh) or Enter (Windows).

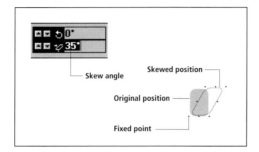

Removing transformations

To immediately restore any single transformation, choose Edit > Undo.

To restore a transformed object (except a PageMaker line) to its original, untransformed state at any time after transformation, choose Element > Remove Transformation.

CROPPING A GRAPHIC

When you import a graphic from another program or publication, you can crop parts of the graphic that you do not want to print by adjusting the size of its surrounding bounding box.

After you crop a graphic, you can control which portions of it appear in your publication by moving the graphic within the visible area. You cannot crop to resize the visible area of locked objects, but you can change what portion of the image shows within the cropped area.

To save printing time, crop graphics before you import them into PageMaker.

If you crop an imported graphic and later relink to a different graphic, select the Retain Cropping Data option in the Place Document or Link Info dialog box (depending on whether you are replacing or relinking the graphic). Otherwise, PageMaker imports the entire graphic to fit within the cropped area, which can distort the graphic.

The Retain Cropping Data option applies only to objects you replace or relink using linking options in PageMaker. PageMaker automatically retains cropping information for OLE-linked or OLE-embedded graphics, Macintosh edition files, and also when you relink to a file that PageMaker could not find while opening or printing your publication. See "Managing Linked Text and Graphics" on page 369 for more information.

Note: If you crop an inline graphic with the Control palette, you can only crop from the center. To crop from any other point, use the cropping tool in the toolbox.

TIP: IF YOU ARE PRINTING TO A POSTSCRIPT PRINTER, CROPPED DRAW-TYPE PICT FILES MAY NOT PRODUCE THE DESIRED RESULTS. WHEN SAVING DRAW-TYPE GRAPHICS ON THE MACINTOSH, SELECT THE EPS OPTION WHENEVER POSSIBLE.

To crop a graphic using the cropping tool:

1 Select the cropping tool, and select the graphic that you want to crop.

2 Position the cropping tool so that a handle shows through the center of the tool.

3 Hold down the mouse button to turn the cropping tool into a two-way arrow, and drag until only the part of the graphic you want in your publication remains. To show more of the graphic, drag away from the center of the graphic.

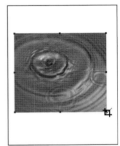
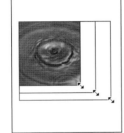

4 To move the graphic within the frame, position the cropping tool at the center of the graphic and hold down the mouse button. (In Windows, hold down the left mouse button.)

5 When the hand appears, drag until you see the part you want to appear in your publication. Then release the mouse button.

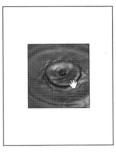

To crop a graphic using the Control palette:

1 Select the graphic.

2 Click the Cropping option on the Control palette.

3 Click or double-click to select a reference point on the Proxy:

• If you click to select a reference point, it appears as a small rectangle on the Proxy, and the equivalent location on the selected object remains stationary as you crop the object. To crop the right side of a graphic, for example, select a reference point on the left side of the Proxy.

• If you double-click to select a reference point, it appears as a two-way arrow, and the equivalent location on the selected object moves as you crop the object.

• To crop evenly from all sides, select the center reference point.

4 Change the values for X and Y or for H and W.

The X and Y options will crop the graphic only if the reference point is a two-way arrow.

WRAPPING TEXT AROUND GRAPHICS

One of the best ways to create visual impact in a publication is to wrap text around graphics.

To wrap text around a graphic:

1 Select a graphic or image.

2 Choose Element > Text Wrap.

3 Click the middle Wrap Option. (The rightmost icon is not available unless you have customized the text wrap, as described later.)

4 Specify a Text Flow option.

The leftmost Text Flow icon jumps text over a graphic and continues the text on the next page or column. The middle icon allows text to jump over a graphic and continue on the same page. The rightmost icon creates a rectangular text wrap around all sides of a graphic.

5 Enter standoff values for the boundary. The standoff values determine the distance of the text from each side of the graphic.

6 Select Wrap Text on Same Layer Only if you want text on other layers to ignore the text wrap boundary.

7 Click OK.

To customize text wrap around a graphic:

1 Apply text wrap as described above.

2 With the object selected, do any of the following:

• Add a new handle by clicking on the graphics boundary where you want the handle to appear.

• Reshape the boundary by dragging handles or line segments. (You can hold down Shift as you drag handles or segments to constrain movement to vertical or horizontal.)

TIP: YOU CAN SPACE MULTIPLE INLINE GRAPHICS EVENLY BETWEEN THE LEFT AND RIGHT EDGES OF A TEXT OBJECT: CREATE THE GRAPHICS IN A ONE-LINE PARAGRAPH CONTAINING NO TEXT, INSERT A SPACE BETWEEN EACH PAIR OF GRAPHICS, AND SELECT TYPE > ALIGNMENT > FORCE JUSTIFY.

• Delete a handle by dragging it onto an adjacent handle.

Note: *As you modify the graphic's boundary, you can hold down the spacebar to temporarily prevent text from rewrapping. When you release the spacebar, the text rewraps.*

A

B

C

A The default shape of a text wrap boundary is a rectangle

B Drag handles and boundary lines to shape the text boundary

C Click boundary lines to create additional handles

To restore a custom boundary back to a rectangular boundary:

1 Select the graphic.

2 Choose Element > Text Wrap.

3 Click the middle Wrap Option icon.

Tips for wrapping text

To wrap text around another text block, select the text block around which you want text to wrap, and then choose Element > Group. PageMaker now treats the text block like a graphic. With the grouped text block selected, apply a text-wrap option.

To wrap text around only three sides of a graphic, position either the left or right edge of the graphic against a column guide. Alternatively, you can increase the standoff values enough to put the graphics boundary next to the column guide.

ATTACHING A GRAPHIC TO TEXT

When you want a graphic to remain with specific text, place the graphic as an inline graphic.

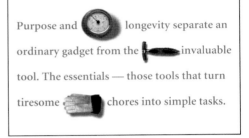

Purpose and longevity separate an ordinary gadget from the invaluable tool. The essentials — those tools that turn tiresome chores into simple tasks.

Any graphic that you can use as an independent graphic, you can also use as an inline graphic, with the exception of a grouped object. You can:

• Import a graphic directly into a text object or quickly change an existing graphic in your publication into an inline graphic.

• Insert a graphic anywhere in a paragraph containing text or create a paragraph containing only art.

• Transform an inline graphic when you transform the text object containing it or transform the graphic independently of the text object.

• Maintain linking information for an inline graphic exactly as you do for an independent graphic.

You can import an inline graphic when you are working in layout view or in story editor by placing it, linking it, embedding it, or (Macintosh only) subscribing to it. Because you can view only text in story editor, you'll see an icon (▧) representing each inline graphic. See Chapter 11, "Importing, Linking, and Exporting," for more information about importing graphics.

To change an independent graphic to an inline graphic:

1 Select the frame or graphic.

2 Choose Edit > Cut or Edit > Copy to store it on the Clipboard.

3 Select the text tool.

4 Click an insertion point in the text where you want the frame or graphic to appear.

5 Choose Edit > Paste.

To make an inline graphic an independent graphic, simply reverse the procedure: cut the graphic from the story and, with the pointer tool selected, paste it into layout view.

Note: Because inline graphics are part of a story, any inline graphics you have added in PageMaker will be lost if you: select the story, choose File> Place, and then select Replacing Entire Story, or if you update a link to the story (including links to OLE-linked or OLE-embedded files and Macintosh edition files).

Modifying inline graphics

In many ways, you can treat inline graphics as you would independent graphics—you can resize, transform, and crop them. You can align an inline graphic so it is flush left, flush right, or centered, but you cannot apply other character attributes, such as font, type style, width, and size, to an inline graphic. This section describes techniques that apply specifically to inline graphics.

Because an inline graphic is in a text object, you can rotate, reflect, or skew the graphic with the text object. If the inline graphic is already rotated, reflected, or skewed when you transform the text object, the effect is cumulative. For example, if you rotate an inline graphic 20 degrees, and then rotate the text object 35 degrees, the graphic is rotated a total of 55 degrees.

Inline graphic rotated 20 degrees independent of text object

Text object, including inline graphic rotated 35 degrees

To move or transform an inline graphic with the text object, select the text object using the pointer tool, and then alter it as you would normally. To transform an inline graphic independently, select the graphic (not the text object) using the pointer tool, and then transform it as you would normally.

For more information about transforming, see "Rotating, Skewing, and Reflecting an Object" on page 204.

Adjusting the leading and tracking for an inline graphic

Spacing around an inline graphic is determined by the leading and tracking of the text with which it is associated. By default, PageMaker assigns Auto leading (vertical spacing based on the size of the graphic) to an inline graphic, even if the leading of surrounding text is different. (A line always adopts the highest leading value in the line: a large graphic, for example, will increase the leading of the line.)

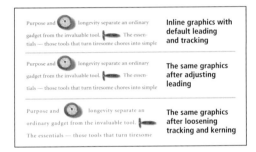

To adjust the leading and tracking of an inline graphic:

1 Using the text tool, select the graphic.

2 Do one of the following:

• Specify leading and tracking using Type menu commands or using the Control palette.

• Choose Type > Character to open the Inline Specifications dialog box, and then set leading and tracking values.

Note: Low leading values can cause a graphic to spill onto the line above or below. If you encounter this problem, reduce the size of the graphic, move it up or down to offset its baseline, or change the leading.

Adjusting the baseline of an inline graphic

PageMaker aligns the baseline of an inline graphic with the baseline of the text around it. The default position of an inline graphic's baseline is two-thirds of the distance from the top of the bounding box to the bottom, regardless of the leading method specified for the paragraph.

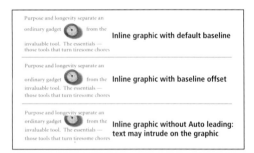

To adjust the baseline of an inline graphic:

1 Go to layout view.

2 Select the pointer tool, and use either of these methods:

• Drag the graphic up or down (relative to the sides of the text object).

• Choose Window > Show Control Palette, and adjust the Baseline-Offset option on the Control palette by nudging or by typing a positive or negative value. A value of 0 aligns the base of the graphic with the baseline of the text in which the graphic is placed.

There is a difference between the baseline shift attribute (which applies to both inline graphics and text characters) and the baseline-offset attribute (which applies only to inline graphics). The baseline offset is relative to the baseline shift setting for an inline graphic. To move an inline graphic outside the range of allowable values for Baseline-Offset (the range is from 0 to the height of the graphic), use the Baseline-Shift option in character view on the Control palette. For more information on baseline shift, see "Shifting Baselines" on page 171.

USING IMAGE CONTROL ON A BITMAP

PageMaker lets you modify 1-bit and grayscale (but not color) bitmap images by increasing or decreasing the lightness or contrast of an image, and by applying a line or dot halftone screen and a halftone screen ruling value for an image. (PageMaker prints gray areas of images with a round halftone dot.)

You can control the following factors:

• Contrast: Adjust the look of different objects inside the image by making them lighter or darker in relation to their background. (On the Macintosh, you can also vary the contrast for one or more levels of gray.)

• Brightness: Adjust the overall percentage of lightness. (On the Macintosh, you can also vary the lightness for one or more levels of gray.)

• The screen pattern: Specify a line screen for special effects, otherwise PageMaker automatically prints a dot screen.

If you are printing to a PostScript printer, you can customize the following items:

• Screen angle: Enter a different screen angle in the Image Control dialog box to override the printer default, which is typically 45 degrees.

Contrast *Lightness* *Screen pattern* *Screen angle*

• Number of lines per inch (Lines/In): Enter a screen-ruling value to override the printer default, which is typically 53 lines per inch (lpi) for 300-dpi LaserWriters and either 90 or 150 lpi for imagesetters (the default for an imagesetter depends on the version of PostScript installed).

If you are using a Macintosh, you also have the following options:

• Black and White: If the selected graphic is a 1-bit, paint-type image, this option is selected automatically.

• Screened: Select this option when you have selected a black-and-white image and want to change the screen that will be applied to the image when it is printed.

• Gray: If Gray is selected when you display a gray-scale TIFF image, the screen ruling selected in the Color printing dialog box is used when printing the image. To specify a different screen ruling, select Screened and enter a value in the Lines/In text box.

• Gray-level patterns: Click an icon to change the pattern.

Default gray pattern *Reverse gray levels* *Posterize effect* *Solarize effect*

To modify lightness, contrast, and halftone screen settings:

1 Select the image.

2 Choose Element > Image > Image Control.

3 Adjust the lightness and contrast as follows:

• On the Macintosh, use the up or down arrows to adjust the overall image, or drag individual slider bars to create custom effects. Alternatively, click one of the four standard effects. Click Apply to preview the modified image.

- In Windows, adjust the values in the Lightness and Contrast text boxes from -100 to +100 %. The greater the percentage, the greater the lightness or contrast. To reverse an image, type **-50%** for Contrast. Click Apply to preview the modified image.

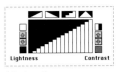

Macintosh   *Windows*

4 To specify a line-screen pattern, click on the rightmost icon in the Screen option (called Screen Patterns in Windows).

5 To override the PostScript printer defaults for lines per inch (or Screen Frequency) and screen angle, type new values for those options. The screen angle can range from -360 to 360 degrees; the Lines/In or Screen Frequency setting can range from 10 to 300 lpi. To restore the printer's defaults, type "DFLT."

Note: *On the Macintosh, click Screened in the Image Control dialog box to activate the Screen, Angle and Lines/In options.*

USING PHOTOSHOP EFFECTS

To further enhance RGB or CMYK TIFF images, you can apply Adobe Photoshop-compatible plug-ins (including Kai's PowerTools and Adobe Gallery Effects) directly within PageMaker. Adobe Gallery Effects® are automatically

installed with PageMaker. For native Photoshop filters, you must use those included with Photoshop version 3.0.4 or later.

When you add a plug-in to the Effects folder within the Plug-ins folder (within the PageMaker RSRC folder), and restart PageMaker, the plug-in becomes available to PageMaker. Alternatively, you can create a shortcut (Windows) or alias (Macintosh) to Photoshop's Filters folder, rename the shortcut or alias "Effects," and store the shortcut or alias file in the Effects folder within the Plug-ins folder (within the PageMaker RSRC folder). You can then use PageMaker to select from the filters available in Photoshop's Filters folder.

For information on using a specific plug-in, see the documentation included with your plug-in, or click the Help button within the dialog box that appears when you choose that plug-in.

Some plug-ins are memory-intensive and may need more RAM than the minimum PageMaker system configuration requires.

To modify an image with a Photoshop Effect:

1 Select the image.

2 Choose Element > Image > Photoshop Effects.

3 Type a new file name to create a modified copy of the original image. Alternatively, type the original file to overwrite the original TIFF with the modified copy.

If you make a copy of the image, it is stored in the same folder as the original and PageMaker links to the modified copy.

4 Choose a plug-in filter.

5 Click OK. If a filter-specific dialog box appears, complete the options, and then click OK.

COMPRESSING AND DECOMPRESSING A TIFF IMAGE

Because TIFF images sometimes require a large amount of disk space, PageMaker provides built-in TIFF compression capabilities. Work with compressed TIFF images in PageMaker exactly as you work with uncompressed TIFF images: place them, link them, OLE-link or OLE-embed them, or subscribe to them.

When you compress a TIFF image, PageMaker compresses a copy of the image without altering the original. Although you can then delete the original from your hard drive, note that using maximum compression can result in loss of detail and image quality in the compressed copy, and you might therefore want to keep the original version available. (If you need to use a compressed TIFF image in another program that does not support Lempel-Ziv & Welch [LZW] compression, you can always use PageMaker to decompress and save it.)

PageMaker provides two levels of compression: maximum and moderate. Maximum compression produces the smallest files on your hard drive, but may change colors and cause banding or loss of detail in the screen image and printed versions of grayscale and color images. Moderate compression produces larger files, but improves the screen image of grayscale and color images and does not noticeably degrade print quality. (PageMaker automatically decompresses images when printing the publication.)

Note: *PageMaker also imports bitmap image files saved and compressed as JPEG (Joint Photographic Experts Group) files. Adobe Photoshop, for example, can save an image with JPEG compression, applying one of several quality settings to determine the trade-off between file compression and loss of image data. With JPEG compression, some image data is discarded to achieve the highest compression ratio.*

When you compress or decompress a TIFF image, PageMaker places a copy of the file on your hard disk and in your publication. PageMaker renames the compressed copy by appending an identifier to the filename, overwriting up to two characters of the original filename, if necessary. For example, a maximum-compressed copy of REDCHAIR.TIF would be named REDCHA_L.TIF in Windows and REDCHAIR.TIF(L) on the Macintosh.

TIFF image compression/decompression filename identifiers			
Type of TIFF image	Moderate	Maximum	Decompressed
1-bit	_P or (P)	_L or (L)	_U or (U)
Palette color (16- or 256-color)	_P or (P)	_L or (L)	_U or (U)
Grayscale or full color	_D or (LD)	_M or (LD2)	_U or (U)

To compress or decompress a TIFF image:

1 Choose File > Place.

2 Select the file you want to compress or decompress, and hold down the following keys while you click OK, and for at least two seconds after clicking OK.

• For moderate compression, hold down Command + Option (Macintosh) or Ctrl + Alt (Windows).

• For maximum compression, hold down Shift + Command + Option (Macintosh) or Shift + Ctrl + Alt (Windows).

• For decompression, hold down Command (Macintosh) or Ctrl (Windows).

Note: You can also use TIFF images compressed by other programs that use LZW compression, such as Adobe Photoshop.

VIEWING IMAGES ON-SCREEN AT DIFFERENT RESOLUTIONS

PageMaker provides a number of options to display images. For example, if layout is finalized and you are proofing text only, you can reduce redraw time by graying out all images.

High resolution   *Standard*   *Grayed out*

You can use one of three preference settings to control the display of all images in the publication, and another preference setting to control the default resolution at which graphics normally display. You can also temporarily override the preference setting for one image at a time.

A graphic's links must be up-to-date to display in high resolution.

Note: Display settings determine print quality when you print to PCL devices, since PageMaker rasterizes information directly from the screen. For best print quality, use the highest screen resolution settings when you print.

To set image-display preferences:

1 Choose File > General Preferences.

2 Select Gray Out, Standard, or High Resolution for the Graphics Display option.

Graphics display: ○ Gray out
　　　　　　　　● Standard
　　　　　　　　○ High resolution

3 Click More.

4 For Define Standard Display By, select one of two methods:

• Select Size, and type a value from 8 to 1024.

• Select Monitor Resolution, and select or type a percentage from 0 to 100.

This setting determines the amount of memory used to create the screen display of each image when Standard is selected in step 2. Use this option to improve the on-screen resolution of graphics (type a higher value) or to reduce the size of the publication and reduce the memory (and time) it takes to redraw graphics (type a lower value). A graphic whose file size or display resolution is smaller than the setting is not affected. This setting has no impact on printing time or print resolution unless you are printing to a PCL device and links to a graphic are lost.

To temporarily display graphics in the current view at full resolution:

Press Control (Macintosh) or Ctrl + Shift (Windows) as you place the graphic, or as the page with the graphic redraws. (To force the screen to redraw, choose the page view currently selected in the View menu.)

KEYLINING

Some designs require a thin border to surround (or keyline) objects on the page. PageMaker can create the border automatically by drawing a box (or oval, for oval objects or oval clipping paths) around the object, and grouping the object and keyline together. You also use Keyline to change or remove keylines created with PageMaker 6.0 or 6.5.

To keyline an object:

1 Select one or more objects. Do not include a group.

2 Choose Utilities > Plug-ins > Keyline.

```
Keyline                           OK
Extends  0.5   points outwards    Cancel
● Bring keyline to front of object   Remove
○ Send keyline behind object      Attributes...
☐ Knock out under keyline
   Overlap interior by  0   points
```

3 Type the distance you want to extend the keyline from the object's bounding box for Extends __ Points Outward.

For example, if you type 5 points, the outside edge of the keyline (whatever its line weight) will begin 5 points from the object's outside edge.

4 Click Attributes to open the Fill and Line dialog box, and then set fill and line attributes such as line weight and fill color.

One use of Keyline is to fill the keyline shape with the color Paper, so that it forces a knock out of any background color below the object you are keylining.

5 Select a position for the keyline—in front of the object or behind it, depending on how you want the keyline to appear in relation to the object—and click OK.

CREATING NON-PRINTING OBJECTS

You may want to create objects that appear on-screen, but not on printed or portable document versions of your publication. This technique is useful when working with a low-resolution representation of a high-resolution scanned image that will be stripped in later, or when you want to attach comments to the publication without having them appear on the page. (You can also use PageMaker's layer feature to accomplish similar effects; see "Using Layers" on page 224 for more information.)

Non-printing objects display by default, but you can hide them so that the screen displays what you'll see on the final output. Non-printing objects must be visible in order to select them.

To make an object non-printing:

1 Select the object.

2 Choose Element > Non-Printing.

To view or hide non-printing objects:

Choose View > Display Non-Printing Items.

To allow non-printing objects to print:

1 Choose File > Print.

2 Select the Ignore "Non-Printing" Setting.

USING LIBRARIES

The Library palette provides an efficient way to manage collections of frequently used text and graphic objects. It lets you store, organize, view, search for, and retrieve items from a floating palette.

Note: You cannot use libraries created in earlier versions of PageMaker with PageMaker 6.5. Instead, using PageMaker 5.0 or 6.0, insert the contents of the library you want to reuse into a publication, open that publication in PageMaker 6.5, and add the contents into a new PageMaker 6.5 library

You can create many different libraries. Within each library, you can identify and later search for each item by title, author, the date it was added to the library, and descriptive words (key words). In this way, a library acts like a database, letting you find and preview only the objects you need at the moment. A selected object on the Library palette is surrounded by a thick line.

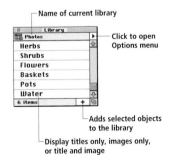

Name of current library

Click to open Options menu

Adds selected objects to the library

Display titles only, images only, or title and image

You can have only one library open at a time; if a library is open when you create a new library or open an existing one, the open library closes.

To create a new library:

1 Choose Window > Plug-in Palettes > Show Library.

If you have previously created a library, the palette opens to the most recently used library.

2 Choose New Library from the Library palette menu.

3 Type the name of the library, specify a location in which to store it, and click OK.

To open an existing library:

1 Choose Window > Plug-in Palettes > Show Library.

2 Choose Open Library from the Library palette menu, locate the library you want, and then click Open.

To delete a library:

1 Go the Finder (Macintosh) or Explorer (Windows).

2 Locate the library you want to delete.

Libraries are stored in the folder that was active at the time the library was created. In Windows, you can recognize a library file by its .PML filename extension.

3 Move it to the trash (Macintosh) or choose File > Delete (Windows).

Moving objects to or from a library

You can quickly add objects to or remove objects from a library. PageMaker lets you add any object that it can copy to the Clipboard, and it copies all linked information about the object. On Macintosh only, you can import items from Adobe Fetch and add them to your library. This gives you quick access to graphics stored on network servers, compact disks, and internal or external hard drives.

To add an object to a library:

1 If the Library palette is not currently visible, open or create a library as described previously.

2 Select one or more objects in the publication window and click the add button (the plus sign) on the Library palette.

To import Adobe Fetch items (Macintosh):

1 In Fetch, open a catalog and select the items you want to import to the Library palette. (You cannot import sounds or QuickTime movies into the Library palette.)

2 In Fetch, choose Edit > Copy References > Include Thumbnails.

3 Start PageMaker 6.5 or, if PageMaker is already running, click the PageMaker 6.5 window to make it active.

4 In the Library palette, choose Import Fetch Items from the Library palette menu

To place a library object on a page:

1 Open a library.

2 Go to the page where you want to place the object.

3 Drag the library object to the page.

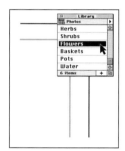 

Select an object   Drag it to the page

To delete an object from the library:

1 Select the object on the Library palette.

2 Choose Remove Item from the Library palette menu.

3 Click OK when PageMaker asks you to confirm the action.

To set library display characteristics:

1 Open a library.

2 From the Library palette menu, choose the appropriate display option (Display Images, Display Names, or Display Both). On the Macintosh only, you can choose Preferences from the Library palette menu and then click Make Color Thumbnails to control whether images are color or grayscale.

Cataloging library items

You can attach information to library items to help you locate them quickly as your library grows. You can give an object a title, enter the name of the person who created or placed the object in the library, enter the date the object was placed in the library, or add one or more key words that describe the object. (To increase legibility and keep track of information, separate key words by commas and spaces.)

To automatically display the Item Information dialog box as each item is added to the library, do the following:

• Macintosh: Choose Preferences from the Library palette, and then click Edit Items After Adding.

• Windows: Choose Edit Items After Adding from the Library palette menu.

To add or edit library information:

1 Open a library.

2 Double-click an object on the Library palette.

3 Type or edit the desired information.

Searching for objects in a library

Using the Library palette's search features, you can locate objects based on the author, date, key word, or other categories. For example, you can locate (and limit the display to) all objects cataloged under Photos but exclude photographs by a particular author.

To search for objects:

1 Open the library you want to search.

2 Choose Search Library from the Library palette menu.

3 To search by key word, by title, or by author, complete the information for those options.

4 To search by more than one key word, enter the key word you want to find in the first edit box, and choose an option from the pop-up menu to define the search: One Key Word Only, And, Or, or But Not. Enter the second key word in the second text box.

5 Click Search.

The library appears with only the objects that meet the search criteria.

If you enter information in more than one search option (key word, author, or title), the search displays only those objects that fulfill all search options.

To display all objects after a search:

Choose Show All Items from the Library palette menu.

USING LAYERS

Each PageMaker 6.5 publication includes one or more *layers*. Think of layers as transparent sheets of film that are stacked on top of each other. You can see through them to any other visible layers (except where opaque objects block the view of objects on lower layers).

By using multiple layers you can create and edit specific areas or kinds of content in your publication without affecting other areas or kinds of content. For example, if you placed your type on a specific layer, and your images on another layer, you could temporarily hide the image layer to make fine-tuning typography and proof

About layers • Layers are like sheets of transparent film stacked one on top of the other, each containing one or more objects. You can display, print, lock, and reorder layers as distinct units. By using multiple layers, you gain greater control over the design and production process.

The layers palette

reading that much easier. Or create multi-language versions of the same publication by placing each text translation on its own layer.

By default, a new publication, or one converted from an earlier version of PageMaker, uses just one layer—it's called [Default], and it cannot be removed or renamed. You can add one or more layers to the document at any time. You can even create new layers with no publication open so that all subsequent new publications have multiple layers. The number of layers a document can have is limited only by your computer's memory.

Note: Layers apply throughout a publication—all pages in a document share the layers, including master pages. For example, if you hide Layer 1 while editing page 1 of your document, the layer becomes hidden on all pages until you decide to show it again.

Three rules affect objects and their order on layers:

• Within each layer, objects are stacked according to their stacking order. See "Changing the Stacking Order of Objects" on page 190 for more information.

• Master page objects can be placed on any layer, but on publication pages they display behind all other objects on the page, regardless of how layers are arranged. See "Changing the Order of Layers" on page 229 for more information.

• Objects in a group always occupy the same layer, and frame content always occupies the same layer as the frame itself. If you group objects from different layers, all objects are placed on the frontmost layer of the group, directly behind the frontmost object in the group.

Displaying the Layers palette

You use the Layers palette to create, edit, lock, and delete layers. The Layers palette also lets you show and hide individual layers, determine the order in which layers appear, and lets you move an object from its current layer to a different layer.

To display the Layers palette:

• Choose Window > Show Layers.

Use the scroll bars or resize the palette to see additional layers.

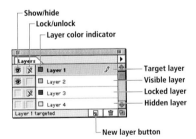

The Layers palette lists the layers in a document, with the frontmost layer appearing at the top of the palette.

The target layer, or the layer to which new objects are added, is always highlighted (the pencil icon and status bar also indicate the target layer). Only one layer can be active (targetted) at a time.

When an object is selected, a small colored dot appears to the right of the layer name on the palette to indicate the layer to which the object is assigned.

Creating layers and setting layer options

You add layers using the New Layer command on the Layers palette menu or the new layer button at the bottom of the Layers palette. Once you create a new layer it becomes the target layer, and you can add objects to it by creating new objects with the text or drawing tools; by importing, placing, or pasting text or graphics; or by selecting objects on other layers and then moving them to the new layer.

To create a new layer and set options for it:

1 Choose Window > Show Layers, and choose New Layer from the Layers palette menu.

2 Type a name for the layer in the Name text box. By default, layers are named according to the order in which they were created, with [Default] being the backmost layer.

3 Select a color from the Selection Color pop-up menu, or accept the default assigned automatically.

The selection handles for objects selected on a layer appear in the color specified for that layer. That lets you tell at a glance whether the currently selected objects are on the same layer or not. The layer color also appears in a box to the left of the layer name on the palette.

4 Select or deselect the Show option to display or hide the layer. (Hidden layers do not print and cannot be edited.)

5 Select or deselect the Lock option to lock or unlock objects on the layer. For more information, see "Locking Layers" on page 231.

6 Click OK.

To add a new layer using default settings:

Press Option (Macintosh) or Alt (Windows) and click the new layer button ( ) at the bottom of the Layers palette.

A new, visible, unlocked layer is created, and is named according to the order in which it was created. The selection color is assigned automatically.

Adding objects to layers

Any new object created in a document is placed on the layer selected in the Layers palette.

To select a layer on which to work:

Click the name of the layer you want on the Layers palette.

Moving or copying an object to a different layer

You can move or copy objects from one layer to another by using the Layers palette.

To move objects to a different layer using the Layers palette:

1 Use the pointer tool to select the objects you want to move.

A small colored dot appears to the right of the layer name in the Layers palette, indicating the current selection.

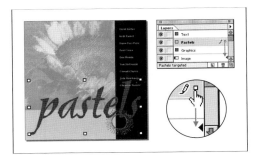

2 Drag the colored dot to the layer to which you want to move the object.

If you selected objects from two or more layers in step 1, repeat step 2 until only the destination layer shows a colored dot to the right of its name.

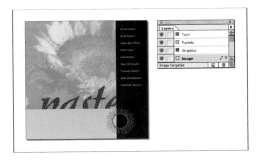

To copy objects from one layer to another:

1 Use the pointer tool to select the objects you want to copy.

A small colored dot appears to the right of the layer name in the Layers palette, indicating the current selection.

2 Press Command (Macintosh) or Ctrl (Windows) and drag the colored dot to the layer to which you want to copy the object.

If you selected objects from two or more layers in step 1, repeat step 2 until only the destination layer shows a colored dot to the right of its name.

Selecting all objects on a layer

You can quickly select all objects on a page or two-page spread that are assigned to a particular layer.

To select all objects on a particular layer:

1 Press Shift if you want objects currently selected to remain selected.

2 Press Command + Option (Macintosh) or Ctrl + Alt (Windows) and click the name of the layer you want to select objects from.

To select all objects on the target layer:

1 Click a layer name on the palette to set the target layer.

2 Choose Select Target Layer from the Layers palette menu.

About layers and pasting

If you use the Paste command to move objects from one page to another, remember that pasting works differently depending on whether the Paste Remembers Layering option on the Layers palette menu is selected:

• If the Paste Remembers Layering option is selected, then objects cut or copied from different layers retain their layer assignments when pasted to the new page or position.

• If the Paste Remembers Layering option is *not* selected, objects cut or copied from different layers are pasted together onto the selected layer.

To paste objects to a different page or position and retain layering information:

1 Choose Paste Remembers Layering from the Layers palette menu.

2 Select the object that you want to move, and choose Edit > Cut or Edit > Copy.

3 Turn to the new page if necessary.

4 Choose Edit > Paste to paste the objects onto the same layers they had been on originally.

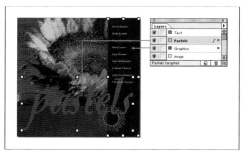

Objects on different layers copied from page 1…

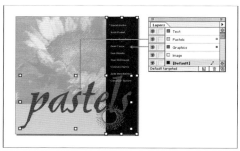

retain layers when pasted on page 2, if Paste Remembers Layering is selected…

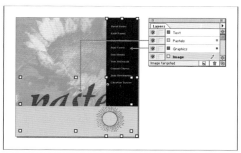

or appear on target layer on page 2, if Paste Remembers Layering is not selected.

To move an object to a different layer using the Paste command:

1 Make sure that the Paste Remember Layering option on the Layers palette menu is not selected.

2 Select the object that you want to move, and choose Edit > Cut or Edit > Copy.

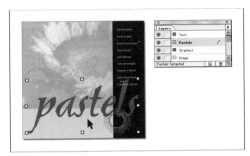

3 Select any object on the layer to which you want to move the cut object, or select the layer name in the Layers palette.

4 Choose Edit > Paste to paste the object into the center of the artwork as the frontmost object on the selected layer.

Once the object is pasted, you can move it and use the commands in the Element > Arrange menu to change the stacking order of the object on its new layer.

Changing the order of layers

By rearranging the layers on the Layers palette, you can change the order of layers in your document.

To change the order of layers:

In the Layers palette, drag the layer you want to move to its new location. You can also press Shift (Macintosh) or Ctrl (Windows) to select multiple layers; when you drag two or more layers to a new position, they maintain their layer order relative to one another.

Image layer moved to top of Layers palette

Result

Deleting and merging layers

You can remove layers from your document by using the Delete Layer or Delete Unused Layers commands on the Layers palette menu. The objects assigned to a deleted layer on every page of the publication are either deleted or added to a specified layer, depending on the option you choose.

The Merge Layers command on the Layers palette menu also deletes layers, as described later in this section.

Important: Remember that each layer appears on every page of a publication, not just on a specific page. Before deleting a layer, you might want to hide all the other layers first, and then turn to each page of the publication to view the objects on the layer you are about to delete.

To delete a layer:

1 Select the layer name in the Layers palette.

2 Choose Delete "layer name" from the Layers palette menu, or click the trash button at the bottom of the palette. (You can also drag the layer to the trash button.)

3 In the Delete Layer dialog box, select an option:

• Select Assign Items From Deleted Layer To, and choose the name of the layer to which you want the objects moved. Remember that this can change the way objects overlap in your publications. Double-check your pages after merging layers in this way.

• Select Delete Items on All Pages From Layer to remove all objects throughout the publication assigned to that layer.

To delete the selected layer (with all its objects) and prevent the Delete Layer dialog box from appearing, hold down Option (Macintosh) or Alt (Windows) as you complete step 2.

To delete all layers that lack objects:

1 Choose Delete Unused Layers from the Layers palette menu.

2 In the dialog box that appears, you are prompted to delete the first unused layer (click Yes) or to preserve it (click No). Click Yes To All if you want to automatically delete the unused layers without being further prompted, or click No To All to cancel the action.

To prevent the dialog box from appearing, hold down Option (Macintosh) or Alt (Windows) as you choose Delete Unused Layers.

To merge layers:

1 Press Command (Macintosh) or Ctrl (Windows) and select two or more layer names in the Layers palette.

2 Choose Merge Layers from the Layers palette menu.

Objects from all selected layers are moved to the first layer you selected in step 1 (since clicking the first layer makes it the target layer). Of the layers you select to merge, only the target layer will remain in the publication; the other selected layers are deleted.

Locking layers

Objects on locked layers cannot be selected or edited.

To lock or unlock one layer at a time:

Click the rightmost box to the left of the layer name. The lock icon (🔒) appears, indicating that the layer is locked. Click again to hide the icon and unlock the layer. You can drag up or down to lock or unlock other layers.

To lock all but the target layer:

1 With no layers locked, click a layer name to make it the target layer.

2 Choose Lock Others from the Layers palette menu, or press Option (Macintosh) or Alt (Windows) and click the rightmost box to the left of the target layer name.

To unlock all layers:

Choose Unlock All from the Layers palette menu, or press Option (Macintosh) or Alt (Windows) and click the lock icon to the left of any locked layer.

Showing and hiding layers

Hiding a layer controls not just whether a layer displays or not, but whether it prints and whether it can be edited.

To show or hide one layer at a time:

Click the leftmost box to the left of the layer name. The eye icon (👁) appears, indicating that the layer is showing. Click again to hide the icon and hide the layer. You can drag up or down to show or hide other layers.

To hide all layers but those selected in the palette:

1 Select the layer or layers you want to view.

2 Choose Hide Others from the Layers palette menu, or press Option (Macintosh) or Alt (Windows) and click the eye icon to the left of selected layers.

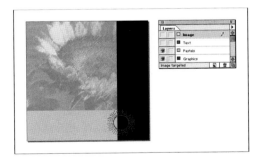

To show all layers:

Choose Show All from the Layers palette menu, press Option (Macintosh) or Alt (Windows) and click the leftmost box to the left of any hidden layer's name. The eye icon appears, indicating the layers are visible.

Choosing a selection color for layers

Selecting a different color for each layer makes it easy to distinguish layers in your publication as you work. When you select an object, its handles display in the color specified for that layer. A layer's selection color is displayed in the box to the left of the layer name in the Layers palette.

To specify a selection color for a layer:

1 Double-click the layer you want in the Layers palette.

2 Choose a color from the Selection Color pop-up menu, and then click OK.

Chapter 7: Indexes, Contents, and Pagination

Many publications—from annual reports to catalogs to multi-volume manuals—are compilations of separate publications such as a table of contents, chapters, and an index. PageMaker lets you produce these long documents in the manner that best fits your working style and situation.

In a workgroup setting, long document features allow individuals to work on separate publications simultaneously. In this way, you can maintain connections between the publications to complete tasks such as repagination and printing.

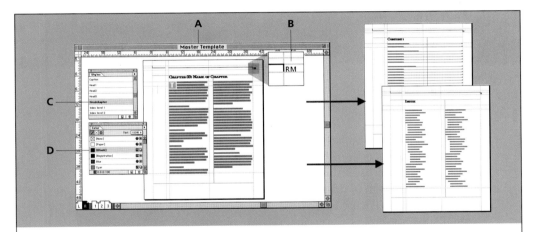

Tips for planning a long document • Save time and effort by planning a multiple-publication document in advance:

A Create a master template that includes common elements in your book, such as margins and columns, text styles, colors, headers and footers, and other design elements.

B Set up page-number markers in the master template, and add prefixes or change the numbering format for each section template or publication.

C Use paragraph styles to make it easy to generate a consistent table of contents.

D Specify colors only once in the master template. This ensures that the colors are consistent in all publications based on the template.

Long document features also include support for Portable Document Format (PDF) versions of publications. In a PDF file, you can jump from each index or table of contents page-number reference to the corresponding publication page. For more information on PDF and online publishing, see Chapter 13, "Distributing a Publication Electronically."

ASSEMBLING PUBLICATIONS INTO A BOOK

Assembling multiple publications into a book associates them, so you can work with them as a whole—creating an index and a table of contents, and printing the book—while retaining the ability to work with each publication independently. Creating a book helps keep publication file sizes relatively small, so you can work more efficiently.

Assemble a book by creating a book list in one of the publications that you want to include in the book, such as the table of contents or the index. A book list tells PageMaker which publications you want to assemble into a book. When you generate the index or print the book, PageMaker looks at the book list in the active publication, repaginates the book, and compiles index or table of contents information. If the active publication does not contain a book list, PageMaker performs these tasks only on the active publication.

The order in which publications appear in the book list determines the order in which Page-Maker repaginates and prints them. It is important to list publications in their correct sequence, so that page numbers and index entries are accurate and headings appear in the correct order in the table of contents.

A publication can be part of more than one book and, consequently, can appear in more than one book list. This is a handy feature if you want a publication to appear in many documents. However, a publication can only contain one book list at a time.

To create a book list:

1 Open the publication in which you want to create the book list.

2 Choose Utilities > Book.

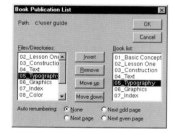

3 Double-click the name of each file you want to add. You can add publications from various locations on your hard drive or network.

TIP: IF YOU PLAN TO NUMBER THE PAGES IN A MULTIPLE-PUBLICATION DOCUMENT, ADD PAGE-NUMBER MARKERS TO THE MASTER PAGES IN YOUR TEMPLATE BEFORE YOU CREATE EACH PUBLICATION.

4 Click the Move Up or Move Down option to change the selected publication's position in the list or click Remove to delete it from the list, and then click OK.

See "Numbering Pages Within a Book" on page 240 for more information.

Copying a book list

You can copy a book list to every publication in the book. This lets you create an index or table of contents spanning all chapters in the book and print all chapters from any publication in the list.

When you copy a book list into a publication that already contains a book list, you replace the existing book list with the one you are copying.

Note: The publication from which you're copying the book list must be named before you can copy its book list into other publications.

To copy a book list:

1 Open the publication containing the book list.

2 Press Command (Macintosh) or Ctrl (Windows), and then choose Utilities > Book.

PageMaker copies the book list into every publication in the list. If you later modify the book list in one publication, you will need to recopy the list to update the other publications.

NUMBERING PAGES IN A MULTIPLE-PUBLICATION DOCUMENT

PageMaker has a variety of page-numbering options. When you add page numbers to your publication, you can add prefixes to the page numbers, such as *A-*, or *1-*, to identify sections of your document; number pages in associated publications sequentially or restart the numbering sequence for each publication; and select among various number formats.

About paginating PDF documents

If you plan to create one Portable Document Format (PDF) version of your booked publication, be aware of how pages are counted in the PDF file format.

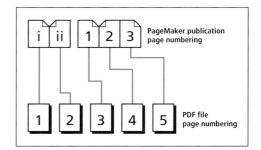

The first publication page in the first booked publication is always considered Page 1 in the PDF version, even though it may be numbered with a Roman numeral i in PageMaker. This difference can result in incorrect links and page references in a PDF file.

For more information on designing publications for PDF file format, see Chapter 13, "Distributing a Publication Electronically."

Adding page numbers

In PageMaker you add page-number markers to the pages you want to be numbered. PageMaker automatically updates the page number when repagination occurs (such as when you add, remove, or insert pages).

You can type the page-number marker on a publication page or you can place page-number markers on the master pages to automatically number all pages in a publication.

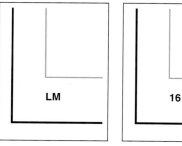

Master page with
page-number marker

Publication page with
page number

Since you'll typically want page numbers to appear in the exact same place and with the exact same formatting, use caution if you are working with several master pages. If possible, add the page number marker to the document master

page, and then create other masters based on the document master. See "Using Master Pages" on page 68 for more information.

To add page-number markers to master pages:

1 Turn to a master page in your publication.

2 Click an insertion point with the text tool.

3 Press Command + Option + P (Macintosh) or Ctrl + Alt + P (Windows).

4 Choose Edit > Select All to select the text, and format the text as necessary.

5 Repeat steps 3 and 4 for all master pages in the publication.

Page-number markers appear as *RM* (right master) or *LM* (left master) on the master pages but display the page number on publication pages.

If your publication has facing pages, add the page-number marker on both the right and left master pages, and to any single-sided master pages. See "Setting Up Pages" on page 65 for more information.

Note: *If your publication contains a book list, PageMaker renumbers the pages in your book each time you show or generate an index, create a table of contents, or output the book.*

Adding a prefix to page numbers

You may want to add a page-number prefix, such as *1-* or *A-*, before the page numbers of your publication. You can add separate page-number prefixes to the actual pages and to the page references in the table of contents and the index.

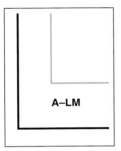 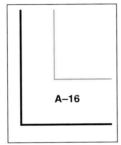

Master page with prefixed page-number marker   *Publication page with prefixed page number*

It's especially useful to use separate prefixes for page numbers and page references when creating an index or table of contents for a set of publications. For instance, if you are creating a year-end index for a monthly newsletter, you can add a page-reference prefix to each issue of the newsletter (such as *Jan-*, *Feb-*, and so on), and then generate a single index referencing all 12 issues.

To add a prefix to a page-number marker:

1 On each master page in your publication, use the text tool to click an insertion point before the page-number marker.

2 Type the prefix you want for the page number.

If you add a prefix to a page-number marker and want it to appear in the table of contents and index, you'll need to add the prefix to your publication page references as described below.

To add page-reference prefixes to a table of contents or index:

1 Open the publication to which you want to add a page-reference prefix.

2 Choose File > Document Setup.

3 Click Numbers.

4 Type the page-number prefix in the TOC and Index Prefix text box. You can enter up to 15 characters.

Repeat this procedure to add page-reference prefixes to other publications in your book.

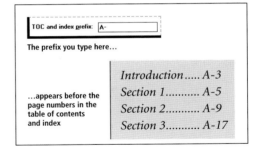

Numbering pages within a book

With PageMaker, you can number the pages of a multiple-publication document consecutively from the first publication through the last, restart the page numbering in each publication, or combine the two methods. You can also tell PageMaker to begin each successive publication on the next odd or even page number.

Note: An individual publication can only have one numbering scheme, and you cannot restart page numbering in the middle of a publication.

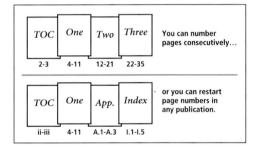

To number pages consecutively in a multiple-publication document:

1 Open the publication containing the book list.

2 Choose Utilities > Book.

3 Select an option for Auto Renumbering to specify the page on which you want numbering to begin in each subsequent publication:

• The None option prevents automatic renumbering. Each publication in the book list retains the page numbering specified in the Document Setup dialog box for that publication.

• The Next Page option numbers publications in a book list consecutively from the first publication to the last. For example, if the first publication ends on page 54, the second publication begins on page 55. PageMaker continues numbering consecutively to the end of the book, or until it finds any publication that has the Restart Page Numbering option selected in the Document Setup dialog box.

• The Next Odd Page and Next Even Page options number publications in a book list so that each publication begins on an odd- or even-numbered page. If necessary, PageMaker creates a blank page at the end of a publication to ensure that the next publication in the list begins with an odd or even page number.

Note: Specifying an Auto Renumbering option will not add numbers to publications that do not have page-number markers.

TIP: CHECK THE SPELLING IN THE ENTIRE DOCUMENT BEFORE SELECTING WORDS TO INDEX. WHEN YOU INDEX A WORD, PAGEMAKER ADDS IT TO THE TOPICS LIST, SO IT SHOULD BE SPELLED CORRECTLY.

Restarting page numbering

You can restart the page numbering of any publication in the document—an appendix, for example. Each time PageMaker repaginates the entire long document, it restarts page numbering in the publication at the number you specified using the New or Document Setup command and continues numbering consecutively in subsequent publications.

To restart page numbering in a publication:

1 Open the publication in which you want to restart the page numbering.

2 Choose File > Document Setup.

3 Click Restart Page Numbering.

4 Type the desired starting page number in the Start Page # text box, and then click OK.

Specifying a page-number format

You can use alphabetic, Arabic, or Roman numerals to number the pages in a publication, regardless of the numbering format used in other publications in the book. For example, you can specify Roman numerals for front-matter and Arabic numerals for chapters.

Alphabetical numbering styles use A–Z to represent the numbers 1–26. Double-letters AA–ZZ are used for 27–52. For alphabetical numbers 53 and higher, and Roman numbers 5000 and higher, PageMaker reverts to Arabic numerals.

Note: Changing the format of page numbers does not affect the overall page-numbering sequence of a publication.

To specify a page-number format:

1 Open the publication in which you want to reformat page numbers.

2 Choose File > Document Setup.

3 Click Numbers.

4 Select a numbering format from the list, and then click OK.

INDEXING A PUBLICATION

You can create a simple key-word index or a comprehensive guide to the information in the book. PageMaker lets you focus on the planning and structure while it does the hard work: tracking index entries as pages change, even across several publications.

An index entry is composed of two parts: a topic and a reference. Usually the reference is to a page number, but it can also be a cross-reference to another topic. For example, in the *Fonts* entry of the manual index shown below, a discussion on installing is shown as appearing on page 23; in the entry *Formatting,* see also *Applying,* readers are directed to a related topic (*Applying*) that contains additional information.

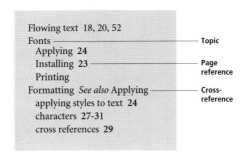

Indexing guidelines

The index is frequently the first place readers look for information. Creating a well-planned and complete index is a challenging and time-consuming task, but it makes the information in your document immediately accessible to your readers. Here are a few guidelines to consider:

• Think about how you want your index to look. How many levels will it have? Will it refer the reader to other related topics? Will a simple key-word index suffice, or do you want a more thorough index?

• Anticipate alternate ways that your readers might look up information. For instance, a reader may search for information on type by looking under *Type, Typography, Text,* or *Fonts.*

• Some indexers prefer to create a list of topics ahead of time, while others prefer to index topics as they come to mind and refine the index later.

• Add index entries when the content of your document is fairly stable. If you delete large portions of your text later, you'll lose your indexing work as well.

• Review your index several times before generating the final index. Look for duplicate entries, weak areas, misspellings, and other problems.

• Make corrections to the index entries themselves. Edits you make to the index story will not be saved if you regenerate the index later.

ABOUT THE INDEXING PROCESS

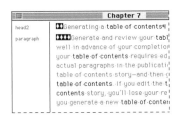

1 Add index entries • In each story you want to index, use the Index Entry command to add an index marker for each topic or cross-reference you want to appear in the index. The marker flows with the text, and specifies the wording, level (main topic or sub-topic), and the page range or cross-reference for the topic.

2 Edit index entries • Use the Show Index command to preview and edit topics and cross-references compiled from all indexed publications in the book (or from the current publication only). You can quickly change almost any aspect of a topic or delete a topic in this dialog box, but you cannot add a topic here.

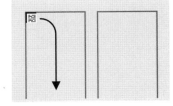

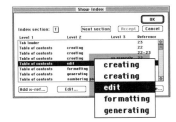

3 Generate the index • Use the Create Index command to generate and format the index information. PageMaker compiles all entries from all publications in the book (or from the current publication only) into a single story.

4 Flow the index story • Use automatically-generated paragraph styles to change type and paragraph attributes for the index story. Do not add, delete, or edit entries in the placed index story, since PageMaker does not update the corresponding index markers with your changes. Use the Index Entry or Show Index commands to make content changes.

Understanding index entries

When you define an index entry, PageMaker inserts an index marker (▐) in the text to indicate that an index entry exists. This marker, visible only in story editor, stores the indexing information for a particular entry. When you generate an index, PageMaker scans the active publication's book list, repaginates each publication, compiles and alphabetizes index entries from the publications, and creates the index.

Although index markers move as text is added or deleted to a story, the text before or after a marker is not connected to the index marker. In fact, if you delete the text, but not the marker, the index entry remains.

Note: When you import or export stories, you lose certain index information associated with the marker, including cross-references, sorting information, and page ranges.

The same passage of text might have several markers associated with it—in other words, an entry for each place in the index where the audience might look up the topic. For example, you might index an important point about applying fonts with entries under *Fonts, Typefaces, Type Attributes,* and *Formatting.* Each of these entries would refer to the same publication page where the font discussion occurs.

Each entry includes two key pieces of information about the topic: the topic level, and the page range.

About topic levels

In a simple index, all entries might be primary topics—that is, entries without subcategories associated with them. But a more detailed index will use secondary-level topics and even tertiary-level topics, subordinate to the primary topics. In the following example, secondary topics are indented under the primary topics, tertiary topics under secondary topics.

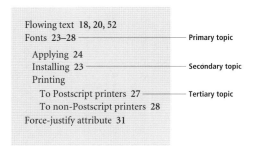

PageMaker automatically collects all entries with the same primary topic (such as *Fonts*) under that one section of the index. PageMaker allows up to three topic levels in an index.

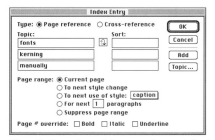

Three Topic text boxes define up to three topic levels.

About page ranges

As shown in the previous example, an index entry can direct the reader to a single page, a series of pages (23-28), or several pages at different points in the book (18, 20, 52). PageMaker determines the right pages to refer to based on the Page Range option you select in the Add Index Entry dialog box. Your options are:

• The Current Page option is appropriate for short, specific discussions that aren't likely to span more than one page.

• The To Next Style Change option is useful for discussions that occur over several paragraphs that have the same paragraph style (for example, *Body text*) and end when another paragraph style occurs (for example, *Heading 1*).

• The To Next Use of Style option is useful if the discussion occurs over several paragraphs that might have more than one style applied, but ends when a certain paragraph style occurs. From the menu, select the paragraph style that signals the start of another topic.

• The For the Next __Paragraphs option is useful if you know the number of paragraphs in which the discussion occurs.

• The Suppress Page Range option is useful if you do not want to immediately refer to a page, but want to create a placeholder to index later.

Creating index entries

This section describes how to use the Utilities > Index Entry command to create an index entry. Once an entry is created, you can select its index marker, and then use Utilities > Index Entry to edit or update the information you initially specified.

When you create index entries in the Add Index Entry dialog box, you enter each topic, specify whether the topic has a page reference or a cross-reference to another index entry, and tell PageMaker how to sort topics. You can also specify a page range for your entry or the kind of cross-reference you want, and change the type style of the page references and cross-references.

To create an index entry:

1 Click an insertion point in front of the text you want to index (or select the text you want to use for the index entry).

2 Choose Utilities > Index Entry.

If you selected text in Step 1, the text appears in the first-level Topic text box.

3 Select Page Reference for type of entry.

To create a cross-reference, see "Creating a Cross-Reference" on page 249.

4 Enter up to three topic levels in the Topic text boxes, as follows:

• Type information for one or more levels.

• Click Topic and select a pre-existing topic from the list in the Select Topic dialog box. This method ensures that you use the exact terminology and spelling as other entries, so as not to create two or more topics unintentionally (for example, *Font* and *Fonts* or *St. Petersburg* and *Saint Petersburg*).

Note: *In the Select Topic dialog box, press Command (Macintosh) or Ctrl (Windows) as you click OK if you want to add the selected topic to the Add Index Entry dialog box without overwriting the existing topic level information.*

Use the Promote/Demote button to move the text in Level 1 to Level 2, Level 2 text to Level 3, and Level 3 text to Level 1. For example, if in step 1 you selected the text "Fonts" and want to create an index entry for *Fonts* under the primary topic *Type attributes*, click the Promote/Demote button once, and then type **Type attributes** in the Level 1 text box.

The page reference appears in the index beside the lowest topic level you enter. See "About Topic Levels" on page 244 for more information.

5 Specify the page range denoting where the discussion of the subject begins and ends, so PageMaker can supply page numbers for the reference.

See "About Page Ranges" on page 245 for more information.

6 Select any of three Page # Override options—bold, italic, and underline—for emphasizing index-entry page numbers.

Selecting any of these options causes the type style of the page numbers to be reversed from the rest of the index entry. For example, if the paragraph style for page numbers is Normal, selecting Italic changes the type style to italic ("Typeface *25, 73–85, 206*") and vice versa. PageMaker applies that setting to all new entries until you change it.

7 Click Add to add more entries (follow steps 3-6), or click OK to add the entry and close the dialog box.

The Add button in the Add Index Entry dialog box lets you save the current index entry, and create another one without closing the dialog box. This is useful, for example, when you create a primary index entry, such as *Fonts*, and want to use *Fonts* as a second-level topic under *Type attributes*, or create another primary index entry, *Typefaces*.

Sorting topics

Index entries are spelled in the index as they appear in the Topic text boxes but are sorted alphabetically according to the spelling in the Sort text boxes. For example, if the topic reference is *St.* and you want it to be sorted in the index as *Saint*, type **Saint** in the Sort text box next to *St.* You can do this as you create the index entry, or later, when you use Show Index to edit entries.

Indexing proper names and other simple entries

Once you understand the basics of adding index entries, you can use the shortcuts in this section to speed up your work.

To index selected text using a keyboard shortcut:

1 Select the text in your story that you want to index.

2 Press Command + Shift + Y (Macintosh) or Ctrl + Shift + Y (Windows).

PageMaker creates an index entry using the selected text as the topic and the current page as the page reference.

To index a proper name, last name first:

1 In the story you are indexing, select the proper name.

2 Press Command + Opt + Y (Macintosh) or Ctrl + Alt + Y (Windows).

The name will appear—last name first—in your index with the current page as its page reference. For example, *Mary Shelley* is indexed as *Shelley, Mary*.

To index proper names of more than two words (or names that include titles), position nonbreaking spaces between titles, first names, and middle names or initials. Then PageMaker sees the name as only two words. For example, to index *Hans Christian Andersen*, place a nonbreaking space between *Hans* and *Christian*. PageMaker indexes the name as *Andersen, Hans Christian*. To insert a nonbreaking space, press Option + spacebar (Macintosh) or Ctrl + Alt + spacebar (Windows).

To index all occurrences of words or phrases with the Change command:

1 Identify the key words you want to index.

2 In story editor, click an insertion point at the beginning of any story in the publication you want to index.

3 Choose Utilities > Change.

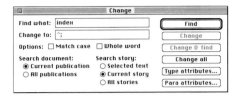

4 Type a key word in the Find What text box.

5 Type ^**;** (caret + semicolon) in the Change To text box.

The caret (^) and semicolon (;) characters tell PageMaker to index the term without changing the story text.

Note: *Type ^z (caret + z) instead of ^; (caret + semicolon) to format the index entry as a proper name—last name first—without changing the story text.*

6 Use one of the following options:

• Click Change All to index all instances of the word as it appears in the story.

• Click Find to evaluate each instance of the key word before you create an entry for it.

• Click Change and Find to index the current instance of the key word and then go to the next instance.

See "Finding and Changing Text and Text Attributes" on page 139 for more information.

7 Repeat this procedure for each key word you want to put in the index.

At any time in the process you can pause to customize the entry with the Index Entry command.

Indexing with a topics list

Many professional indexers prefer to base index entries on a topics list—a predefined list of subjects to which the index will refer. Using a topics list as you create index entries can help you index concepts and terms consistently and save time. In a multiple-publication index, you can use the same topics to index each publication by importing the topics used to index other publications in your document. You can then select these topics, instead of typing new topics, as you create index entries in the active publication.

To create a topics list:

1 Choose Utilities > Index Entry.

2 Click Topic.

3 Type a topic for one or more levels in the text boxes, and then click Add to add the topic to the list.

4 Enter additional topics, or click OK to close the Select Topic dialog box.

5 Click Cancel in the Add Index Entry dialog box to return to your publication.

Note: *You are not adding entries to the index at this point. Topics added to the topics list do not create an index marker in the text, and they do not appear in the index until you use them in an index entry.*

To copy a topics list:

1 Open the publication to which you want to copy the list.

2 Create a book list, if necessary, or copy one containing the publications with the topics you wish to copy.

See "Assembling Publications Into a Book" on page 236 for more information.

3 Choose Utilities > Index Entry.

4 Click Topics.

5 Click Import.

All index topics (but not index entries) from the publications in the book list are added to the topics list in the current publication.

To print a topics list:

1 Create a new publication.

2 Add the publications in your document to the new publication's book list.

3 Copy the topics list (see previous procedure).

4 Create an index entry using each topic in the list.

5 Generate, place, and print the index for the new publication only.

You can remove unused topics from the topics list, but first be sure you won't need them. If you remove unused topics too soon, you may need to re-create them.

To remove unused topics from the topics list:

1 Choose Utilities > Create Index.

2 Click Remove Unreferenced Topics, and then click OK.

The unused topics will be removed from the index topics list when the index is generated.

Creating a cross-reference

Cross-references tell readers which other topics contain related or additional information. A cross-reference entry does not generate an index marker or reference a page location, so the position of the cursor in your story is irrelevant.

To create a cross-reference:

1 Choose Utilities > Index Entry.

2 Select Cross-Reference for Type of entry.

The dialog box changes when you select the Cross-Reference option.

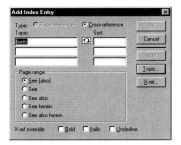

3 Enter the index entry topic.

This is the topic that the reader will look up in the index. You can enter up to three levels in the text boxes or you can click Topics to select a topic from the topics list.

4 Click X-Ref.

5 Enter the related topic to which the reader will be referred.

You can enter up to three levels in the text boxes, or you can select a topic from the list displayed in the bottom portion of the dialog box.

6 Click OK to close the Select Cross-Reference Topic dialog box.

7 Select the Denoted By option that describes your cross-reference, as follows:

• See [also]: When you select this option, PageMaker decides whether to use *See* or *See also* for a cross-reference. If you specified a topic with a page reference, PageMaker supplies a *See also* cross-reference; if you specified a topic without a page-reference, PageMaker uses a *See* cross-reference.

• See: Refers the reader to other topics.

• See Also: Refers the reader both to the current topic and to the topics mentioned in the cross-reference.

• See Herein: Refers the reader to subentries (Level 2 or 3 entries) within a topic. For example, a book on desserts might have so many entries under *Pies* that it would be helpful to list types of pies. You might include a reference such as "Pies. *See herein* Quiche."

• See Also Herein: Refers the reader both to the page references of the main entry and to subentries (Level 2 or 3 entries) within the index entry.

For example, in a general cookbook discussion of pies in various categories (*Desserts, Light Meals,* and so on), you could include a reference to *Pies* as "Pies *117-139, 153-177. See also herein* Quiche."

8 Select an X-Ref Override option if you want to override the current formatting of the cross-reference.

9 Click Add (to continue adding cross-references) or OK (to close the dialog box).

Reviewing and editing an index

The more complex your index, the more time you should allot to reviewing it, as you may need several review cycles. First review the index on the screen, where you can revise on the fly, and then review a printed copy.

To review a printed copy of your index, generate an index story by following the steps listed in "Generating an Index" on page 254 Place the resulting index story in your publication and print.

Edit internal index entries using the Index Entry or Show Index commands. (When you edit the index story, your revisions only affect the text, not the internal index entries.) You can see the contents of a particular index marker in story editor using the Index Entry command, but you'll probably make most of the changes to your index using the Show Index command, which lets you edit index entries from all of your booked publications.

Show Index dialog box

A Select the alphabetical section you want to display.

B Click to display the next alphabetical section with at least one entry.

C Click to accept any changes you've made to entries. The dialog box stays open so you can make further changes.

D Index entries and cross-references for the selected section appear in the list.

E Click to add cross-references, and to edit, remove, or capitalize entries.

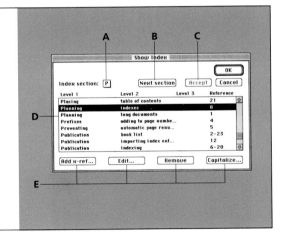

If you create index entries that refer to text that PageMaker cannot locate on a publication page, PageMaker references those entries as follows:

- PB: Pasteboard

- LM: Left master page

- RM: Right master page

- OV: Text that spills outside text objects (in layout view), sometimes called overset

- UN: Unplaced story (in story editor)

- ? (question mark): Text included in a page range that may have changed

- HI: Entry placed on a hidden layer

To view or edit a single entry:

1 Switch to story editor, and select the index marker.

Be sure to select only the index marker you want to see; PageMaker creates a new index entry if additional characters are selected.

2 Choose Utilities > Index Entry.

3 Make changes to any aspect of the entry.

4 Click OK.

To review and edit an index using Show Index:

1 Open the book's index publication or open the publication with index entries you want to edit.

2 Choose Utilities > Show Index or, to review only the index from the active publication, hold down Command (Macintosh) or Ctrl (Windows) and choose Utilities > Show Index.

Unless you press Command (Macintosh) or Ctrl (Windows), PageMaker repaginates the publications in your book list and compiles index information from each, so you can review all of the index entries for the entire booked publication at one time.

3 Select the alphabetical section containing the entries you want to work with, and select the index entry you want to revise.

4 Revise the entry using one of the following methods:

- Click Add X-Ref to add a cross-reference.

- Click Edit to edit the entry.

- Click Remove to remove the entry.

- Click Capitalize to capitalize the selected entry, all level one entries, or all entries in the index. This can help prevent unintended duplicate entries due to differing capitalization (for example *Fonts* and *fonts*). See "Capitalizing Index Entries" on page 254 for more information.

Note: *After you edit an index entry, PageMaker may display a "?" under the Reference heading indicating that the page reference has changed. When you regenerate the index, PageMaker displays the correct page range.*

5 Click Accept to register changes. Continue revising the index, and then click OK to close the dialog box.

Note: If you see two letters instead of a page reference or a cross-reference next to an entry, it means that the entry is somewhere other than on a publication page. These entries will not be included when you generate the index. See "Reviewing and Editing an Index" on page 251 for more information.

Shortcuts for deleting and restoring index entries

The techniques listed below can save time and work when you make extensive edit changes to an index.

Note: When you click Remove to eliminate the selected index entry from the index, you remove the index entry itself but not the index topic. When you generate the index using the Utilities > Create Index command, you have the option of removing unreferenced topics (topics to which no index entries refer).

Additional Show Index dialog box techniques

To do this...	Press this (Macintosh)...	Press this (Windows)...
Delete all entries added since you last clicked Accept or since you opened the dialog box.	Option + Add X-Ref	Alt + Add X-Ref
Restore all entries deleted since you last clicked Accept or since you opened the dialog box.	Option + Remove	Alt + Remove
Delete all page references.	Command + Option + Remove	Ctrl + Alt + Remove
Delete all cross-references.	Command + Shift + Remove	Ctrl + Shift + Remove
Delete all index entries.	Command + Option + Shift + Remove	Ctrl + Alt + Shift + Remove

Capitalizing index entries

You can automate the capitalization of one or more topic levels within a single publication's index, but not within a compiled index of booked publications. To change a specific index entry, you must select it before opening the Capitalize dialog box.

To capitalize index entries:

1 Hold down Command (Macintosh) or Ctrl (Windows) and choose Utilities > Show Index.

This step ensures that the index is compiled from the active publication only.

2 Select a specific entry to modify.

3 Click Capitalize.

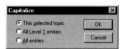

4 Select one of the following, and then click OK:

• The This Selected Topic option capitalizes the first letter in Level 1 of the selected index entry.

• The All Level 1 Entries option capitalizes the first letter in Level 1 for all entries in the index.

• The All Entries option capitalizes the first letter in all levels (Levels 1, 2, and 3) of all entries in the index.

Moving index entries

You can move index markers by cutting and pasting them in story editor. The markers contain the information about the index entry. If you paste the markers in another location, the information for the markers remains the same; however, the page reference will reflect the new position of the markers.

To move an index entry:

1 Select the index marker in story editor.

2 Choose Edit > Cut.

3 Click an insertion point in your story where you want the index marker to appear.

4 Choose Edit > Paste.

Generating an index

You can generate an index at any time. When you generate an index, PageMaker repaginates the publications in the book list and creates a new story containing the compiled index information. If an index already exists in the active publication, you can replace the existing index with the new one.

Note: To create an index for an entire book and place it in a separate publication, you must copy the book list into the index publication before generating the index story. See "Assembling Publications Into a Book" on page 236 for more information.

To generate an index:

1 Open the publication in which you want your index to appear.

2 Create a book list, if necessary, of all the publications you want to include in the index.

3 Choose Utilities > Create Index.

4 Type an index title (up to 30 characters), and then select from the following options:

• Select the Replace Existing Index option to replace an existing index (or the most recent index, if you have more than one) with the index you are generating. Deselect the option to keep the existing index if, for example, you want to compare it with the new one.

• Select the Include Book Publications option to generate a single index for all publications in the book list and renumber the book's pages. Deselect this option if you want to generate an index for the active publication only.

• Select the Remove Unreferenced Topics option to remove topics without page or cross-references when you generate the index. An unreferenced topic may be a topic you imported for cross-referencing but didn't use, or a topic

for which all index entries were deleted, or a topic left in the Topics list after you've removed an index marker in the publication. Selecting this option does not remove the entries in which you elected to Suppress Page Reference.

• Select Include Entires on Hidden Layers only if you want to index stories on hidden layers. Deselect this option if you are using layers to store various text translations and only printing one translation at a time.

5 Click Format to open the Index Format dialog box and specify formatting options, as described in the next section.

6 Click OK, and then place the generated index in your publication.

Note: *If you are going to create a Portable Document Format (PDF) version of your publication, and you edit a placed index story in layout view, be careful not to press the Delete key when the insertion point is directly in front of a topic or page-number reference: this will remove the (invisible) bookmark/hyperlink text token from the publication and disable the PDF file's hypertext link for that index entry or page reference.*

Formatting an index

You can format an index in two ways: specify how text in individual index entries will be arranged or change text style attributes applied to the index story.

Use the Index Format dialog box to specify whether to include section headings in the index, to determine if second- and third-level index entries are placed on their own lines indented under the first-level topic (nested format) or rather presented in a single paragraph with the first-level topic (run-in format). You can also specify which characters will separate parts of an index entry.

The specifications you set apply to the active publication when a publication window is open. To set defaults for all future publications, enter index format specifications when no publication window is open.

To specify an index format:

1 While generating an index, click Format in the Create Index dialog box.

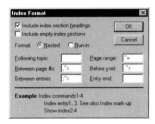

2 Select from the following options:

• Select the Include Index Section Headings option to include headings (symbols, A, B, C, and so on) at the beginning of each index section. When you deselect the option, PageMaker eliminates the section headings but keeps a space between alphabetical sections.

• Select the Include Empty Index Sections option to include all 27 sections–Symbol (where PageMaker puts entries that do not begin with alphabetic characters) plus A through Z–in the index, whether or not they contain any entries. Empty sections will contain the phrase "no entries."

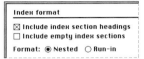

• Select Nested if you want an indented format in which each subentry (level 2 or 3 entry) is a separate paragraph; or select Run-in if you want the levels of your entry to be included in one paragraph. The example at the bottom of the Index Format dialog box illustrates the selected choice.

3 In the remaining text boxes, enter spaces, punctuation marks, or special characters (such as tabs, em spaces, and so on) to separate parts of your index entry as follows:

• Following Topic: Enter characters to separate the entry from the first page number. The default is two spaces.

• Between Page #s: Enter characters to separate multiple page references for a single entry. The default is a comma and a nonbreaking en space.

Note: *A nonbreaking character prevents PageMaker from adding a line break where the character appears. If your index entries appear too crowded in your final index, substitute a regular (breaking) space for the nonbreaking en spaces.*

• Between Entries: Enter characters to separate second- or third-level entries in a run-in format or to separate cross-references in any index entry. The default is a semicolon and a non-breaking en space. (To enter characters after each second- or third-level entry in a nested format, use the Entry End text box.)

• Page Range: Enter characters to separate the first and last numbers in a range of pages. The default is a nonbreaking en dash.

• Before X-Ref: Enter characters to appear before a cross-reference. The default is a period and a nonbreaking en space.

• Entry End: Enter characters to appear at the end of every referenced entry (in nested format) or to follow the last cross-reference in the topic (in run-in format). The default is no character.

The example at the bottom of the Index Format dialog box illustrates the selected choice. See Appendix A for a complete listing of special characters.

About index paragraph styles

When you generate an index, PageMaker creates special index paragraph styles and applies them to the index story.

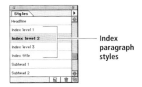

Index paragraph styles

You can edit these index styles just as you edit other styles, but you should not change the index style names. Each time you generate the index, PageMaker looks for the original index style names. If it doesn't find them, PageMaker will re-create the index styles and apply them to the new index. You must then re-apply your revised styles or modify the re-created PageMaker styles.

For more information about styles, see "Using Paragraph Styles" on page 136.

CREATING A TABLE OF CONTENTS

You can create a table of contents (TOC) for any document in PageMaker, regardless of its size or the number of publications involved. You can even have multiple tables of contents in a publication—for example, a list of chapters, and a list of illustrations.

As with an index, each table of contents is a separate story which compiles information, including correct page numbers, from pages throughout a publication or set of booked publications. The process for creating a table includes three main steps:

• Apply the paragraph-level text attribute, Include in TOC, to the paragraphs you want to appear in the table of contents. You can apply the setting to individual paragraphs, but the most efficient method is to apply the setting as part of a paragraph style, so that all paragraphs with a particular paragraph style applied are cited in the table of contents.

• Use the Create TOC command to format and generate the table of contents story.

• Flow the table of contents story and use automatically-generated paragraph styles to change type and paragraph attributes for the table. If you add, delete, or edit entries in the placed table of contents story, you will lose the changes if you later regenerate the table of contents.

Note: If the page numbers in the publications have prefixes, such as A-1 or 1-1, see "Numbering Pages in a Multiple-Publication Document" on page 237 to include the prefixes in your table of contents.

Setting up a table of contents

The most efficient way to set up a table of contents is to determine which paragraphs, such as chapter titles and section headings, should be included. When you define those paragraph styles, you can specify that they be included in the table of contents. You can also mark individual paragraphs for inclusion in the table of contents. Do so sparingly, however, because your table of contents will be more consistent if you include paragraph styles rather than mark individual paragraphs for inclusion. For information about defining styles, see "Using Paragraph Styles" on page 136.

To mark a paragraph style for inclusion in a table of contents:

1 Choose Window > Show Styles.

2 If the style already exists, press Command (Macintosh) or Ctrl (Windows) click it in the Styles palette to edit it. If you are defining a new style, click the new style button in the Styles palette, and then type a name for the style in the Style Options dialog box.

3 In the Style Options dialog box, click Para.

4 Click Include in Table of Contents.

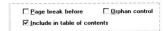

5 Click OK to close each open dialog box.

To mark a paragraph for inclusion in a table of contents:

1 Click an insertion point in the paragraph.

2 Choose Type > Paragraph.

3 Click Include in Table of Contents.

4 Click OK.

Generating a table of contents

Generate and review your table of contents well in advance of your completion deadline. If your table of contents requires editing, edit the actual paragraphs in the publications—not the table-of-contents story—and then generate a new table of contents. If you edit the table of contents story, you'll lose your revisions when you generate a new table of contents.

Note: *If you want to create a table of contents for an entire book and place it in a separate publication, you must copy the book list into the table-of-contents publication before you generate the table-of-contents story. See "Assembling Publications Into a Book" on page 236 for more information.*

To generate a table of contents:

1 Open the table-of-contents publication, or create a new publication.

2 If you are creating a table of contents for multiple publications, verify that the book list is complete and that all publications are listed in the correct order. See "Assembling Publications Into a Book" on page 236 for more information.

3 Choose Utilities > Create TOC.

4 Type a title, up to 30 characters, and then select the appropriate settings, as follows:

• Select the Replace Existing Table of Contents option to replace an existing table of contents with the table of contents you are generating. To generate a new table-of-contents story without altering the existing one, deselect this option.

• Select the Include Book Publications option to create a single table of contents for all publications in the book list and renumber the book's pages. Deselect this option if you want to generate a table of contents for the active publication only.

• Select Include Text on Hidden Layers only if you want to list paragraphs on hidden layers in your TOC. Deselect this option if you are using layers to store various text translations and only printing one translation at a time.

5 Select a formatting option to define the appearance and position of page numbers in the table of contents.

6 In the Between Entry and Page Number text box, specify what characters you want between the table-of-contents entry and its page number.

The default is ^t (caret + t), which tells PageMaker to insert a tab. You can enter up to seven characters in the text box. See Appendix A for a complete list of special characters.

TIP: LEADERS, INCLUDING
DOT LEADERS, ADOPT
THE FORMATTING CHAR-
ACTERISTICS OF THE
SPACE THAT PRECEDES
THEM. YOU CAN EASILY
FORMAT LEADERS BY
INSERTING A SPACE
BEFORE THE LEADER TAB
AND APPLYING TYPE
SPECIFICATIONS TO
THE SPACE.

Unless you choose otherwise, PageMaker places page numbers at the right margin of the table of contents following a row of dot leaders. To change the tab stop or leader, edit the table-of-contents styles as described in the following section.

7 Click OK and, when the loaded text icon appears, place the table-of-contents story as you would any other text.

Note: *If you are going to create a Portable Document Format (PDF) version of your publication, and you edit a placed table-of-contents story in layout view, be careful not to press the Delete key when the insertion point is directly in front of a TOC entry or page-number reference: this will remove the (invisible) bookmark or hyperlink text token from the publication and disable the PDF file's bookmark or hyperlink for that table-of-contents entry or reference.*

Formatting a table of contents

When you generate a table of contents, PageMaker creates styles for the table of contents and applies them to the new table of contents. The TOC style name is based on the original paragraph style name and shares the style attributes of the original paragraph style.

For example, a paragraph formatted with the Heading 1 style appears in the table of contents with the TOC Heading 1 style applied to it.

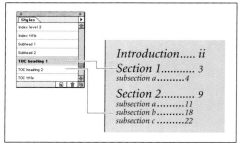

PageMaker creates new TOC styles, then applies those styles to the table-of-contents entries.

You can edit TOC styles just as you edit other styles, but do not change the TOC style names. Each time you generate a table of contents, PageMaker searches for the original TOC style names. If it doesn't find them, it will re-create them and apply them to the new table of contents. You will then need to re-apply your revised styles or modify the re-created PageMaker styles. For information about editing paragraph styles, see "Using Paragraph Styles" on page 136.

Note: *Table-of-contents entries generated from paragraphs without text styles are not assigned styles in the table of contents. The type size and style (such as 10-point bold) of these entries are the same as the original paragraphs.*

ADOBE ACROBAT, INDEXES, AND TABLES OF CONTENTS

PageMaker inserts a bookmark or hyperlink text marker (▲) in front of each index topic and page reference in the placed index story and in front of every table-of-contents entry and page reference in the placed table of contents story. These bookmark/hyperlink text markers are visible only in story editor. PageMaker uses the location of the marker to produce an accurate bookmark or page reference in Adobe Acrobat. You can click the hand tool to view and follow the index and table-of-contents hyperlinks in layout view.

If you generate a Portable Document Format (PDF) version of the publication, the bookmark or hyperlink marker jumps to the corresponding PDF page when you click a bookmark or page number reference in the PDF index or table of contents.

Any changes you make to existing index or table-of-contents entries in the placed story are registered by the hyperlink text marker and so appear in the PDF file; however, any new entries you add to the placed index or table-of-contents story are not detected, and will not have a hyperlink jump in the PDF file.

Note: If you converted a PageMaker 4.x-5.0 publication to PageMaker 6.5 and, before conversion, you made changes to a placed index or table-of-contents story, you must regenerate the index and the table of contents stories after conversion. Otherwise, a PDF version of the publication will not include hyperlink jumps in its index and table of contents.

For more information on creating PDF files, see Chapter 13, "Distributing a Publication Electronically."

Chapter 8: Defining, Applying, and Trapping Color

T his chapter describes how to use color effectively in a PageMaker publication. Whether you are defining, applying, or trapping colors, you need to understand the requirements of your commercial printer. If you are unfamiliar with the process of working with a commercial printer, consult the *Adobe Print Publishing Guide*. If you are using a color management system to ensure the colors you see on screen match output from your printing devices, see Chapter 9, "Color Management." For online publishing color issues, see Chapter 13, "Distributing a Publication Electronically."

About default colors in PageMaker • PageMaker provides the following default colors or object attributes in the Colors palette list.

A [None] removes a color applied in PageMaker to an object or an EPS graphic. Applying [None] to a PageMaker-drawn object changes its fill or line attribute to None; applying [None] to an EPS graphic restores the EPS to its original colors.

B [Paper] refers to the paper color on which you're printing. Objects behind a paper-colored object won't print where the paper-colored object overlaps them. Instead, the color of the paper on which you print shows through. You can edit [Paper] to simulate the actual paper color on your screen, but you can't print the edited color.

C [Black] is a 100% process-color black. Unless you change the default using File > Preferences > Trapping, [Black] overprints when applied to text at type sizes under 24 points, and knocks out when applied to objects. See "Overprinting Colors," on page 277.

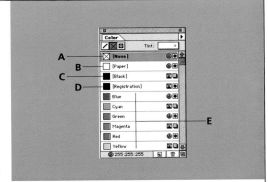

D [Registration] is an attribute that you can apply to design elements so that they'll print on every separation from a PostScript printer. For example, if you want your company name and telephone number to appear outside the page area on every separation, you can apply [Registration] to the text.

E Blue, Cyan, Green, Magenta, Red, and Yellow are provided as a starting point for color work.

SETTING UP PUBLICATION COLORS

Each PageMaker publication contains its own collection of colors, available through the Colors palette. The colors can be ones you define from scratch, select from a color-matching system installed with PageMaker, copy from another publication, or import with an EPS graphic. Several default colors are also provided.

When you add a color to a publication, its name appears in alphabetical order on the Colors palette and in any dialog box, such as the Fill and Stroke dialog box, that lists colors.

When you define a color, you specify whether it is a spot color, process color, or a tint (lightened tones) of a spot or process color. You can also select predefined spot, process, and high-fidelity colors from color-matching systems installed with PageMaker, such as the Trumatch® color library and the PANTONE MATCHING SYSTEM®.

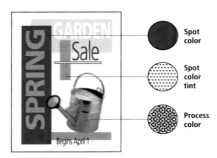

Spot
color

Spot
color
tint

Process
color

Whether you're specifying a spot or process color or selecting a color from a library, do not select a color based on how it looks on your color monitor unless you are working with a color management system supported by PageMaker and you understand its limitations. To specify accurate colors, always use the values printed on process-color charts or the inks printed in spot- and high-fidelity -color swatch books. (Replace your swatch books regularly, as the colors fade over time.) For more information see Chapter 9, "Color Management."

Specifying a spot or process color

Creating new spot and process colors in PageMaker is simple, but to get the printed results you want—the correct colors at a reasonable price—you need to understand how spot and process colors are printed. If you're unfamiliar with the differences between these two types of color, refer to the *Adobe Print Publishing Guide.*

For process-color work, you can use the standard CMYK inks, or, if your commercial printer supports high-fidelity color output, use more than four process inks to define a color. See "About High-Fidelity Colors" on page 267 for more information.

To create a spot or process color:

1 Choose Window > Show Colors.

2 Click the new color button (⊡) at the bottom of the Colors palette or choose New Color from the Colors palette menu.

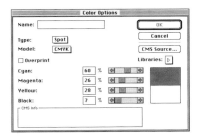

3 Type a name for the color.

4 Choose Spot or Process to specify the type of color.

5 Choose RGB, HLS, or CMYK to select the color model that you want to use.

For process colors, you can use the RGB or HLS model to create a process color, but PageMaker will convert those values to the approximate CMYK values when you print separations or color composites. To control the final printed colors in your publication, use the CMYK model to specify process colors.

6 Type values or adjust the scroll bars to specify the color.

7 Select Overprint if you want objects to which the color is applied to print on top of any objects that appear behind it on a page.

See "Overprinting Colors" on page 277 for more information.

8 Click OK.

About high-fidelity colors

PageMaker supports high-fidelity colors—that is, colors comprised of more than four process inks. High-fidelity colors extend the range of printed colors beyond the range conventional CMYK printing makes possible. Be sure to consult with your commercial printer about using high-fidelity colors since special equipment is required to reproduce them. For more information see "Working With a High-Fidelity Color Publication" on page 286.

There are two ways to specify a high-fidelity color in PageMaker:

• Select colors from one of the two Pantone® Hexachrome™ libraries installed with PageMaker. (One library supports coated paper stock, the other uncoated paper stock.) The Pantone Hexachrome system of high-fidelity colors uses six process inks: Cyan, Magenta, Yellow, Black, Orange, and Green (all names begin with the "Hexachrome" prefix). See "Specifying a Color from a Color-Matching System" on page 268 for more information.

• Create a custom library that defines high-fidelity colors composed of two to eight inks in any combination of inks. See "Creating Custom Color Libraries" on page 284 for more information.

Note: *You can import an object that was created with high-fidelity colors (including EPS graphics saved from PageMaker 6.0-6.5) and thus add high-fidelity colors to a publication in that way. Once you use a high-fidelity color in a publication, you can then copy it into other publications, just as you can with other kinds of colors.*

Specifying a color from a color-matching system

One of the most challenging aspects of specifying colors for commercial printing (whether you're working traditionally or electronically) is reproducing those colors accurately on a printing press. To achieve the closest color match possible, specify standardized spot and process colors from a reputable color-matching system.

PageMaker provides many licensed color-matching systems for spot and process colors. (The colors you can choose from are stored in color libraries, which are accessible from all PageMaker publications.) The vendors who provide color-matching systems have developed rigorous specifications for their colors, which they license to commercial printers. In accepting a

license, the commercial printers agree to maintain the specified color standards so that they can produce consistent colors.

Note: *Before you select a color from a color-matching system, ask your commercial printer which color-matching systems they support, which they prefer, and why. Also, to ensure predictable printed results, select colors from swatch books for the color-matching system rather than relying on their appearance on your monitor.*

To specify a color from a color matching system:

1 Choose Window > Show Colors.

2 Click the new color button (🔳) at the bottom of the Colors palette, or choose New Color from the palette menu.

3 Select a color library name from Libraries.

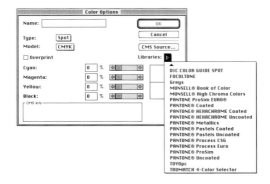

TIP: IF YOU USE CERTAIN COLORS OFTEN TO CREATE PUBLICATIONS, SPECIFY THOSE COLORS ONCE IN A PUBLICATION, AND THEN USE THE CREATE COLOR LIBRARY COMMAND TO STORE THEM IN A LIBRARY YOU CAN OPEN FROM WITHIN ANY PUBLICATION. SEE "CREATING YOUR OWN COLOR LIBRARY" ON PAGE 270 FOR MORE INFORMATION.

If no library names appear, either the color-picker file or the individual library information files are not in the correct location on your hard drive or network server. For more information, see the *Adobe PageMaker 6.5 Getting Started* book.

4 Select a color by clicking on it or by typing its name.

5 Click OK.

Specifying a tint

Adding a second spot color to a publication may increase your printing costs significantly, especially if you print in small quantities. You can, however, expand the palette of colors you use in a publication without affecting your printing costs by creating tints of spot colors. (Tints are screened shades of an ink, and print on the same separation as the ink they are based on.) PageMaker also lets you create tints of high-fidelity and process colors (in effect, lighter process colors) and even tints of other tints.

There are two different kinds of tints:

• *Color-level tints* are defined and named with the New Color command on the Colors palette menu. They appear on the Colors palette and in dialog boxes that display colors.

• *Object-level tints* simply specify the percentage of base color to apply to an object. This kind of tint is not a selectable, editable color as is a color-level tint. You create an object-level tint as you

create or edit an object (you do not define the tint separately as with color-level tints). See "Applying Colors" on page 271 for more information.

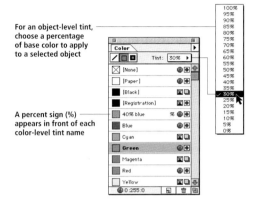

For an object-level tint, choose a percentage of base color to apply to a selected object

A percent sign (%) appears in front of each color-level tint name

PageMaker lets you specify and print tints in 1% increments. (When you specify a tint in 1% increments, the increment subsequently appears on the Tints menu.)

Note: Versions of PageMaker earlier than 6.0 let you apply percentage tints as fills to rectangles and ellipses in preset, 10% increments from the Fill menu. Those fills are converted to object-level tints when you open the publication in PageMaker 6.5.

To create a color-level tint:

1 Choose Window > Show Colors.

2 Click the new color button (🗅) at the bottom of the Colors palette, or choose New Color from the palette menu.

3 From the Type pop-up menu, choose Tint to specify the type of color.

4 Type a name for the tint.

5 Select a spot or process color as the base color for the tint from the Base Color menu.

6 Type a value, or adjust the slider bar to specify the exact percentage of your tint.

7 Click OK.

Copying colors from another PageMaker publication

If you specify colors in one PageMaker publication and want to use them in another publication, you can quickly copy the colors between publications. All the colors in the publication you select are copied into the active publication, where they appear in the Colors palette list and in any dialog box that lists colors.

To copy colors from another publication:

1 Choose Window > Show Colors.

2 Choose Import Colors from the palette menu.

3 Double-click the PageMaker 6.5 publication that contains the colors you want to copy into your current publication.

To copy one color at a time (without copying all colors from a publication), you can drag an object with that color applied to it into another publication.

Note: If one of the colors you're copying has the same name as a color in the active publication but has different color specifications, PageMaker asks if you want to replace the color in the active publication. If you click Cancel, PageMaker doesn't import that color. If the two colors have the same name and specifications, PageMaker ignores the imported color.

Creating your own color library

PageMaker lets you name and save the group of colors on your Colors palette (with the exception of tints), so that you or others in your company or work group use the same colors on future jobs. For example, if your company has a suite of approved colors that it specifies for production jobs, use this feature to save the colors. Then, when you need to use the colors in a different publication, select the library name from the list of libraries within the Color Options dialog box.

To create a color library:

1 Add colors to your Colors palette.

You can use colors from any installed color library, define your own colors, or copy them from other publications.

2 Choose Utilities > Plug-ins > Create Color Library.

3 Enter a name for the library you are creating.

The name you type will appear in the Library menu within the Color Options dialog box. The library's filename (which you see in the Finder or Explorer) can differ.

4 Type the number of rows and columns your library will contain (up to a maximum of ten rows and ten columns).

5 Optionally, in the Notes text box, type comments or information that you want to appear when you click the About button in the Library dialog box.

6 Click a button to save the file, as follows:

• Click Save to store the color library as a binary color file (BCF) named Custom.BCF.

• Click Save As (Macintosh) or Browse (Windows) to specify a different name or location (such as if you are saving to a network to share the file).

PageMaker automatically appends the filename with the BCF extension.

All color files must reside in the Color folder which is either inside the RSRC folder (Macintosh) or inside the language folder (Windows). If you click Save in Step 6, the file is stored in the correct location by default.

APPLYING COLORS

You can apply colors and tints to many different objects, including text and graphics created in PageMaker, and monochrome or grayscale bitmap images (such as TIFF images) or EPS graphics that you import into PageMaker.

As with any other text or graphic attribute, you can set the color for text or PageMaker-drawn graphics as you create them. For example, you can set text color in the Character Specifications dialog box for a story you are about to type. Or, you can apply the color at any time after the text in an object has been created, as described in this section. For information on setting text and graphic attributes as you create them, see "About Formatting Text" on page 121, and "Changing Strokes and Fills" on page 180.

To apply color to most objects (lines, text, and certain imported images), you simply select the text or the object, and then click the color name in the Colors palette. Applying color to PageMaker-drawn rectangles, polygons, or ellipses (including frames) involves slightly different steps because you can apply colors separately to the stroke and the fill of those shapes.

In some instances, you might want to use the Element > Fill and Stroke command rather than the Colors palette. You can use this command to apply fill and stroke colors for PageMaker-drawn rectangles, polygons, or ellipses (including frames); specify whether the stroke or fill of the object should overprint; and also set an object-level tint for either the stroke or the fill.

When you apply a color to an imported EPS graphic, the color of the graphic does not change on-screen; however, the graphic prints on the separations of the applied spot or process color. If you remove a color applied in PageMaker, PageMaker uses the color information in the imported EPS graphic to determine on which separations it prints.

Using the Colors palette • Use the Colors palette to apply colors or view the name or kind of color applied to the selected text or object.

A Click the fill button to change the fill color of a rectangle, polygon, ellipse, or frame.

B Click the stroke button to apply a color to the line on a rectangle, polygon, ellipse, or frame.

C A % sign indicates a color-level tint.

D Indicates color imported with an EPS graphic.

E Displays the CMS applied to the color, its color model, and ink values or tint percentage.

F Cick the both button to apply the same color to both the stroke and the fill.

G Specify a tint percentage to apply object-level tints of the base color applied to the selection.

Icons to right of color names indicate *model*—RGB (■), HLS (■), CMYK (■), or multiple ink (■)—and *type:* Spot (●), or Process (■). To hide these, choose the bottommost commands on the palette menu.

TIP: IN PAGEMAKER FOR THE MACINTOSH YOU CAN USE THE APPLE COLOR PICKER TO EDIT COLORS. CHOOSE WINDOW > SHOW COLORS, SELECT THE COLOR YOU WANT TO EDIT, AND CHOOSE MacOS COLOR PICKER FROM THE COLORS PALETTE MENU.

To apply a color with the Colors palette:

1 Select the object or text you want to color.

You must select text with the text tool to apply color to it.

2 Choose Window > Show Colors.

3 If you selected a frame or a PageMaker-drawn rectangle, polygon, or ellipse in Step 1, specify whether you want to change the stroke, fill, or both.

Stroke color is active   *Fill color is active*   *Both stroke and fill are active*

4 Click the name of the color you want to apply.

5 Optionally, to adjust the percentage of color applied, select a percentage from the Tint menu on the palette to apply an object-level tint.

To apply a color with the Fill and Stroke command:

1 Select the object.

2 Choose Element > Fill and Stroke.

3 Select the type of fill or stroke you want.

For more information, see "Changing Strokes and Fills" on page 180.

4 Select colors for the fill and stroke.

5 Optionally, to adjust the percentage of color applied, type a percentage or choose one from the Tints menu to apply an object-level tint.

6 Select the Overprint option if you want to make a stroke or fill print over colored objects placed behind it when imaging color separations or color composites.

See "Overprinting Colors" on page 277 for more information.

7 Click OK.

REPLACING AND REMOVING COLORS

If you create and apply a color and then decide to use another color instead, you can replace that color with another. PageMaker removes the original color from your publication and applies the replacement color to any objects that have the original color applied. Any tints based on the original color also change to the replacement color.

Replace one color…   *with another color.*

You can also remove colors you don't need. When you remove a color, PageMaker applies the color [Black] to any text or graphic to which the color you remove was applied. Tints that used the removed color change to tints of [Black]. You can remove a color from a PageMaker-drawn graphic, remove a color from the active publication, and remove all unused colors (that is, colors defined but not applied) from the active publication.

Note: *You can't remove the colors [None], [Paper], [Black], and [Registration]. Also note that you can remove colors imported with an EPS graphic only if the EPS graphic itself has been deleted from the publication. To limit the colors imported within EPS graphics, see "Working With Imported EPS Colors" on page 275.*

To replace one color with another:

1 Choose Window > Show Colors.

2 Press Command (Macintosh) or Ctrl (Windows) and click the color that you want to replace.

3 Change the name of the original color to exactly match the name of the color you want to replace it with, and then click OK.

4 When PageMaker displays an alert asking to confirm the change of colors, click OK.

To remove a color from an object:

1 Select the object.

2 For PageMaker-drawn rectangles, polygons, and ellipses (including frames), use the fill and stroke buttons to specify whether it is the fill or stroke color you want to remove.

3 Click the [None] option on the Colors palette.

To remove colors from a publication:

1 Choose Window > Show Colors.

2 Do one of the following:

• Click a color that you want to remove, and choose Delete Color from the Colors palette menu.

• Drag the color from the palette to the trash button (🗑) at the bottom of the palette.

• Choose Remove Unused Colors from the palette menu to delete all colors not applied in the publication (including unused inks specified as part of a high-fidelity color). When you select Remove Unused Colors, a dialog box appears in which you can choose to remove all unused colors at once, or remove unused colors one by one. Alternatively, you can remove unused inks when you print. Just click the Remove Unused button in the Print Color section of the Print dialog box.

EDITING A COLOR

As with paragraph styles, when you edit a color, PageMaker automatically updates any objects to which you applied the color. You can even edit the ink values for a high-fidelity color, but the color adjustments appear only on the color separations—the appearance of the color on screen and in a composite proof does not change.

Note: You can edit the definition of a spot color imported with an EPS graphic, but you cannot change its name or its Overprint setting.

To edit a spot or process color:

1 Choose Window > Show Colors.

2 Press Command (Macintosh) or Ctrl (Windows) and click the name of the color you want to edit.

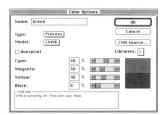

3 Change the name or the color specifications, or whether or not it overprints other colors.

4 Click OK.

When editing a color, you can switch its type from Spot to Process (or vice versa). However, some spot colors, like metallic gold, cannot

be reproduced accurately with process inks. If you choose to convert a spot color to process, you may need to adjust the resulting color values (using a printed swatch book as a reference) for the converted spot color to print as you expect.

To switch a spot color to a process color or vice versa:

1 Deselect all objects, and choose Window > Show Colors.

2 Click the name of the color that you want to change.

3 Choose the Convert to Process or Convert to Spot command from the Colors palette menu.

WORKING WITH IMPORTED EPS COLORS

PageMaker lets you choose what kind of colors are imported with an EPS graphic (and with native Adobe Illustrator 5.x-6.x files you import directly). Since all spot and process colors defined in the document that generated the EPS are embedded with the EPS graphic, the control PageMaker provides can limit the kind of colors added to your publication.

PageMaker also lets you edit individual spot colors imported with an EPS graphic. By editing spot colors in an EPS file so that they merge with colors already in your publication, you reduce the number of color separations PageMaker will produce, saving you time and money.

To control the colors imported with an EPS graphic:

1 Choose File > Place.

2 Select the EPS file you want to import.

3 Press Shift as you double-click the file name. (You do not need to press Shift if the Show Filter Preferences option is selected.)

4 In the dialog box, select options to specify the kinds of colors to include.

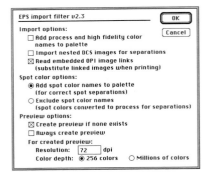

• The Add Process Color Names to Palette option adds the process and high-fidelity colors to the Colors palette.

• In the Preview Options section, select the preference you want. If you are printing to a non-PostScript printer, you can experiment with values greater than the 72 dpi default setting (the optimum value depends on your printer's dpi setting), and select Millions of Colors. Another reason to use higher resolution and greater color depth is if you are exporting to HTML or PDF (where the exported image is derived from the screen preview).

• The Import Nested DCS Images for Separations option includes all the color and image data PageMaker requires to color-separate DCS images embedded in the EPS graphic. If this option is not selected, PageMaker prints a low-resolution version of the DCS image to a single color plate.

• The Add Spot Color Names to Palette option ensures that PageMaker has accurate color data to spot-color separate the EPS graphic.

• The Exclude Spot Color Names option converts the spot colors to their CMYK equivalents during printing. Use this option if you want process-color separations only, and it is acceptable that the process equivalents do not exactly match the original spot colors.

If you import an EPS color that has the same name as a color in your publication, PageMaker displays an alert. If you press Cancel, PageMaker does not import the color or list it in the palette. When you print, however, the EPS color images on the correct separation. If you click OK, PageMaker replaces the color in your publication with the EPS color.

To edit a spot color in an imported EPS file:

1 Choose Window > Show Colors.

2 Press Command (Macintosh) or Ctrl (Windows) and click the name of the color you want to edit.

3 Do one of the following:

• To change the spot color's definition, edit the percentages of its color components (CMYK, RGB, or HLS).

• To make the spot color a process color, choose Process from the Type pop-up menu.

• To merge an EPS spot color with another color, choose Tint from the Type pop-up menu, and then select another color as its base color. Accept the default of *100%* for the tint percentage. This makes the spot-colored areas of the EPS file print on the same separation as the base color.

4 Click OK to save your changes.

Note: *Changes you make to imported EPS spot colors apply when you print on a PostScript printer with the Preserve EPS Colors option deselected in the Print Color dialog box (File > Print). When Preserve EPS Colors is selected, EPS files print using their original colors. This option is not available when printing on a non-PostScript printer.*

OVERPRINTING COLORS

When you print overlapping color objects on a printing press, you typically want the top object to print and the bottom object not to print where the top object overlaps it. In other words, you want the top object to *knock out* the bottom object.

In some cases, however, you do want a spot or process color to overprint another color—to compensate for misregistration, or the unintentional gap or hue shift between colors, that occurs when colors printed from separate plates are misaligned on the printed piece.

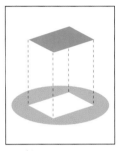 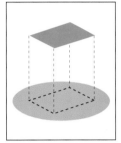

Knocking out   *Overprinting spot colors*

When imaging separations from PageMaker 6.5, all graphics, whether you create them in PageMaker or import them from other programs, knock out objects behind them by default. Black text however, overprints by default provided its type size is smaller than 24 points. There are several ways to override the default behavior if you need to. You can:

• Overprint the fill or stroke of a particular object (called object-level overprinting). Use the Element > Fill and Stroke command to set overprinting as a fill or stoke attribute. See "Applying Colors" on page 271 for more information.

• Overprint a color wherever it is applied (color-level overprinting). Use the Color Options dialog box to specify that a color overprints. Then all objects—imported images, lines, ellipses, polygons, rectangles, even text—to which that color is applied will overprint. See "Specifying a Spot or Process Color" on page 266 or "Editing a Color" on page 275 for more information.

• Specify that all black strokes, or all black fills, or all black text (below a certain point size) either overprint or knock out. Use the File > Preferences > Trapping Options command to control how black objects print. See "Trapping Text" and "Trapping Black" on pages 280-281 for more information.

To overprint a color when applied to some objects but not to others, you can create a 100% tint of the color, and set the tint to overprint and the base color to knock out. (This technique does not work for black objects set to overprint with the Auto-overprint settings in the Trapping Preferences dialog box.)

Note: When PageMaker traps a publication, it does not trap objects set to overprint (because overprinting compensates for misregistration). Make sure you understand the requirements for producing your publication before you override PageMaker's overprinting defaults.

TRAPPING COLORS

In commercial printing, it is crucial to anticipate misregistration. When imaging separations to PostScript output devices, PageMaker can help compensate for potential gaps between two adjoining colors with a technique called trapping. Even if text or a PageMaker-drawn object overlaps several different background colors, PageMaker applies the correct trapping techniques on different parts of the object. The trapping adjustments are made automatically throughout the publication, although PageMaker gives you control over settings that help define how to trap in particular situations. The effects of trapping appear only on color separations and composites; you do not see the results on-screen.

When colors print out of register, visible gaps appear between adjacent objects

What PageMaker traps

PageMaker traps text to underlying PageMaker-drawn objects (rectangles, polygons, lines, ellipses, and filled text frames), and traps PageMaker-drawn objects to each other, but it ignores imported graphics. If you need to trap complex images or illustrations within your publication, use the trapping features in the illustration or image-editing program that created the artwork, or use a separate, trapping program such as Luminous TrapWise®.

For information on basic trapping concepts, refer to the *Adobe Print Publishing Guide*.

How PageMaker traps

PageMaker decides whether to trap based on ink density values, and places the traps based on the neutral densities (relative lightness or darkness) of abutting colors, in most cases spreading lighter colors into adjacent darker colors.

In all cases, PageMaker uses the overprint trapping technique—the trap color prints over the darker of two abutting colors. For this reason, traps are not correctly represented in color-composite output devices.

The trap color PageMaker uses depends on the component inks of the two abutting colors:

• For adjacent process colors that require a trap, PageMaker creates the trap color using only the CMYK values in the lighter color that are higher than those in the abutting color.

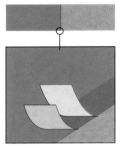

Process color trap

• For a process or spot color next to a spot color, PageMaker uses the lighter color as the trap color.

Trapping a publication

The following procedure presents the basic steps you take to trap a publication. To understand how to set each trapping parameter in PageMaker, read the subsequent sections on setting trap widths, trapping text, trapping black, and other trapping options.

To trap a publication:

1 Open the publication.

2 Choose File > Preferences > Trapping.

3 Click Enable Trapping for Publication.

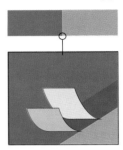

4 Set the trapping options you want, and then click OK.

See the following sections in this chapter for descriptions of each set of options.

5 Choose File > Print.

6 Complete the Print dialog box settings and click Print.

Setting trap widths

The File > Preferences > Trapping command provides two different settings for trap width (the amount of overlap for each trap):

• Default specifies the trap width for trapping all colors except those involving solid black.

• Black Width specifies the trap width for trapping colors next to or under solid blacks. Typically, the Black Width is set 1.5 to 2 times the value of the default trap width.

The value you set for Black Limit determines what PageMaker considers a solid black or a rich black (a process color consisting of solid black with one or more layers of C, M, or Y inks). For details on trapping to black, see "Trapping Black" on page 281. For illustrated details on rich blacks, see the *Adobe Print Publishing Guide*.

Differences in paper characteristics, screen rulings, and press conditions require different amounts of trap. To determine the appropriate trap widths for each job, consult with your commercial printer.

Trapping text

PageMaker traps text characters to underlying PageMaker-drawn graphics (including text frames with fills). A text character overlapping different background colors traps accurately to all colors it overlaps.

Note: *PageMaker does not trap foreground elements to text in the background, nor does it trap text characters to other text characters.*

Make sure you use PostScript or TrueType fonts in your publication because bitmap fonts do not trap. Also note that PageMaker does not trap text in imported graphics.

PageMaker traps text at point sizes greater than the point size you enter for the Trap Text Above option. For black text, you can use the Black Attributes section of the Trapping Options dialog box to specify a threshold below which the text overprints. Text colored black overprints if it is below the point size you specify ; black text above the threshold knocks out the background objects and traps to the background.

Trapping black

The value you type for Black Limit in the Trapping Options dialog box determines what PageMaker considers a solid black and a rich black (a process color consisting of solid black with one or more layers of C, M, or Y inks). The default value of 100% specifies that colors containing 100% black are considered solid blacks.

Note: the Black Width and Black Limit settings do not apply to the Hexachrome Black color used in high-fidelity color publications.

The Black Limit setting is useful when you must compensate for extreme dot gain (as when using low-grade paper stock). These situations cause black percentages lower than 100% to print as solid areas. By screening back (using tints of solid black) blacks or rich blacks and decreasing the Black Limit setting from its default of 100%, you can compensate for dot gain and ensure that PageMaker will apply the proper trap width and placement to black-colored objects.

When trapping involves a color whose percentage of black is equal to or greater than the percentage you specify for Black Limit, PageMaker applies the trap size specified for Black Width to all solid and rich blacks, and uses a keepaway placement for rich blacks. (Keepaways ensure that the rich-black support screens stay away from edges of reversed-out or light elements in the foreground, so that the light elements retain their sharpness.)

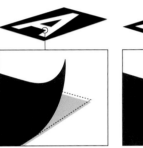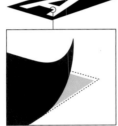

With no black width, support screens may show through.

Adding a black width chokes back the support screens.

You can automatically overprint the strokes, fills, or both, of PageMaker-drawn frames, rectangles, polygons, ellipses, and strokes that are black. If you select the Fill and Stroke options in the Black Attributes section of the Trapping Preferences dialog box, PageMaker overprints the strokes or fills, and does not trap them.

Centerline traps

When colors have similar neutral densities, neither color defines the edge. To trap these colors, PageMaker adjusts the trap position from spreading the lighter color into the darker one to straddling the centerline between them, and thus creates a more elegant trap. (Centerline traps use the highest ink components from both of the abutting colors.)

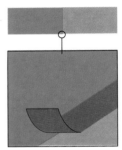

Example of centerline trap

In the Trapping Options dialog box, the Centerline Threshold value determines when PageMaker uses a centerline trap placement. The value refers to the proportion of the lighter color's neutral density value to a darker, abutting color's neutral density value. For example, setting the Centerline Threshold value to 70% causes PageMaker to change the trap placement to centerline when the lighter color exceeds 70% of the darker color in neutral density (lighter color's neutral density ÷ darker color's neutral density > 0.70).

You can specify a threshold from 0% to 100%. At 0%, all traps default to centerline; at 100%, centerline trapping is turned off, forcing a full spread or choke regardless of the neutral density relationship of the adjacent colors.

Adjusting trapping tolerance

Some jobs need only the most extreme color changes trapped, while others require traps for even the most subtle color changes. The Step Limit value specifies the threshold at which PageMaker considers a trap necessary.

To change how much the component inks in abutting colors can vary before causing PageMaker to trap those colors, increase or decrease the value for Step Limit in the Trapping Options dialog box. The lower the Step Limit percentage, the more often PageMaker creates traps between colors.

Trapping and imported graphics

The Trapping Options dialog box includes an option that should be deselected in almost all cases: Traps Over Imported Objects. If a foreground object generated by PageMaker overlaps an imported graphic, chances are that you do not want to trap it, since the object will trap not to the graphic, but to any PageMaker-drawn object underneath it, creating undesirable effects. Trapping over imported objects would be desirable only if the PageMaker element overlapped an evenly-colored area in the imported graphic (such as a cloudless blue sky) and the PageMaker-drawn object beneath the imported object had a matching color applied to it.

Adjusting ink neutral density values

In certain cases, you might want to alter the ink neutral density (ND) values PageMaker uses to determine the precise placement of traps. You can click the Inks Setup button in the Trapping Options dialog box to do so.

The default ND values for process inks are based on the neutral density readings of process ink swatches that conform to industry standards in different parts of the world. The language version of PageMaker determines which standard it adheres to. For example, the ND values for the U.S. English and Canadian versions of PageMaker conform to the Specifications for Web Offset Publications (SWOP) solid ink density values published by the Graphic Arts Technical Foundation of North America. PageMaker lets you adjust process ink neutral densities to match printing industry standards in a different part of the world. Ask your commercial printer what values you should enter in the dialog box.

PageMaker derives the ND values for a spot color from its CMYK equivalent. For most spot colors, the ND values of their CMYK equivalents are accurate enough for proper trap creation. Pastel, metallic, or other spot inks that are not easily simulated using process inks, however, may need their ND values adjusted so that PageMaker traps them correctly. By typing new values, you can ensure that an ink that is observed as darker or lighter is perceived that way in PageMaker; the appropriate trap placement is then applied automatically.

Note: Changing the neutral density for a spot color only affects how that color will trap. It will not change the appearance of that color in your publication.

Use the following guidelines for adjusting ND values:

• Metallic and opaque inks: Metallic inks are usually darker than their CMYK equivalents, while opaque inks typically obscure any ink beneath them. In general, you should set the ND values for both metallic and opaque spot colors much higher than their default values to ensure that these spot colors won't spread.

• Pastel inks: These inks are normally lighter than their process equivalents. You may want to set the ND value for these inks lower than their default values to ensure that they spread into adjacent darker colors.

• Other spot inks: Some spot inks may be significantly darker or lighter than their CMYK equivalents. You will need to compare printed swatches of the actual spot inks to printed swatches of their CMYK equivalents. You can adjust the spot ink's ND value as high or low as necessary.

The most accurate method of determining an ink's ND is to use a commercial densitometer to measure a swatch of the ink color. Read the "V" or visual density of the ink (do not use process filters). If the value differs from the default setting, type the new value in the ND text box, and click Set. You can restore the default for a selected ink by clicking Default.

If you are unsure of the ND of an ink or do not have a commercial densitometer available, obtain its ND value from your commercial printer.

CREATING CUSTOM COLOR LIBRARIES

If the color libraries included with PageMaker do not suit your needs, you can create your own from scratch. This section shows how the Adobe Color File (ACF) format defines a color library.

To create a custom color library:

1 Open the sample Crayon.ACF file in a text-editing program.

The Crayon.ACF file is installed in the Color folder (within the PageMaker RSRC folder).

2 Add values to the key words in the file.

All of the key words must appear in the file in the order shown in the following example, even if you do not include values for them. Callouts on the next page provide more information about each key word.

3 Save the file as a text file.

Make sure that the file is in the Color folder and that ACF is specified as the filename extension.

```
ACF 2.1  Ⓐ

  Sample color library  Ⓑ

  LibraryVersion: 1.0  Ⓒ

  Copyright: ©Adobe Corp.  Ⓓ

  AboutMessage: High-fidelity
  color library sample  Ⓔ

  Names: Partial  Ⓕ

  Rows: 4  Ⓖ

  Columns: 4  Ⓗ

  Entries: 16  Ⓘ

  Prefix:  Ⓙ

  Suffix:

  Type: HiFi  Ⓚ

  Models: RGB CMYK HiFi  Ⓛ

  PreferredModel: HiFi  Ⓜ

  Inks: 6  Ⓝ
  cyan, 15.0, 21.0, .8
  magenta, 75.0, 50.0, .5
  yellow, 0.0, 67.5, .16
  black, 45.0, 90.0, 1.7
  orange, 15.0, 9.33, .34
  green, 75.0, 38.0, .65

  Data:  Ⓞ

  0 28600 28600
  1 0 0 .5
  0.2 0.0 0.8 0.0 0.44 0.0
  Bluespruce
```

A Identifies the library to PageMaker.

B Type a name for the custom library (up to 31 characters). The name you specify appears in the Library menu in the dialog box.

C Type a version number for the library (optional).

D Type any necessary copyright information (optional). This information appears in the Library dialog box that displays the custom library colors.

E Type text to appear when you click About in the Library dialog box (optional).

F Type **Full** to display color names with their prefixes and suffixes. Type **Partial** to display color names only. Type **None** to hide color names.

G Type a number between 1 and 10 to specify the number of rows that appear in the Library dialog box.

H Type a number between 1 and 10 to specify the number of columns in the Library dialog box.

I Type a number indicating the total number of colors in the library. This number must match the number of colors defined in the color library.

J Type a prefix (up to 11 characters), a suffix, or both to be included with each color name when the value for the Names field is Full (optional).

K Type **Spot** to define a library of spot colors, **Process** for a process-color library, **HiFi** for a high-fidelity color library, **Lab** for a CIE Lab color, or **mixed** for a library with spot and process colors.

L Type **CMYK** to define colors by their CMYK (process ink) components; **RGB** to define colors for accurate display on-screen; **HiFi** for a high-fidelity color; or **Lab** for a CIE Lab color. One of the models must be RGB or CMYK for PageMaker to recognize a color, and both RGB and CMYK must be present if Hi-fi is too. When you list more than one model, separate them with a space or a tab. The order in which you list the models is the order in which you'll need to specify the values for each color.

M Type **CMYK, RGB, HiFi,** or **Lab** to specify the default color model. Type just one model. If HiFi is the preferred model, you must also specify HiFi for the Type field.

N This field is required only if you are specifying high-fidelity colors. Type the number of inks required to reproduce the colors. Then type the following information for each ink:

Ink name (up to 31 characters long).

Angle: used to print halftone screens (optional). Type a value from 0 to 360.

Frequency: indicates the screen ruling to use in a halftone (optional). Type a value from 0 to 1000.

Density: sets the neutral density of the ink for trapping (optional). Type a value from 0.000 to 10.000.

O Define and name colors for your library. Type the values on the line after the keyword. Use the following guidelines to define colors:

For RGB color, specify the values for red, green, and blue with values from 0–65535 where 0 = 0% and 65535 = 100%. Type the color name (up to 17 characters) below the CMYK and/or RGB values.

For CMYK color, specify the values for cyan, magenta, yellow, and black with values from 0–1, where 0 = 0% of the ink and 1 = 100% of the ink.

For high-fidelity color, specify the values for each ink with values from 0–1 where 0 = 0% of the ink and 1 = 100% of the ink. You must list a value for each ink, and include RGB and CMYK values.

For lab color, specify values for L, a and b. L range is from 0–100. The a and b range is from -127 to 127. A fractional value rounds to the nearest integer.

For mixed colors, each set of color values must be followed by the type of corresponding color type. For example, after typing **spot color values**, type **spot**, and then type the name of the color.

Working with a high-fidelity color publication • High-fidelity color is a variety of print processes designed to achieve a larger gamut range than traditional CMYK color output processes. PANTONE Hexachrome is a system that uses 6 inks in combination to accurately simulate over 90% of the current PANTONE solid and spot inks. Those inks are: cyan, magenta, yellow, black, orange, and green (CMYKRG). Although Hexachrome uses 6 inks, only a maximum of 4 inks will be used at one time in combination (cyan and orange use the same screen angle; likewise, magenta and green use the same screen angle). Hexachrome CMYK inks are different than traditional CMYK inks.

Set up your PageMaker Hexachrome colors and CMS preferences

• Choose colors from a Pantone Hexachrome color library (there's one for coated and one for uncoated stock; for best results, use a high-quality, coated paper). Because there are no source profiles available, these colors cannot be color-managed. Use the PANTONE Hexachrome Color Selector Guides (available from Pantone) to get the most consistent color results. You can also create a custom high-fidelity color library.

• Always use the Hexachrome black rather than PageMaker's default Process black. Since Hexachrome black does not automatically overprint objects, create new color that is a 100% tint using Hexachrome black as the base color, set the new color to overprint, and apply that color to the elements you need to overprint.

• For CMS preferences, choose File > Preferences > General, and click CMS Setup. Turn CMS on, and select the Kodak-ICC CMS (currently the only system that supports Pantone Hexachrome).

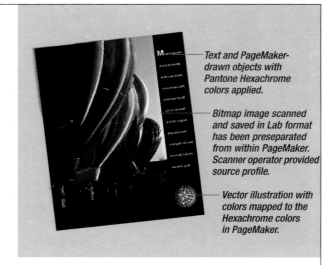

Text and PageMaker-drawn objects with Pantone Hexachrome colors applied.

Bitmap image scanned and saved in Lab format has been preseparated from within PageMaker. Scanner operator provided source profile.

Vector illustration with colors mapped to the Hexachrome colors in PageMaker.

• In the CMS Setup Preferences dialog box, select Pantone Hexachrome CMYKRG for the separations printer destination profile. Two destination profiles are available for different press operating conditions: Normal SID Output (Solid Ink Density), which produces the clearest, sharpest images and closely matches the SID and dot-gain characteristics of the inks as printed in the Pantone Hexachrome Color Selector; and High SID, which has a slightly wider tolerance for heavy inking (especially black) on press. It also produces excellent separations with minimal loss of clarity and sharpness in images.

• Also in the CMS Setup Preferences dialog box, choose a calibrated monitor profile from the Monitor pop-up menu, and choose "Separations printer" from the Monitor Simulates pop-up menu. These settings will result in the closest possible color match on screen.

Create and prepare imported graphics

Create and trap vector illustrations in an illustration package, keeping the following points in mind:

• Since most illustration packages do not support Hexachrome inks, use the overprinting method for traps; that way, when the colors you use in the art are mapped to Hexachrome inks in PageMaker, the trap still works. Note that, to date, no post-processors trap Hexachrome colors.

• Use spot colors in the illustration, and, after importing into PageMaker, make each imported spot color a 100% tint of a Hexachrome color in the publication. See "Working with Imported EPS colors" on page 275 where this technique is described in detail.

• For bitmap images, work with the scanner operator to bypass CMYK conversion (which defeats the purpose of the high-fidelity model) to create a raw-RGB or Lab TIFF image (to preserve the largest possible color gamut). Ask the scanner operator to create and provide a device profile for the scanner when the images are scanned, or to provide the device profile to which the operator calibrates the scanner.

• Choose File > Place, select the bitmap image in the list of files, and click CMS Source. In the CMS Source Profile dialog box, choose Kodak ICC for This Item Uses, and then assign the source profile provided by the scanner operator (or, for Lab TIFF images, you can assign the Adobe: Photoshop CIELab profile).

Output the PageMaker publication

• For faster separation time, preseparate bitmap images using the File > Export > Graphic command (be sure to select the Relink to New Image option).

• In the Printing dialog boxes, ensure that the Preserve EPS Colors option is deselected.

• If you use traditional screening, do not change the default screen frequency of 175 lpi for the Hexachrome inks.

Proofing and commercial printing

Keep in mind that colors on-screen and on proofs are only approximate.

• Print laser separations to verify that all objects separate to the correct plates.

• For off-press proofing, use either the AGFA Proof System II or the DuPont Chromalin proofing systems.

• If your proofs reveal a need to fine-tune color, remember that PageMaker 6.5 lets you edit the ink values of Hexachrome colors directly in PageMaker (choose Color Options from the Colors palette menu with the appropriate color selected). The edits do not appear on-screen; they only appear in the separations.

Where to go for more information on high-fidelity

• The *High-fidelity Production Guide*, a PDF document from Adobe, is available in the Adobe Technical Info folder on the PageMaker 6.5 CD-ROM. It describes in greater depth how to produce high-fidelity output using PageMaker 6.5; it also includes a listing of other sources of information. Use Adobe Acrobat Reader or Exchange to view and print the file, which is named "HifiProdGuide.PDF."

• The *Adobe Print Publishing Guide*, included with PageMaker, provides guidance on working with your printer to derive the best results for your project. Coordination with your printer is especially important for producing high-fidelity publications.

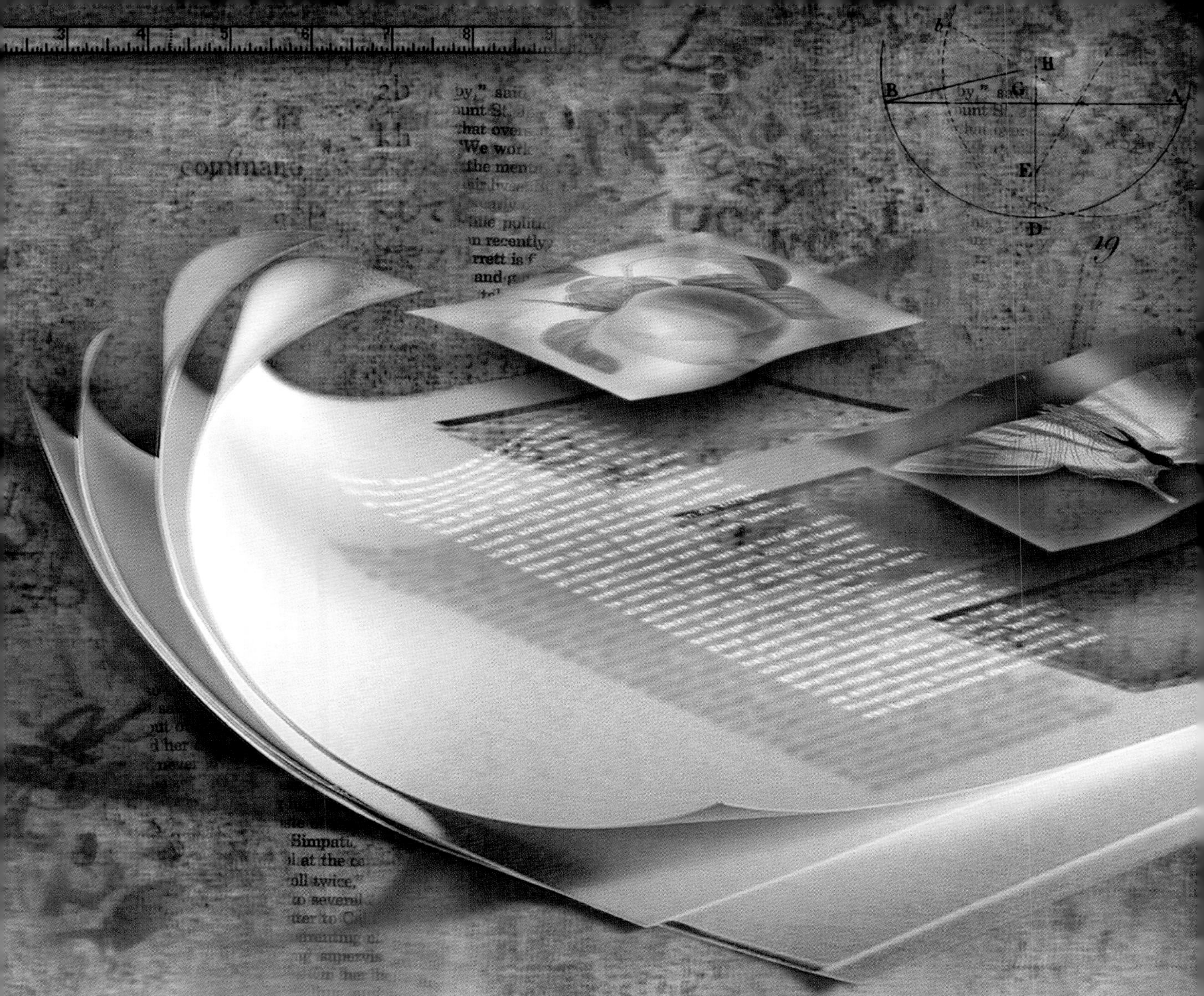

Chapter

9

COLOR MANAGEMENT

CHAPTER 9: COLOR MANAGEMENT

PageMaker's open architecture lets you use a compatible color management system (CMS) to better manage the colors displayed on-screen and printed in your final output. PageMaker 6.5 supports two International Color Consortium (ICC) compatible systems: the Kodak Digital Science Color Management System on Macintosh and Windows, and the ColorSync 2.x standard on the Macintosh. How you use a color management system with PageMaker depends on your particular workflow and your publication. This chapter describes a CMS, how it can improve your output, and how to use a CMS with PageMaker.

The color publishing process is an exercise in trying to reproduce color on a series of devices that have progressively diminishing color-reproduction capabilities. The human eye discerns a wide color spectrum, while a color monitor displays only a fraction of those colors, and a printing press reproduces even fewer colors. A color management system adjusts the color relationships between devices to ensure consistent color throughout the publishing process.

Most color is device-dependent; the color that you get depends on the device (monitor, printer, scanner, or press) that produces it. On open systems—computer systems with components from a variety of vendors—the color you see at one stage of design is not the same as the color you see at another stage unless you use color management.

WHAT IS A CMS?

Each device you use to create a publication—scanner, monitor, desktop printer, and printing press—can reproduce or display a limited set of colors. The spectrum of color that a device can reproduce is called its color gamut. The color gamut of the many devices is recorded by the manufacturer in a file called a device profile.

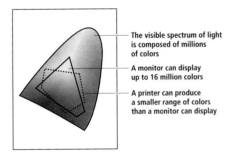

The visible spectrum of light is composed of millions of colors

A monitor can display up to 16 million colors

A printer can produce a smaller range of colors than a monitor can display

A CMS translates colors from the color gamut, or color space, of one device into a device-independent color model, and then fits that color information to another device's color gamut by a process called color mapping. A CMS obtains the color characteristics of each device from its device profile, and then maps this device-dependent color information between devices.

Color management is most important with devices that have small color gamuts, such as desktop printers. The smaller the color gamut, the more valuable it is to reconcile color gamut differences with a CMS.

There are several methods that a CMS can use to reconcile the color gamuts of various devices. One method preserves the relationship between colors by shifting all colors into the device's color gamut. Another method maps only the out-of-gamut colors to colors that the device can produce without preserving the relationships between the colors.

Using a CMS with PageMaker 6.5: An overview

- Determine how to use a CMS.
- Create a work environment for color management.
- Calibrate your input devices.
- Choose a CMS.
- Set CMS preferences.
- Define colors using a CMS.
- Import bitmap images using a CMS.

DETERMINING HOW TO USE A CMS

How you use a CMS depends on the type of colors you use, the quality and accuracy of your devices, and your expectations of final output quality. A CMS can manage colors in many different ways, but how you use a CMS for managing colors in a publication can be broken down into roughly two different workflows.

CMS-oriented workflow

A CMS-oriented workflow relies on the quality of color information provided by your input devices and device profiles. This color information, and the corrections made by the device profile, influences how accurate the color appears on your monitor and how well the final output device reproduces the color.

Correct color values—the numeric values that define a color—are critical to the success of a CMS-oriented workflow. The accuracy of the color coming into the CMS greatly influences the colors that print. Your input devices must accurately represent color values, and those color values depend on how well the devices and the device profiles work together.

Output-oriented workflow

An output-oriented workflow focuses on final color produced with specified inks. Colors and bitmap images are converted to ink values early in the process. Preseparated bitmap images, such as CMYK TIFF images or DCS files, can be imported.

Colors are specified using CMYK and spot color libraries or swatch books, not on the basis of how colors appear on-screen. You can also use a CMS to print an accurate representation of your publication on your desktop color printer.

CREATING A WORK ENVIRONMENT FOR COLOR MANAGEMENT

Your immediate work environment influences how you see color on your monitor and on your final output. You must control the colors and light in your work environment to get accurate color by doing the following:

• Control the ambient light. Sunlight can change the way colors appear on your screen, as can artificial lighting. Keep shades drawn. View your publication in an environment that provides consistent light. To eliminate the yellow cast from fluorescent lighting, consider installing 5000 degree Kelvin lighting.

• View your publication in a room with neutral-colored walls and ceiling. A room's color can effect the perception of both monitor color and printed color. The best color for a viewing room is polychromatic gray.

• Match the light intensity in the room you use to the light intensity of your monitor. View continuous-tone art, printed output, and bitmap images on-screen under the same intensity of light.

• Remove background patterns on your desktop. Busy or bright patterns surrounding an image interfere with accurate perception of the colors in your publication. Select a desktop color scheme of neutral grays.

• On your monitor, the Contrast knob changes overall intensity, and the Brightness knob changes the level of black. Display an image that is predominantly black. Adjust Brightness so that the monitor reproduces true black on the screen. Make sure that the adjustment isn't so high that the black image appears to be surrounded by dark gray. Put a piece of tape over the Brightness knob so the setting does not change, and then adjust the Contrast knob to suit your preference for display intensity. For more information on monitor calibration, see "Calibrating Your Monitor" on page 295.

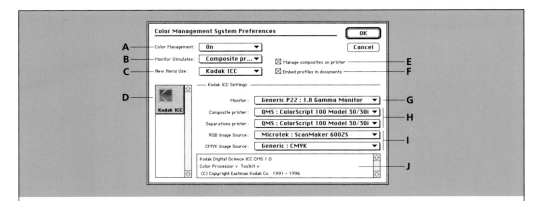

Setting color management system preferences • You can select a CMS and choose device profiles for your system components. The default settings are used when you import a bitmap image or create a color in PageMaker.

A Select on or off from the pop-up menu.

B Select Composite Printer or Separations Printer to proof your color publication on-screen. The color gamut of the selected device is used to display on-screen colors. Select None to turn off this feature.

C Choose a CMS to have PageMaker automatically assign device profiles to new colors and imported bitmap images. Choose None to turn off the automatic assignment of device profiles.

D Select a color management system from those installed on your system and display its current settings.

E Select this option if you are printing composites to a PostScript Level 2 device, and want to let the device perform the color management using its default color rendering dictionary. Be sure to deselect the option if you want to assign a profile from the Composite pop-up menu (otherwise the menu reads "Printer's Default" and is unavailable).

F Select the Embed Profiles in Document option to store the source profiles in a publication. Use this option only when you save a PageMaker file for another computer, and deselect it immediately after. If you leave this option selected, it will cause a significant drop in performance.

G Select a device profile that describes the color characteristics of your primary monitor.

H Select device profiles that describe the color characteristics of your composite and separations printers.

I Select device profiles for your scanner or other devices you use to create RGB and CMYK images.

J The information window gives additional specifications about the device profile or CMS selected.

• After you create a publication using a CMS, retain the files, proofs, and the final printed publication. These materials can be used as references to understand how colors defined using a CMS appear in the final printed piece.

CALIBRATING YOUR MONITOR

Manufacturer's device profiles are based on a particular set of calibration settings for a given monitor. To effectively use a color management system, you need to calibrate the monitor you use to match the expected performance defined in the device profile. You can also create a custom device profile tailored to your monitor. The quality of your results depends on how closely your monitor matches the device profile.

Several monitor calibration tools are available. Active feedback tools from Radius and Barco can interpret the colors your monitor displays and create a custom device profile for your monitor.

CHOOSING A CMS

PageMaker lets you use compatible CMS software produced by a variety of manufacturers. A CMS used with PageMaker can manage colors in graphics and bitmap images that are not already targeted to a final output device. A CMS can manage colors applied to PageMaker objects and colors in RGB bitmap images, and spot colors in EPS files.

A CMS can color manage the RGB screen image of a CMYK TIFF file so that it is color corrected for output to a color composite proofing device. You can also use a CMS to change the targeted final output device of a CMYK TIFF if necessary. You cannot color manage DCS files. WMF and PICT files are not color managed because the image colors are rendered by the printer driver when printed.

PageMaker 6.5 comes with support files for two color management systems: the Kodak Digital Science Color Management System and the Apple ColorSync Color Management System (Macintosh only).

• The Kodak CMS is complete and ready to use after you install it.

• To use the Apple ColorSync CMS in PageMaker 6.5 for the Macintosh, the ColorSync 2.x control panel device and extension (both available from Apple Computer) and profiles must be installed and running at the time that you start PageMaker; you can then select ColorSync as the CMS you want to use for a publication.

SETTING CMS PREFERENCES

Before you start a publication, select a default CMS and set the default device profiles for all devices. The default device profiles should be changed when you change input devices, monitors, or output devices.

Device profiles are designed for a specific device. A custom device profile created for your input device or monitor provides the best results. A manufacturer's device profile can provide good results, depending on how well your device fits the characteristics of the input device or monitor it was created for. Avoid using a device profile not intended for use with your input device or monitor; using the wrong device profile when selecting your CMS preferences can produce unacceptable results in your final output.

Choosing device profiles

You can choose device profiles for the following devices:

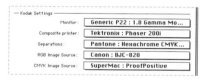

- The Monitor option lets you select the device profile that matches your monitor type.

- The Composite Printer option lets you select the device profile that matches the output device you use for color composite output. Choose a printer, such as a color wax transfer printer, that prints all page elements and colors on one page.

Note: If you are printing composites to a PostScript Level 2 device, and you want the device to perform color management using its default color rendering dictionary, select the Manage Composites on Printer option. (Be sure to deselect that option if you want to assign a profile from the Composite pop-up menu; otherwise the menu reads "Printer's Default" and is unavailable.)

- The Separations Printer option lets you select the device profile for the output device you use to create color separations. For example, if you are using the Kodak CMS and your publication will be printed by a commercial printer, choose one of the SWOP device profiles—either Kodak SWOP Proofer CMYK- Coated stock or Kodak SWOP Proofer CMYK- Uncoated stock. This profile ensures that the final printed output made from the film separations will meet SWOP standards for coated and uncoated stock.

- The RGB Image Source and the CMYK Image Source options let you select the device profiles for the devices you use to create RGB and CMYK bitmap images. The Default RGB device profile can be a scanner or a monitor device profile. The Default CMYK device profile can be any device you use to produce CMYK bitmap images.

Note: *If you color-correct images and save them as RGB bitmap images using image-editing software such as Adobe Photoshop, the default RGB device profile should match your monitor's device profile.*

To choose a CMS and to select CMS preferences:

1 Choose File > Preferences > General, click CMS Setup, and choose On from the Color Management pop-up menu.

2 Choose one of the following options:

• If you want PageMaker to automatically color-manage new colors and imported bitmap images, choose a CMS from the New Items Use pop-up menu.

• If you prefer to color-manage bitmap images and new colors individually, choose None from the New Items Use pop-up menu.

• If you are printing composites to a PostScript Level 2 device, and want the device to perform color management using its default color rendering dictionary, select the Manage Composites on Printer option.

3 Click the icon of the CMS you want to use, and then select the device profile for each device you use. Click OK.

Adding new device profiles

The PageMaker installer lets you choose from device profiles for the most commonly used equipment, but because of the large number of equipment manufacturers, it is not possible to supply profiles for every device. If your device was not listed when first installing device profiles, use the default CMS configuration or contact the device manufacturer to obtain a device profile.

You can create custom device profiles tailored to your input device using the Kodak Digital Science Color Calibration kit or other ICC-compliant editors. A custom profile can compensate for variations in a device, so it is more accurate than a generic device profile.

To add additional profiles to your system:

1 On the Macintosh, copy all profiles (including Kodak-ICC profiles) to the ColorSync folder in the Preferences folder within your System folder. On Windows 95, copy files into the Windows\System\Color folder. On Windows NT, copy files into the Windows\System32\Color folder.

2 Restart PageMaker.

Simulating printer colors on a monitor

Monitor simulation displays an on-screen approximation of the colors your printer can reproduce. The CMS calculates the exact colors to be displayed on your monitor

The Monitor Simulates option lets you select either your composite printer or your separations printer to use as the color gamut for displaying on-screen colors. Your monitor then displays colors in the gamut of the selected output device.

If your publication will be printed by a commercial printer, choose the separations printer for your Monitor Simulates setting.

To set monitor simulation:

1 Choose File > Preferences > General, and then click CMS Setup.

2 Choose one of the following options:

• To turn on monitor simulation, choose either Composite Printer or Separations Printer from the Monitor Simulates pop-up menu.

• To turn off monitor simulation, choose None from the Monitor Simulates pop-up menu.

3 Click OK to exit the CMS Preferences dialog box, and then click OK again.

DEFINING COLORS USING A CMS

You manage spot colors and process colors in different ways. Colors that you create in PageMaker can be color-managed by a CMS, either by assigning a source profile to the color or by having the CMS automatically assign a source profile to the color using the New Items Use option. A color management system adjusts the component values of a color to represent the color gamut of the color's source profile.

Colors defined in the RGB or HLS color models use the monitor device profile as the source profile. If these colors are converted to process colors, the CMYK values are estimates of the on-screen color. Colors defined in the CMYK color model use the separations printer device profile. The on-screen color is the RGB equivalent of the final output color.

Color managing spot colors

You can color manage spot colors in imported EPS files and from color-matching libraries to get a closer approximation of the color on your proofing device and monitor. If you are creating spot-color separations, changing the RGB color values will not affect the printed color because spot colors are reproduced with premixed inks and do not rely on settings in PageMaker. Changing the RGB color values of a spot color in PageMaker can dramatically change the color if you convert the spot color to a process color.

Color manage spot colors when you want the displayed color or the color output on your proofing device to be a close approximation of the final printed color. Remember that it is difficult to match the color of a spot color on-screen or on a proofing device because of the differing color models. For more information on color models, see the *Adobe Print Publishing Guide*.

To assign a source profile to a spot color:

1 Choose Windows > Show Colors.

2 Choose New Color from the Colors palette menu, and type a name for the new color in the Color Options dialog box.

3 Define a color using one of the following techniques:

• Define your own color by selecting the Type, Model, and color values for the color.

• Select a spot color from a predefined color-matching library.

Color managing a publication • A color management system (CMS) is a color translator that interprets color between various devices, such as scanners, color monitors, and printers.

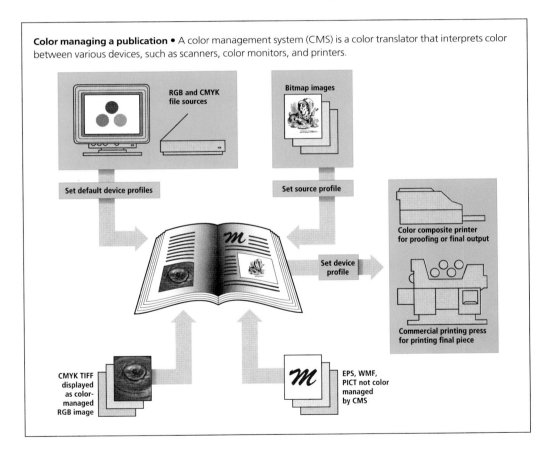

RGB and CMYK file sources

Bitmap images

Set default device profiles

Set source profile

Color composite printer for proofing or final output

Commercial printing press for printing final piece

Set device profile

CMYK TIFF displayed as color-managed RGB image

EPS, WMF, PICT not color managed by CMS

4 Click CMS Source in the Color Options dialog box.

5 Select a Source Profile based on the following guidelines:

• If you are creating an RGB spot color, choose the same device profile you assigned to your monitor as the source profile for your new color.

• If you are creating a CMYK spot color, choose the same device profile that you assigned to your Separation printer as the source profile for your new color.

6 Click OK to return to the Color Options dialog box.

7 Click OK.

To have a CMS automatically assign a source profile to new spot colors:

1 Choose File > Preferences > General, and then click CMS setup.

2 Choose the color management system to use for assigning source profiles to new colors from the New Items Use option. PageMaker assigns the Monitor profile to new RGB colors and the Separation Printer device profile to new CMYK colors. To turn off color management for new colors, choose None.

3 Click OK to exit the CMS Preferences dialog box, and click OK.

Color-managing process colors

When defining a process color using a CMS, select your colors from a process color-matching library. You should not change the CMYK values of process colors since the values assigned to these library colors are predefined to achieve the best printed results.

The CMYK values assigned to color-managed process colors are critical to color accuracy when printing your publication on a commercial press. Process colors should always be created with the final output device in mind. When defining a process color to be color-managed, always choose as the source profile the same device profile as your Separation printer. Current CMSs do not color-manage process colors in imported EPS files.

USING HIGH-FIDELITY COLOR WITH A CMS

PageMaker can create separations for up to eight inks in any combination. This includes both process and spot colors, varnishes, and high-fidelity colors.

High-fidelity color printing uses additional process inks to increase the gamut of printed colors by as much as 20%. For example, PANTONE Hexachrome colors are reproduced using cyan, magenta, yellow, black, orange, and green inks. High-fidelity printing solutions often use

Frequency Modulation (FM) or stochastic screening. For more information on high-fidelity color, see "Working with a High-fidelity Color Publication" on page 286.

PageMaker, using the Kodak CMS, can separate high-fidelity colors defined with any combination of custom inks, including inks in high-fidelity color systems. To create high-fidelity colors, you can either select the colors from a high-fidelity color library, such as the PANTONE® Hexachrome™ library, or define your own high-fidelity color library using specifications from a high-fidelity color swatch book.

In PageMaker, you can define high-fidelity colors and separate them with high-fidelity inks without choosing a Separations Printer device profile that supports high-fidelity color. You can also define spot and process colors, and image them to an output device using a device profile that supports high-fidelity color.

If you want to edit a high-fidelity image in Photoshop, you must take special steps to preserve the colors. For more information, see "Preseparating Bitmap Images" on page 302.

IMPORTING BITMAP IMAGES USING A CMS

A color management system's strength is in correctly representing color in bitmap images. Bitmap images can originate from a variety of sources, such as a drawing or paint program, or a scanner. A bitmap image can have a CMS source profile contained in the file if it was created with an application using a CMS. A source profile indicates to a CMS the color gamut used to produce colors in the file. This source profile can be from any installed CMS on your computer, or images can have a different source profile from a CMS on a different computer. For more information, see "Importing Photo CD Images" on page 306.

When you place a bitmap image and a color management system is selected in the New Items Use option, PageMaker reads the image and applies a CMS and source profile based on the following criteria:

• If the bitmap image was created using any Kodak Digital Science-supported application, PageMaker applies the Kodak CMS and the source profile.

• If the source profile specified in the image file is not available, PageMaker applies the default CMS and selects the default profile.

• If the bitmap image file does not specify a source profile, PageMaker applies the default CMS and the source profile that matches the color model of the image, either the RGB Image Source or the CMYK Image Source. If you need to change the source profile setting determined by PageMaker, you can identify what type of image it is, based on the preferred profile applied, and then select the correct CMS and source profile.

If you need to color-correct an imported bitmap image in an image-editing application, such as Adobe Photoshop, you may need to update its source profile after editing. Incremental changes, such as changing size or cropping, do not require resetting the source profile, but any color changes, such as retouching or color correction, require changing the source profile of the image to the device profile of your monitor.

Note: If you plan to print a bitmap image on different output devices, always save an RGB or Lab copy of the bitmap image. RGB and Lab color models represent larger color gamuts than most output devices can reproduce, so the bitmap image retains the maximum amount of information before being mapped to a smaller color gamut for output.

To apply a source profile when placing a bitmap image:

1 Choose File > Place.

2 Select the graphic you want to import, and then click CMS Source.

3 Select a device profile from the Source Profile pop-up menu.

4 Click OK.

To select a source profile for a bitmap image in a publication:

1 Select the bitmap image. You can also select multiple bitmap images with the same color space by holding down Shift while you click each image.

2 Choose Element > Image > CMS Source. You can also choose a different CMS or turn color management to None for the bitmap image.

3 Select a device profile from the Source Profile pop-up menu.

4 Click OK.

PRESEPARATING BITMAP IMAGES

PageMaker can convert bitmap images from RGB to CMYK or high-fidelity ink separations, or it can retarget a CMYK TIFF image to another CMYK (or high-fidelity) output device. Converting images to CMYK and targeting the bitmap image to the proper output device before printing can shorten the time it takes to image a file. Color management must be on to convert or retarget bitmap images.

Preseparating bitmap images lets you change from a CMS-oriented workflow to an output-oriented workflow by converting your color-managed bitmap images into separated, device-dependent images. Preseparate bitmap images in these cases:

- You are ready to create separations.

- The next step in your publication process does not support color management. For example, if you submit the files for trapping or other pre-press work using dedicated postprocessing programs.

- You are going to create CMYK images to store on an OPI server.

- You are not going to make any on-screen changes to the bitmap image.

PageMaker creates a new CMYK or high-fidelity color TIFF file (or a DCS file) from the original bitmap image. The new image can contain a preview image that you can color-manage. You can automatically link to the preseparated file or maintain the link to the original file.

Note: PageMaker separates the image using the Separations Printer device profile specified in CMS preferences. No preseparated image is created if the source profile for the TIFF image matches the device profile of the Separations Printer.

The Source Space and Separation Space information in the Export Graphic dialog box provide information on the device profile assigned to the bitmap image and the device profile that will be used to create the separated image. For best results, verify that these profiles are accurate before you create the separated image.

You can choose to create a screen preview that is saved with the preseparated image file. If a screen preview is not created when preseparating, PageMaker must analyze the entire bitmap image to create a screen preview when a preseparated image is imported. A preseparated bitmap image with a screen preview imports faster than one without a screen preview.

If you choose not to include a screen preview for images preseparated using a multi-ink device profile such as Hexachrome, the screen preview is a gray box when you import the preseparated image.

To preseparate a bitmap image:

1 Choose File > Preferences > General, click CMS Setup, and make sure the correct CMS is turned on, and that the correct profile is selected for Separations Printer.

2 In the publication, select the bitmap image you want to separate.

3 Choose File > Export > Graphic.

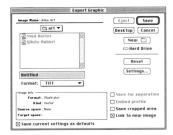

4 Type a name for the separated file, and choose a folder in which to store the file.

5 For Save as Type, select TIFF or DCS.

Typically you'll select the TIFF format, and only select DCS as the output format if you want to use Adobe Photoshop to edit an image containing high-fidelity inks. To do that, you'll need to use the Channel 24 plug-in (available separately from VISU technologies BV) with Macintosh Photoshop 3.0.4 or later. For information on the Channel 24 plug-in, use your Web search engine to find the VISU technologies website.

6 Select the Save for Separation option.

7 Select the Embed profile option if the image will be used in publications on other computers which may lack that profile. Deselect the option if you want to keep file size to a minimum, or if a high-fidelity profile is specified for your

separations printer, or if the source image is auto-relinked to the preseparated image and won't be reimported elsewhere.

8 Click Settings and specify options as follows:

For TIFF images:

• For Compression, select the method you prefer. See "Compressing and Decompressing a TIFF Image" on page 217 for details.

• For Preview, choose Draft to save a low-resolution (36 dpi) screen preview with the image, Best to save a 72 dpi screen preview with the image, or Do Not Store in Image for the smallest file size. If a high-fidelity profile is specified for your separations printer, the Do Not Store in Image option uses a gray box for a screen preview; otherwise the screen preview is generated from the source image.

• For Data Format, choose Optimize for Separation.

• Select the Strict TIFF 6.0 Compliance option if you want the preseparated TIFF optimized for best compatibility with other applications. To ensure best compatibility with PageMaker, make sure the option is not selected.

For DCS images:

• For Display Preview and for Composite Preview, specify the way you want the DCS to display on screen (Display Preview) and in print (Composite Preview); the Full Size option sets the image to display and print at its full resolution, which is set by the application that created it. A full size preview can create a large image file, and slow down screen display and composite print times.

• For PostScript Encoding, select Binary (unless you are using Windows PageMaker) to get the best performance and the smallest image size, or ASCII to get the best compatibility with other applications, but with an image size twice as large as the Binary option produces. (ASCII is recommended if printing from Windows.)

• For Format, choose Multiple Files if you want a TIFF created for each separation plate required to print the image (plus one composite and screen preview EPS), or Single File to keep the image information together in one file.

9 Click OK in the Settings dialog box.

10 Select Save Current Settings as Default if you intend to save additional images for separation and want to apply the same settings you've applied during this procedure to those other images.

11 If it is not selected, click Relink to New Image to replace the original bitmap image in the publication with the new separated file.

12 Click Export.

COLOR MANAGING PAGEMAKER 4.X-5.0 PUBLICATIONS

When you convert a PageMaker 4.x-5.0 publication to PageMaker 6.5, PageMaker does not automatically apply the default CMS, so elements are not color managed in the converted publication. You can change the CMS preferences and set source profiles for each bitmap image or color after conversion. (If you use a CMS to add new colors to your converted publication, remember that new colors are managed by the CMS, but the converted colors are not automatically color-managed.)

COLOR MANAGING PAGEMAKER 6.0/6.01 PUBLICATIONS

When you use PageMaker 6.5 to open a PageMaker 6.0 or 6.01 publication managed with the Kodak Precision CMS, a special conversion process takes place. The Kodak Precision CMS is no longer supported: it has been replaced by the Kodak Digital Science CMS. Kodak source profiles used in PageMaker 6.0/6.01 (where they were called Precision Transforms) are mapped to an equivalent ICC-compliant profile included with PageMaker 6.5. If you used a Precision Transform other than one supplied with PageMaker 6.0/6.01, PageMaker 6.5 cannot do the mapping automatically;

in that case, the default source profile specified in the CMS Preferences dialog box will be None. PageMaker warns you during publication conversion if this condition occurs; you can then apply a ICC-compliant profile to the color or image that used the older source profile.

IMPORTING PHOTO CD IMAGES USING THE KODAK DIGITAL SCIENCE CMS

To place Photo CD images into PageMaker, you must choose the Kodak CMS set as your default CMS. To get accurate color, the Photo CD filter requires you to select a source profile when you import a Photo CD image (required profiles are installed automatically when you choose to install the Photo CD filter). For more information, see "Importing Photo CD Images" on page 365.

To import a Photo CD image with the Kodak CMS:

1 Choose File > Place.

2 Select a Photo CD image.

3 In the Import Photo CD Image dialog box, click Source.

4 Select a device profile from the Source Profile pop-up menu and click OK.

5 Click OK.

Note: Many Photo CDs come with a device profile for the scanning device used to create the bitmap images on the Photo CD. Use this device profile as your source profile when importing Photo CD images.

CHANGING OUTPUT DEVICE PROFILES BEFORE PRINTING

You can change your device profile selection for your composite or separations printer from the print dialog box. Before you print on a different output device, change the device profile in CMS Preferences to match the output device.

For best results, don't change the Separations Printer device profile when using color management. Color-mapping decisions are often based on the separations printer device profile, and changing the separations printer device profile late in the color management process may not give the best results.

To change your output device profile before printing:

1 Choose File > Print.

2 If you are printing on a PostScript printer, select the appropriate PPD for your output device.

3 Click Color, and then click CMS Setup.

4 Select a device profile for your composite or separations printer, and click OK.

5 Select one of the following options:

• Select any additional print options, and then click Print.

• Hold down the Shift key and click Done to save the new settings without printing.

TURNING OFF COLOR MANAGEMENT

Sometimes you may not want to use the color management system. You may want to turn color management off in these situations:

• If you don't use bitmap images and only use spot colors in your publication.

• If you use only preseparated bitmap images.

• If your imported graphics include only DCS files and EPS files that contain only process colors.

• If you use a postprocessing application to create separations of your publication.

Since displaying and printing using the CMS requires mapping colors from one gamut to another, screen redraw and printing are faster when the CMS is turned off.

In some situations, you may want to color-manage your publication but not color manage a particular image. Turning off color management for a particular image file allows the color

information in the file to "pass through" the CMS without being changed. The color information is still available to the output device but it has not been color-managed by the CMS in PageMaker. Turn off color management in the following situations:

• If you create CMYK TIFF files in an image-editing program, such as Adobe Photoshop, and have targeted the images for the final output device.

• If your bitmap images are separated by your prepress service provider and you are using low-resolution images for layout and positioning only.

To turn color management off:

1 Choose File > Preferences > General.

2 Click CMS Setup.

3 Choose Off from the Color Management pop-up menu, and then click OK.

To turn off color management for a bitmap image:

1 Select the bitmap image.

2 Choose Element > Image > CMS Source.

3 Choose None from the This Item Uses pop-up menu, and then click OK.

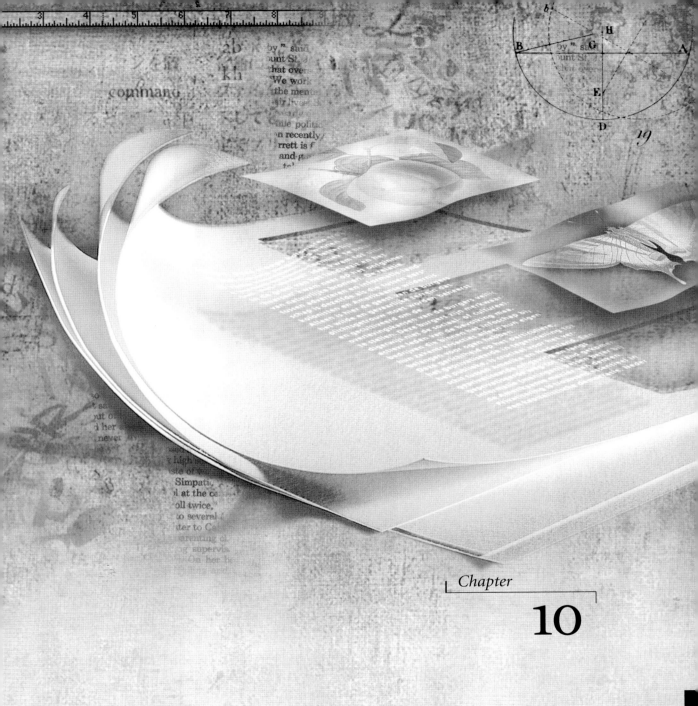

Chapter

10

CHAPTER 10: USING ADOBE TABLE

This chapter describes how to create and edit tables using Adobe Table 3.0—a stand-alone utility included in PageMaker 6.5—and then import them into your publications. You can:

• Export the table as a text-only file or as a graphic and then import the text or graphic file (either as an EPS or as a draw-type graphic) into a PageMaker publication.

• Import an OLE-linked or embedded version of a table. With the OLE-embedded option you do not create a native file on the hard disk or an exported version of the file; you must have enough RAM for PageMaker and Adobe Table to run simultaneously. See "OLE: Object Linking and Embedding" on page 357 for more information.

Once the table is imported into PageMaker, you can manipulate it as you can any other imported graphic.

For more information on comparing importing methods, see "Choosing an Importing and Updating Method" on page 333.

STARTING ADOBE TABLE

Adobe Table is installed in the Extras folder within the PageMaker folder on your hard drive or network. You can start the application as you would any other application—for example, by double-clicking the application icon.

You can also start the application from within PageMaker, which lets you import a table as an OLE-embedded object. See "Creating, Importing, and Updating a Table Using Adobe Table" on page 354 for more information.

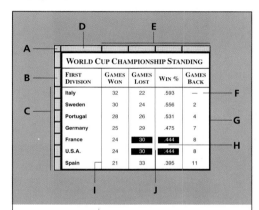

Working in Adobe Table • This example shows the basic components of a table.

A Table-select button

B Row-select button (non-printing)

C Rows

D Column-select button (non-printing)

E Columns

F Cell

G 1-point outside border

H 1.5-pica gutter between rows

I .5-point vertical borders between cells

J 1-pica gutter between columns

SETTING UP A NEW TABLE

Each time you start Adobe Table, and when you choose File > New after starting up, the Format Cell dialog box appears, where you specify the number of rows and columns you want (up to 100 each), and the height and width of the table (up to 40 inches by 40 inches). You can also specify the kinds of borders you want around the table and inside it, as well as the size of the gutter, or space, you want between text in neighboring rows and columns. You can change any of the settings at any time while working in Adobe Table.

To create a new table:

1 Start Adobe Table and choose File > New.

2 Type the number of rows and columns you want, and the height and width of the table.

The dimension of the table determines the height of the rows and the width of the columns.

3 In the Table Gutters section, specify the horizontal space between blocks of text in columns and the vertical space between blocks of text in rows.

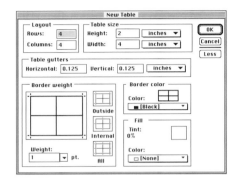

4 Click OK or click More to further define border and fill attributes.

5 To change the border weights, select the borders you want to specify, as follows:

• Click a line in the borders proxy. The dashes appear at the end of the line that is selected.

• Click the outside icon to select all borders on the perimeter of the table.

• Click the internal icon to select all borders within the table (excluding the borders on the perimeter).

• Click the all icon to select all vertical and horizontal lines.

6 Select the line weight you want, as follows:

• Type a value from 0 to 36 points in .1 increments.

• Select a preset line weight, or select None to make the border invisible.

7 To change the color applied to all borders with widths, select a defined color from the Colors pop-up menu. Selecting the color None resets all border weights to 0 pts.

8 To apply a fill (a color background) to all cells in the new table, select a defined color from the Colors pop-up menu in the Fills section of the dialog box. Then, use the Tint option to type or select a percentage of the fill color to apply. You can type a percentage value between 0 and 100% in 1% increments.

9 Click OK.

OPENING AN EXISTING TABLE FROM WITHIN ADOBE TABLE

You can open the following files in Adobe Table:

• Tables saved in the Adobe Table 2.5 or 3.0 native file format. You can open Adobe Table files created on the Windows platform directly from the Macintosh platform, and vice versa.

• Tables created with Table Editor version 2.x (included with earlier versions of PageMaker for Windows) and version 1.01 (included with PageMaker 4.x for the Macintosh). Table Editor files open as untitled copies of the original. All the table formatting is converted, including grouped cells and number formats, with the exception of dashed or dotted lines, which are converted into solid lines.

If you also own Adobe Table 1.0, included with Adobe Persuasion® 3.0 for Windows and Macintosh (or Aldus Table 1.0 if you own Aldus Persuasion 3.0), you must use that version of the application to open the OLE tables it created; Adobe Table 3.0 does not open them.

You can have as many tables open at the same time as allowed by the amount of RAM available. The names of open tables are listed in the Window menu.

Note: *If you created and imported a table as an OLE-embedded object into a publication and want to open it from within PageMaker, see "Updating and Saving a Table" on page 314.*

To open a table:

1 Choose File > Open.

2 Select the table file you want.

3 Specify whether you want to open the Original version or a Copy. (You can open the original version or a copy of an Adobe Table 3.0 file.)

4 Click OK.

If the fonts applied in the table you are opening are not available on your system, Adobe Table alerts you and asks if you want to continue opening the file. If you click Continue, Adobe Table opens an untitled copy of the table. On the Macintosh, Adobe Table substitutes Times for the missing font; Adobe Table for Windows substitutes Times New Roman for the missing font.

Updating and saving a table

How you save changes depends on whether you opened the active table from within Adobe Table (using the New or Open commands) or from within PageMaker (using the Edit > Insert Object or Edit Original commands).

To save a table opened from within Adobe Table:

1 Complete the changes you want to save.

2 Use either of the following options as appropriate:

• Choose File > Save if the table has been saved previously.

• Choose File > Save As if the file is being saved for the first time or if you want to change how the file is saved.

3 If you chose Save As, specify a name for the file and a folder in which to save it, and whether you want to save the table as a template or as a table.

Adobe Table templates work just like they do in PageMaker; they let you create new, untitled documents using the content and formatting of the template as a starting point.

4 Click OK.

To save a table opened as an embedded OLE document from within PageMaker:

1 Make the changes you want.

The changes appear automatically in PageMaker 6.5. If you use Adobe Table to embed a table in an application that only supports OLE 1.0 (such as PageMaker 5.0), you can choose File > Update to apply the changes to the version of the table stored in the application file.

2 Optionally, choose File > Save Copy As to save the OLE document to disk. In the dialog box that appears, specify a name for the file and a folder in which to save it, and whether you want to save the table as a template or as a table.

For more information on creating, editing, and updating OLE tables from within PageMaker, see "Creating, Importing, and Updating a Table Using Adobe Table" on page 354.

CLOSING TABLES AND QUITTING ADOBE TABLE

Use the File > Close command to close the active table. Use the File > Quit (Macintosh) or File > Exit (Windows) commands to close all tables and end the Adobe Table work session. If you have made changes to a table without saving or updating at the time you close the table or end the work session, Adobe Table prompts you to save the changes.

VIEWING AND SELECTING

The kind of changes you can make to various aspects of a table depend on what is selected at the time you make a change. For example, to format text in one or more cells, you must first select those cells; to change a column's width, you must first select the column.

To make a table active:

Either click any part of the table's windows to select it, or choose the name of the table you want from the Window menu in Adobe Table.

To change how open tables are displayed:

Windows only: Choose Window > Tile to arrange open tables side-by-side within the application window. Choose Window > Cascade to arrange open tables in an overlapping stack so that title bars are visible behind the active window.

Use the following methods to display the part of the active table you need to select:

• Use the scroll bars on the right and bottom sides of the window to scroll the table vertically or horizontally.

• Choose a new display size from the View menu. A check in the View menu marks the current display size. All display sizes are proportional to the actual size of the printed table.

To hide or display rulers on the top and left sides of the active table:

Choose View > Show Rulers.

As with PageMaker rulers, you can set the zero point to any position—just click in the zero point window and drag.

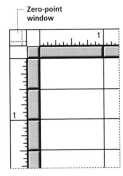

Zero-point window

Selecting text, cells, rows, and columns

To select one or more cells:

1 Click an insertion point in the cell.

2 To select additional cells, use one of the following techniques:

• To select contiguous cells, either drag in any direction, or press Shift and click another cell to select all cells between it and the first cell you selected.

• To select a discontiguous range of cells, press Command (Macintosh) or Ctrl (Windows) and click the cells you want.

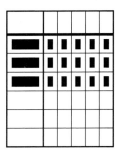 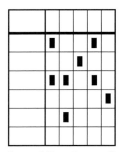

Range of contiguous cells   *Range of discontiguous cells*

To select entire rows or columns:

1 Make sure the View > Show Selection Buttons command is selected.

The select zones appear along the top and left sides of the table.

2 Click the button at the start of the row or top of the column you want to select.

Working with color • If you know how to create, copy, and edit colors in PageMaker, you are ready to work with color in Adobe Table. The Adobe Table color dialog boxes are virtually identical to those in PageMaker; you can even use the same color libraries supplied with PageMaker.

You can apply color to any range of text characters, to any range of cells (the color becomes a fill background in the cell), or apply a single color to the borders throughout a table. You can also apply tints of fill and border colors.

Note: PageMaker converts OLE information to PostScript for high-quality printing. If you use a spot color in a table which you then OLE-link or embed into PageMaker, be sure to add that color to the PageMaker Colors palette before you print. Otherwise the color will not be available for separations printing.

Adobe Table provides a set of default colors to choose from. Of these, Black, Cyan, Magenta, and Yellow are process colors; the remaining ones are defined as spot colors. You can use the Format > Define Colors command to create additional colors, edit existing colors, or copy other colors from existing Adobe Table files, much like you do in PageMaker. See Chapter 8, "Defining, Applying, and Trapping Color" for information on these tasks.

3 To extend the selection, press Command (Macintosh) or Ctrl (Windows) and click the Select button for each row or column you want.

To select all rows and columns:

Click in the upper left corner of the Select Button area, or choose Edit > Select All with one or more cells selected. (If you choose Select All with text or an insertion point selected, Adobe Table selects all the text in the cell.)

┌── Select All zone

WORLD CUP CHAMPIONSHIP STANDING				
FIRST DIVISION	GAMES WON	GAMES LOST	WIN %	GAMES BACK
Italy	32	22	.593	—
Sweden	30	24	.556	2
Portugal	28	26	.531	4
Germany	25	29	.475	7
France	24	30	.444	8
U.S.A.	24	30	.444	8
Spain	21	33	.395	11

To select text in a cell:

Drag-select a range of text or, to select all the text in a cell, click an insertion point in that cell, and then choose Edit > Select All.

Shortcut: *Position the cursor in a cell's gutter and click to select the cell (including all its text). You can also double-click a word to select it, or triple-click to select the paragraph.*

TYPING, EDITING, AND FORMATTING TEXT

Click in a cell to type, edit, and format text within it. Formatting changes can also affect all text in a selected range of cells.

Typing text

When you type, text automatically wraps to fit within the width of the column; if necessary, the height of the row expands to accommodate the text you add.

The row height expands to accommodate the text you add.

Use the following keys and key combinations when typing text:

• Press Tab to move to the next column to the right. If you press Tab with the insertion point in the last cell in the table, another row appears.

• Press Shift + Tab to move to the next column to the left.

• Press Option + Tab (Macintosh) or Ctrl + . (period) (Windows) to insert a tab at the insertion point.

• Press Return (Macintosh) or Enter (Windows) to create a new paragraph in the cell.

• Press Shift + Return (Macintosh) or Enter (Windows) to create a new line within the current paragraph.

• Press the arrow keys to move line-by-line (up or down arrows) or character-by-character (left and right arrows) through text in the cell, or to the next cell in the row or column.

To view non-printing markers representing tabs and other invisible characters:

Choose View > Show ¶.

FORMATTING TEXT IN TABLES

You should be familiar with text formatting in PageMaker before using Adobe Table to format text. The character- and paragraph-level text attributes you can set are a subset of those that PageMaker offers, with only two exceptions: the Vertical and Decimal alignment options (described below).

For more information on the text attributes Adobe Table shares with PageMaker, see "About Formatting Text" on page 121.

To format text in the active table:

1 Select the range of text you want to format, or select one or more cells containing text you want to format.

2 Choose Window > Show Text Palette, or Format > Format Text.

3 Specify the settings you want.

Using the vertical alignment option • You can position the top line of text along the top of the cell's text block; position the bottom line of text along the bottom of the cell's text block; or center text vertically within the cell's text block. (Vertical alignment is a cell attribute, not a paragraph-level attribute.)

Using the decimal alignment option • In columns that contain numbers with decimals, you can ensure that the decimals align regardless of the number of digits before or after the decimal point. This feature is similar to the Decimal tab stop in PageMaker.

Vertical alignment option

Decimal alignment option

To set text defaults for all new tables you create:

1 Close all open tables.

2 Choose Format > Set Default Text Format.

3 Specify the settings you want, and click OK.

To align numbers in a column:

1 Select the paragraphs that contain the numbers you want to align, choose Window > Show Text Palette, and select decimal-horizontal alignment.

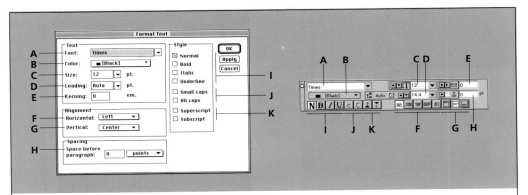

Applying text attributes • Adobe Table is similar to PageMaker in the methods it provides for applying text attributes. When formatting text, you have two options: use the Format > Text Format command, or use the Text palette. The Text palette is similar to PageMaker's Control palette in Character or Paragraph view. To open it, choose Window > Show Text Palette. The state of the palette changes to reflect the text attributes of selected cells.

A Font

B Color

C Size

D Leading and autoleading

E Kerning

F Horizontal Paragraph Alignments: Left, Right, Center, Justify, Decimal

G Vertical Cell Alignments: Top, Center, Bottom

H Space Before Paragraph

I Type Style

J Small Caps and All Caps

K Superscript/Subscript

2 Insert a single tab—Option + Tab (Macintosh) or Ctrl + . (period) (Windows)—immediately before each number you want to align by decimal point.

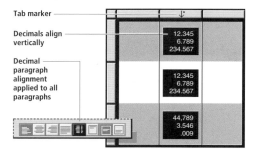

Tab marker

Decimals align vertically

Decimal paragraph alignment applied to all paragraphs

If you want to override the default position of the tab stop (the place where the decimal point is positioned within the column), complete steps 3 and 4.

3 Make sure the View > Show Tab Markers and View > Show Selection Buttons commands are selected.

4 In the Select Button of the column containing the numbers you are formatting, drag the tab marker to where you want the decimals to appear.

The position of the decimal point is a column-level setting, so that all paragraphs with the Decimal alignment attribute have the same tab position within a column.

Setting other type options

Several options for formatting text—the Autoleading percentage, and Super/Subscript size and position—are available in the Text Positioning dialog box. (If you choose the command with no table open, you change the attributes for all new tables you create.) These type options are identical to the options in PageMaker. For more information on auto-leading, see "Selecting a Leading Value" on page 164. For information on Super/Subscript size and position, see "Changing Case and Position" on page 172.

CHANGING BORDERS AND APPLYING FILLS

You can enhance the look of a table by using different line weights for borders and fills within cells, rows, or columns. You can apply different fill colors to different cells within the same table, but borders in a table share the same color.

You first define the line weights for a table's borders in the Format Cell dialog box, but you can change any border at any time using the Table palette. You also use the Table palette to add fills (percentages of a specified color) to one or more cells. By default, cells have no fill applied.

Note: You can change the borders of the entire table, or apply a fill to all cells, by selecting the entire table and choosing Format > Format Cell.

TIP: IF YOU ARE USING THE TABLE PALETTE, YOU CAN CLICK A NUDGE BUT-TON TO RESIZE THE ROW OR COLUMN IN FINE IN-CREMENTS. TO RESIZE BY 10 TIMES THE DEFAULT AMOUNT, PRESS COM-MAND (MACINTOSH) OR CTRL (WINDOWS) AND CLICK A NUDGE BUTTON.

To open the Table palette, choose Window > Show Table Palette. The state of the palette changes to reflect the border and fill attributes of selected cells.

Using the borders proxy

The borders proxy in the Table palette lets you specify which borders in the selected cells you want to change. Remember, only the borders that are selected (indicated by dashes at the end of lines in the proxy) will change when you specify the new line weight you want. You click lines in the proxy to select or deselect borders.

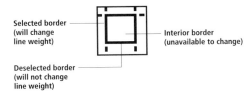

Selected border
(will change
line weight)

Interior border
(unavailable to change)

Deselected border
(will not change
line weight)

Shortcut: *Double-click on a blank section of the proxy to select all outside borders, and triple-click to select all borders along the outside edge and within the selection.*

To change the borders in the table:

1 Select the cell or range of cells you want to change.

2 Choose Window > Show Table Palette.

If the selection of cells is rectangular, the outside edge of the proxy represents the top, bottom, left, and right sides of the selection, and the lines inside the proxy represent all vertical and horizontal lines within the selection.

If you selected a single cell, or a discontiguous range of cells, the outside edge of the proxy represents the top, bottom, left, and right sides of the selected cell or each cell in the selected range; the lines inside the proxy are unavailable.

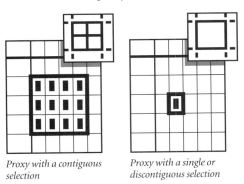

Proxy with a contiguous selection

Proxy with a single or discontiguous selection

3 To change border widths, select the borders you want to specify, as follows:

• Click a line in the borders proxy. The dashes appear at the end of the line that is selected.

• Double-click the proxy to select all borders on the perimeter of the selection.

4 Select the line weight you want for the selected borders, as follows:

• Type a value from 0 to 36 points in .01 increments.

• Select a preset line weight.

5 To change the color applied to all borders in the table with widths, select a defined color from the Colors pop-up menu. Selecting the color None resets all border weights in the table—not just in the selection—to 0 pts.

To apply a fill:

1 Select the cells you want to fill.

2 Choose Window > Show Table Palette.

3 In the fills section of the palette, do either or both of the following:

• Choose a color from the Color pop-up menu. Choosing None from the menu makes the selection transparent. (Any objects behind the table when placed into PageMaker will show through the cells with the None attribute applied.)

• Type (in 1% increments) a fill percentage in the Tints text field, or select a preset fill from 10% to 90% from the Tints pop-up menu.

RESIZING ROWS AND COLUMNS

Adobe Table provides several options for resizing rows and columns.

• Drag to resize a row or column button (displayed along the left and top sides of the table). If you press Shift as you drag, the adjacent row or column resizes as well, so that the height or width of the table is preserved.

• Use the Cell > Row/Column Size command or the resize section of the Table palette to set the size of selected rows and columns. Both options change the height or width of the table without changing the adjacent rows or columns.

• Use the Format > Format Cells command to change the size of the table. The rows and columns are resized uniformly to adjust to the new height and width.

To move a row or column boundary:

1 Choose View > Show Selection Buttons.

2 To preserve size of the adjacent row or column, drag the boundary you want to move. Otherwise, press Shift and drag the boundary.

The adjacent column does not change size when you drag.

 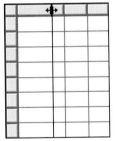

The adjacent column does change size when you press shift and drag.

To resize rows and columns by typing values:

1 Select the rows or columns you want to resize.

2 Choose Cell > Row/Column Size or Window > Show Table Palette.

3 Type the new row height or column width.

4 Click OK in the Row/Column Size dialog box, or press Return (Macintosh) or Enter (Windows) in the Table palette to apply the changes.

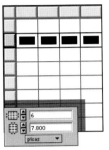 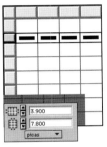

Resizing a row with the Table palette

To resize rows and columns by changing table height or width:

1 Choose Format > Format Cells.

2 Type the new height or width you want.

3 Click Apply to preview the changes without closing the dialog box, or click OK to make the changes and return to the table.

To set the default unit of measure for row and column size (with no table open):

1 Choose Cell > Row /Column Size Preferences.

2 Choose the unit of measure you want.

3 Click OK.

Understanding row height

Several factors determine the height of rows. If you cannot decrease row height by the amount you want, you have a number of alternatives.

• Increase the width of one or more columns (so that the text takes up less vertical space).

• Decrease the size of the horizontal gutters.

• Decrease Type Size, Leading, or Space Before Paragraph attributes in the cell with the most text.

• Edit to eliminate words in the cell with the most text.

ADDING AND DELETING ROWS AND COLUMNS

The easiest way to add new rows to a table is by pressing Tab with an insertion point selected in the table's last cell. You can add rows and columns to a table by choosing commands on the Cell menu, or by using the Format > Format Cells command to change the table layout. The following sections describe the differences between these two methods.

Using Cell menu commands to insert rows or columns

Commands on the Cell menu let you insert new rows or columns anywhere in the table. Depending on the command you select, new rows are inserted above or below the currently selected row, and new columns are inserted to the left or right of the currently selected column. The table expands to accommodate the new rows or columns.

New rows and columns appear with the same default text attributes, borders, fills, and row height or column width as those of the row or column selected when you choose the command. The number of rows or columns selected when you choose the command determines the number of new rows or columns inserted.

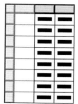 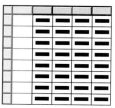

Before: Two columns selected when Insert Column After is chosen. *After: Two columns inserted to the right of the rightmost column in the selection.*

 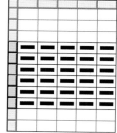

Before: Three rows selected when Insert Row Above is chosen. *After: Three rows inserted above topmost row in selection.*

To insert rows or columns with commands on the Cell menu:

1 Select one or more cells in the row or column where you want the new row or column to appear. (To insert more than one row or column, select entire rows and columns rather than individual cells.)

2 Choose a command from the Cell menu to determine the placement of the new row or column:

- For Rows, choose the Cell > Insert Row Above or Insert Row Below command.

- For Columns, choose the Cell > Insert Column Before or Insert Column After command.

Using the Format Cell command to insert rows or columns

When you increase the number of rows or columns with the Format Cell command, the new rows are inserted at the bottom of the table, and new columns are inserted at the right side of the table. By default, the table expands to accommodate the new rows or columns. You must reset the Height and Width values back to the original settings if you want the existing rows and columns to resize to accommodate the new rows or columns.

To insert rows or columns with the Format Cell command:

1 Choose Format > Format Cell.

2 Type the number of rows and columns you want, and click Apply or OK.

Deleting rows and columns

You use the Cell > Delete command to remove the selected row or column and all its contents from the table. If you only want to remove the text from the row or column (for example, to place new text into the cells within the row or column) you can use the Edit > Cut or Clear commands. See "Cutting, Copying, and Pasting Information"on page326 for more information.

When you use the Cell > Delete command to remove selected rows and columns, the table decreases in size accordingly. You must leave at least one row and one column in a table.

To delete rows or columns:

1 Select the rows or columns.

2 Choose Cell > Delete Row or Delete Column.

GROUPING AND UNGROUPING CELLS

You can combine individual selected cells into one cell—for example, to create a heading that spans two or more columns. The new grouped cell takes on the fill of the cell in the top-left corner of the selected cells (the anchor cell). Text in cells other than the anchor cell is added to the anchor cell when the cells are grouped.

Cells before grouping   *Cell after grouping*

To group cells:

1 Select the cells you want to combine.

2 Choose Cell > Group.

To restore a group to individual cells:

1 Select the grouped cell.

2 Choose Cell > Ungroup.

CHANGING GUTTERS

You can change the size of horizontal or vertical gutters at any time. The change applies to all rows or columns in the current table; not just selected parts.

When you change the gutter, the text areas within the cells are adjusted first. Adobe Table only changes the height of rows or width of columns (and the overall height and width of the table) if the text area cannot be adjusted further (for example, due to the amount of text in a cell).

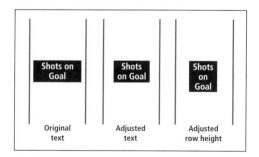

Original text   Adjusted text   Adjusted row height

To change gutters:

1 Choose Format > Format Cells or Window > Show Table Palette.

2 Type a new value for the horizontal or vertical gutters.

If you are using the Table palette, you can click a nudge button to resize the gutter in fine increments. To resize by 10 times that amount, press Command (Macintosh) or Ctrl (Windows) and click a nudge button.

CUTTING, COPYING, AND PASTING INFORMATION

The Adobe Table Edit menu includes the standard editing commands—Cut, Copy, Paste, and Clear—for moving information back and forth from a table to the Clipboard (or with Clear, for removing information entirely). Note that these commands apply only to text and fills (not borders), with one exception: if the entire table is selected when you choose Cut or Copy, the table is placed on the Clipboard as a PICT (Macintosh) or as an Enhanced Metafile (Windows).

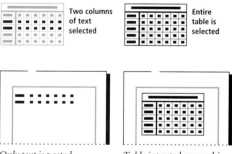

Two columns of text selected

Entire table is selected

Only text is pasted   *Table is pasted as graphic*

The Paste command changes to read Paste Text, Paste Cells, or Paste Table depending on the contents of the Clipboard. When you paste text into one or more cells, the text attributes of the Clipboard contents are preserved. (The vertical alignment of the cell into which you paste text is preserved, since vertical alignment is a cell attribute, not a text attribute.)

Guidelines for cutting and pasting

• If you choose Paste when the Clipboard contains more cells than are in the currently selected range of cells, Adobe Table asks whether you want to cancel pasting or paste as much of the text as the selected range can accommodate.

• When you paste text from Adobe Table into another application, a tab indicates the end of a cell; a soft return (also called a line feed) indicates the end of a paragraph; and a paragraph return indicates the end of a row. Tabs typed within cells are removed when pasted into the other application.

• If you choose Cut or Copy with the entire table selected, you can then choose Paste Table to replace an entire table with an exact copy of the table on the Clipboard, or to paste in the text on the Clipboard only.

SETTING DEFAULTS AND PREFERENCES

Like PageMaker, Adobe Table has two kinds of defaults:

• Application defaults, which you set when no table is open and which are applied to all new tables you create. For example, if you choose Format > Set Default Cell Format before you open a table and, in the Format Cell dialog box, change the number of rows to six, then all new tables you create will have six rows.

• Cell-range defaults, which you set with one or more cells selected and which are applied only to selected cells. For example, if you select all of Row 1 and choose Center paragraph alignment from the Text palette, then any new text you type in Row 1 is aligned to the center of the cell.

Adobe Table also has a Preferences command which controls various attributes of tables.

To set preferences:

1 Choose File > Preferences.

2 For the Language option, select the version of English you want to appear in Adobe Table dialog boxes, messages, and palettes.

3 Click OK.

The settings stay in effect until you change them.

IMPORTING AND EXPORTING

Although you'll typically want to import a native Adobe Table file directly into your publication by embedding or linking the table as an OLE document, you can also choose to export a table as a text-only file or as a graphic. This section also describes how to import text-only files into Adobe Table (you cannot import graphics).

Exporting tables from Adobe Table

You can choose the File > Export command to save a table as a text or graphics file that other applications can read directly from disk. When exporting text, you can export the entire table or a selected range of cells. When you export as a graphic, you must export the entire table.

When you export a table as a graphic, you can format the file as an EPS graphic (with or without fonts), as PICT (Macintosh only) or EMF (Windows only).

If you are printing to a PostScript printer, we suggest you use the EPS format, since it is supported on both Windows and Macintosh platforms and offers the best printing results. If you are certain your printer (or service bureau) has the fonts you used to create the table, you can save the EPS without fonts. If you choose to include fonts (to avoid font substitution problems), the file size of the exported graphic will be much larger than the same file saved without fonts.

If you export a table as a text-only (.TXT) file, the borders, fills, and text attributes applied in Adobe Table are not retained when you import the file into another application.

When you place an exported table into PageMaker, PageMaker does not link its internal version of the table to the original Adobe Table file (the table from which you created the exported file). Rather, PageMaker links its placed version of the table to the external text or graphic file you exported from Adobe Table.

To export a table as text or a graphic:

1 If exporting text, select an insertion point or a range of cells as follows:

• To export part of a table, select the cells you want to export.

• To export the entire table, click an insertion point in any cell, or select the entire table.

When you export as a graphic, the entire table is exported regardless of what is selected when you choose Export.

2 Choose File > Export > Text, or File > Export > Graphic.

3 Specify a name for the file and folder in which to save the file.

4 Select the file format you want (for a graphic) or the delimiter format you want (for text).

5 Click OK.

Importing text

You can import text-only files into all or part of a table. If the file you are importing contains more cells than are in the entire table (or in the selected range), Adobe Table asks you whether you want to cancel the action or import as much of the information as the table (or the selected range) can accommodate.

How the file is imported depends on whether the application that saved or exported the text used tabs or commas as delimiters—that is, as the marks to indicate a new cell or new row.

To import text:

1 Select an insertion point or a range of cells, as follows:

• To import text into part of a table, select the cells into which you want to import text.

• To import text starting at a particular point in the table, click an insertion point in the cell where you want to insert the imported text.

2 Choose File > Import.

3 Select the file you want to import.

4 Specify the delimiter that separates cells in the text file.

In comma-delimited text, commas enclosed in quotes are interpreted as punctuation and do not act as delimiters.

5 Click OK.

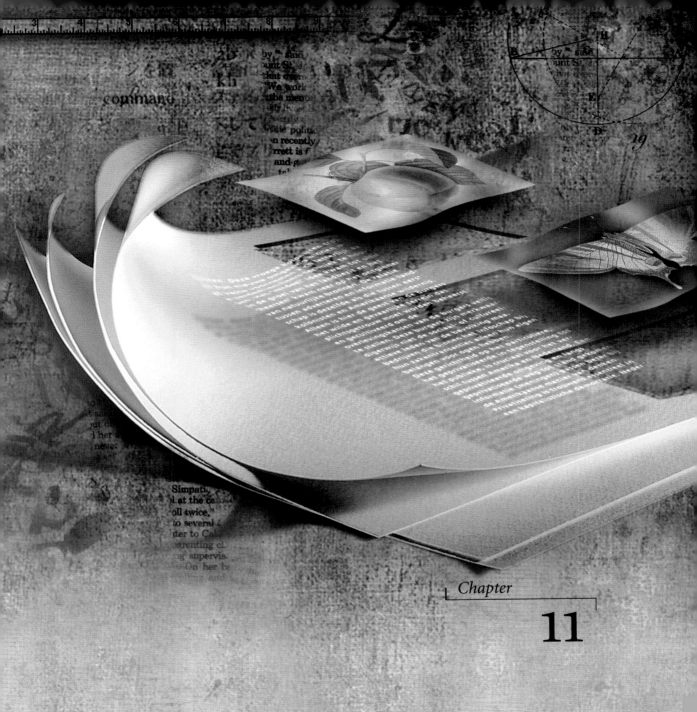

CHAPTER 11: IMPORTING, LINKING, AND EXPORTING

PageMaker's versatile importing, linking, and exporting capabilities make it a powerful integration tool for all types of publications. A PageMaker publication can contain line art, bitmap images, text, and spreadsheet and database files from a variety of applications and formats. In most cases, you can edit and update a graphic using the application in which it was created, directly from PageMaker.

CHOOSING AN IMPORTING AND UPDATING METHOD

PageMaker offers many ways to import and manage text and graphics, and your selection of importing and updating options can influence how much PageMaker improves your workflow and efficiency.

Choosing an importing and updating method based on its capabilities

Importing and updating	Place	Paste	Paste link (Paste Special)	Insert object	Subscribe (Macintosh)
Can update a link	•		•	•	•
Converts imported text so that you can edit it using PageMaker	•	•			1*
Can open an imported object directly in its original application, if that application is installed on your computer	•		•	•	•
Can simultaneously update multiple instances of an object in one or more publications	•		•		•

* See footnotes on next page

continued on next page

Choosing an importing and updating method based on its capabilities continued from previous page

Importing and updating	Place	Paste	Paste link (Paste Special)	Insert object	Subscribe (Macintosh)
Can import a portion of a saved file		•	•		•
File management and version control					
Stores an imported graphic inside a publication	5	•	•	•	•
Saves disk space by storing imported EPS, TIFF, and other images outside a publication with a link	5				
Includes an option to update a linked file automatically or manually	•		•		•
Can edit and update an imported graphic without an external saved file				•	
Printing					
Supports prepress-quality EPS and TIFF files	•				2
Can print an imported object without a saved external file	3	•	4	•	4

1   If you edit text that was imported using subscribe, the link to the original text is broken.
2   True when the edition file is published in EPS format.
3   True if you chose to include the object inside the publication.
4   Prints the most recently received update of an object, even if it was created on a different platform.
5   You may choose to store a graphic inside or outside a publication.

The importing method you choose determines the kind of link (if any) to the original file and your ability to edit or update the object later. If you import an object by placing, OLE linking or embedding, or subscribing, you may be able to update the object in PageMaker each time the original document changes. In addition, you may be able to start the application in which you created an object directly from PageMaker, if the application is on your computer.

PLACING AND LINKING

The Place command is PageMaker's primary importing method. When you place text or a graphic, PageMaker establishes a link to the source file on your hard drive (unless the file is an HTML document). The link allows PageMaker to update the version of the document that is in your publication, and can minimize the size of your publication by allowing you to store an imported graphic outside the publication.

You can use the File > Links Manager command to manage the updating attributes of almost any file you place. You can check the link status and relink or unlink source files as necessary. Together, the Place and Links Manager commands support most of the features of the other importing and linking methods. See "Managing Linked Text and Graphics" on page 369 for more information.

What happens when you place a file? •
PageMaker imports the file and creates a link to the original file.

Importing: After creating a file in the source application **A**, you place the file into a PageMaker publication **B**. As the object imports, PageMaker creates a link **C** between the object and its original file. If you copy the object to other parts of the publication or to other PageMaker publications, PageMaker creates additional links to the original file.

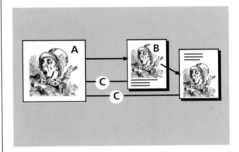

Updating: When you want to edit the object, you can open the original file in the application that created it, directly from PageMaker **A**. When you finish editing **B**, PageMaker can update the file in the publication automatically **C**, or it can prompt you to update the file manually.

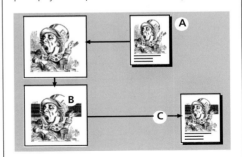

TIP: WHEN YOU CHOOSE THE PLACE COMMAND IN WINDOWS, YOU CAN LIST ALL FILES IN A FOLDER, REGARDLESS OF THE TYPE OF FILE, BY TYPING *.* FOR A FILE NAME AND THEN PRESSING ENTER OR RETURN.

Before you place a file, make sure you've installed the import filters that support the file formats you use. To find out which filters are installed, press Command (Macintosh) or Ctrl (Windows) while choosing About PageMaker from the Apple menu (Macintosh) or Help menu (Windows).

If you want to edit a linked file directly from PageMaker, the application that created the file must be on your computer or accessible over a network.

To place text or a graphic in layout view:

1 Choose File > Place.

If you use the text tool to click an insertion point in a text object before choosing Place, and then you select a graphics file, it imports as an inline graphic contained within the text object. To override this default, select As Independent Graphic in the Place Document dialog box or select the pointer tool before you choose Place.

2 Select the file you want to import, select importing options, and then click OK or Open.

You may be prompted to specify additional options in another dialog box. For example, if you want to place a text-only file, PageMaker displays the Text-Only Import Filter dialog box. If you want to place a story from a PageMaker 5.0 or 6.0 publication, PageMaker displays the Place

PageMaker Stories dialog box. Select options, and then click OK. See "Options for Placing" on page 337 for more information.

3 Do one of the following:

• To make the graphic or text independent of a frame, position the loaded icon where you want the upper-left corner of the graphic or text block to be, and then click.

• To position the item within an existing frame, click within the frame.

• To size the graphic or text block as you place it, drag the mouse and then release the mouse button.

Size a graphic or text block by dragging as you place the file.

To place text or a graphic in story editor:

1 In story editor, click an insertion point where you want the imported object to appear in the story, or select text that you want to replace with imported text or an inline graphic.

2 Choose File > Place.

3 Select the file you want to import, select importing options, and then click OK.

In story editor, placed graphics appear as small, shaded boxes.

For more information on choosing options, see "Options for Placing" on page 337.

Note: If you have not placed the story in the active story window on the page in layout view, or if you import text as a new story, PageMaker asks you to place the story when you close story editor. If you click Place, PageMaker loads the text icon, which you can then place on the appropriate page in layout view.

Controlling how large graphics files affect publication size

If you place a graphics file that is 256K or larger, PageMaker displays an alert message asking if you want to store a complete copy of the graphic in the publication. If you don't want to store the complete graphic, PageMaker imports a low-resolution version of it for display only, which reduces the size of your publication file and establishes a link to the original file. This original file must be available and linked when you print

the publication; otherwise PageMaker prints only the low-resolution version of the graphic. You can increase or decrease the file size that PageMaker stores in your publication.

To adjust file size for storing a copy of a graphic in a publication:

1 Choose File > Preferences > General.

2 Click More, and then specify a file size for the Alert When Storing Graphics Over option.

3 Click OK to close each dialog box.

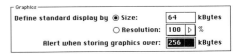

OPTIONS FOR PLACING

The options available in the Place Document dialog box depend on whether you select a text, spreadsheet, database, or graphics file to place, and whether you have an object or frame selected when you choose File > Place. The dialog box displays files whose formats (Macintosh) or extensions (Windows) PageMaker recognizes as compatible.

If the Show Filter Preferences option is selected when you click OK or Open in the Place dialog box, additional options associated with certain filters become available in a secondary dialog box. Alternatively, you can press Shift and double-click a file in the Place dialog box to open the additional dialog box.

Options for placing text

The following options appear when you choose File > Place and select a text file (some options are not available for HTML files):

• The As New Story option adds the file as a new story, separate from any existing stories in the publication.

• The Replacing Entire Story option deletes the selected story and replaces it with one you select, flowing it into the existing text objects. PageMaker preserves the position, size, and orientation of the original text objects.

• The Inserting Text option places text at the insertion point, without deleting any existing text.

• The Replacing Selected Text (or Place Within Frame) option deletes selected text (or the text in the selected frame) and replaces it with new text.

• The Retain Format option imports any character and paragraph formatting and the style sheet, if there is one, with the file.

• The Convert Quotes option converts quotation marks and apostrophes into typographer's quotation marks and apostrophes. This option also converts double dashes to em dashes.

• The Read Tags option applies paragraph styles to text. See "Importing Text with Style-Name Tags" on page 344 for more information.

Options for placing graphics

The following options appear when you choose File > Place and select a graphics file:

• The As Independent Graphic option adds the graphic to your layout, independent of text blocks.

• The Replacing Entire Graphic (or Place Within Frame) option deletes the selected graphic (or the graphic within the selected frame) and replaces it with the graphic you select, retaining the sizing and text wrap applied to the old graphic, as well as any rotation, skewing, or reflecting applied in PageMaker.

• The As Inline Graphic option adds a graphic to your publication at an insertion point in the text.

• The Retain Cropping Data option replaces a graphic that you have already cropped and applies the original cropping to the new graphic. This option is only available when the Replacing Entire Graphic (or the Place Within Frame) option is selected.

Choosing a graphics file format • Most applications can save or export files in several different formats. Choose an appropriate graphics format based on final output.

If your final output is...	Do this...
High resolution (over 800dpi) PostScript imagesetter	Use EPS for vector graphics. Use TIFF for bitmap graphics. These file formats support precision output for text and graphics at high resolutions.
Process-color separations	Use EPS for vector graphics. Use CMYK TIFF or DCS EPS for color bitmaps, and TIFF for grayscale bitmaps. These file formats support high-resolution output devices and consistent CMYK color.
High-fidelity-color separations	Use Lab TIFF or Raw RGB for color bitmaps. These file formats preserve the largest possible color gamut.
Portable Document Format (PDF)	Use any compatible file format. An EPS or TIFF graphic is likely to print most consistently. (If final output is the screen, which is low resolution, you can avoid high-resolution graphics.)
Low-resolution PostScript printer	Use any compatible file format. An EPS or TIFF graphic is likely to print most consistently.
Non-PostScript printer	Use any compatible file format and avoid graphic effects that require a PostScript printer.
HTML document	Use JPEG or GIF graphics. PageMaker can also export other graphics as JPEG or GIF images when you export. See "Exporting a Graphic in a Different Format" on page 378 for details.

File-format icons for placing a graphic

	Bitmap (paint) image		Scrapbook (Macintosh only)
	EPS graphic (Macintosh)		TIFF, GIF, JPEG, PhotoCD image
	EPS graphic (Windows)		Vector (draw) graphic

Graphics file formats you can place in PageMaker

Graphics file format	Macintosh PageMaker	Windows PageMaker	Filename extension	Preferences dialog box
Adobe Illustrator 5.0 or later	•	•	.AI	yes
CGM graphics	•	•	.CGM	yes
CorelDRAW! 3.0-5.0 / 5.0 Clip Art		•	.CDR/.CMX	yes
Desktop Color Separation (DCS)	•	•	.DCS	yes
Dynamic Exchange Format (DXF)	•	•	.DXF	yes
Encapsulated PostScript (EPS)	•	•	.EPS	yes
Graphics Environment Manager (GEM)	•	•	.GEM	yes
Graphics Interchange Format (GIF)	•	•	.GIF	no
Hewlett-Packard Graphics Language (HPGL)		•	.PLT	yes
Joint Photographics Expert Group (JPEG)	•	•	.JPG	no
Kodak Photo CD and Pro Photo CD	•	•	.PCD	yes
Lotus Graphics PIC		•	.PIC	yes
Macintosh Picture (PICT)	•	•	.PCT	yes
MacPaint	•	•	.PNT	no
Microsoft Excel 3.0-4.0		•	.XLC	no
PC Paintbrush	•	•	.PCX	no
QuickTime movie (specified frame only)	•	•	.MOV	yes
Scitex Continuous Tone	•	•	.SCT	no
Table Editor 2.1		•	.TBL	no
Tektronix Plot		•	.PLT	no
TIFF	•	•	.TIF	no
Windows Bitmap	•	•	.BMP	no
Windows Metafile or Enhanced Metafile	•	•	.WMF/.EMF	no
WordPerfect Graphics 1.0-2.0		•	.WPG	yes

Note: Select Show Filter Preferences to make preferences dialog boxes appear automatically. PageMaker remembers the preferences settings used the last time you imported a graphic. Those settings become the defaults for files subsequently imported in that format until you change the settings or restart PageMaker.

IMPORTING TEXT FEATURES

You can import text into PageMaker from many different sources, including:

- Other PageMaker publications.

- Word-processing applications, such as WordPerfect, Microsoft Word, and Microsoft Works, with most character, paragraph, and style attributes intact.

- HTML files

- Text or table editors or any application that can export text-only (ASCII) format.

- Spreadsheet files in Excel and Lotus 1-2-3 formats.

- Database files, such as those created by dBASE and dBASE-compatible applications.

Selecting an import format

PageMaker imports as much character and paragraph formatting as possible from text files but ignores most page-layout information, such as page breaks, margins, and column settings, which you can set in PageMaker.

If your word-processing application can save files in more than one file format, we recommend that you use the richest format available to ensure that PageMaker imports as much text formatting as possible—either the application's native format or an exchange format, such as RTF (rich text format).

Converting text formats with Macintosh Easy Open (Macintosh only)

Macintosh Easy Open is an Apple Macintosh system 7.5 Control Panel item that can be used to translate various text file formats. When you want to import a text file that cannot be imported using one of PageMaker's import filters, you may try to obtain and install an Easy Open translator for it.

If PageMaker doesn't have a filter to import the specified file and an Easy Open preference for the file type doesn't exist, a Translation dialog box appears. You can choose from a list of available translators to proceed with the import. If no filter or Easy Open translator is available, an error message will appear.

If PageMaker uses an Easy Open translator to import a file, you may see an additional progress indicator as you place the file, indicating that Easy Open is translating a file into a format that PageMaker can recognize with one of its filters. A file translated using Easy Open is stored in the same folder as the original file unless the original resides on a write-protected disk. In this case, PageMaker creates a folder called Converted Doc in the PageMaker RSRC folder, where the translated file is stored. When the file has been successfully placed into PageMaker, the translated file is deleted and links are established to the original file.

Text or database file formats you can place in PageMaker

Text or database file format	Filename extension	Macintosh import	Macintosh export	Windows import	Windows export	Preferences dialog box
ClarisWorks 1.0-4.0		•				no
Document Content Architecture 2.0	.DCA	•	•	•	•	no
HTML	.HTM / .HTML	•	•	•	•	yes
Lotus 1-2-3 versions 1.0-5.0	.WKS			•		yes
Symphony 1.0-3.0	.WRK / .WRI			•		yes
MacWrite II		•	•			no
MacWrite Pro 1.0-1.5		•				no
Microsoft Excel 3.0-5.0	.XLS	•		•		yes
Microsoft Excel for Windows 7.0	.XLS	•		•		yes
Microsoft Write for Windows 2.0	.WRI			•		no
Microsoft Word for Windows 2.0	.DOC			•		yes
Microsoft Word 3.0 / Word 3.0 for DOS	.DOC	•	•	•		DOS only
Microsoft Word 4.0 / Word 4.0 for DOS	.DOC	•	•	•		yes
Microsoft Word 5.0 / Word 5.0 for DOS	.DOC	•		•		yes
Microsoft Word 6.0 / Word for Windows 6.0	.DOC	•		•		yes
Microsoft Word for Windows 7.0	.DOC	•		•		yes
Microsoft Works 2.0-4.0	.WKS	•				no
Open Database Connectivity (ODBC)				•		yes
PageMaker 5.0-6.01 stories		•		•		yes
Rich Text Format (RTF)	.RTF	•	•	•	•	no
Tagged Text (ASCII)	.TXT	•	•	•	•	no
Text-only (ASCII)	.TXT	•	•	•	•	yes
WordPerfect for Macintosh 2.x		•				yes
WordPerfect for Macintosh 3.0 / 3.1		•				no

continued on next page

Text or database file format	Filename extension	Macintosh import	Macintosh export	Windows import	Windows export	Preferences dialog box
WordPerfect 4.2 (DOS)	.WP4	•				no
WordPerfect 5.x (DOS and Windows)	.WP5	•		•	•	yes
WordPerfect 6.x (Windows)	.WP6	•		•		no
WordStar 3.3-6.0	.WS / .WST			•		no
WriteNow 2.0-3.0		•	•			no
XyWrite III or III+	.XY3	•	•	•	•	Win only

Text or database file formats you can place in PageMaker continued from previous page

Importing paragraph styles from a word-processing application

Styles are named sets of formatting attributes that you can apply to selected paragraphs. If your word-processing application supports styles and PageMaker has an import filter for the application, you can import the styles along with the text file.

If your word-processing application does not use styles, you can mark your word-processing file with style-name tags to match the styles in your PageMaker publication. PageMaker applies those styles to the marked paragraphs when you place the file. For information about PageMaker styles, see "Using Paragraph Styles" on page 136.

Note: *When you import an HTML document, you can map each HTML format (an element similar to a paragraph style), to a PageMaker style.*

When you import styles, PageMaker generally imports all formatting information specified in the word-processing application. Features that are not available in PageMaker are not imported. For example, PageMaker does not support character-based styles.

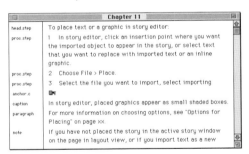

Styles imported into PageMaker

PageMaker adds imported styles to the list of existing styles for the publication, placing a disk icon next to each imported style name in the Styles palette. If an imported style has the same name as an existing PageMaker style, PageMaker overrides the imported style definition, and no icon appears next to the style name.

Importing text with style-name tags

A style-name tag is a name enclosed in angle brackets (for example, <Title> or <Body text>) at the beginning of a paragraph in your word-processed document. The tag tells PageMaker which style to apply to the paragraph. An empty tag (< >) indicates No Style. The tag must have no spaces or characters preceding it and all characters, including angle brackets, must have the same formatting; otherwise PageMaker imports the tag as text instead of as a style-name tag.

Style-name tags at the beginning of each paragraph

Styles have to be defined in PageMaker prior to importing text with style-name tags. If a style-name tag does not exactly match an existing PageMaker style, PageMaker creates a new style based on the formatting applied to the style-name tag in the word-processing application.

You can also import text tagged with PageMaker Tags. See Appendix D, "PageMaker Tags," for more information.

PageMaker applies the style specified by the first tag it finds to every subsequent paragraph until the end of the file or until it encounters a new tag. If you select Retain Format in the Place Document dialog box before you import the text, PageMaker applies the styles as well as any additional formatting, such as an italicized word in the middle of a paragraph.

To import a document with style-name tags:

Choose File > Place and select the Read Tags option. (You cannot transfer style-name tags through the Clipboard.)

Note: *In Windows, the Read Tags option is available only if the selected file uses a standard file-name extension and you have installed an import filter for that file type.*

Importing format-specific text options • When you place files from the applications and formats listed below, you can select format-specific options in a dialog box. PageMaker remembers the settings used the last time you imported text. Those settings become the defaults for files subsequently imported in that format until you change the settings or restart PageMaker.

Format	Options	To open the dialog box*
HTML	HTML format mapping to PageMaker styles; retain hyperlink information; import graphics as inline or independent.	Click OK/Open in the Place dialog box
Microsoft Word for Windows Microsoft Word 4.0-6.0 (Macintosh)	Table of contents; index; character spacing, width, kerning, and tracking; page breaks; tables.	Hold down the Shift key as you click OK/Open in the Place dialog box.
Microsoft Word 3.0-6.0 for DOS	Source of style names.	Hold down the Shift key as you click OK/Open in the Place dialog box.
PageMaker 5.0-6.0 stories	Place selected stories as one; list stories only over length x; story preview.	Click OK/Open in the Place dialog box.
Text-only (ASCII or ANSI)	Remove extra carriage returns (contiguous, at each line, or between paragraphs); retain tab-delimited tables; replace spaces with tabs; import text as Courier; import text with no conversion.	Click OK/Open in the Place dialog box.

* The dialog box opens automatically if Show Filter Preferences is selected in the Place dialog box.

Transferring text between PageMaker publications

You can import stories from PageMaker 5.0 and 6.0x publications using the Place command, which allows you to transfer text between PageMaker publications without opening another publication, copying, or pasting. To import text from a PageMaker 6.5 publication, you must first use the File > Save As command to save a copy of the publication in PageMaker 6.0 format.

The Place PageMaker Stories dialog box appears when you double-click a PageMaker 5.0 or 6.0x publication in the Place Document dialog box. The dialog box lists all stories in the publication, although you can specify a minimum number of characters for stories to be listed so that short stories, such as captions, don't appear in the list. Select the View Story option to preview a selected story before you place it. If you select more than one story to import in the list, the selected stories import as one continuous story.

The story importer retains character formatting and named styles from other publications but has the following limitations:

• Index entries with cross-references are not imported. Index entries with ranges other than Current Page or For Next Paragraphs are converted to Current Page.

• Inline graphics are not imported.

• Manual-kerning information from the original PageMaker publication is ignored and replaced with the pair-kerning instructions for the paragraph into which you insert the story.

• Text that you have rotated is imported but the text is not rotated when you place it in the publication.

To import a story from another PageMaker publication:

1 Choose File > Place.

2 In the list box, select a PageMaker publication, and then click OK.

3 To list only stories longer than a certain length, specify a number of characters in the List Only Stories Over _ Characters Long option, and then click Relist.

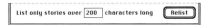

4 To preview a story in the Story Importer dialog box, select a story and click View Story.

5 Select one or more stories from the list or click Select All, and then click OK.

IMPORTING HTML FILES AND OTHER INFORMATION FROM THE WORLD WIDE WEB

In PageMaker 6.5 you can import HTML files directly from your hard disk or mounted volume, complete with embedded images, hyperlinks, and HTML formats. Additionally you can import directly from the Web using the following techniques:

• Specify a URL (uniform resource locator) to open in the Place dialog box (click the Place URL button). PageMaker communicates with the Web to copy the specified document to disk and then imports the file.

• Drag-and-drop text, graphics, and QuickTime movies from a Web browser window into the PageMaker window. If the text or graphic you select is hyperlinked to another location on the network, you have the option of dropping in the content of the URL referenced by the hyperlinked element. Not all browsers support drag-and-drop in the same way, so your results may vary depending on the browser you use.

Note: Importing HTML files or other information from the World Wide Web differs from importing other files in that a link is not maintained in the Links Manager dialog box to the HTML file or Web file. However, GIF or JPEG images imported directly or as part of an HTML file are stored locally and linked to the publication.

Setting up online preferences

To place URLs or to drag-and-drop from your Web browser, you must first set up PageMaker to communicate with the Internet; you can also indicate the folder on your hard drive in which to store information downloaded from the Web.

Note: You can skip step 1 of the following procedure if you are using Netscape Navigator (version 1.1 or later). You can also skip this step if you have a direct connection to the Internet, provided your Internet server uses port number 80, which is the standard HTTP port. If your company uses a firewall to provide a secured (indirect) connection to the Internet (and you are using a browser other than Netscape Navigator), then be sure to perform step 1.

To set online preferences:

1 Launch your Web browser, open the dialog box in which your Proxy / Proxy Port configuration is specified, and copy or write down the information exactly as it appears in the dialog box for:

• HTTP Proxy and Port.

• No Proxy On.

For example, in Internet Explorer 3.0, choose View > Options, click the Connections tab, and then click Settings. For other browsers, refer to your product documentation for setting up proxies. You can also get the appropriate information from your network administrator.

2 In PageMaker, choose File > Preferences > Online.

3 If you completed step 1, paste or type the information you determined from your browser in the Proxies / Port and No Proxies fields; otherwise leave the settings as they are.

4 In the Web Browser section, click Browse, select the browser you want, and then click OK.

5 For Download To Folder, click Browse to specify a folder on your hard disk, and click Open. You can also type in a folder name; PageMaker creates the folder if it does not exist. Files downloaded from the Web to be imported by PageMaker are stored in the folder you specify.

6 Click OK in the Online Preferences dialog box.

Importing HTML files

This section describes the various ways to bring HTML documents in whole or in part into your publication. Most of the import methods cause the Import HTML dialog box to appear. The subsequent section, "Setting HTML Import Options," describes the specific options available in the Import HTML dialog box.

To import an HTML file or URL with the Place command:

1 Turn to an empty page where you want to insert the HTML file, or, to replace existing text, click an insertion point in a new or existing text object, or select a text block with the pointer tool.

If you do not turn to an empty page (and you are not replacing existing text), PageMaker will insert one or more new pages after the currently selected page and place the HTML file on the new pages.

2 Choose File > Place, specify place options (including Inserting Text if you clicked an insertion point in step 1), and do one of the following:

• Double-click the HTML file you want to place.

The file must have an .HTM or .HTML extension.

• Click Place URL, type or paste the URL for the information you want to place, and click OK. The URL type must be http, ftp, file, or Gopher.

Using the Place URL option makes PageMaker communicate with the Web. Factors such as a slow network connection or a busy server can hamper PageMaker's ability to place the file quickly. If delays occur, it might be more efficient to switch to your Web browser and use it to open the URL, and then switch back to work in PageMaker until the browser indicates the Web document is fully available. Then you can use the browser's Save As feature to store the

Web document to your hard drive (make sure the Save As format is set to source, not text), and import it directly into PageMaker from there.

3 When the Import HTML dialog box appears, select the options you want, and click OK.

The options are explained in the next section.

To place all or part of an HTML document with drag-and-drop:

1 Turn to an empty page where you want to insert an entire HTML file, or to the page where you want to import selected text, graphics, or movies from an HTML file.

2 Position the PageMaker window and your browser window side-by-side.

3 In the browser, go to the page with the text, graphic, QuickTime movie, or hyperlink reference you want to import.

4 Do one of the following:

• If you want to import the contents of the file a hyperlink refers to, press Option (Macintosh) or Alt (Windows), and drag the hyperlink to the PageMaker window.

• If you want to bring only the selected text, graphic, or movie into PageMaker, drag the selection to the PageMaker window.

Note: If you drag and drop a GIF or JPEG image from Netscape Navigator into PageMaker, a screen preview of the image is imported. To import the actual image, either use your Web browser to save the image to disk and then place the image into PageMaker, or choose File > Place, click Place URL, and type the URL for the graphic.

5 Release the mouse button when the cursor appears at the desired location.

6 If you pressed Option or Alt while dragging, the Import HTML dialog box appears. Complete dialog box options as described in the next section, and then click OK. If you dragged a movie (or hyperlink reference to a movie) the QuickTime Import Filter dialog box appears; complete dialog box options as described on page 368.

Setting HTML import options

Regardless of how you import an HTML file, PageMaker can retain all hyperlinks in the file (they appear in the Hyperlinks palette for easy management), all GIF and JPEG images, as well as horizontal rules and HTML formats specified in the file. (You can freely map HTML formats to the paragraph styles defined in the active publication.)

PageMaker accepts HTML files compliant with version 3.2of the HTML specification, and supports a limited number of extensions to the HTML specification. The following subset of features are not imported into a publication:

• Character-level text attributes (other than bold, italic, underline, and superscript/subscript) such as color and type size.

• Java applets.

• Form elements, such as pop-up menus and text entry fields.

• Image mapping data (the image map graphic— a single image which links to multiple destinations—is imported without its hyperlinks).

The Import HTML dialog box gives you control over the way HTML formats are mapped to PageMaker paragraph styles in the active publication and how images referenced by the file are imported. If you import the file from within story editor you cannot control how images are placed: they come in as inline graphics.

To complete options in the Import HTML dialog box:

1 Make sure the Keep Hyperlinks option is selected if you want hyperlinked text and graphics in the HTML file to remain hyperlinked in PageMaker.

If the option is not selected, the hyperlink elements are imported but are not hyperlinked.

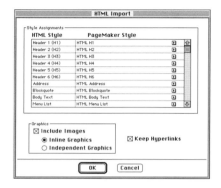

2 Select an option for importing graphics:

• Select Inline Graphics if you want the images to import as inline graphics that flow with the text.

Respecting and Complying With Intellectual Property Laws • Some of the materials you bring into PageMaker from the World Wide Web or other sources may be subject to restrictions on use or copying based on copyright, trademark, or other laws. Familiarize yourself with pertinent laws if you intend to reuse any material obtained from another source; it may be necessary to secure permission first. (Many Web pages include a footer or other section that notes copyright stipulations and whom to contact for permission or other information.) Issues of professional courtesy and integrity aside, the failure to comply with legal restrictions may have serious repercussions.

- Select Independent Graphics if you want the images added as independent graphics.

The images are sized as closely as possible to the original size, and are kept with the text they were associated with in the HTML file. If your page margins or column widths force the images to a smaller size, PageMaker scales the images proportionally. Horizontal rules are imported as paragraph rules.

IMPORTING A SPREADSHEET FILE

If you are using a spreadsheet application that supports OLE, you can OLE-link or OLE-embed an entire spreadsheet, a specified range, or a graphic. On the Macintosh, you can also publish a spreadsheet or databasee—if your application has this capability—and then subscribe to the published edition file in PageMaker.

If there is no PageMaker import filter for your spreadsheet application, and the application does not support OLE or editions, you can import a text-only (space- or tab-delimited ASCII) version of a spreadsheet, and then format and edit it in PageMaker. For more information about importing text-only files, see "Importing Text Features" on page 341.

The range or spreadsheet you import cannot contain more than 40 visible columns. PageMaker has a limit of 40 tabs per paragraph and uses tabs to separate spreadsheet columns. If you try to place a range with more than 40 columns, PageMaker warns you that it will place only the leftmost 40 columns.

Formatting imported spreadsheet text

When you place a spreadsheet as text, PageMaker generates one paragraph for each row in your spreadsheet with tabs between columns. (If you specify a three-dimensional import range for Lotus 1-2-3 release 3.0, PageMaker places the sheets in the range one after another as if you had printed the same range in Lotus 1-2-3.)

Note: When you import an Excel, Lotus 1-2-3, or Symphony spreadsheet as text, PageMaker converts each row in the spreadsheet to a paragraph and separates columns with tabs, matching the column widths in the original spreadsheet. If you plan to format the text in PageMaker in a font larger than that of the original spreadsheet, you may need to widen the columns in the spreadsheet application to accommodate the larger font.

PageMaker creates a style and applies it to the imported spreadsheet text (the WKS style for Lotus 1-2-3 and Symphony and the XLS style for Excel). The default for WKS is 10-point Courier with tabs based on that font and size. The default for XLS is the font you were using in Excel with tabs based on that font and size.

If you create a style named WKS or XLS before placing the spreadsheet, PageMaker applies the style attributes to the imported spreadsheet. However, PageMaker overrides all tab settings when importing and sets tabs to match the column widths in the spreadsheet application. To change column spacing, adjust the column widths in the spreadsheet before you import it, or adjust tabs in PageMaker after importing the spreadsheet.

Importing a spreadsheet or chart as a graphic

To import a spreadsheet or chart as you place any other graphic, you must first export it in a PageMaker-compatible graphic format. PageMaker places charts as graphic images, which you can manipulate in PageMaker (by cropping, transforming, and applying color) as you would any other graphic.

You can also paste an Excel chart as an OLE-linked or OLE-embedded object, or publish the chart as an edition file. See "OLE: Object Linking and Embedding" on page 357 for more information.

IMPORTING A DATABASE (WINDOWS ONLY)

To import native database files you must have both of the following components installed on your system:

• The ODBC (Open DataBase Connectivity) version 2.5 drivers and data sources. If you haven't installed them previously with your spreadsheet or database programs, you can install them from the Adobe PageMaker 6.5 CD-ROM; refer to the *Adobe PageMaker 6.5 Getting Started* book for installation instructions.

• The PageMaker ODBC filter or plug-in. The filter lets you import "flat" data files (no relational links or complex structure), and automatically update the links to them. The plug-in lets you import more complex data files, and allows for more in-depth SQL query editing—however, the imported files are not updated automatically as are linked files. You must run the ODBC plug-in to update the publication if the database file has changed since you imported it.

To import a flat data file with the ODBC filter:

1 Choose File > Place.

2 Select the name of the file you want to import.

3 Select the import options to specify how the text file is placed, and click OK or Open.

The Select Content dialog box appears, and lists each column (or field) in the file you selected.

4 In the Select Content dialog box, select each column you want to import, and then click the Add button to move it into the Selected Columns list box (or click Add All to import all the available columns). Optionally, you can edit the SQL query used to import the data. Click OK when you've completed specifying content.

5 In the dialog box that appears, format the data you are about to import, and click OK.

To import a new data file with the ODBC plug-in:

1 Choose Utilities > Plug-ins > ODBC.

Note: If you are not running the ODBC plug-in for the first time, a list appears of the previously placed ODBC files. Click the New button.

2 Select the layout option you want, and then click Next.

3 Select the Data Source for the file you want to import, and then click Next.

4 Select the table you want to import, and then click Next. Optionally, you can apply a custom query to define the information you want to import from the selected table.

The Select Content dialog box appears, and lists each column (or field) in the table you selected.

5 In the Select Content dialog box, select each column you want to import, and then click the Add button to move it into the Selected Columns list box. Optionally, you can edit the SQL query used to import the data. Click Next when you've completed specifying content.

6 Follow the instructions on screen to complete the import process. The exact steps depend on the Data Source you selected.

To update a data file imported with the ODBC plug-in:

1 Choose Utilities > Plug-ins > ODBC.

2 Select the previously-imported file you want to update, and do one of the following:

• Click Update to reimport the data as specified the last time you imported the file.

• Click Change to revise the import specifications you applied the last time you imported the data. For example, you might want to add or remove columns.

3 Click Done to close the dialog box.

IMPORTING A TABLE

You can import a table from another application in several ways:

• Create an embedded table by opening Adobe Table 3.0 from within PageMaker.

• Place or paste a table as a graphic. Use this method when you want to preserve graphics attributes created in another application.

• Place a table as tab-delimited text. Use this method when you want to edit the table text in PageMaker.

Creating, importing, and updating a table using Adobe Table 3.0

Adobe Table, a separate application included with PageMaker, can create tables as graphics or as text. One of the simplest ways to use Table is to open it directly from PageMaker and create an embedded OLE table that updates automatically. For existing tables, you can also establish an OLE-link between a PageMaker publication and the table file. See Chapter 10, "Using Adobe Table," for more information.

To create an embedded Adobe Table:

1 In layout view, choose Edit > Insert Object.

2 In the Insert Object dialog box, select Adobe Table from the list, select New, and then click OK.

3 Create a table in Adobe Table.

4 Choose File > Quit & Return.

To edit and update an OLE-embedded or OLE-linked Adobe Table:

1 In layout view, press Option (Macintosh) or Alt (Windows) and double-click on the table.

2 Edit the table.

3 When you are finished, choose File > Quit & Return.

You can also create a table in Adobe Table, export it to a file, and place it into PageMaker. In PageMaker, you can import any of the text or graphics formats that Adobe Table can export. However, if you are printing a table as a graphic to a PostScript printer, we recommend exporting the table as an EPS file. EPS is also the best option if you are going to export to HTML—the EPS preview can be converted to a GIF or JPEG image compatible with HTML.

Importing a table as a linked object

If you want to create a linked table that can update when you modify and save the original table file, use one of the following methods:

• Place the table saved as a graphic.

• Insert it as an embedded or linked OLE object.

You can use any application that supports the file formats that PageMaker can place, embed, or subscribe to. You can then manage the file links from the Links dialog box in PageMaker.

Importing a table as a graphic

If you created a table with graphics features that you want to preserve, import the table as a graphic. If you are printing to a PostScript printer or exporting the publication to HTML, we recommend that you export the table as an EPS file. For a list of file formats PageMaker can place, see the table on page 340.

Importing a table as text

If you want to be able to edit a table in PageMaker, export the table from the original application as a tab-delimited text file, which means that the columns are separated by tabs and the rows are separated by carriage returns. When you import the text file into PageMaker, the text takes on your publication's default type attributes. For a list of file formats PageMaker can place, see the table on page 342.

COPYING AND PASTING

You can use the Paste command to transfer text or graphics from one page to another within a PageMaker publication, or between publications.

If you use the Paste command to transfer a graphic from another application into PageMaker, the original attributes of the object may not be preserved. When transferring text, however, PageMaker will preserve most formatting if the original application copies text to the Clipboard using rich text format (RTF). You can paste text or graphics whether you're working in layout view or story editor.

If you paste a graphic into story editor, it imports as an inline graphic, which moves with the surrounding text. In layout view, you can paste a graphic as an inline graphic when you have an insertion point in a text object. (Graphics paste as independent objects when there is no insertion point in a text object.)

Pasting text or a large graphic into PageMaker may require more random-access memory (RAM) than importing the text or graphic by using the Place command. If you encounter memory problems when pasting objects, try importing data using the Place command instead.

How PageMaker handles formatting for objects imported from the Clipboard

When you paste an object from another application, it imports as either an unlinked or an OLE-embedded object. To paste as an OLE-linked object, use the Paste Special command.

Different applications support varying formats, so an application may copy more than one format to the Clipboard. PageMaker pastes the format that provides the most information about the object.

When you paste graphics created in an application that supports OLE, PageMaker embeds an OLE object. When you paste any object created in an application that is not an OLE source application, the object is pasted into the publication with no links to the original file.

When you paste rich text format (RTF) text, even from an application that supports OLE, PageMaker by default pastes a version of the text that is neither OLE-linked nor OLE-embedded, so that you can edit it in PageMaker. (You cannot edit OLE-linked or OLE-embedded text in PageMaker.)

To find out if the object on the Clipboard is available in rich text format, choose Edit > Paste Special.

When PageMaker cannot read the type specifications of text on the Clipboard, text pasted into an existing text block has the font, size, spacing, style, and paragraph specifications of the preceding character (or, if you insert at the beginning of the text block, of the following character). Additional type-style properties (such as boldface) applied to the text before you placed it on the Clipboard are retained.

To paste text or a graphic:

1 Select the text or graphic and choose Edit > Copy to copy to the Clipboard.

Use the text tool to select text; if you use the pointer tool, text may paste as an uneditable graphic.

2 Activate your PageMaker publication, and then choose Edit > Paste.

Pasting a specified format

When there is more than one format on the Clipboard and you choose Edit > Paste, PageMaker automatically uses the compatible format that best preserves the appearance of the original file. When you paste text, PageMaker gives priority to a format that allows you to edit the text in PageMaker while preserving formatting.

You can select the paste format from the PageMaker-compatible formats that another application copies to the Clipboard. In the Paste Special dialog box you may view and choose to import any one of the listed formats. The Paste Special command is not available in story editor.

To paste using a specified format:

1 With an object on the Clipboard, choose Edit > Paste Special.

2 Select a format in the Paste Special dialog box.

If the object supports OLE linking, click Paste Link if you want to paste it as an OLE-linked object.

3 Click OK.

DRAGGING AND DROPPING

You can select an object in another OLE 2.0 application and drag it into PageMaker, or vice versa, using the drag-and-drop method. (On the Macintosh, the application must be drag-and-drop aware.) You can also use drag-and-drop to copy or move an object from one PageMaker publication to another or from one position to another within the same PageMaker window. For more information, see " Duplicating an Object" on page 188.

Be aware of the difference between copying and moving. When you copy an object by dragging, PageMaker creates a copy of the object at the drop destination. When you move an object by dragging, it is deleted from the original position. If you are dragging an object into PageMaker, check the source application documentation to verify how the application specifies a copy or move operation.

You can drop a dragged object into PageMaker if the source application you dragged from makes the dragged object available in one of the following formats:

- Rich text format (RTF)
- Object linking and embedding (OLE)
- Encapsulated PostScript (EPS)
- Macintosh PICT
- Text
- Enhanced metafile (EMF)
- Windows metafile (WMF)
- Windows bitmap (BMP)

To copy an object from PageMaker to another application:

1 Make sure both the source and destination windows are visible.

2 Drag the object from the source window into the desired position in the destination window. In Windows only, press Ctrl while you do this, otherwise the object is moved rather than copied.

3 Release the mouse button.

To cancel copying or moving when dragging:

Drop the object outside of all windows, or drag it back to its original position, or (in Windows only) press the Esc key.

To move an object from PageMaker to another application (Windows only):

Drag the object to the destination. This deletes the object in the original position and moves it to the new location.

OLE: OBJECT LINKING AND EMBEDDING

Object linking and embedding are two ways to update an imported object when the object's original file is modified. PageMaker supports the object linking and embedding (OLE) protocol, a standard for exchanging data between applications.

PageMaker is an OLE 2.0 container, meaning it can import OLE objects from other applications. PageMaker is not an OLE 2.0 server, so it cannot create an OLE object.

For OLE to import an object properly, the source application must be an OLE server, and your system must have enough RAM for both PageMaker and the other application to run simultaneously and to accommodate the size of the object.

You can link or embed an entire document or any portion of a document that you can copy to the Clipboard and which is smaller than the pasteboard in PageMaker. The exact amount you can copy depends on the amount of available RAM when you copy. Importing large objects using OLE may require more RAM than using the Place command.

Note: Do not use OLE to import more than one page of continuous text, because OLE does not support multiple-page objects.

You manage linked and embedded OLE objects the same way you manage PageMaker links and edition links, using the Links command. A linked object updates automatically when the original document is modified, as long as the original document remains linked to the PageMaker publication and Update Automatically is selected in the Link Options dialog box. See "Managing Linked Text and Graphics" on page 369 for more information.

Using OLE to import text

PageMaker imports OLE text as a graphic whether you paste it independently or into a text object. You cannot edit OLE text using the text tool; you can only edit it in its source application. If you want to import editable text, use the Paste or Place command to import it.

Note: You cannot link or embed OLE objects in story editor because the Paste Special and Insert Object commands are not available in story editor.

To import a linked OLE object by pasting:

1 In the source application, create and save the text or graphic you want to import.

2 Select the text or graphic, and copy it to the Clipboard.

3 Activate the PageMaker publication, and then choose Edit > Paste Special.

4 In the Paste Special dialog box, click Paste Link.

5 Click OK.

To import an existing file as a linked OLE object that updates automatically:

1 In PageMaker, choose Edit > Insert Object.

2 Click Create From File, and select a file from the list.

3 Click Link, and then click OK.

The item being linked or embedded is automatically placed on the page.

To create an embedded OLE object:

1 In PageMaker, choose Edit > Insert Object.

2 Click New, and select an application from the list.

3 Click OK.

4 Create or open an object in the source application.

5 Choose File > Exit in the source application.

Note: *If you cannot find File >Exit in the source application, see its documentation for more information.*

What happens when you link using OLE?

Importing • After creating an object in the source application **A**, you import it from the Clipboard **B** into a PageMaker publication **C**. As the object imports, a link is created **D** between the object and its original file. If you copy the object to other publications **E**, additional links are created to the original file **F**.

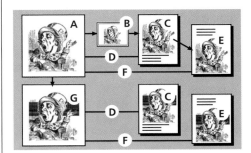

Updating • When you want to edit the object, it automatically opens in the application that created it **G**. When you finish editing, all files that contain a copy of the object are updated.

What happens when you embed using OLE?

Importing • When you want to insert a new object from another application into a PageMaker publication **A**, you select a file or an application from PageMaker. The file imports or the application opens with a new, empty file **B**. When you import or finish creating the object, it is inserted into your PageMaker publication and a link **C**, is created between the object and its original application.

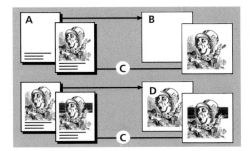

Updating • When you want to edit the object, it automatically opens in the application that created it **D**. When you finish editing, the object is updated in the PageMaker publication.

To import an existing file as an embedded OLE object:

1 In PageMaker, choose Edit > Insert Object.

2 Click Create From File, and select a file from the list.

3 Click OK.

The item being linked or embedded is automatically placed on the page.

Editing an OLE object

When you want to update any OLE object, the application that created the object must be available on your hard drive with sufficient unused RAM.

When you intend to update a linked OLE object, you must maintain a separate saved file containing the original text or graphics on a mounted volume or disk. An embedded OLE object is completely contained within PageMaker, so no external file is required.

To update a linked or embedded OLE object:

1 In PageMaker, select the object, and then choose Edit > Edit Original, or double-click the object.

2 Edit the object after it opens in the source application.

3 Choose File > Exit in the source application.

Note: *If you cannot find File > Exit in the source application, see its documentation for more information.*

PUBLISH AND SUBSCRIBE (Macintosh only)

You may be able to publish text or graphic elements from the application in which they were created and then import them into a publication by subscribing to the resulting edition, a method called publish and subscribe. When you subscribe to an edition, you can automatically update the imported object (the subscriber) to reflect changes in the original document.

The Subscribe To command is useful when you want to revise imported text or graphics that you use in more than one instance, such as in a series of illustrations.

You can also subscribe to edition files using the Place command. By default, editions to which you subscribe are updated automatically, while editions you place adopt the links setting for placed objects. See "Managing Linked Text and Graphics" on page 369 for more information.

You can subscribe to text or graphics editions in layout view or in story editor.

To subscribe to an edition:

1 Choose Edit > Editions > Subscribe To.

2 Select the edition file to which you want to subscribe.

3 Click Subscribe, or if you are placing a text edition and you want to import a PICT (graphic) version of the text, press Shift as you click Subscribe. (This only works with some types of text editions.)

4 Click the loaded icon where you want the upper left corner of the subscriber to be (or click in a selected frame); or drag to define the size of the subscriber, and then release the mouse button.

What happens when you publish and subscribe?

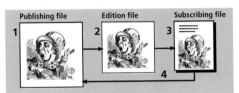

Exporting: After you create text or graphics in the publishing file (source file) **1**, publish (export) a version of the object as an edition file **2** on disk. You can publish one edition per page.

Importing: After you publish an edition file **2** from a publishing file, you can open a subscribing file (destination file) **3** and subscribe to (import) the edition file. When an edition is inside a subscribing file, it is called a subscriber. You can subscribe to more than one edition file per publication or page.

Updating: When you want to edit the object, the Macintosh automatically opens the edition file in the publishing file that created it **4**.

When do revisions take effect?

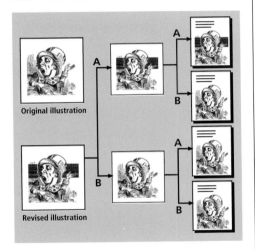

If you specify automatic updating **A** for either a publisher or a subscriber, changes affect an edition file or a subscriber when you save the publishing file. If you specify manual updating **B**, changes take effect only when you request them.

To modify a subscriber using the application that created it:

1 In PageMaker, select the subscriber.

2 Choose Edit > Edit Original. PageMaker opens the edition file in the application in which it was created.

3 Modify the edition file, and then choose File > Save.

4 Close the publishing application or choose PageMaker 6.0 from the application menu to return to PageMaker.

Deleting an edition

It is best to delete an unwanted edition file from the application that published it. If you delete an edition by putting it in the Trash, the link to an edition's publisher is not deleted, so you may see messages asking you to link to a file you deleted.

To delete an edition:

1 Open the application that published the edition.

2 Choose Edit > Editions > Publishing Options.

3 Click Cancel Publisher.

Note: The location of the Cancel Publisher option may vary depending on the application. For example, some applications provide it as a command on a submenu of the Edit menu.

VERSION CONTROL FOR EDITION FILES

Once you subscribe to an edition file, you can specify whether changes affect the PageMaker subscribing publications automatically or only when you request an update. Because you can subscribe to more than one edition per publication, you can set options uniquely for each subscriber.

The result of the subscriber options you select in PageMaker is affected by two other factors: the publishing options set by each publishing application, and the general linking settings specified in PageMaker placing and linking options.

A subscriber updates only when the edition file to which it subscribes is in the same volume or disk from which it was originally placed. If you must store the original file on another volume or disk, mount that volume or disk when prompted or the link will permanently break when you save the publication.

Subscriber options and publisher options

The publishing file that created an edition file can have its own updating settings, and their interaction with PageMaker's subscriber options will affect how a PageMaker subscriber actually updates. To simplify file management, apply publisher and subscriber options consistently across your project.

Updating and linking options for a subscriber

New subscribers are updated automatically. PageMaker uses the default settings selected in the Place Document and Link Options dialog boxes when you choose Subscribe To.

For more information about the interactions between subscriber options and PageMaker's linking and updating options, see "Setting Linking Options for a Subscriber (Macintosh)" on page 374.

You can move an edition file to any location on its current volume, and PageMaker will still be able to find and update it. However, you cannot move it to another volume unless you re-establish its links by resubscribing to it or by using the Links Manager command.

To import edition files using options other than the default settings:

1 Choose File > Place and select the edition file.

2 Select the options you want in the Place Document dialog box, and then click OK.

To set subscriber options:

1 Select a subscriber.

2 Choose Edit > Editions > Subscriber Options.

3 Specify options as follows, and then click OK.

• The Subscriber To option displays the name and location of the edition file.

• The Get Editions option lets you specify when PageMaker updates edition files. To update PageMaker whenever the edition file changes, click Automatically. To update PageMaker only when you click Get Edition Now, click Manually.

• The Get Edition Now option updates the subscriber in your publication.

• The Cancel Subscriber option breaks the link to the edition file and converts the subscriber to the format in which it was published.

Note: *You can re-establish links to the edition file by selecting the object, choosing Element > Link Info (in layout view), locating the file to link, and clicking Link in the Link Info dialog box.*

• The Open Publisher option closes the dialog box and opens the edition file in the application in which it was created. The portion of the file that was in view in PageMaker will display in the publishing application.

Stopping all edition updates

Choose Edit > Editions > Stop All Editions to temporarily suspend all updates to subscribers. For example, if you are part of a workgroup, you may want to selectively update subscribers in your publication.

Restarting all edition updates

To turn on automatic updating again and immediately update all subscribers with their latest editions, deselect Stop All Editions. To turn on automatic updating without also updating subscribers (thereby discarding recent changes), press Shift while you choose Stop All Editions.

Updates are suspended for all publications opened and closed during the current PageMaker session. If you quit PageMaker and then restart, publications are automatically updated again.

You can override the Stop All Editions command for a particular edition file or for all edition files (and other linked files) in a publication publication by clicking Update or Update All in the Links dialog box.

Note: Update All in the Links dialog box does not update an edition that is set to Manually in Subscriber options.

For more information about editions, publishers, and subscribers, see your Macintosh system documentation.

ACQUIRING A TIFF IMAGE

PageMaker supports TWAIN, a cross-platform interface that lets you create a TIFF image using a device (such as a scanner, video-capture board, or digital camera) attached to your computer and import the image into your publication without leaving PageMaker. Your device must support TWAIN in order for you to take advantage of this feature.

Be sure to install on your hard drive both the Source Manager and TWAIN Data source files that come with a TWAIN-compatible device. On Macintosh System 7.1 or later, the Data source file should be in the TWAIN folder within the Preferences folder in the System folder. In Windows, the Data source filename has a DS extension and should be in the TWAIN folder inside the Windows folder, or in a folder inside the TWAIN folder. Once the Data source file is installed, you can operate the device from within PageMaker.

Note: Check with your device manufacturer for the latest Source Manager and TWAIN Data source files.

To select a TWAIN- compatible device:

1 Choose File > Acquire > Select Source.

2 Select the input device.

3 Click OK.

To create and import a TIFF image without leaving PageMaker:

1 Make sure your image-acquisition device is ready to create an image.

Also make sure your scanning software application is inactive, since the next step in the procedure activates it.

2 Choose File > Acquire > Acquire Image.

3 Specify a name, location, and other available options for the image, and then click OK.

4 In the dialog box that opens, specify options according to your device documentation, and then click the button that creates the TIFF image.

The name of the button varies with the device; in most cases it is OK, Scan, or Acquire.

If your device requires physical operation (a hand scanner, for example) it is ready for you to begin creating the image at this point. Otherwise, the image software acquires the image and saves it to your hard drive. If you are in layout view and do not have an insertion point in a text block, the pointer changes to a loaded TIFF icon when the image is complete. Otherwise, the image imports as an inline graphic.

5 In PageMaker, click the loaded cursor where you want the upper left corner of the image (or click a frame to add the TIFF to the frame). To size the image as you place it, drag the mouse and then release the mouse button.

IMPORTING PHOTO CD IMAGES

PageMaker supports the Kodak Photo CD standard for importing images. Photo CD images are available in a range of resolutions, depending on the Photo CD disc format in which they were stored. If your publication will be printed on a commercial printing press, images should be stored using the Photo CD Master or Photo CD Master Pro formats.

Note: To import a PhotoCD image you must turn on the Kodak-ICC CMS (choose File > Preferences > General and click CMS Setup).

Images are stored on Photo CD discs in landscape (wide) orientation; the same orientation as they appear on a negative filmstrip. When you import an image into PageMaker, the Kodak Photo CD import filter enables you to change the orientation and specify other options, such as image size and resolution.

The Photo CD Master format has five default resolution settings; the Photo CD Master Pro has six. When you import a Photo CD image, the filter takes into account both image size and the resolution you specified in the Document Setup dialog box, and then assigns the optimum default resolution. You can override this setting in the Kodak Photo CD import filter dialog box.

Before you deliver Photo CD images to a prepress service provider for final output, determine how they prefer to receive the images. For example, your service provider may not own a Photo CD-compatible CD-ROM drive, and may prefer to receive images in TIFF format. For more information, see "Saving Photo CD Images as CIE Lab TIFFS" on page 367.

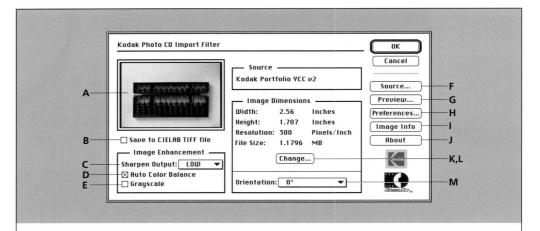

Kodak Photo CD import dialog box

A This area shows a thumbnail of the stored image.

B Click to save the image as a CIE Lab TIFF.

C Choose a sharpening effect from the pop-up menu.

D Click to balance the colors of the image using the lightest part of the image as the white point (the whitest part of the image). Use this option only if the lightest part of the image was originally white.

E Click to convert the image to a grayscale image with 256 levels of gray.

F Click to choose the film-type used to create the image. This option fine-tunes the image based on the original medium of the image. Also click to choose a different device profile for color managing the image.

G Click to see a preview of the image that reflects the orientation, grayscale, and color balance selections. Sharpness is not shown in the preview.

H Click to change the unit of measure displayed, and to turn off alert messages.

I Click to view image information, including the type of device used to scan the image and the original medium of the image.

J Click to view the Kodak Photo CD import filter version number.

K Click, then type a value to specify image size.

L Click, then type a value to specify resolution.

M Click to select an option to rotate or to flip the image either clockwise (CW) or counter-clockwise (CCW).

To place a Photo CD image:

1 Choose File > Place.

2 Select the Photo CD image you want to import, and then click OK.

3 Set options in the Kodak Photo CD import filter dialog box, as follows:

• To crop the image, click the Preview button, and hold down the mouse button and drag across the image preview to select the part of the image you want. The Kodak Photo CD import filter limits cropping to the image sizes supported by the Photo CD format.

• To change the image size and resolution attributes, type new values in the Quality and Size areas of the dialog box. The Kodak Photo CD import filter limits the image size to the maximum supported by the Photo CD format.

• To sharpen the image, choose the degree of sharpening from the Sharpening pop-up menu. The effects of sharpening do not appear in the preview or thumbnail images; sharpening takes place when the image is imported, and may take some time.

• To rotate or flip the image, choose an orientation from the Orientation pop-up menu. You will see the correct orientation in the Kodak Photo CD import filter dialog box preview window, not in the thumbnail view on the CD itself.

For additional options, see the Kodak Photo CD import dialog box overview on page 366.

4 Click Preview to view the image in its own window at the current settings.

5 Click OK to close the preview window and make additional changes, and then click OK to import the image.

Saving Photo CD images as CIE Lab TIFFs

The CIE L*a*b model is an international standard for color measurement that is device-independent; that is, it creates consistent color regardless of the specific device that you use to create or output the image. The CIE Lab TIFF format maintains color fidelity when moving images between systems and when printing to PostScript Level 2 printers.

For fastest results using Photo CD images, choose the Save as Lab TIFF option for each image. The image is converted to a CIE Lab TIFF and stored on your hard disk (hard disks have faster access times than CD-ROM drives). Saving the Photo CD image as a Lab TIFF also stores the image in a format that does not require a Photo CD-compatible CD-ROM drive to open the image.

Saving images as Lab TIFFs also allows you to give each image a unique name, rather than using the generic Photo CD naming scheme (IMG001.PCD; IMG002.PCD and so on).

Note: *To re-import an image saved as a Lab TIFF, re-save the original Photo CD as a Lab TIFF image when importing. Do not use the Replace option in the File > Place dialog box.*

IMPORTING A QUICKTIME MOVIE FRAME

You can import any frame within a QuickTime movie as a linked TIFF image; the image is defined with RGB color and its resolution is 72 dpi. If you later export to Portable Document Format (PDF) or Hypertext Markup Language (HTML), the exported file automatically includes a hyperlink to the movie so that the viewer of the PDF or HTML document can play the movie (provided the movie file is stored in the same folder as the PDF or HTML document, and the necessary movie-viewing components are available on the computer used to view the movie).

For the Macintosh, you must have QuickTime 2.0 or later installed on your system, and the movie file must have the file type "moov." For Windows, QuickTime version 2.1.1 or later must be installed on your system, and the movie file must have the filename extension .MOV. In Windows, the movie must be flattened with QuickTime-compatible software, such as Adobe Premiere or the MoviePlayer utility from Apple Inc.

Note: *In the QuickTime Frame Import dialog box, you preview movies frame by frame, but you actually select a specific time, not a specific frame, to import. If the movie is edited and the link is updated, PageMaker imports the new frame associated with the time you selected when you first placed the image.*

To import a QuickTime movie frame:

1 Choose File > Place.

2 Select the name of the movie you want to import from, the place options you want, and then click OK or Open.

In Windows, you might need to select the More Importable Files option in the Place dialog box in order to make the .MOV file available.

3 When the movie preview appears in the dialog box, use the player controls to display the frame you want to import.

You can click the play, rewind, and forward buttons, or use the slider bar to find the frame you want.

4 With the desired frame selected, click OK.

Once the image is imported, you can double-click the image to replace it with a different frame from the same movie file.

MANAGING LINKED TEXT AND GRAPHICS

You can modify how linked objects link and update. Objects with links can be placed objects, linked OLE objects or, on the Macintosh, placed or subscribed edition files.

Note: *Do not confuse links with hyperlinks in PageMaker. For information on hyperlinks see Chapter 13, "Distributing a Publication Electronically."*

Use the Links Manager, Link Info, and Link Options commands to identify and monitor objects in your publication that are linked to external text and graphics files or applications. Use these commands to update linked text or graphics, to re-establish links when external files are moved from their original folders, to unlink a file from the active publication, and to minimize the size of the publication by storing large graphic images externally:

• The Links Manager command lets you view or modify links for single and multiple objects throughout a publication.

• The Link Options command or option lets you view or modify updating options for an individual object or for link defaults.

• The Link Info command or option lets you view or modify a selected object's link to its original file.

To view the link status of all files in the publication

Choose File > Links Manager.

The Links Manager dialog box • Shows the status of all links in the publication.

A Document: Lists the filename of each linked, OLE-linked, and subscriber object in the active publication.

B Kind: Lists the type of each linked file.

C Page: Lists the page numbers where the linked objects appear, and may also include page indicator symbols. (See table on page 371.)

D Link status indicators: Symbols appear in this column, indicating the state of linked files. When no indicator appears beside the filename, the object is either up-to-date or it is no longer linked.

E Status area: Describes the current status of the link.

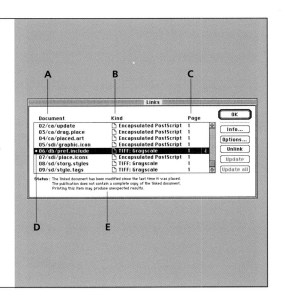

TIP: YOU CAN ALSO
MODIFY A LINKED
OBJECT'S LINK SETTINGS
BY CHOOSING FILE >
LINKS MANAGER,
SELECTING A FILE
FROM THE LIST,
AND THEN CLICKING
INFO OR OPTIONS.

Setting link options

It's a good idea to determine how you want imported files to link and update, and then set linking defaults to match your work process. This way, imported files automatically conform to your workflow.

Note: You cannot change link options for an OLE-embedded object, because it has no source file.

To set default link options:

1 With no object selected, choose Element > Link Options.

2 Select options, and then click OK.

To set link options for the selected object, page, or publication:

1 In layout view, do one of the following:

• To change just one object, select the object and choose Element > Link Options

• To change all links on the current page or throughout the publication, choose Utilities > Plug-ins > Global Link Options.

2 If you chose the Global Link Options plug-in, specify the range you want the options to apply to (either the current page or the entire publication) and the scope (text, graphics, or both).

3 Specify options as follows, and then click OK.

• The Store Copy in Publication option determines whether an imported file is stored inside or outside the publication. (Text files are always stored in the publication, so you can edit the text.)

• The Update Automatically option updates the copy of the file stored inside the publication when its original file is modified. This option is always on for externally stored objects.

• The Alert Before Updating option presents a dialog box notifying you when PageMaker is about to update a link, and asks you to approve the update.

Setting link options for an EPS graphic

PageMaker can add Open Prepress Interface (OPI) comments to an EPS graphic so that you can use a low-resolution version of it for layout and then substitute a high-resolution scan of the image before imaging or printing to disk. PageMaker not only adds OPI comments to your print file when you print a composite PostScript file disk, it can also read OPI comments when you import an EPS graphic.

To set link options for an imported EPS graphic:

1 Choose File > Place.

2 Select the EPS file you want to import.

3 Press Shift and click OK.

4 In the EPS Import Filter dialog box, select the Read Embedded OPI Image Links option.

Note: OPI comments embedded in an EPS will not be read if the Omit Images option is selected in the Print dialog box or if you are printing to a .SEP or .EPS file.

A guide to page and link-status indicator symbols in the Links dialog box

Page indicators in the Links dialog box

UN The linked inline graphic or text is in a story that has not yet been composed; the page number is therefore unknown.

LM The linked item is on a left master page.

RM The linked item is on a right master page.

PB The linked item is on the pasteboard.

OV (Overset text) The linked inline graphic is not displayed in layout view because it is part of a text block that has not been fully flowed.

X (Macintosh) The linked text is in an open story window and has not yet been placed.

> Indicates that a link established in a Macintosh PageMaker publication is not supported in Windows PageMaker.

Link-status indicators in the Links dialog box

NA Indicates that the object has no source document because it was pasted without links or is an OLE-embedded object.

Ø Indicates that the link is broken because the object is an EPS graphic that contains links to one or more Open Prepress Interface (OPI) images, and PageMaker cannot find the original OPI images referenced by the links.

? Indicates that the link is broken; PageMaker cannot find the linked object's external file.

◆ (Macintosh) or **+** (Windows) The object is linked to an external file that has been modified since it was imported into or exported from the publication.

◇ (Macintosh) or (Windows) The object is linked to an external file that has been modified since it was imported into or exported from your publication, and the Update Automatically option is turned off for this object.

△ (Macintosh) or **!** (Windows) The object is linked to an external file and both the internal and external copies of the object have been modified. Resolve this situation carefully—updating the link will replace the changed internal object with the changed external object, and if the changes were different in each copy, some changes may be lost.

X (Windows) The object is linked to a file stored outside the publication, and the external copy has been modified.

¿ Indicates that an object will not print in high resolution (because a linked file is missing, a required filter or OLE object-handler is not available, the print image has not been translated for the current platform), or that high-resolution printing may not provide the expected results.

Updating a single file manually

A manual update is only possible when an externally linked file is out of date. Updating a link replaces the current internal version of a linked object with its current external version. If both the internal and external copies of a linked object have been modified, PageMaker asks you to verify that you want to discard the changes made to the internal copy.

If PageMaker cannot locate the object, choose File > Links Manager and then click Info to find it.

Note: An added inline graphic is considered a change to an internal copy of a story, so it will be discarded if you update the story with a newer external version.

To update a file manually:

1 Choose File > Links Manager.

2 Select an object from the list.

3 Click Update.

To update all linked files simultaneously:

1 Choose File > Links Manager.

2 Click the Update All button.

3 Click OK.

Note: This option is available only for those objects that are set to Update Automatically.

Unlinking an object

Sometimes you may want to unlink objects from their original publisher (Macintosh) or file. Most often, you break links to prevent an imported object from being updated when the source files change, such as when your source file is a spreadsheet.

If you unlink a Macintosh edition, it becomes the equivalent of a non-OLE graphic that you paste from the Clipboard. If you unlink a PageMaker linked file, PageMaker does not check or update the status of the file.

Note: You cannot unlink OLE objects.

To unlink an object:

1 Choose File > Links Manager.

2 Select the object that you want to unlink in the Links dialog box.

3 Click Unlink, and then click OK.

Relinking a broken link

Each time you open or print your publication, PageMaker tries to link to all imported files listed in the Links dialog box. If a file has been moved or is on an unmounted volume or disk, it will not be found. You must reestablish the link to allow future updates.

When you relink to a file, PageMaker reimports the file. PageMaker preserves resizing, rotating, skewing, and reflecting modifications applied to the object in your publication. Any other changes you make to imported files are lost when you relink.

Note: You can only relink a text file to another text file, or a graphics file to another graphics file.

To re-establish a broken link:

1 Choose File > Links Manager.

2 Select the file that has a broken link.

3 Click the Info button.

4 Locate the original file (or a replacement),

5 If you are relinking to a graphic you cropped in PageMaker and you want to preserve existing cropping, select Retain Cropping Data.

6 Click Link, and then click OK.

KEEPING LINKED FILES WITH THE PUBLICATION

Although the ability to link files gives you the flexibility to edit text and graphics you import into PageMaker, it also makes it essential that your links are in order before you print your publication. This is especially true if you take your publication to a service bureau or prepress service provider for printing: you'll need to provide the service bureau with copies of certain linked files in order for your publication to print correctly.

Note: Your service bureau might prefer that you use the Save For Service Provider plug-in, which saves files for remote printing and checks the status of links, fonts, and other attributes of the publication. See "Using the Save for Service Provider Plug-in" on page 411 for more information.

PageMaker always stores a copy of text files and pasted non-OLE objects inside the publication, but editions and large imported graphics may be stored outside the publication. Your publication will not print correctly if objects stored outside the publication are missing when you print the publication at a service bureau; you must copy all the files you need to print or work with a publication onto another storage device.

To copy linked files with your publication:

1 Choose File > Save as.

2 Select Files for Remote Printing in the Save Publication As dialog box, select a location on a storage device for the files (such as a hard drive or removable cartridge), name the publication file, and then click OK.

PageMaker saves the file and copies all linked files needed for printing (those not stored in the publication) into the same location as the publication files. For complex publications with many linked files, you may want to create a new folder before saving the publication with its linked files.

To copy all linked files instead of only those needed for printing, select All Linked Files in the Save Publication As dialog box.

Updating links and resolving font conflicts

After you select a publication to open, PageMaker searches for text and graphics files linked to the publication and matches the fonts used in the publication with those available in your computer.

If a font used in the selected publication isn't available, PageMaker will display the PANOSE Font Matching dialog box. See Appendix B, "Font Substitution," for more information.

If you open a publication that has links to external files that are set to update automatically, PageMaker prompts you with a Cannot Find dialog box if a file cannot be located (for example, if the file is not in the location you originally specified, or if the file or location has been renamed). Use this dialog box to locate the file or to tell PageMaker to stop searching. Set options as follows:

• Click the Link option to re-establish the link after you have located the file and selected it in the list box. PageMaker searches that location for any other links it cannot find. To re-establish a link for one file without adding that folder to the search set (for example, if there are no more linked files at that location), hold down Option (Macintosh) or Ctrl (Windows) while you click Link.

• Click the Ignore option to end the search for a file. Another Cannot Find alert appears if more links need to be re-established.

• Click the Ignore All option to end the search for all files linked to the publication you want to open. This lets you open the publication directly. You can relink files after opening a publication by choosing File > Links Manager.

Setting linking options for a subscriber (Macintosh)

On the Macintosh, a subscriber you imported has linking and updating options that exist in addition to PageMaker options. Fortunately, changes you make to one set of linking options also appear in the other. You can specify whether you want PageMaker to update a subscriber whenever the edition file is revised or only when you specify.

To set subscriber options:

1 In layout view, select a subscriber.

2 Choose Edit > Editions > Subscriber Options.

3 Select options, and then click OK.

For more information about options in the Subscriber Options dialog box, see "Subscriber Options and Publisher Options" on page 362.

Effect of Subscriber Options settings on Link Options settings

In the Subscriber Options dialog box, click...	...to change your options in the Link Options dialog box from...	to...
Manually ☒ Update Automatically ☒ Alert before updating	☒ Store copy in publication ☐ Update Automatically ☐ Alert before updating	☒ Store copy in publication
Manually ☒ Update Automatically ☐ Alert before updating	☒ Store copy in publication ☐ Update Automatically ☐ Alert before updating	☒ Store copy in publication
Automatically ☐ Update Automatically ☐ Alert before updating	☒ Store copy in publication ☒ Update Automatically ☐ Alert before updating	☒ Store copy in publication
Manually	☐ Store copy in publication ☐ Update Automatically ☐ Alert before updating	☒ Store copy in publication ☐ Update Automatically ☐ Alert before updating

Effect of Link Options settings on Subscriber Options

In the Link Options dialog box, these settings...	...change your update option in the Subscriber Options dialog box to...
☒ Store copy in publication ☒ Update Automatically ☒ Alert before updating	Automatically
☒ Store copy in publication ☒ Update Automatically ☐ Alert before updating	Automatically
☒ Store copy in publication ☐ Update Automatically ☐ Alert before updating	Manually
☐ Store copy in publication ☐ Update Automatically ☐ Alert before updating	Automatically

Alternatively, you can set subscriber options using the Element > Link Options or File > Links Manager commands, as you can for most other imported files. The dialog box reflects the most recent settings, regardless of the command used.

REVISING IMPORTED OBJECTS

Although you can import objects into PageMaker in several different ways, you can revise most imported objects in the same way, regardless of how you imported them.

You can use the Edit Original command to edit an imported object in the application that created it, directly from PageMaker, or to edit the object using a different application than the one in which it was created.

You cannot use the Edit Original command to edit unlinked text or graphics (graphics that you did not OLE-link or OLE-embed, or that you have unlinked in the Links dialog box). A graphic in a simple paint or draw format may be edited by pasting the graphic into the application in which it was created.

To edit an imported object in the application that created it, directly from PageMaker:

1 Select the text or graphic object.

2 Use one of the following selection methods:

• Choose Edit > Edit Original. (If the object is an OLE object, Edit Original on the Edit menu is replaced by the object format, such as Excel Worksheet Object.)

• Use the pointer tool to select any object you placed or to which you subscribed, and then hold down Option (Macintosh) or Alt (Windows) as you double-click the object.

• Double-click an OLE object.

• Select the subscriber in your publication, choose Edit > Editions > Subscriber Options, and then click Open Publisher (Macintosh only). PageMaker starts the application that created the object, with the original text or graphics document open. (The application must be available on your hard drive or network drive.)

3 Edit and save the object.

Note: *In story view, you must use Edit Original to edit linked text in its originating application; to edit an inline graphic, select only the graphics marker, and then choose Edit Original.*

To edit a linked object using a different program than the one in which it was created :

1 Select the text or graphic object (except subscribers on the Macintosh and OLE objects).

2 Hold down Shift, and then choose Edit > Edit Original.

3 Select an editor in the Choose Editor dialog box, and then click Launch.

Alternatively, you can select the object, and then hold down Shift + Option (Macintosh) or Shift + Alt (Windows) as you double-click the object.

EXPORTING TEXT

You can save all or part of a PageMaker story in a file format that you can open in a variety of applications. Each story in a publication exports to a separate document, although you may combine exported stories using an indirect method. Except for PICT graphics on the Macintosh, inline graphics are not exported with a PageMaker story.

Note: *You can also export a publication as an HTML file complete with text, hyperlinks, HTML formats, and GIF or JPEG images. See "Exporting as HTML" on page 455 for more information.*

PageMaker can export text in several file formats, listed in the Export dialog box. The formats listed are used by other applications, which retain the type specifications, indents, and tabs set in your document. The line length is the default specified by your word-processing application. If the word-processing application to which you want to save the text is not listed, you may need to install the appropriate export filter.

If PageMaker doesn't have an export filter for your word-processing application, you may be able to transfer the file to your word processor in either RTF (rich text format) or DCA/RFT format. RTF retains the most formatting. If your word-processing application doesn't support these formats, use the text-only (ASCII) format. (Exporting in ASCII format removes all character attributes from the text.)

Note: *If your file contains text attributes that PageMaker does not support, you may want to preserve the original file by exporting it as a new file under a different name.*

To export a story:

1 Select the text tool and click in the story you want to export (or open the story in story editor). Alternatively, use the text tool to select a portion of the text to export.

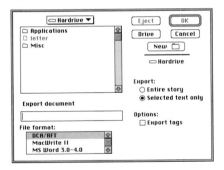

2 Choose File > Export > Text.

3 Select a file format and options, name the file, and then click OK.

Exporting a range of text

You may export all or part of a story. The Entire Story option is selected when you place an insertion point in the story. The Selected Text Only option is selected when text is selected, although you can override this option by selecting Entire Story.

To combine and export stories from a publication:

1 Open the publication from which you want to combine and export stories, choose File > Save As, and save the publication as a PageMaker 6.0 publication.

2 Open a new PageMaker publication.

3 Choose File > Place, select the publication from which you want to combine and export stories, and then click OK.

The Place PageMaker Stories dialog box appears, listing every story in the publication in the order in which they were placed.

4 Click Select All to combine all stories in the publication, or hold down Shift while clicking on the stories you want to combine, and then click OK.

The pointer changes to a loaded icon.

5 Click the loaded icon, and then, using the text tool, click an insertion point in the story you just placed.

6 Choose File > Export > Text, select a file format and options, and then click OK.

Exporting paragraph style tags

If you plan to import text back into PageMaker, and you're exporting in a file format that does not support styles (such as Windows Write, DCA/RFT, or text-only format), select Export Tags in the Export To file dialog box. PageMaker then exports paragraph style names as tags with the text, so that you can edit the text in a word-processing application that does not support defined styles. If you place the file back into PageMaker with the style-name tags intact, PageMaker can apply its styles to the text. Leave Export Tags deselected (the default) to export a file without its tags. For more information about style tags, see "Importing Text with Style-Name Tags" on page 344.

EXPORTING A GRAPHIC IN A DIFFERENT FORMAT

You can export almost any kind of imported graphic in a publication in any one of four formats: TIFF, JPEG, GIF89, or DCS. This section describes how to export graphics for general purposes, but note that PageMaker includes export features designed for special publishing tasks:

• If you are exporting graphics for color separation purposes, or exporting a high-fidelity color image for editing in Adobe Photoshop, see "Preseparating Bitmap Images" on page 302.

• If you are exporting your publication to HTML, you can use the File > Export > HTML command to convert graphics to GIF89 or JPEG automatically as the HTML document is created; see "Exporting as HTML" on page 455 for more information. However, if you export images individually as described in this section, you have more control over GIF89 and JPEG export options such as color palette (the colors included in the image for display purposes) and compression quality.

To export a graphic in a different format:

1 Select the graphic to export.

2 Choose File > Export > Graphic.

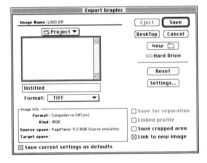

3 Type a name for the exported graphic, and choose a folder in which to store the file.

4 Select the new format you want from the Format pop-up menu.

The DCS option is available as the output format only if you are using color management. See "Preseparating Bitmap Images" on page 302 for more information on saving in the DCS format.

5 Select the Embed Profile option if the color-managed image will be used in publications on other computers which may lack that profile. Deselect the option if you want to keep file size to a minimum, or if a high-fidelity profile is specified for your separations printer, or if the source image is auto-relinked to the preseparated image and won't be reimported elsewhere.

6 Click Settings and specify options as follows:

For TIFF images:

• For Compression, select the method you prefer. See "Compressing and Decompressing a TIFF image" on page 217 for details on PageMaker compression schemes.

• For Preview (available only if saving for separations) choose Draft to save a low-resolution (36 dpi) screen preview with the image, Best to save a 72 dpi screen preview with the image, or Do Not Store in Image for the smallest file size.

• For Data Format, choose Basic TIFF unless saving for separations (in which case choose Optimize for Separation) or working with an image scanned at a very high resolution (choose Optimize for Large Images).

• Select the Strict TIFF 6.0 Compliance option if you want the preseparated TIFF optimized for best compatibility with other applications. To ensure best PageMaker printing, make sure the option is not selected.

For GIF89 images:

• For Palette and Color depth (options available only for full-color images), choose the setting that best matches your needs. See "Image Compression and Color on the Web" on page 381 for details on your choices.

• For Transparency, choose White or Black if the graphic includes a white or black background and you want that background to be transparent (for example, so that an HTML document's page background color or tiled background image appears rather than the opaque white or black area).

• For Resolution, choose Image if you want to use the exported file in a publication designed for print (including PDF documents designed for on-demand printing), or Screen if the graphic is intended to be viewed online (for example, in an HTML document). If you choose the Image option for images resized within PageMaker, the images may revert to their original dimensions.

• In the Caption field, type an image caption if desired. The text is included along the bottom of the exported image, overlaying the image. Some graphics applications can read these captions; however, PhotoShop 3.x, Netscape Navigator 1.0-3.0, and Internet Explorer 1.0-3.0 cannot read or display the caption.

• Select Interlaced if the image will be included in an HTML document. Interlacing improves the speed at which GIF images display and download over the Web.

For JPEG images:

• For Image Quality, choose the level you want. The higher the image quality, the lower the amount of compression. The loss of image detail caused by higher compression is permanent; you cannot resave an image with a higher level of image quality to restore the lost detail. Therefore, always preserve the original image.

• For Resolution, select Image if you want to use the exported file in a publication designed for print (including PDF documents designed for on-demand printing), or Screen if the graphic is intended to be viewed online (for example, in an HTML document). If you select the Image option for images resized within PageMaker, the images may revert to their original dimensions.

7 Click OK in the Settings dialog box.

8 Select Save Current Settings as Defaults if you intend to export additional graphics and want to apply the same settings you've applied during this procedure to those other graphics.

9 If it is not selected, click Link to New Image to replace the original bitmap image in the publication with the new file.

10 Select Save Cropped Area if you cropped the image with the cropping tool and want to retain only the cropped (visible) portion of the image.

11 Click Save.

IMAGE COMPRESSION AND COLOR ON THE WEB

Your Web publication will be viewed by computers on a variety of platforms, using different Web browsers and computer monitors. To make your work accessible and attractive to audiences with 8-bit color monitors and less-than-ideal Internet connections, do the following:

• Keep image file sizes to a minimum (within acceptable image quality standards).

• Use the appropriate image format and color palette option (for GIF images) for best representing each particular image on a broad range of monitors.

With those goals in mind, take the following points into account when exporting images for the Web:

JPEG is designed for 24-bit photographic (continuous tone) images, and includes several compression levels so you can balance image display quality against image compression.

For other images, GIF89 (an 8-bit and below format) is probably the best option. With the GIF format, PageMaker lets you take advantage of interlacing (for faster downloading over the Web) and transparency.

JPEG   GIF

Setting palette options for GIF89 files

In the Export GIF89 Settings dialog box, you can specify the most appropriate color palette for full-color images being saved in the GIF format. The color palette determines the range of colors available to use to display the image over the Web.

Exact: Available if the original image included 256 or fewer colors, this option uses the same colors for the exported image's color palette as those in the original image.

Adaptive: The Adaptive palettes use colors sampled from the more commonly used areas of the color spectrum that appear in the selected image. To simulate the colors not in the palette, monitors *dither*, or mix the pixels of available colors. If you choose the Adaptive (no dither) option, monitors will not simulate an unavailable color in that way, but instead use the palette color closest to the missing color. The result is a sharp transition between shades of color in the image. Adaptive (dither) works better than the Netscape palette for 8-bit (256 color) photographs or continuous-tone images, especially if the original image was a 24-bit image.

Netscape: This option uses the colors that browsers such as Netscape Navigator and Internet Explorer use on 8-bit monitors. Use this palette if you want to avoid dithering. 216 of the 256 colors in the palette are consistent across Macintosh and Windows platforms.

System: A set of 256 default colors in the Windows or Macintosh operating system. The Netscape Navigator and Internet Explorer browsers convert these colors into their own 8-bit palette.

After you specify the color palette, set the color depth to specify the number of colors that can be displayed at one time. The lower the number of colors, the lower the image quality, and the lower the file size.

Chapter 12: Printing Publications

PageMaker provides a range of printing features to help you create professional publications. You can print everything from simple black-and-white newsletters on a desktop laser printer to high-fidelity color separations on a PostScript imagesetter. This chapter describes the printing features that you can use to print your publications and offers techniques for printing publications efficiently.

If you plan to have a prepress service provider image your publication on a high-resolution imagesetter, talk to the service provider before you start your publication. Discuss your plans for the publication, ask what type of imagesetter will be used, and determine the appropriate output resolution. You'll use this information to create your publication. For more information on working with a service provider or a commercial printer, refer to the *Adobe Print Publishing Guide*.

PAGEMAKER 6.5 PRINTER COMPATIBILITY

With the latest compatible drivers installed, PageMaker can print to any PostScript printer connected directly to a compatible Macintosh or Windows computer or connected via a network. PageMaker can also print to non-PostScript printers including QuickDraw (Macintosh) printers and PCL printers (Windows). For infor-

mation on setting up your printer and selecting the appropriate printer driver, see the *Adobe PageMaker 6.5 Getting Started* book.

PAGEMAKER 6.5 PRINTING BASICS

You can print a black-and-white, grayscale, or color publication on a range of output devices. When you open a new publication, the default print settings let you print a composite (all page elements print on the same page, as opposed to separations where page elements print on different pages, depending on their color and page assignment).

If you print to different printers for proofing and final output, your Document Setup settings should match those of your final output device.

PageMaker has print options for creating a large tiled piece, printing several sections of a publication at once, and printing proofs without graphics. These options are covered later in this chapter.

To print using the default settings of a publication:

1 Choose File > Print.

2 If you are printing on a PostScript printer, select a PPD that matches the printer type.

3 Select the Document printing options you want. See the following section for more information.

The Print Document dialog box • When you choose File > Print, PageMaker displays the printing dialog boxes for the type of printer (PostScript or non-PostScript) you selected.

A Click Print to print your publication.

B Click Cancel to close the printing dialog boxes without printing and to change back to their previous state any of the printing options you set.

C Click Document to display the Print Document options again.

D Click Paper, Options, or Color to view other printing options for PostScript printers.

E Click Features to view printer-specific features for PostScript printers.

F Click Setup, Options, or Color to view other printing options for non-PostScript printers.

G Click Reset to change the printing options in a dialog box back to their original settings.

PostScript

Non-PostScript

4 For PostScript printers, click Paper to check the fit of the publication and to set additional options. For non-PostScript printers, click Setup to set additional printing options. For more information on PostScript printing, see "Viewing the Fit of a Publication" on page 388.

5 Click Print.

GENERAL DOCUMENT PRINTING OPTIONS

Update the Print Document settings each time you print a publication. These are the most frequently adjusted settings since they affect the information PageMaker has about the printer, as well as which pages are printed and how many copies print.

Document printing options

• The Printer field displays the name of the printer currently selected.

• The PPD option, for PostScript printers only, specifies the PostScript Printer Description file that PageMaker will use for printing. For more information on PPDs, see "PostScript Printer Description Files" on page 394.

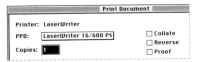

• The Copies option indicates the number of printed copies you want. For some non-Post-Script printers, click Setup to set the number of copies to print.

• The Collate option prints one complete copy of the publication or book (publications specified in the book list) before printing the next copy. Printing is slower when this option is selected.

• The Reverse option changes the order in which pages normally print on the printer. For example, if a printer usually prints the first page of a publication first, it will print the first page last when Reverse is checked.

• The Proof option omits all imported graphics, instead printing rectangles with *X*s in them that match the dimensions of those graphics. Pages print faster with this option selected. For more information on proofing, see "Printing Proofs on a Desktop Printer" on page 400.

Page range options

• The All option prints all of the pages in the active publication, or prints all booked publications if Print all Publications in Book is selected.

• The Ranges option lets you specify the range of pages you want to print in the active publication. Type a hyphen before or after a number to print all of the pages in the publication up to and including, or following and including that page. Typing a hyphen between two numbers tells PageMaker to print all of the pages in that range. You must type the numbers separated by hyphens in ascending order, (*2-4*, not *4-2*.)

Use commas to separate the individual pages or page ranges you specify. Page numbers separated by commas do not have to be typed in any order. For example, you can type -5, 19, 10-11 to print pages 1 through 5, followed by page 19, and ending with pages 10 and 11. You can type up to 64 characters in the edit box.

PageMaker ignores spaces in your page range entry. If you type an unknown character or describe a range incorrectly, PageMaker displays an alert, warning you of the incorrect syntax.

• The Print pages options let you choose which pages to print within the range you specified. Select Both Pages to have PageMaker print all of the pages in the specified page range. Select Even

Pages or Odd Pages to print all of the even or odd pages in your publication or book in the specified page range.

• The Print Blank Pages option prints blank pages in their proper position in the publication.

Element printing options

• The Ignore "Non-Printing" Setting option lets you print objects that are specified as Non-Printing. For more information on non-printing objects, see "Creating Non-Printing Objects" on page 220.

Publication orientation

• The icons in the orientation section specify the orientation of the pages. Click the tall icon in the Orientation section to print your publication in portrait mode (the short edge of your paper is horizontal). Click the wide icon to print in landscape mode (the long edge of your paper is horizontal).

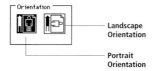

For best results, select the same orientation here as you specified for your publication pages in the Document Setup dialog box; otherwise, parts of your page might not print on the paper.

VIEWING THE FIT OF A PUBLICATION (POSTSCRIPT)

PageMaker lets you view how your active publication pages fit on the chosen paper size before you print to a PostScript printer. The preview in the Fit section of the Print Paper dialog box also shows the publication's orientation, printer's marks, page information, polarity (whether it's negative or positive), and mirror (emulsion) settings. This preview can guide you as you adjust various settings to set up print jobs properly.

The Fit section shows this information as either a graphical representation of a page or as numerical data. The Offset values below the page indicate if the page is too large for the currently selected page size. To toggle between the graphic fit and the numerical fit formats, double-click the page representation in the Fit section.

The document size and the specified page size are scaled in the Fit section in relation to one another; they do not represent a consistent scale when choosing between page sizes. For example, an 8 1/2-by-11-inch page is not shown proportionally smaller than an 11-by-14-inch page.

Note: *PageMaker gets the offset and paper information for the Fit section from the selected PPD. If the PPD does not match the printer's capabilities, the information in the Fit section may be incorrect.*

The Fit section • When you choose File > Print, and click Paper (PostScript printers only), the Fit section shows how your publication fits on the selected page size.

A Paper area outline.

B Document area outline.

C Document area is white when printing a positive image. The area has a black fill when printing a negative image.

D The graphic E indicates the emulsion side (mirror) orientation. Emulsion-side up is indicated by a right-reading E. Emulsion-side down is indicated by a backward E.

E Printer's marks (registration and crop marks, density-control bars, and a color-control bar).

F Page information.

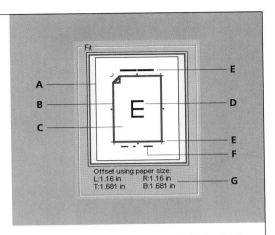

G Offset information indicates numerically the fit of the publication on the selected page size. If the publication and the selected marks are too large for the printable area, the values appear in red.

Paper printing options

• The Size option specifies a paper size. The sizes listed are defined in the selected PPD.

• The Source option determines the paper tray that will be used to print the publication. The options listed are specified in the selected PPD.

• The Printer's Marks option prints crop marks, registration marks, density-control bars, and a color-control bar on separations or composites of your publication. These marks help your commercial printer align separations and judge

color accuracy. The Printer's Marks option requires 0.75 inches (22.2 mm) in addition to the document size. (You can also select Crops and Bleeds Only to limit the kinds of marks that appear.)

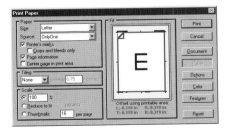

• The Page Information option prints the file-name, page number, current date, and spot- or process-color separation name in 8-point Helvetica (Macintosh) or 8-point Arial (Windows) in the lower-left corner of each sheet of paper or film. The Page Information option requires 0.5 inches (13 mm) along the horizontal edge.

• The Center Page in Print Area option centers the publication page in the printable area for the printer on which you are printing. Some output devices have a printable area that is asymmetrically offset from the edges of the paper; check your printer documentation to determine if your printer uses an offset. Click this option to center your publication within that offset printable area. Leave this option deselected to center your publication on the selected paper size.

Note: *Be sure to select a paper size big enough for your publication, the printer's marks, and the page information. The Printer's Marks and Page Information options together require 0.75 inches (22.2 mm) in addition to the document size. The offset values in the Fit section are red if the publication, printer's marks, or page information do not fit in the printable area defined in the PPD.*

• Double-click the page fit icon (the large E) to access the Offset Calculation option. The Offset Calculation can compensate for the non-printable area common with desktop printers. The Use Paper Size option (the option for black and white printers) assumes the entire paper size is the printable area. Use this setting when imaging on an imagesetter.

The Use Printable Area option (the default for composite color printers) obtains offset information—how far in from the edge of the paper the printable area is located—from the PPD and adjusts the printable area to compensate for the printer's non-printable area. Use this setting when printing on a desktop printer.

MANUALLY DETERMINING THE FIT OF A PUBLICATION

Information about the maximum printable area is not readily available for non-PostScript printers. Consult the printer documentation for specific dimensions or use the following procedure to determine the printable area.

To manually determine the printable area of a printer:

1 Choose File > New.

2 In the Document Setup dialog box, set the Page dimensions to match the paper in your printer, and then click OK.

3 Draw a shaded box that covers the whole page.

4 Chose File > Print, and then print the page.

The box will print only within the printable area for your printer.

Draw a shaded box that covers the page…

and then print the page to see the imageable area.

FONT PRINTING BASICS

The two main font standards are PostScript Type 1 and TrueType. PostScript fonts are the printing industry standard for imaging to any PostScript output device and can be used with a font manager, such as Adobe Type Manager, to print on non-PostScript printers. TrueType fonts work well with most PostScript and non-PostScript output devices. The disadvantage of using TrueType to a PostScript printer is that the font must be converted to a PostScript outline; the quality of the resulting font depends on the quality of the conversion. Other font standards include PCL native fonts.

Windows note: For Windows 95, be sure you are using ATM version 3.02 or greater and the Adobe PostScript printer driver version 4.11. ATM is installed automatically if you use PageMaker's Typical install option. The Adobe PostScript driver is included on the Adobe PageMaker 6.5 CD-ROM. Refer to the Adobe PageMaker 6.5 Getting Started *book for installation instructions. For Windows NT 4.0, use the PostScript driver shipped with the operating system.*

The resolution, scalability, and design of fonts determine how well they print. Since a printer or imagesetter reproduces a page with dots, all fonts at some point in the printing process must be converted into bitmaps, a process called rasterizing.

Where a font resides and where it is rasterized can affect imaging time and output quality. Printer-resident fonts—fonts stored in a printer's memory—are converted to bitmaps at the printer. Printers with resident fonts include PostScript printers and some non-PostScript printers. Other fonts, such as TrueType, are stored on your computer and are converted to bitmaps or PostScript outlines by the operating system, whether in Windows or on the Macintosh (both Macintosh and Windows have built-in type managers for TrueType).

When you print a font in your publication that is not available on your printer, fonts must be transferred from your computer to your printer. When you print a publication that includes non-resident fonts, the font must be created by the operating system or a type manager, and downloaded by PageMaker. PageMaker downloads fonts to your printer as needed, provided that they are installed on your computer's hard disk.

You can use font-matching options provided in PageMaker to substitute fonts when PageMaker cannot find the fonts used in a publication. For more information see Appendix B, "Font Substitution."

Printing fonts on PostScript printers

Printing PostScript fonts on a PostScript printer is the most direct and flexible way to print. All typographical features of PageMaker are supported by PostScript printers. PostScript is the standard for imaging publications on high-resolution imagesetters to create film for commercial printing.

PostScript printers come with built-in printer fonts that are listed in your printer's PPD file. PageMaker reads the PPD and does not download fonts listed there. If PageMaker cannot find the printer font to download, or if your printer does not contain a font listed in the PPD file, the printer substitutes Courier so the missing font can be easily identified and corrected. For more information on PPD files, see "PostScript Printer Description Files" on page 394.

Also available:
rosemary
chamomile
sage
cilantro
chives
&
borage

Also available:
rosemary
chamomile
sage
cilantro
chives
&
borage

If a printer can't find a font... it substitutes Courier.

Printing non-PostScript fonts, like TrueType fonts, to a PostScript printer results in the font being translated into PostScript before being rasterized by the printer. The quality of the font depends on the quality of the conversion; the outline may not have the same quality as the PostScript version of the font.

Printing fonts on Non-PostScript printers

Non-PostScript fonts are either in the format of the printer, such as PCL bitmaps and PCL-5 outlines, or the font is translated into a bitmap. This translation occurs for TrueType fonts, or PostScript fonts using a font manager such as Adobe Type Manager (ATM).

PostScript fonts translated through ATM and TrueType fonts are sent to the printer as graphics or bitmaps. The graphics or bitmaps are created on your computer; large fonts and type effects require more time and processing power. If fonts are sent to the printer as graphics, almost all of typographical features of PageMaker are supported.

Using type managers

Type-management utilities, such as Adobe Type Manager (ATM), translate PostScript printer fonts from smooth, scalable outlines to bitmaps that PageMaker uses to display on-screen and to print on non-PostScript printers. In Windows, ATM creates bitmaps as needed, so screen fonts are not required for PostScript fonts. For more information on ATM, refer to the Adobe Type Manager documentation.

TWO-WAY PRINTER COMMUNICATION (MACINTOSH ONLY)

Two-way printer communication frees PageMaker from relying on the contents of a PPD to obtain information about a PostScript printer. The Query Printer for Font and Memory Information option lets PageMaker determine how much memory is available, allowing PageMaker to make the best use of the available memory. PageMaker also checks to see what fonts have been downloaded to the printer's RAM or added to your printer's hard drive. PageMaker then downloads only the fonts in your publication that are not available to your printer, speeding up the printing process.

When this option is deselected, PageMaker relies on the PPD for information about available fonts and free memory. If the PPD for your printer is up-to-date or your publication contains only printer-resident fonts, you do not need to select this option.

PageMaker polls the printer for RAM and font information… and then downloads fonts and makes the best use of virtual memory

abcdefghijk

To activate two-way printer communication:

1 Choose File > Print.

2 Click Options and make sure Query Printer for Font and Memory Information is selected. PageMaker queries the printer for information when you click Print and periodically as it images your publication.

```
┌─Printer communication ─────────────────────────────┐
│ ⊠ Query printer for font and memory information     │
└────────────────────────────────────────────────────┘
```

Note: *This option is available only if Background Printing is turned off in the Chooser.*

To turn off Background Printing:

1 Choose Chooser.

2 Select a PostScript driver icon.

3 Click Off for the Background Printing option.

4 Close the Chooser.

POSTSCRIPT PRINTER DESCRIPTION FILES

PageMaker uses PostScript printer description (PPD) files when printing on a PostScript printer. PPD files, written by printer manufacturers, provide PageMaker with information about your PostScript printer, including a list of printer-resident fonts, paper sizes, optimized screens, and resolution capabilities. This information is provided by the printer manufacturer and reflects the most common configuration of the device.

PageMaker uses the information in the PPD file to determine what PostScript information to send to the printer when printing a publication. For example, PageMaker assumes that the fonts listed in your PPD file reside in the printer, so they are not downloaded when you print. PageMaker also uses information in the PPD to determine printer-specific features that you can control when you choose File > Print and click Features.

Note: *PageMaker 6.5 does not support the Simplified Printer Description (SPD) files in Windows 95.*

In Windows, PPDs have a file name and a nickname, which is a longer name for the PPD file. For example, "Linotronic 330 v52.3" is the nickname for the PPD file used with the Linotronic 330 imagesetter with a PostScript version 52.3 interpreter, but the filename in Windows is "L330_523.PPD." PageMaker can list PPDs in the Print Document dialog box by either the nickname or the file name. By default, PageMaker lists PPD files by their nicknames.

To list PPDs by filename (Windows):

1 File > Preferences > General.

2 Click More.

3 Click Display PPD Name in the print section of the dialog box.

4 Click OK, and then click OK to close the Preferences dialog box.

Obtaining PPDs

If a PPD file is not available on the PageMaker installation disks or the PageMaker CD-ROM for your printer brand or model, you can obtain the PPD from your printer manufacturer. Many prepress service providers and commercial printers have PPDs for the imagesetters they use. Adobe Systems has several ways you can obtain PPDs that don't ship with PageMaker. See the Help Card that came with PageMaker 6.5 for more information.

Updating a PPD file

Since PPDs represent the standard configuration of your printer when it left the manufacturer, you may need to update your PPD if you add printer RAM, an additional paper tray, or attach a hard disk to your printer. While the original PPD is locked and should not be changed, you can create a new PPD that reflects any changes to your printer.

On the Macintosh and in Windows 95, you can use the Update PPD plug-in to query the printer for available memory and fonts and create a custom PPD containing the updated information.

Update PPD creates a custom PPD file that contains information about your printer that is not in the original PPD. This information supplements the information in the original PPD. When you print using the custom PPD file, PageMaker reads the information in the custom PPD and the original PPD; when information in the two files matches, PageMaker uses only the information from the custom PPD file. When you use the original PPD, PageMaker does not read the information from the custom PPD file. You can update a custom PPD file, or create a new one, whenever printing requirements change.

A PPD can be updated manually as well. The process is explained in FaxYI bulletin #100102 that can be sent to your fax machine by dialing (206) 628-5737 from the phone on your fax machine. In United States and Canada, you can also call from any touch-tone phone.

Creating a custom PPD (Macintosh)

You can create a custom PPD using either the Update PPD plug-in or the Update PPD utility. Both the plug-in and the utility query the current PostScript printer and use the information provided by the printer to create a custom printer description file on your hard disk.Creating a custom printer description file can take several minutes, especially if your printer has a hard disk with many fonts.

Some PPDs don't contain all page sizes supported by a given printer. The Update PPD plug-in lets you include U.S. and European page sizes, your printer's maximum page size, and fonts that are located on the printer's hard disk or in printer RAM.

To create a custom PPD for your current Macintosh printer:

1 Turn off any printer spooling software.

2 Do one of the following:

• In PageMaker, choose Utilities > Plug-ins > Update PPD.

• To launch the Update PPD utility, double-click the utility's startup icon in the Printing folder within the Extras folder in your PageMaker 6.5 folder

Update PPD queries the printer for information. This process may take several minutes.

3 Select the PPD for your printer.

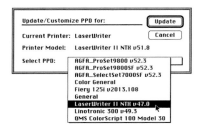

4 Click Options and select one or more of the following options:

• U.S. Page Sizes adds traditional U.S. page sizes that the printer supports; the sizes display in the Size pop-up menu of the Print Paper dialog box.

• European Page Sizes adds European page sizes that the printer supports; the sizes display in the Size pop-up menu of the Print Paper dialog box.

• Max Page Size adds the largest possible paper size for output devices, such as imagesetters, that support custom page sizes; it also adds a set of common Extra and Extra.Transverse paper sizes.

• Include Fonts on the Printer's Hard Disk adds PPD entries for all fonts that are stored on the printer's hard disk.

• Include Fonts in the Printer's RAM adds PPD entries for all fonts currently in the printer's RAM.

• Give Up Waiting for Printer to Respond After determines how long your computer will wait for an answer from your printer. If you want your computer to wait more time or less time before receiving a message from your printer, change the default setting of 2 Minutes to the desired setting.

5 Click Update. Update PPD prompts you for a file name and location for the custom printer file. Save the new custom printer description file in the Printer Descriptions folder, located in the Extensions folder within the System Folder.

Note: *By default a new PPD is created with a bullet character added to the PPD file name. For example, if the original file name of your PPD is "Linotronic 300 v52.3," the new file is named "•Linotronic 300 v52.3."*

6 Click Save.

If Update PPD encounters any corrupted fonts at the printer during creation of the custom printer file, an alert message appears indicating a log file has been created and a valid custom printer file has been created without the damaged font(s).

Note: *Custom PPD files created using Update PPD for the Macintosh cannot be read by Update PPD 2.0 for Windows.*

Creating a custom PPD (Windows)

Updating the amount of memory available to your printer requires communicating direc.ly with the printer. Because Windows does not provide two-way communication between your printer and your computer, Update PPD 2.0 sends a command to your printer, and the printer responds by printing the amount of memory available. You can then enter that information into the custom PPD using the Edit VM dialog box. In addition, Update PPD checks the Win.ini file for resident fonts and adds them to the custom PPD.

To create a custom PPD for your current printer (Windows):

1 Make sure the PostScript printer which you are creating the custom PPD file for is installed in the Printers section of the Windows Control Panel.

2 To start Update PPD, do one of the following:

• In PageMaker, choose Utilities > Plug-ins > Update PPD.

• To launch the Update PPD utility, double-click the application icon in the Explorer. The application is installed in the Print folder within the Extras folder within the PageMaker 6.5 folder.

3 Select the PPD file for your printer.

4 Type a name in the Custom PPD File Name or accept the default name.

5 Type a nickname in the Custom PPD Nickname or accept the default name.

6 Click Edit VM to determine and set the current amount of available virtual memory (VM).

7 Select the printer from the Select Printer pop-up menu and click Print. Click OK to close the dialog box stating that the printer memory information was printed to the selected printer.

8 Type the VM value from the printout in the New VM text box, and Click OK.

Note: *If you use a VM setting that is higher than what is indicated on the printout, PageMaker may send too much information to the printer at one time, causing printing delays or errors.*

9 To add or remove font names listed in the custom PPD file, click Add Fonts and select your printer from the printer pop-up menu.

10 To change the fonts listed in the custom PPD file, choose one of the following options:

• To add fonts to the custom PPD, choose font names from the list box on the left. Select one or more fonts to add to the custom PPD file, and then click Add. To select multiple fonts, press Shift while you click each font name. To add all fonts in the list, click Add All.

• To remove fonts from a custom PPD file, choose font names from the list box on the right and click Remove. Click Remove All to remove all of the font names from the custom PPD file.

Click OK to add or remove font names from the custom PPD file and return to the Update PPD 2.0 dialog box.

11 To edit the custom PPD file or to add a pre-defined patch, click Advanced.

Note: If you know how to program using Post-Script language, you can edit the file by typing PostScript operators into the edit box. Avoid changing the PostScript code without consulting a PostScript language reference.

12 Click OK to close the Advanced dialog box, and click Save in the Update PPD 2.0 dialog box to create a new custom PPD. The default location for the new file is the PM65/RSRC/USENGLSH/PPD4 folder.

PRINTING GRAPHICS ON POSTSCRIPT PRINTERS

PageMaker has several options to make bitmap images, EPS graphics, and native Adobe Illustrator files print most efficiently on PostScript printers.

Note: Non-PostScript printers do not support EPS graphics; EPS graphics are printed as low-resolution screen images.

Preserving EPS colors

When you import EPS graphics or Adobe Illustrator files, you can choose to import the EPS colors so you can modify them in PageMaker. You can print the EPS file with the original colors or the modified colors. Selecting Preserve EPS Colors prints the original EPS colors even if you have modified them in PageMaker.

To print the original EPS colors:

1 Choose File > Print, and then click Colors.

2 Click Preserve EPS Colors.

3 Click Print.

TIP: IF A PAGE WON'T PRINT, USE PROOF PRINT TO DETERMINE IF AN IMPORTED GRAPHIC IS THE PROBLEM. IF A PAGE PRINTS WITH PROOF SELECTED, THEN ONE OF THE GRAPHICS ON THE PAGE IS MOST LIKELY THE CAUSE.

Missing fonts in imported PostScript graphics

When you print on a PostScript printer, you can have PageMaker search EPS graphics and native Adobe Illustrator files for fonts and check the computer for the corresponding fonts. If a PostScript graphic contains fonts for which there are no corresponding screen fonts on the computer, a dialog box appears indicating the missing font, the graphic's file name, and the page on which the graphic first appears.

To have PageMaker scan PostScript graphics for fonts:

1 Choose Utilities > Plug-ins > EPS Font Scanner.

2 Click On, and then click OK.

3 Choose File > Print, set printing options, and click Print.

A warning dialog box appears if fonts are missing.

4 Choose one of the following options:

• Click Print Anyway. If you choose Continue and the outline font is available on your printer's hard disk, the correct font will print. However, if you choose Continue and the outline font is not available, Courier is substituted for the missing font.

• Click Do Not Print. Install the missing fonts on your system and try printing again.

Note: If the Proof option is selected, no missing fonts warning is given because the graphics do not print.

Determining how bitmap images print

When working with high-resolution TIFF images and paint-type graphics, including PCX and GIF, you can save time printing proofs by choosing how bitmap images will print. When printing proofs to a printer with a lower resolution than the final output printer, you can speed printing time by having PageMaker calculate a resolution optimized for your printer. You can also print imported bitmap images at either the normal resolution, at low resolutions, or have placeholders created so that you can link the images to high-resolution versions of the image.

To determine how bitmap images print:

1 Choose File > Print.

2 Click Options, and select one of the following options from the Send Image Data pop-up menu.

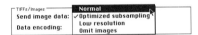

• Select Normal to send all the bitmap-image data to the printer. Use this setting when printing line art or grayscale bitmap images containing black-and-white data.

• Select Optimized Subsampling if your publication contains high-resolution images and you are proofing your work on a low-resolution printer. Use this setting if there is more image data than the printer needs for the linescreen (for color and grayscale images) or for the printer resolution (for black-and-white images). PageMaker prints the images at the best possible resolution for your printer, omitting the image data that your output device cannot use. Use this setting when printing bitmap images with a large tonal range.

• Select Low Resolution to print bitmap images at 72 dots per inch (dpi), reducing printing time.

• Select Omit Images if you do not want bitmap images to print. This option is useful when printing separation (SEP) files to a disk, so that you can link to high-resolution versions of the images with a prepress product that supports OPI. For more information on OPI, see the *Adobe Print Publishing Guide*.

3 Click Print.

PRINTING PROOFS ON A DESKTOP PRINTER

Before you image the final version of your publication, it's a good idea to print a black-and-white or color proof copy to check your layout. This is especially true if you are imaging the final copy on an imagesetter or giving the file to a prepress service provider; reprinting your publication on high-end imagesetters can be time-consuming and expensive.

PageMaker provides several ways to proof a publication:

• Print your publication with placeholders (rectangles) instead of graphics.

• Print thumbnails (miniature versions of the pages) of your publication.

• Print reader's spreads to preview the look of your publication.

The printer on which you print proofs of your publication does not need to match the printer you selected as your final output device. But if your final output device is a PostScript printer, you should print your proofs on a PostScript printer. Proofs of color separations can not be accurately printed on a non-PostScript printer.

To get accurate color from a color proofing device, use a color management system. For more information, see Chapter 9, "Color Management."

Printing proofs without graphics

When you print using the Proof option, PageMaker prints imported images as rectangles with *X*s in them, reducing printing time. These rectangles are the same sizes as your imported graphics, so you can check sizes and positioning.

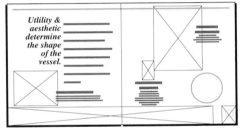

A publication printed with the Proof option selected.

To print a proof without imported graphics:

1 Choose File > Print.

2 If you are printing on a PostScript printer, select a PPD that matches your printer type.

3 Select the Proof option.

4 Set your print options, and then click Print.

Printing thumbnail proofs

PageMaker lets you create miniature versions of your pages so you can review the overall design of your publication.

If you specify page ranges when creating thumbnails of a publication, each range starts a new page of thumbnails. For example, if you specify a page range of "1, 3-5," a thumbnail of page 1 will print on one page, and thumbnails of pages 3–5 will print on the next page.

A publication printed with Thumbnails selected.

To print thumbnail proofs:

1 Choose File > Print.

2 If you are printing on a PostScript printer, select a PPD that matches your printer type and click Paper. If you're printing on a non-PostScript printer, click Options.

3 Click Thumbnails. Type the number of thumbnails (from 1 to 1000) to print on each page. The number of thumbnails per page determines the size of the thumbnails.

4 Click Print.

Printing reader's spreads

Reader's spreads let you view pages together as if they were bound. This is useful for evaluating the look of the publication. Select the Reader's Spreads option in the Print Document dialog box to print two facing pages on a single sheet of paper.

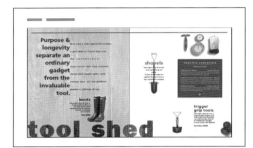

A publication printed with Reader's Spreads selected

Note: *The Reader's Spreads option is not available if the publication does not have facing pages.*

To create reader's spreads:

1 Choose File > Print.

2 Select the Reader's Spreads option.

3 Click Print.

DEFINING A CUSTOM PAPER SIZE FOR POSTSCRIPT IMAGESETTERS

PageMaker lets you define a custom paper size provided that the printer type you select for PPD supports custom paper sizes. You can also specify how the page prints on the roll of paper or film.

To define a custom paper size:

1 Choose File > Print.

2 Select the PPD for your imagesetter.

3 Click Paper and select Custom from the Size pop-up menu.

Page orientation • Most imagesetters can accommodate regular page sizes, such as letter and tabloid, as well as transverse page sizes, where the regular page size is rotated 90 degrees when printed. The transverse orientation is often a more efficient use of imagesetter media.

The Page Orientation specified in Document Setup and the Orientation specified in the Print Document dialog box should always be the same, whether you print normal or transverse. For example, select Tall with Portrait and Wide with Landscape. The orientation of the page (Portrait or Landscape) does not affect the paper orientation (Normal or Transverse). If you don't know what page size is best, consult your prepress service provider.

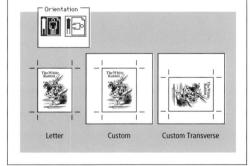

4 Type dimensions for your custom paper size, or accept the default dimensions.

The default custom paper dimensions are equal to the size of your publication page plus the space required for any printer's marks specified.

5 Select Normal or Transverse from the Page Orientation pop-up menu.

6 Click Print.

Note: You can save these print settings for reuse. See "Saving Print Settings Using Printer Styles" on page 414 for more information.

FILM PREPARATION

When you prepare files for imaging separations, consult with your commercial printer about special requirements for film preparation. Ask, for example, whether your printer requires the separations imaged as negatives or positives, or if the film should be emulsion-side up or emulsion-side down. (Emulsion is the photosensitive substance on the film surface.) The answer depends on the type of press used and how information is transferred from the film to the printing plates. This setting is critical when you hand off

a PostScript file instead of a PageMaker publication. By default, PageMaker prints pages as positive images, emulsion-side up.

Original image   *Negative*   *Negative with emulsion-side down*

To image with the emulsion-side down or as a negative image:

1 Choose File > Print.

2 Click Color.

3 Click Mirror to print your publication with the emulsion-side down.

4 Click Negative to print a negative image of your publication.

5 Set other print settings as needed, and click Print.

PRINTING COLOR

You can print either a composite, where all page elements and colors print at one time, or separations, where each ink is output separately. You can print your publication on a wide variety of PostScript and non-PostScript printers. You can proof your color publication on a desktop printer before imaging, but you should proof color separations only on a PostScript printer.

For more accurate color reproduction on your desktop color printer, use a color management system. For more information, see Chapter 9, "Color Management."

Printing color composites

You can print a color or grayscale composite of a color publication on a desktop printer. Most desktop color printers can only approximate the final colors produced by a printing press. You can print a color composite to verify that the correct colors are applied to your objects and to get a sense of how the final printed piece will look. However, you should adjust color based on printed swatches from a color-matching system, and talk to your prepress service provider about other color-proofing options.

When you print a grayscale composite, PageMaker prints visually correct grays. The gray that prints to simulate a 20% tint of yellow, for example, is lighter than a 20% tint of black, since yellow is visually lighter than black. When printing a color composite, remember that knockouts will not show on a composite print and overprinting and traps are not represented.

When you choose Print Colors in Black, colors print as the tint of black (gray) necessary to print the color correctly on film. For example, if you specified a 20% tint of black and a 20% tint of a spot-color green, the 20% tints of black and

green would be identical grays when printed. If you are printing a simple publication using spot colors that do not overlap, you can use this option to create a composite of your color publication that your prepress service provider can use to make separations. Consult your service provider before selecting this option for your final output.

Windows Note: *Non-PostScript printers have the option of using the PCL printer driver to create halftones. Click Allow PCL Halftoning in the Print Color dialog box to use the printer driver halftone settings instead of the Image Control settings.*

To print a composite of a publication:

1 Choose File > Print.

2 If you are printing on a PostScript printer, select a PPD that matches your printer type.

3 Select the Document printing options you want.

4 Do one of the following:

• If printing on a PostScript printer, click Paper to check the fit of the publication and to set additional options. Click Options to access PostScript printing options and to set options affecting how bitmap images print.

• If printing on a non-PostScript printer, click Setup to set printer options and to check the paper selection.

5 Click Color, click Composite, and click Color or Grayscale.

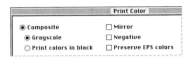

Note: *When printing on a PostScript printer, PageMaker displays Color or Grayscale depending on the capabilities of the printer PPD you select.*

6 Click Print.

PRODUCING COLOR SEPARATIONS ON A POSTSCRIPT IMAGESETTER

PageMaker lets you image spot-, process-, and high-fidelity color separations of your publications on a PostScript imagesetter using paper or film. When you print separations, you get one sheet of paper or film for each spot or process ink you print. Your commercial printer uses these separations to prepare plates for the printing press. For further information on the process of creating color separations, see the *Adobe Print Publishing Guide*.

First spot-color separation   *Second spot-color separation*   *The printed page (before trimming)*

When you print process colors, you need to control two factors to ensure the quality of your printed work: the number of halftone dots that print per inch (called the screen frequency or screen ruling) measured in lines per inch (lpi) and the angle at which they print (called the screen angle). If you don't specify these factors carefully, the inks may not print correctly in relation to one another, and you'll see moiré patterns or cross-hatching in the final printed colors that distract from their effect. The default screen settings in your PPD are based on specifications from the printer manufacturer and are optimized for your printer. Your prepress service provider may suggest different settings if the job requires them.

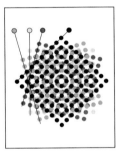
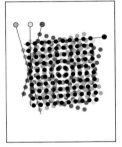

The screen angles for the four process inks produce a rosette pattern.   *When the angle of a process ink is incorrect, an undesirable moiré pattern results.*

The PPD file for each PostScript printer contains information about the best screen frequency and screen angle to use to print each ink on a particular printer. When you select Separations in the

Print Color dialog box, PageMaker displays the information found in the PPD file for the Optimized Screen option, and the Angle and Frequency fields. Although you can enter your own values for Angle and Frequency, we recommend using the optimized screen settings in the PPD file (unless you're experienced at using other settings). For more information, see "PostScript Printer Description Files" on page 394.

If you're giving your file to a prepress service provider to print the color separations on film, you may want to set options for printing color separations and print the separations to a PostScript file. For more information, see "Handing-Off to a Prepress Service Provider" on page 410.

The four process inks (cyan, magenta, yellow, and black) always appear in the ink list in the Print Color dialog box, whether or not you use process colors in your publication. Spot inks and high-fidelity inks also appear in the ink list, as well as any spot inks used in imported EPS files. For information on high-fidelity colors, see "Using High-Fidelity Color with a CMS" on page 300.

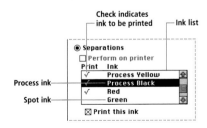

Removing unused colors and inks

PageMaker creates a separation for each ink selected in the ink list and used in your publication. The ink list may reflect colors from graphics that are no longer in your publication. Removing these unused colors and inks gives you a more accurate list of the separations PageMaker creates.

You can remove colors you created in PageMaker or EPS colors from graphics that have been deleted from the publication. Removing colors from the ink list also removes the associated colors from the Colors palette.

To remove unused colors and inks:

1 Choose File > Print.

2 Click Color, and then click Separations.

3 Click Remove Unused.

PageMaker prompts you for the first unused color in the list and gives you the following options:

• Click Yes to remove the color and to continue being prompted to remove additional unused colors.

• Click Yes to All to remove all unused colors without being prompted.

• Click No to retain the unused color and to continue being prompted to remove additional unused colors.

• Click No to All to retain all unused colors from that point on without being prompted.

4 Click Print to create separations. To save the edited ink list without printing, press Shift and click Done.

PERFORMING A PREFLIGHT CHECK BEFORE IMAGING

Perform a quality-control check on your publication by first printing proofs of your color publication, and then creating a list of all publication information for your prepress service provider. For more information on performing a preflight check of your publication, see the *Adobe Print Publishing Guide*.

Proofing color separations

You can print proofs of color separations on a black-and-white desktop printer to verify that objects appear on the correct separations and that colors overprint or knock out as expected. For more information on specifying colors to overprint or knock out, see "Specifying a Spot or Process Color" on page 266.

If your separations printer is a PostScript Level 2 imagesetter, the Perform on Printer option becomes available in the Print Color dialog box. Select this option to speed the printing process by allowing the separating to occur on the printer rather than on your computer. Devices with in-RIP capability can work with PageMaker 6.5 to process separations much more quickly in some

cases than a conventional printer. (Do not select the option if you need to color separate spot color blends created by Adobe Illustrator 5.0-6.0, or multi-tone—i.e., duotone, tritone, or quadtone—images created by Adobe PhotoShop 3.0 or later.)

To proof separations on a PostScript desktop printer:

1 Choose File > Print.

2 Select the PPD for your printer.

3 Click Color, and then click Separations.

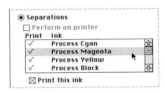

4 Select the inks you will use in your final separations. Click each ink, and then click the Print This Ink option for each ink. (Or simply double-click each ink you want to print.)

Note: *If an ink in the ink list isn't used in the publication, PageMaker does not create a separation for that ink.*

5 Click Paper to check that your publication fits on the selected paper size. Consider using Reduce to Fit or Tiling if the publication does not fit on the selected paper size.

6 Click Print.

To image color separations:

1 If your publication contains PageMaker elements that need to be trapped, choose File > Preferences > Trapping. Click Enable Trapping for Publication, set trapping options, and then click OK. For more information on trapping, see "Trapping Colors" on page 278.

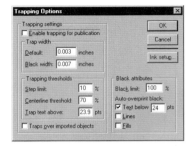

2 Choose File > Print.

3 Select a PPD for your printer type.

4 Click Color, and then click Separations.

5 Determine the angle and screen frequency for each ink as follows:

• Spot and high-fidelity inks normally print at the angle specified in the PPD for Custom Color, which is usually 45 degrees. Use the default setting in the PPD for best results. To print a spot ink at an angle other than 45 degrees (for example, to create a special effect), select the spot ink and type a new value for Angle. Repeat for other spot inks you want to print.

• For process colors, select the name of a process ink, and then verify the values for Optimized screen. Repeat for each process ink you want to print. We recommend using the optimized screen settings.

6 Select the name of each ink you want to print, and click Print This Ink. Alternatively, you can double-click the name of each ink you want to print. To select all inks, click Print All Inks.

7 Select the Mirror and Negative options as needed.

For information about these options, see "Film Preparation" on page 403.

8 Click Paper to check that your publication fits on the selected paper size and to choose printer's marks and page information.

9 Click Print.

Overprinting inks

Spot colors knock out by default: if two spot colors overlap each other in a publication, the spot color on top prints and the spot color (or any other color) beneath it does not print where the two colors overlap. Generally, you want inks to knock out so that the inks don't mix on the press and create an undesired third color. In some instances, however, you may want an ink to print on top of, or overprint, another ink to create a new color. For more information, see "Overprinting Colors" on page 277 and the *Adobe Print Publishing Guide*.

Printing spot colors with process inks

When you image process-color separations on a PostScript imagesetter, you can specify that any spot-color inks in your publication (including spot-colors in imported EPS files) be temporarily converted to their process-color (CMYK) equivalents. You may want to make this conversion if you have created more spot colors than you wish to have plates for, if your printer does not have the spot ink, or if you wish to image only the four process-color separations.

Note: The process-color equivalents may not exactly match the original spot colors. Selecting this option can also affect overprinting and trapping settings in your file.

To print all spot colors with process inks:

1 Choose File > Print.

2 Click Color.

3 Select Separations and click All to Process.

4 Click Continue.

The All to Process button changes to Revert to Spot once you've used it to convert your spot colors to process colors. To restore your spot colors, click Revert to Spot.

5 Click Print.

If you want to permanently convert certain spot colors to process colors, you can do so for each color using the Define Colors command. Unlike the All to Process option, this conversion preserves trapping and overprinting settings. See "Specifying a Spot or Process Color" on page 266 for details.

Printing high-fidelity colors

You can create color separations based on the extended color gamut available when using high-fidelity inks. For more information, see "Using High-Fidelity Color with a CMS" on page 300.

If you are printing high-fidelity colors, work with your commercial printer to determine the best proofing system. Some proofing systems cannot accurately represent the final output of high-fidelity printing.

To successfully print high-fidelity colors, use one of the following techniques:

• Use a high-fidelity color library to define high-fidelity colors. For more information on defining high-fidelity colors, see "About High-Fidelity Colors" on page 267 and "Using High-Fidelity Color with a CMS" on page 300.

• Set the device profile for your Separations printer to be a high-fidelity compatible device. For more information, see "Choosing Device Profiles" on page 296.

HANDING-OFF TO A PREPRESS SERVICE PROVIDER

You can give your prepress service provider either a PageMaker file or a PostScript file made from your publication. Hand off PageMaker files when you want your service provider to be able to make changes to your file, verify print settings, or perform prepress tasks. When you hand off a PostScript file, you maintain more control over the final output, but you are also responsible for choosing the correct print settings for your job.

If you have a prepress service provider image your publication, you may need to print your publication to a disk and set your print settings, instead of handing off a PageMaker publication.

When you print a publication to a disk, you create a PostScript file that contains a description of everything in your publication, including information about linked files and instructions tailored to the output device. The size of a PostScript file is usually larger than the original PageMaker document. Once you create the PostScript file, you can copy it to a disk (or a removable storage unit, such as a SyQuest disk) or use a modem to send it to the service provider. The service provider can then send the file directly to the imagesetter.

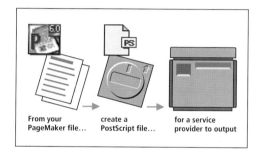

From your
PageMaker file...   create a
                         PostScript file...   for a service
                                                   provider to output

Printing a PostScript file to a disk gives you three advantages over taking the publication file to a remote location:

• You do not have to have the same version of PageMaker, the platform, or the version of system software that your service provider has.

• PostScript files can contain OPI and DCS comments that allow you omit large scanned images from your PostScript file and have your service provider incorporate them in your publication before imaging.

• PostScript files can contain downloadable fonts used in your publication, so your fonts image correctly even if the service provider doesn't have the fonts you used. (However, including fonts in a PostScript file unnecessarily increases imaging time if the service provider has the fonts you need, so consult your service provider before including them.) For more information about downloading fonts, see "Font Printing Basics" on page 391.

Consult your prepress service provider before printing a file to a disk. Make sure that you have the correct PPD file for the high-resolution imagesetter. When you deliver a PostScript file to the service provider, include a written report on your file.

Using the Save for Service Provider plug-in

Using the Save for Service Provider plug-in, you can copy your publication, all linked image files, fonts, and other files required to print your document. Save for Service Provider also helps you resolve broken links by prompting you to locate the folders containing linked files. Similarly, this plug-in can also check the status of links and fonts in a PostScript file generated by PageMaker 6.5.

You can also create a concise report of the information your service provider needs to create output from a PageMaker or PostScript file. The report includes details about fonts, linked graphics, a summary of your print settings, as well as information about who to contact regarding your publication.

To save files and generate a report using Save for Service Provider:

1 Choose Utilities > Plug-ins > Save for Service Provider.

The Summary dialog box opens.

The plug-in works on the active publication if you click Preflight Pub. If you want to check a PostScript file, click Preflight.PS, and then double-click the PostScript file you want to send to the service provider.

2 Click Fonts, Links, Printing, or Colors to see a detailed report on that aspect of the publication or PostScript file. You can print the status information by clicking Print at any time.

3 If the Links dialog box shows one or more linked files needing attention, click Relink or Relink All, and navigate to the correct image files.

4 To save the publication, click Package, and set options as follows:

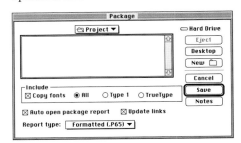

• From the Report Type pop-up menu, choose Formatted (for a PageMaker publication) or Text only (for an ASCII text-only file).

• Select Auto Open Package Report if, after saving the publication and associated files, you want to display the summary report in a new window on your desktop.

• Select Update Links to bring out-of-date links up-to-date in the original publication before making a package.

• For Include, select Copy Fonts to avoid missing fonts at print time, and then select the kind of fonts—All, Type 1 (PostScript), or TrueType.

• Click Notes to enter contact information, such as your name and phone number, any comments on printing the publication, and then click OK.

5 Specify a location in which to save all necessary files.

6 Click Save to copy the necessary files to the destination folder.

Selecting a data encoding option (PostScript only)

Data encoding refers to the format used to save TIFF images or paint-type graphics in PostScript files. The format choice affects how a network transmits the data from your computer to a network printer. Data encoding also affects file size; a binary image file is half the size of an ASCII image file and takes half the time to transmit.

On the Macintosh, both AppleTalk and Ethernet support binary transmissions. When creating PostScript files on the Macintosh from your publications, PageMaker's default setting saves TIFF images and paint-type graphics in binary format.

Many PC networks do not support binary data transmission, so the data encoding default is ASCII in PageMaker for Windows. The binary option is available when you print to disk.

To select a data encoding option (PostScript only)

1 Choose File > Print, and then click Options.

2 Select Send Binary Image Data or Send ASCII Image Data from the pop-up menu.

To print a PostScript file to a disk:

1 Choose File > Print.

2 Select a PPD for your printer.

Note: If you are giving the PostScript file to a service provider, select the PPD that matches the imagesetter on which the service provider will image your file.

3 Select the Document, Paper, and Color printing options you want to use, such as page range, paper size, printer's marks, page information, and composite or separation options.

4 Click Options, and then click Write PostScript to File.

5 Choose one of the following PostScript file types:

• Click Normal to print the same PostScript data to a file that you would send to the printing device if you simply printed the file. The default filename is the publication name (truncated if necessary) followed by a PS extension. For example, a PostScript file created from a publication named CHAPTER1 is named CHAPTER1.PS.

• Click EPS to create an EPS file of each page you print, which you can import into another program that imports EPS images. The default filename is the publication name (truncated if necessary) followed by an underscore, the page number, and the EPS extension. For example, an EPS file created from page 47 of a chapter named CHAPTER3 is named CHAPT_47.EPS. PageMaker produces EPS files for the active publication only.

Windows Note: *EPS files created in PageMaker for Windows don't contain a screen image, but they print correctly to PostScript output devices, and image correctly when imported back into PageMaker.*

• Click For Prepress to create a DSC-(Document Structuring Conventions) compatible separation file, which you can open in a postprocessor, such as Luminous TrapWise. This file also contains OPI comments. The default filename is the publication name followed by a SEP extension. For example, a file separated from a publication named CHAPTER1 is named CHAPTER1.SEP.

If you print to a disk with For Prepress and Print All Publications in Book selected, each publication in the book is created as a separate file.

Note: *Since this option creates a composite PostScript file for a postprocessing program, the Separations option in the Print Color dialog box is unavailable.*

6 Accept the default name and location, or type a new name in the edit box. The default filename changes depending on the type of PostScript file you create. Click Save As (Macintosh) or Browse (Windows) to specify a location for the file created, and then click OK (Macintosh) or Save (Windows).

7 Select one of the following options from the Downloadable Fonts pop-up menu:

• Download PostScript and TrueType fonts

• Download just TrueType fonts

• None to omit fonts from the PostScript file

8 Click Extra Image Bleed to extend the bleed for images from the default of 1/8 inch to 1 inch (25 mm).

9 Click Page Independence if you want PageMaker to download font information separately for each page in your publication. The font information is stored with each page so that pages can be moved or printed in a different order. This option is automatically selected for SEP and EPS files. If you are printing directly to a printer, deselect this option for faster printing.

Macintosh Note: If PageMaker cannot find all of the fonts to download, it displays an error message once the file has been printed to disk.

10 Click Save to create the PostScript file.

PREPARING YOUR PUBLICATION FOR POSTPROCESSING (MACINTOSH)

If you use Luminous TrapWise or PrePrint Pro on the same computer as PageMaker, you can select Launch Postprocessor in the Print Options dialog box to automatically open the SEP file in one of these programs. PageMaker tries to open TrapWise first. If TrapWise is not available, PageMaker looks for PrePrint Pro.

You can print separations directly from Page-Maker, including publications containing RGB TIFF images; however, postprocessing programs let you control sophisticated printing features, such as dot gain and undercolor removal. Most postprocessors can also link to high-resolution scanned images stored on an OPI-compatible system, such as a Color Central® server or a Scitex, Crosfield, or Linotype-Hell system.

SAVING PRINT SETTINGS USING PRINTER STYLES

The Printer Styles command lets you save, retrieve, and apply print settings to any publication.You can define a printer style to ensure that your publications print consistently to a specific printer. Once you save a printer style, you can reuse it without fear of forgetting to set a particular setting, since the style stores almost every setting that can be specified in the printing dialog boxes except page ranges and the angle and frequency settings for non-process inks.

For example, if you print proofs on a desktop laser printer and image the final versions on an imagesetter, you can create a printer style that contains the correct printer settings for your desktop laser printer and create another style that contains the correct settings for a high-resolution imagesetter.

Note: Printer style settings are saved in a defaults file called Printer Styles (Macintosh) or PSTYLES.CNF (Windows). Deleting this file removes all printer styles.

To create a new printer style:

1 Choose File > Printer Styles > Define.

2 Click New.

3 Type a name for the printer style, and click OK.

4 Click Edit.

5 Select the desired settings from the Print dialog box, click OK, and then click OK again to close the Define Printer Styles dialog box.

To use a printer style:

1 Choose File > Printer Styles > the printer style.

2 Click Print, or click Save if the printer style is for creating a PostScript file.

Shortcut: *To bypass the print dialog when using Printer Styles, hold down Shift as you select the printer style name.*

To modify an existing printer style:

1 Choose File > Printer Styles > Define.

2 Select a printer style.

3 Click Edit.

4 Select the desired settings from the Print dialog box, click OK, and then click OK again to close the Define Printer Styles dialog box.

Note: *To rename a printer style, double-click the style name in the Printer Styles dialog box.*

PRINTING BOOKED PUBLICATIONS

When you create long documents, such as technical manuals or books, you typically divide them into individual PageMaker publications. (You might, for example, create a separate publication for each chapter, the table of contents, the index, and the front matter.) Dividing a book into separate publications reduces the size of a single file and lets several people work on individual files throughout the writing and production of the book. When you print, you can print the files individually or combine them to print all at once.

PageMaker lets you link individual publications together as a book so that you can generate a table of contents or an index or print the entire book. For detailed information on creating a book list, see "Assembling Publications into a Book" on page 236.

TIP: HOLD DOWN
COMMAND (MACINTOSH)
OR CTRL (WINDOWS)
AND CLICK STYLE TO
SAVE CURRENT PRINTER
SETTINGS AS A PRINTER
STYLE. HOLD DOWN THE
SHIFT KEY AND CLICK
DONE TO SAVE
THE CURRENT PRINT
DIALOG SETTINGS IN
THE PUBLICATION
WITHOUT PRINTING.

If you print separations of a book, you must print all inks in the book, rather than selecting individual inks to print. For more information on creating separations, see "Producing Color Separations on a PostScript Imagesetter" on page 405.

When you print booked publications all at once, PageMaker prints all of the publications in the book using the print settings specified in the active publication, with the following exceptions:

• PageMaker always uses the paper Orientation setting saved with each publication.

• If All is selected in the Range section of the active publication, then PageMaker prints all of the pages in the book. If Ranges is selected, PageMaker prints the range of pages specified.

• If Write PostScript to File is selected, PageMaker prints the entire book to a PostScript file. For more information on creating PostScript files, see "Handing Off to a Prepress Service Provider" on page 410.

To print booked publications:

1 Open a new publication or an existing publication file that is part of the long document you want to print.

2 Choose Utilities > Book.

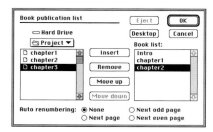

3 In the list on the left side of the dialog box, locate the files you want to print as a book. Double-click each filename to add it to the book list on the right side of the dialog box, and then click OK.

4 Select one of the Auto Renumbering options to control the page numbering of the publications in the book list.

• Select the None option to prevent automatic renumbering. Each publication in the book list retains the page numbering specified in the publication.

• Select the Next Page option to renumber publications in a book list consecutively from the first publication to the last. For example, if the first publication ends on page 54, the second publication begins on page 55.

• Select the Next Odd Page option to number each publication in a book list so that each publication begins on an odd-numbered (right-hand) page. If necessary, PageMaker creates a blank page at the end of the publication to ensure that the next publication in the list begins with an odd page number.

• Select the Next Even Page option to number each publication in a book list so that each publication begins on an even-numbered (left-hand) page. If necessary, PageMaker creates a blank page at the end of the publication to ensure that the next publication in the list begins with an even page number.

5 Click OK.

6 Choose File > Print.

7 If you print on a PostScript printer select a PPD that matches your printer type.

8 Select the Print Blank Pages option to print blank pages in their proper position in the publication.

9 Select the Print All Publications in Book option to print all the publications in the book list of the active publication.

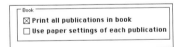

If you deselect this option, only the active publication prints, even if there are other publications in your book list.

10 When printing on a PostScript printer, select the Use Paper Settings of Each Publication option to print using the Size and Source settings in the Print Paper dialog box saved in each publication. For more information, see "Paper Printing Options" on page 389.

Note: *When printing on a non-PostScript printer, the Size, Source and Orientation settings are saved in the printer driver instead of in the publication. PageMaker only uses the settings specified in the driver when printing.*

11 Click Print.

USING BUILD BOOKLET TO CREATE MULTIPLE-PAGE SPREADS

The Build Booklet plug-in lets you create publications in which pages are arranged for printing multi-page spreads. The arrangement of pages printed on a single sheet or form is called an imposition. The Build Booklet plug-in creates multiple page spreads that print on a single sheet and assume the correct page order when folded. When you stack, bind, and trim the folded double-sided booklets, the result is a single book with correct pagination.

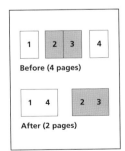

Pages as arranged in PageMaker.

Pages after printing and folding new booklet.

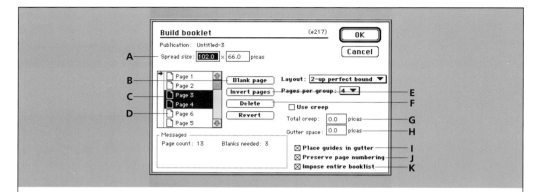

Build Booklet plug-in

A Spread Size values are automatically calculated when you choose an imposition layout. Adjust these measurements to provide room for printer's marks if necessary. A warning appears in the Messages box if the current spread size is not large enough for the publication or it exceeds the maximum page size.

B To add a blank page, select the page in the list box above where you want the new blank page to appear and click Blank Page.

C To select more than one page, click a page icon to select it, and then hold down Shift and click another page icon to add the page to the selection. Press Command + Shift (Macintosh) or Ctrl (Windows) and click a page icon to select nonconsecutive pages.

D To move pages, press Option (Macintosh) or Alt (Windows) and drag the selected pages. Nonconsecutive selections appear consecutively after you reposition them.

E Click Invert Pages to change between ascending and descending order.

F To delete pages, select the pages and click Delete.

G To adjust page placement to account for page thickness, click Use Creep and type a value for Total Creep. This does not change the spread size. Consult your commercial printer to determine the value for creep.

H To add space between pages, type a value for Gutter Space. When you specify a Gutter Space value, the Spread Size values automatically increase by the appropriate amount.

I To add nonprinting ruler guides, click Place Guides in Gutter.

J Click Preserve Page Numbering to include page numbers. Build Booklet numbers any blank pages, renumbers subsequent pages, and places a manual page number on each page corresponding to the page-number markers on the master pages. Deselect Preserve Page Numbering to eliminate page numbers. Build Booklet deletes any page-number markers copied onto the new publication from the original publication's master pages. For example, you might use this option when preparing a brochure and choosing the 3-up consecutive layout option.

K Click Impose Entire Booklist to impose all booked publications into the new publication.

When you choose an imposition layout (and later if you specify a gutter size), Build Booklet automatically calculates the spread size and displays it in the Spread Size option. You can adjust these measurements to provide room for printer's marks. A warning appears in the Messages section if the current spread size is not large enough for the publication or if it exceeds the maximum page size.

Running Build Booklet should be the final step before printing your publication. Build Booklet closes the current publication and creates a new, untitled publication with the page size equal to the size of the imposition. Build Booklet then calculates the proper page sequence and transfers the master and publication page items from the original publication to the correct pages in the new publication. Build Booklet can rearrange pages in the active publication or for all publications in a book list.

The Build Booklet plug-in gives you several options to determine how the final publication will look. You can place additional blank pages, revise the order of pages, or delete pages. Build Booklet can also automatically adjust the placement of the page items to account for paper thickness, increase the space between publication pages, and invert the pages for printing. Any change you make affects the publication copy, not the original publication.

After the new publication is created, you can manually edit the publication, for example, you can delete page numbers from blank pages.

The master pages of the new publication, however, are blank; all master page information has been copied to each page of the new publication.

Choosing a layout

The number of pages in a signature must be a multiple of a certain number, depending on the option you selected for Layout. For example, the 2-up Saddle-stitch and Perfect Binding options require a multiple of four, since pages are paired and then printed back to front.

The message area indicates the number of pages you need to add (if any) to meet the correct page count for the specified layout. If the layout option you've chosen requires blank pages and you do not add them, Build Booklet inserts the needed blank pages at the end of the publication.

With the Build Booklet plug-in, you can create a publication in the following layouts:

• 2-up Saddle-Stitch imposition is designed for standard booklet printing, where double-sided pages are folded once and fastened along the fold. The first page prints on the same printed sheet as the last page, second page on the same sheet as the second-to-last page, and so on. When you print the produced pages front to back and fold them, the pages are in proper sequence.

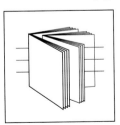 

Inserted signatures   *Saddle-stitch binding*

• 2-up Perfect Bound imposition creates a series of folded booklets, where a group of folded booklets are bound with adhesive along the spine. When you select this option, you also specify the number of pages per booklet and PageMaker calculates the number of booklets needed to produce the publication. If you select 2-up Perfect Bound, select 4-, 8-, or 16-page signatures for Pages per Group.

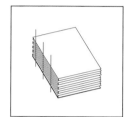

Gathered signatures   *Perfect binding*

• 2-, 3-, or 4-up Consecutive imposition creates multi-page spreads. Each set of 2, 3, or 4 pages in the original publication are combined side-by-side onto a single page in order to save paper or film when printing or imagesetting. These options also let you quickly create 2-, 3-, or 4-panel brochures, centerfolds, and so on.

4-up Consecutive imposition   *Trimmed and folded spread*

• The None option creates a new publication, but does not rearrange the pages nor change the spread size. You can, however, manually adjust the page arrangement, increase the page size, or insert blank pages.

Preparing files for imposition

Before you impose a publication, verify that your publication and your system meet these requirements:

• The Build Booklet plug-in requires disk space on the start-up disk to create a copy of your publication and to sort pages. It's best to have available hard drive space equal to two-and-one-half times the size of the finished publication.

• Make sure your text and layout is complete. Because the Build Booklet plug-in creates a new publication with text and graphics arranged for the format you specify, changes other than minor text and graphic edits can disrupt its organization.

• Generate and place the table of contents and index stories so that they accurately reflect the original page numbers.

• Check that the publication starts on an odd-numbered page. If your first page begins on an even number, insert a blank page before the first publication page.

• Make sure that the publication is smaller than 500 pages. If the publication is too large, divide it into smaller documents.

• Check that the page size in the Document Setup dialog box matches the size of an individual page of the booklet or book. For example, if the final page size is 5.5 inches by 8.5 inches, the page size specified in the Document Setup dialog box should be identical. However, the actual size of the signature—the spread size—depends on the Layout option you choose.

• PageMaker's maximum page width is 42 inches (1029 mm). Be sure that the imposition layout you've chosen does not exceed this amount (including gutters): the original page width or height cannot exceed 21 inches (514.5 mm) for 2-up impositions, 14 inches (343 mm) for 3-up impositions, and 10.5 inches (257.25 mm) for 4-up impositions. Also, make sure your pages fit within the printable area of your printer.

About creep • Creep occurs when the edges of the folded sheets do not lie flush but instead lie offset from each other due to the bulk of the paper. When you trim the edges to make them even, the inner and outer margins—relative to the edge of the page—are inconsistent within the signature, which detracts from the quality of the publication.

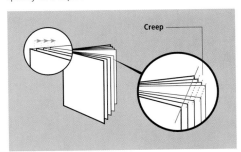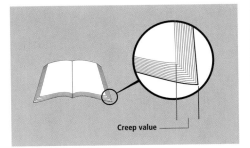

Creep occurs when the inner pages of a signature project outwards. Estimate creep with a mock-up of the signature.

The amount of creep that occurs depends on factors such as the thickness of the paper you are using, the size of the signature or section, and the direction of the fold (with or against the grain of the paper). Your commercial printer can recommend a value to compensate for creep.

To estimate creep, create a mock-up of one signature on the same paper stock that will be used for the final printing. Arrange and fold the paper, staple the binding edge, and trim the facing edge. Then, lay the signature flat and measure the difference in the page width from the inside to the outside of the signature to find the total creep value.

To impose a publication using the Build Booklet plug-in:

1 Open the publication you want to impose. Save the publication if you have not already done so.

2 Choose Utilities > Plug-ins > Build Booklet.

3 Select the Layout option from the pop-up menu.

4 Add, delete, or reorder the publication pages.

5 Select the imposition options and click OK.

PRINTING ON BOTH SIDES OF A PAGE

Some printers, such as the Hewlett-Packard LaserJet 4Si MX, let you print on both sides of the paper. When you select a printer that supports double-sided (duplex) printing, PageMaker lets you specify duplexing options.

Page size restrictions dictate when double-sided printing can occur. Check your printer documentation for page size limits.

Duplex printing • The combination of page orientation and duplex option allows you to create these types of publications:

Page orientation	Duplex option	Result	Example
Tall	Short edge	Horizontal	Wall calendar
Wide	Long edge	Horizontal	Wall calendar
Tall	Long edge	Vertical	Book
Wide	Short edge	Vertical	Book

To print duplex pages:

1 Select a target printer that lets you print on both sides of the page.

2 Choose File > Print.

3 If you're printing on a PostScript printer, select the PPD for your printer type, and then click Features. For non-PostScript printers, click Options.

4 Choose options for duplex printing. Some common print options are:

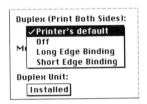

• To use the duplex settings set on the printer, select Printer's Default.

• To print pages on both sides so that they read correctly when bound along the long edge of the paper, select Long Edge Binding.

• To print pages on both sides so that they read correctly when bound along the short edge of the paper, select Short Edge Binding.

Note: The terms in the Duplex pop-up menu differ depending on the printer and PPD you use. For example, some printers use the term Duplex Tumble for Long Edge Binding and Duplex No Tumble for Short Edge Binding.

5 Click Print.

PageMaker will complete the printing of both sides of the last page in a series. For example, if you specify pages 1-5 to print, page 6 also prints.

PRINTING OVERSIZED PUBLICATIONS

You can create and print PageMaker publications as large as 42 inches by 42 inches (1066.8mm by 1066.8mm). Most desktop printers, however, cannot print such large pages. If you want to print an oversized publication on your desktop printer, you can print each page of your publication in pieces, called tiles, and then trim and assemble those pieces. Alternatively, you can scale the publication to fit the available paper size.

Print an oversized publication by…   *creating tiles…*   *or scaling to fit.*

Tiling a publication

You can have PageMaker tile a publication automatically or you can specify the tiles yourself.

Divide an oversized page into four segments and print the tiles.

Align the overlapping sections to assemble the four printed tiles.

When you print tiles automatically, PageMaker calculates the number of pages required, including the overlap, and then centers the print area on the collection of tiles to be printed. Tiling manually lets you control the exact dimensions of the tiles. Each time you print, PageMaker prints a tile for all of the pages you specify to print in the Print Document dialog box.

Note: *This option is unavailable if you are creating a PostScript file.*

To tile a publication automatically:

1 Choose File > Print.

2 Choose one of the following:

• If you're printing on a PostScript printer, select the PPD for your printer type and click Paper.

• If you're printing on a non-PostScript printer, click Options.

3 Select Auto from the Tiling pop-up menu.

4 For Overlap, type the minimum amount you want the tiles to overlap in the unit of measure specified for your publication. The value should be greater than the minimum margin value for the printer. You can specify up to half the size of the shortest side of your publication page to overlap. For example, tiles for a page that measures 11 inches by 17 inches (279.4mm by 431.8mm) can overlap up to 5.5 inches (139.7mm).

5 Click Print. A progress indicator tells you how many tiles are printing.

To tile a publication manually:

1 Reset the zero point of the publication to the upper-left corner of the tile you want to print. Remember to leave room for overlap or for printer's marks and page information.

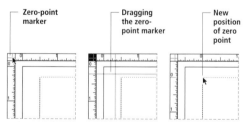

When you drag the zero point to a new position, you set the upper-left corner of the tile that will print.

If the zero point won't move, it may be locked. To unlock the zero point, choose Layout > Guides and Rulers > Zero Lock. For more information, see "Using the Zero Point" on page 80.

2 Choose File > Print.

3 Click Paper if you are printing on a PostScript printer, or click Options if you are printing on a non-PostScript printer.

4 Select Manual from the Tiling pop-up menu.

5 Click Print.

To print additional tiles manually, repeat steps 1 through 3, and then click Print. The Tiling option remains Manual (even if you save, close and reopen the publication) until you select None from the pop-up menu.

Scaling a publication

To fit an oversized publication on a smaller piece of paper, you can also scale your publication by a specified percentage or have PageMaker scale it to fit the paper.

To scale a publication:

1 Choose File > Print.

2 If you're printing on a PostScript printer, select a PPD and click Paper. If you're printing on a non-PostScript printer, click Options.

3 Choose one of the following options to scale your publication:

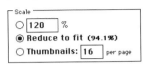

• Type a value from 5 to 1600 to scale your publication by a certain percentage. Not all devices can scale at these values; check your printer documentation for the range of scaling it supports.

• Click Reduce to Fit to scale your publication to fit on the selected paper size.

4 Click Print.

USING THE POSTSCRIPT ERROR HANDLER

You can troubleshoot printing problems by using the information provided by the PostScript error handler. Include PageMaker's PostScript error handler either when you print a file to a disk or when you print on any PostScript device. Then, if a printing problem occurs, the error handler prints the page containing the error with an error message to help you or your prepress service provider troubleshoot the problem. The error message lists the PostScript error, common causes for the error, and remedies for the problem. For more information on the PostScript language, consult the *PostScript Language Reference manual, Second Edition.*

To include the PostScript error handler when printing:

1 Choose File > Print.

2 Click Options.

3 Click Include PostScript Error Handler.

Note: Always consult your service provider before including an error handler with files you hand off. Service providers may not include the error handler or may use their own error handlers when imaging separations.

Using your own PostScript error handler

If you create your own PostScript error handler or your service provider provides you with one, you can substitute that error handler for the one provided with PageMaker.

To substitute your own error handler:

1 Copy the substitute error handler file to the language folder, such as USENGLSH, in the RSRC folder within the PageMaker 6.5 folder.

2 Change the name of the file to P65ERROR.PS.

Note: The error handler is downloaded prior to your publication, provided that you select the Include PostScript Error Handler option in the Print Options dialog box.

FREEING PRINTER MEMORY TO PRINT LARGE GRAPHICS

Problems printing large EPS graphics can often be solved by changing the amount of printer memory PageMaker can use. PageMaker requires additional printer memory when printing large EPS and PICT graphics, and Windows Metafiles. To ensure adequate printer memory, PageMaker can make room for processing large graphics by temporarily removing some or all fonts that have been downloaded to your printer's memory. If your publication generates a low-memory error, such as a limitcheck error, when printing, use this option to free as much printer memory as possible. This action may allow a large graphic to print, but can increase the over-all print time since removed fonts must be downloaded again.

To free the maximum printer memory for printing:

1 Choose File > Preferences > General.

2 Click More.

3 In the PostScript printing section, select Maximum from the pop-up menu.

4 Click OK to accept the change, and then click OK to close the Preferences dialog box.

PostScript Printing Chart

Format (See note 1)	Imaging with default or intrinsic image color(s)			PageMaker-applied color (See note 2)
	Separations made	Overprints	Knocks out (See note 3)	
B&W Bitmap Image	Black plate only	No	Black pixels only	
Grayscale Bitmap Image	Yes	No	Bounding box area only	
RGB Bitmap Image	Yes, with CMS active	No	Bounding box area only	
CMYK Bitmap Image	Yes	No	Bounding box area only	
Vector EPS	Yes	(See note 4)	(See note 4)	
B&W, Grayscale bitmap EPS	Black plate only	No	Bounding box area only	
RGB composite bitmap EPS	No	No	Bounding box area only	Applied color will not print

Notes:

1 Bitmap image formats include TIFF, PCX, BMP, Paint files, JPEG, GIF, and Scitex images. A bitmap image within an EPS graphic prints as described in this chart for the specific bitmap image type; the EPS containing the bitmap prints as described for the specific EPS type. PICT and Metafile formats are not recommended for color-separated print jobs.

2 If you apply a PageMaker color to a black-and-white or grayscale bitmap or EPS image, the color attributes determine how the graphic separates and whether it overprints.

3 Bitmap, EPS, and DCS graphics with clipping paths knock out only within bounds of clipping path.

4 PageMaker honors internal overprint attributes (if applicable). If color applied to object is set to overprint, object will overprint; if color applied to object is not set to overprint, object will knock out.

Key:

 Can apply color to an object

 Applied color displays

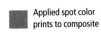 Applied spot color prints to composite

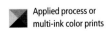 Applied process or multi-ink color prints

continued on next page

PostScript Printing Chart (continued from previous page)

Format (See note 1)	Imaging with default or intrinsic image color(s)			PageMaker-applied color (See note 2)
	Separations made	**Overprints**	**Knocks out** (See note 3)	
"Duotone" EPS	Yes, but see page 407	See note 4	Bounding box area only	Applied color will not print
CMYK bitmap EPS	Process color plates only	No	Bounding box area only	Applied color will not print
Kodak Photo CD	Yes, with CMS active	No	Bounding box area only	
DCS 1.0	Process color plates only	No	Bounding box area only	Applied color will not print
DCS 2.0	Yes	(See note 4)	Bounding box area only	Applied color will not print
Vector PICT	Yes	(See note 4)	Color areas only	
B&W/Grayscale bitmap PICT and metafiles	Black plate only	No	Bounding box area only	
Color bitmap PICT and metafiles	No	No	Bounding box area only	Applied color will not print

CHAPTER 13: DISTRIBUTING A PUBLICATION ELECTRONICALLY

This chapter concentrates on aspects of preparing, viewing, and distributing on-screen publications using PageMaker. PageMaker can export any range of pages into two leading online formats:

• PDF (Portable Document Format) which can be viewed and printed from several different platforms with the page layout and typography of the original document intact.

• HTML (HyperText Markup Language) which is the most prominent standard used on the Internet's World Wide Web. Web browsers control important aspects of an HTML document's appearance, including type color and typeface.

Both the PDF format and the HTML format support hyperlinks, or jumps from one part of the document to another part of the document or to another Internet resource. PageMaker includes a Hyperlinks palette to let you create, manage, and activate these jumps.

If you imported a QuickTime movie frame into your publication, PageMaker adds a hyperlink to the movie in place of the frame when you export to PDF or HTML. In order to play when clicked, the movie file must be stored in the same folder as the PDF or HTML document. See "Importing a QuickTime Movie Frame" on page 368 for instructions.

ABOUT HYPERTEXT LINKS

In PageMaker, any graphic or any range of text can be hyperlinked so that when you export to PDF or HTML, the viewer of the document can click the hyperlink to jump to another object, page, or Internet resource (including movies) on the Web. Hyperlinks also let a viewer of your PDF or HTML file send electronic mail just by clicking the hyperlink.

You can create, import, edit, and manage hyperlinks with the Hyperlinks palette and, in PageMaker's preview mode, test the hyperlinks by clicking them to jump to the associated destination.

Each hyperlink consists of a source (the text or graphic you want to be clickable) and a destination (the object, page, or document you want to appear once the source is clicked). For example if you have the text "Click here to see picture" on page 1 jump to a scanned image on page 4, then the text is the source, and the image is the destination.

Destinations ———————— Sources leading to the associated destination

A destination can be a document on the Web (URL destination)...

or another page within the document (anchor destination)

You use the Hyperlinks palette to associate each destination with source text or graphics. When you establish the connection between the source and the destination, you have a hyperlink. A source can only jump to one destination, but any number of sources can jump to the same destination.

Creating hyperlink destinations

PageMaker supports two different kinds of hyperlink destinations. A destination can be

• Any text or graphic in the same publication as the source (this kind of destination is called an *anchor* in PageMaker).

About hyperlinks, HTML, and PDF • When you export to HTML, which supports a limited set of graphic formats, PageMaker-drawn shapes (other than horizontal lines) are not included in the file. Therefore, do not make them anchors or sources if you are going to export to HTML. For text, remember that the content of text objects is included in exported HTML documents, but not the surrounding object itself (a text frame or a text block). Therefore, if you plan to export to HTML, do not make a text object a source or anchor; instead, use the text tool to select text within the object and make the text itself become a source or anchor.

When you export as PDF, table of contents and index entries are automatically hyperlinked. This special kind of hyperlink does not appear in the Hyperlinks palette. For more information, see "Changing PDF Options for Hyperlinks, Bookmarks, and Articles" on page 449.

• An address on the World Wide Web (this kind of destination is called a *URL destination* in PageMaker). URLs let you specify the location of resources on the Internet (a movie, another HTML page, or a PDF file, for example).

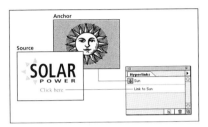

For URL destinations you can use the following URL types:

• http:// (Hypertext Transfer protocol)

• mailto: (Electronic mail address)

• ftp:// (File Transfer protocol)

• gopher:// (the Gopher protocol)

• file:// (Host-specific file names)

• news: (USENET news)

• telnet: (interactive sessions)

• smtp: (Simple Mail Transport protocol)

The section of a URL before the double slashes or colon describes the type of network resource or service. After the double slashes or colon you type the actual Internet address (or e-mail address for the mailto URL). Other information, such as a port number or queries, may be appended to the address.

For example, the URL for the Adobe Systems home page is:

http://www.adobe.com

The Adobe Systems home page URL is an example of an absolute or explicit URL. That is, the address is specified in non-relative terms independent of any other location. However, if the documents you hyperlink to are stored in the same hierarchy of folders, you can use relative URLs, a method by which you designate the location of a resource in terms of its relationship to the file that hyperlinks to it. For example, if your home page, an HTML document, has a hyperlink to your resume—a document called "Resume.PDF" stored in the same folder as the HTML document—the URL address for the resume is simply the PDF filename. However, if the resume is stored in the folder above the folder in which the home page is stored, the URL address is

../Resume.PDF

Most reference materials about HTML and the Internet, including many documents available on the World Wide Web, provide complete details on URLs and addressing schemes.

To create an anchor destination:

1 Choose Window > Show Hyperlinks.

2 Select the range of text or the object you want to be the anchor.

3 Choose New Anchor from the Hyperlinks palette menu, or click the new anchor button () at the bottom of the palette.

4 Type a name for the anchor—that is, the way you want it to be listed in the palette—and click OK.

If you press Option (Macintosh) or Alt (Windows) while you perform step 3, the anchor appears immediately in the Hyperlinks palette with the name "Anchor*n*" (where *n* is an automatically-assigned number). You can edit the anchor name at any time.

To create a URL destination:

1 Write down or copy to the Clipboard the URL you want to be the destination.

URL destination for site on World Wide Web

2 Choose Window > Show Hyperlinks.

3 Choose New URL from the Hyperlinks palette menu.

4 Type (or paste) the URL in the dialog box that appears, and click OK.

The URL destination appears in the Hyperlinks palette. The name for the item in the palette is the URL address. You can change the address by renaming the anchor; see "Editing and Removing Hyperlinks" on page 437.

Importing URL destinations

You can also import into the Hyperlinks palette the URLs that are referenced in an HTML file stored on your hard disk (or mounted network volume) or available on the World Wide Web. You can then associate those destinations with source text and graphics in the PageMaker publication.

If you import an HTML file (either by using the Place command or by dragging-and-dropping from a browser), PageMaker retains the hyperlinks intact with the file's content. That means each hyperlink in the file appears in the palette—both the URL destination and the source text and graphics that refer to it. See "Importing HTML Files and Other Information from the World Wide Web" on page 347 for more information.

To import URLs for use as destinations:

1 Choose Window > Show Hyperlinks.

2 Do one of the following depending on whether the HTML file is available on disk or on the Web:

• If the HTML document is available on your hard disk (or mounted network volume), choose Import URLs From File from the Hyperlinks palette menu, and then locate and double-click the HTML file containing the URLs you want to use.

• If the HMTL document is available on the Web and not stored locally on disk, choose Import URLs From Web from the Hyperlinks palette menu, type (or paste) the URL address of the document containing the URLs you want, and then click OK.

The URLs referenced in the file appear in the palette.

Note: If you have trouble importing URLs, you might need to set up PageMaker to communicate with the Internet. See "Setting Up Online Preferences" on page 347 for more information.

Establishing hyperlinks between sources and destinations

Once you've created or imported destinations, you can use the Hyperlinks palette to associate selected text and graphics (sources) with the destinations, establishing the hyperlinks for your document.

By default, PageMaker does not alter the look of text and graphics that you turn into sources. But you can use the hand tool to preview hyperlinks. In preview mode, source text or graphics are outlined in a blue box. See "Previewing Hyperlinks" on page 437.

A source can even be text or graphics on a master page, in which case the source will be available from every publication page to which the master is applied.

To associate source text or graphics with an anchor or URL destination:

1 Select the text or graphic you want to be the hyperlink's source.

2 Choose Window > Show Hyperlinks.

3 Do one of the following:

• In the palette, click the destination you want to hyperlink to, and choose New Source from the Hyperlinks palette menu.

• Click the anchor icon (⊞) or URL icon (⊞) for the destination you want to hyperlink to.

If the selected text or graphic is already hyperlinked to another destination, PageMaker asks if you want to replace the previously-assigned destination with the new one. Click OK or cancel as appropriate.

You can press Option (Macintosh) or Alt (Windows) as you perform step 3 to use the default name "Source*n*" (where *n* is an automatically-assigned number) and bypass the dialog box for naming the source.

 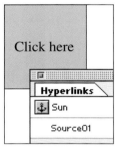

Select text or graphics and click an anchor or URL icon...   *to establish a hyperlink*

4 Specify the way you want the source to be named in the palette, and click OK.

The source appears under the destination in the palette. Remember that a destination can have two or more sources (hyperlinked elements) associated with it; each destination in the palette lists all the sources in the publication that refer to it.

To create a hyperlink with drag-and-drop:

1 Select the text or graphics you want to be a source for a URL destination available on the Web.

2 Position the PageMaker window and the Netscape Navigator window side-by-side.

3 In the browser, activate the page with the hyperlink reference to the URL you want.

4 Drag the hyperlinked item to the PageMaker window, and drop it over the text or graphic you selected in step 1.

The PageMaker selection becomes the source to the URL, and the Hyperlinks palette lists the new source and destination with default names.

Formatting source text

PageMaker provides a script in the Scripts palette to let you quickly apply character-level formatting to all hyperlinked text in a publication. Most online publications use a particular color of type for hyperlinks so that it's clear to viewers that the text jumps to another location. The script is especially useful if you are exporting to PDF, since hyperlinked text is identical to unlinked text unless you manually change the text. If you plan to export to HTML, remember that hyperlinked text is automatically underlined in the Web browser window.

To define and apply hyperlink text formatting:

1 After you've defined all hyperlinks, choose Window > Plug-in Palettes > Show Scripts.

2 Click the Online folder icon in the palette to open that section of the palette.

3 Double-click the Apply Hyperlink Text Style script, and in the dialog box select the type style and color for the hyperlink. Then click OK.

Editing and removing hyperlinks

You can change the way destinations and sources are named in the Hyperlinks palette. For URL destinations, remember that the name is identical to the address, and so the name of a URL destination must be a valid URL address; PageMaker warns you if you type a grammatically-invalid address.

You can also remove destinations and sources from the palette. Renaming or removing sources and destinations from the palette simply removes the source or destination *attribute* assigned to the corresponding text or graphic in the publication, but has no effect on the actual text or graphic.

To rename an item in the palette:

1 Choose Window > Show Hyperlinks.

2 Double-click the item you want to rename.

3 Type (or paste) the new name or URL you want in the dialog box that appears, and click OK.

To remove a source or destination:

1 Choose Window > Show Hyperlinks.

2 Select the item you want to remove.

3 Click the trash button at the bottom of the palette, or choose Delete "[item name]" from the Hyperlinks palette menu, and click OK in the confirmation dialog box that appears.

To delete items and prevent the confirmation dialog box from appearing, press down Option (Macintosh) or Alt (Windows), as you complete step 3.

Previewing hyperlinks

In PageMaker's preview mode, you can see which text and graphics are hyperlink sources, and click them to display the associated anchor or URL destination.

To view and activate hyperlinks:

1 Click the hand tool in the Toolbox to enter preview mode. Alternatively, press Shift + F7.

Hyperlinked text is outlined in a blue box; hyperlinked graphics are framed with a blue line.

If you do not see the hyperlinks indicated in preview mode, then hyperlink display has probably been turned off in the Online Preferences dialog box. See "Setting Hyperlink Preview Preferences" on page 439.

Hyperlinks appear only in preview mode.

Cursor changes when positioned over source text and graphics.

2 Move the cursor over the hyperlink source you want to activate.

When you position the cursor over a hyperlink to an anchor destination, the cursor displays as a pointing hand (🖑). When you position the cursor over a hyperlink to an URL destination, the cursor displays as a pointing hand with a "W" inside it, indicating the destination is a resource on the World Wide Web.

3 Click within the blue border of the hyperlink source to jump to its destination.

By default, PageMaker displays the upperleft corner of the anchor in the center of the window. The page the anchor is on maintains the page-view size last used to view it. See "Setting Hyperlink Preview Preferences" on page 439 if you want to change the default behavior.

For URL destinations, PageMaker switches to your Web browser to display the appropriate page on the Web, or, for mailto URLs, to display the browser's electronic mail feature. PageMaker prompts you to specify a browser if you have not already specified one in PageMaker's Online Preferences dialog box. See "Setting Up Online Preferences" on page 347 for more information.

Redisplaying hyperlinked pages

In the same way most Web browsers provide Back and Forward options so that you can display pages you've already viewed during the browsing session, so PageMaker keeps track of the pages you have turned to within the current publication. You can use the Go Forward and Go Back commands to display pages in this way.

To turn back through the pages you displayed previously:

Choose Layout > Go Back for each page you want to view.

PageMaker turns to the page you most recently displayed. (If you choose the command a second time, you go to the next most-recently displayed page, and so on.) Once you choose Go Back, the Layout > Go Forward command becomes available; choose it to move through the list of more recently displayed pages.

Selecting and navigating to sources and anchors

You can use commands on the Hyperlinks palette menu to quickly locate and select sources and destinations. This saves you the step of switching to preview mode and manually finding and clicking hyperlinked items. If you are editing source text, it's a good idea to use the following procedure to find it, since PageMaker selects the exact characters that make up the source—you don't need to go into preview mode to confirm that you've selected the appropriate characters.

When you select text or graphics that are sources or anchors, a box appears in the Hyperlinks palette beside its source or anchor name. (An item can be both a source and an anchor, in which case a box appears beside the item's source name and by its anchor name.) For text characters that are anchors or sources, you must use the text tool to select all or part of the source or anchor characters to display the box in the palette.

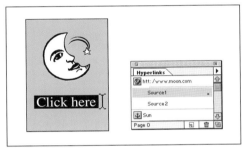

A box indicates the anchor or source name of the selected text or object.

To locate a hyperlink source or destination:

1 Select the item in the palette you want to turn to.

2 Choose Go To "[item name]" from the Hyperlinks palette menu.

If the item was a source or anchor, the text or graphic becomes selected. If the item was a URL destination, PageMaker starts or switches to your Web browser to display the destination.

Setting hyperlink preview preferences

PageMaker's online preferences include settings that help you preview hyperlinks and anchors.

To define online setup for hyperlink display:

1 Choose File > Preferences > Online.

2 Select Outline Link Sources When Hand Tool is Selected if you want borders to appear around hyperlinked text and graphics in PageMaker's Preview mode.

3 Select Center Upperleft of Anchor When Testing Hyperlinks if you want anchors centered in the window when you click a source in Preview mode.

4 Click OK in the Online Preferences dialog box.

CHOOSING FROM DIFFERENT KINDS OF ELECTRONIC DISTRIBUTION

As with printed publications, there are several kinds of electronic publications, and production methods for each kind can vary significantly. Many design and production decisions you make are affected by the kind of electronic distribution you choose.

Creating a publication that must have an acceptable appearance whether printed or viewed on-screen is only partially achievable due to different standard resolutions and design requirements between printed and on-screen documents. Decide which medium is more important and shift compromises in favor of that medium.

On-demand printing

Electronic distribution does not necessarily mean on-screen viewing. If you're creating a publication intended for broad distribution but limited readership, you can design it for the printed page and then create a PDF file from PageMaker, which can be printed as needed, or printed on demand. This approach combines the efficiency and low cost of electronic distribution and storage with the advantages of printing on paper. For more information, see "Preparing a PageMaker Publication for PDF" on page 442.

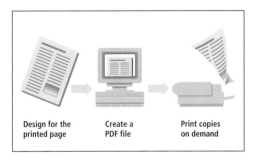

Design for the printed page → Create a PDF file → Print copies on demand

On-screen viewing and distribution

If you're creating a publication intended solely for on-screen viewing and electronic distribution, design it for the screen and then use the File > Export > Adobe PDF command to create a PDF file from PageMaker.

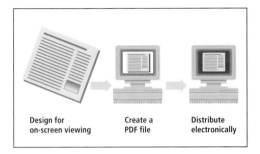

Design for on-screen viewing → Create a PDF file → Distribute electronically

PageMaker and Acrobat: An overview

Adobe Acrobat enables you to take any document from any Macintosh or Windows application and convert it to PDF format as easily as you'd print it. The PDF file retains the page layout, color, graphics, and typography of the original document and can be viewed on-screen or printed using one of the Acrobat viewers: Reader or Exchange.

The Adobe PageMaker 6.5 CD-ROM includes two components of the Adobe Acrobat program, which you must install before you can create and view PDF files from PageMaker:

• Acrobat Distiller, which converts PostScript files to PDF files. Distiller is installed automatically unless you used the Compact Installation option, or unless you specifically deselected Distiller during a Custom install.

• Acrobat Reader, which lets you view and print PDF files. Reader is installed separately from PageMaker. You can also download Reader from the Adobe Systems Inc home page on the Web.

For installation instructions refer to the *Adobe PageMaker 6.5 Getting Started* book.

Publishing on the Internet

If you're creating a publication for distribution on the World Wide Web, design it for the screen and then use one of two ways to prepare the file for the Internet:

• Use the File > Export > Adobe PDF command to create a PDF file that can be distributed electronically across the World-Wide Web. PDF files can be downloaded, viewed, and printed from several different platforms with the page layout and typography of the original document intact.

World Wide Web browser applications, which navigate, view, and retrieve information from the Web, generally do not read the PDF format directly. Acrobat Reader can function as a "helper application" to a browser which supports that feature. For example, when you download a PDF file using a Web browser, the browser can automatically open the PDF in Acrobat Reader. To date, Netscape Navigator 3.0 or later provides the best support for Acrobat; with Acrobat Reader 3.0, Netscape Navigator 3.0 displays the PDF and Acrobat Reader's user interface directly within the Netscape Navigator window.

• Use the File > Export > HTML command to create hypertext-linked pages that you can publish on the World Wide Web. If you select the Preserve Approximate Page Layout option in the Export HTML Options dialog box, PageMaker uses HTML tables to replicate the design of each exported page, including the number and width of columns, and the size and position of graphics on the page.

Although you can use PageMaker to create documents that can be published on the World Wide Web, you will have to set up Web server hardware and software, or set up an account with someone who runs a server in order to make your documents available to Web browsers.

Getting consistent color online • PageMaker includes a color library called Online Colors which consists of the colors most Web browsers use to display text and graphics in HTML documents. The 216 colors in the library are consistent across platforms, because they are the subset of colors that the browers use for both Macintosh and Windows. The library colors are also useful for PDF output, since the colors remain consistent (and do not dither) in all platform versions of Acrobat Reader 3.0.

To add the colors to your color palette, choose Utilities > Define Color, click New, and then choose Online Colors from the Libraries pop-up menu. Press Shift (Macintosh) or Ctrl (Windows) to select multiple colors, and click OK twice to close the open dialog boxes. Then apply the colors, so that you can see how they will appear in a Web browser or in Acrobat Reader 3.0. See Chapter 8 for more information on working with colors and color libraries.

Each color in the library is named with a three-digit value (to sort the colors chromatically); this is followed by the hexidecimal code for the color; the HTML specification defines colors in hexidecimal values. When you select a color in the palette, the Info bar displays its RGB values.

PREPARING A PAGEMAKER PUBLICATION FOR PDF

You may find that electronic distribution is faster than paper distribution, but you must adjust the production process to take the requirements of electronic distribution into account. This section describes the production issues you should resolve when creating a PageMaker file for PDF.

Note: You can use Acrobat Exchange 3.0 (not included with PageMaker 6.5 but available in the full retail version of Adobe Acrobat 3.0) to linearize PDF files for most efficient World Wide Web distribution. Linearization lets a supported Web browser download one page at a time rather than the entire PDF document. Exchange also lets you add interactive links, document security, fill-in form elements, plug-in support, and other enhancements to your document.

For complete discussions about creating PDF files, refer to the *Adobe Electronic Publishing Guide*, a PDF file available in the Adobe Technical Info folder on the Adobe PageMaker 6.5 CD-ROM.

Reconciling page numbering systems

A PDF document always starts on page 1, and supports only one page-numbering system per file. In contrast, a PageMaker document can start on any page number, and a book of publications can use more than one page-numbering system. For example, a booked publication may have front matter numbers with Roman numerals, and the remaining pages may use Arabic numerals, which restart at page 1.

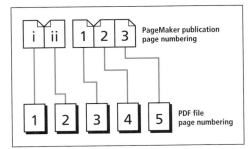

Plan to resolve page-numbering issues if you want to convert a publication that does not start with page 1 or that uses more than one page-numbering system. Otherwise, your bookmarks and hyperlinks will not work properly.

Combining multiple PageMaker files into one PDF file

You may have several PageMaker documents that make up a single publication. If you want to combine the files into a single PDF, gather the publications together using the Utilities > Book command, and then use the File > Export > Adobe PDF command.

Keeping index and table-of-contents links up-to-date

When you create a PDF file from PageMaker, you have the option of converting index and table-of-contents entries into hypertext links or bookmarks, which let readers view and navigate within the publication on-screen. For example, if you click an index entry in a PDF file created from PageMaker, Acrobat can jump directly to the page containing the indexed reference.

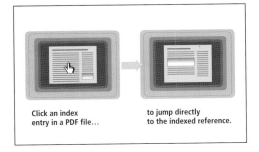

The File > Export >Adobe PDF command in PageMaker can only create hypertext links (using either bookmarks or links) for index or table-of-contents entries that were generated automatically from properly marked words or paragraphs in PageMaker (using the Create Index or Create TOC commands). Acrobat cannot convert manually written index or table-of-contents stories into hypertext links. See Chapter 7, "Indexes, Contents, and Pagination," for more information.

Setting up fonts

One of the challenges in electronic distribution is ensuring that fonts display properly. For example, if a person receives a PageMaker document and does not have the fonts originally used in it, the line lengths of text can change and alter the page layout. You can avoid this problem by creating a PDF file.

Acrobat can embed, or include in the PDF file, the fonts used in the original publication. To minimize file size, you can choose to embed a subset of a given font—that is, only those characters actually typed in the publication. If preserving the exact font is not important, Acrobat can create a working approximation of most fonts so that when the original fonts are missing, character spacing and leading are true to the original publication.

Original font   *Approximation*

Acrobat can only synthesize standard alphanumeric characters. It automatically embeds fonts that are significantly different from standard alphanumeric character shapes, such as script, picture (pi), non-Latin, or symbol fonts.

If you create a PostScript file and distill it on a computer other than the one on which you are running PageMaker, or if you want to use both the PostScript and the PDF files of the same PageMaker print job, we recommend that you select the Include Downloadable Fonts option in the Export Adobe PDF dialog box. This will ensure that Distiller has access to the same fonts that were used in creating the original PageMaker document. The fonts will also be included in the PostScript file for printing to any PostScript printer.

Original font   *Approximation*

To create a PDF version of your PageMaker document:

1 Choose File > Export > Adobe PDF.

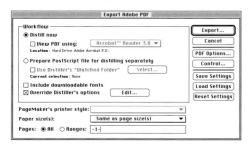

2 Select Distill Now (only available if Distiller is installed).

3 If you want to open and display the PDF file immediately after it has been created, select the View PDF Using option and choose a viewer from the pop-up menu.

4 Specify the range of pages to export, and then click Export.

5 If prompted, specify a filename and location, and then click Save.

Note: Acrobat is the default style on the PageMaker Printer Style pop-up menu. The other printer styles listed are those that have been defined in PageMaker's Printer Styles submenu on the File menu. If the Acrobat style doesn't fit your needs, define and use a new one.

To create a PostScript file to be processed later as a PDF:

1 Choose File > Export > Adobe PDF.

2 Select Prepare PostScript File for Distilling Separately. This prepares a pre-marked PostScript file but doesn't launch Distiller.

3 Select the Use Distiller's Watched Folder option and then click Select to save the file to a watched folder.

If you do not select this option, then you can save the PostScript file anywhere, but you will need to distill it manually.

4 Select a watched folder from the list. (Select the Auto-list from Distiller option to list all watched folders monitored by a specified Distiller.)

5 Click View Options if you want to check the Distiller Job Options specified for the selected watched folder. Click Close to return to the Export Adobe PDF dialog box.

6 Specify the range of pages to export, and then click Export.

7 If prompted, specify a filename and, if you're not using a watched folder, a location, and then click Save.

The PDF file will be processed automatically the next time the Distiller is launched or, if it is already running, after a specified amount of time has elapsed.

For more information about Distiller, see the *Adobe Electronic Publishing Guide* PDF file in the Adobe Technical Info folder on the Adobe PageMaker 6.5 CD-ROM.

Specifying the document area

PageMaker stores two document areas: the page size and the paper size.

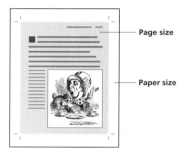

Page size

Paper size

• The page size is the size set in the Document Setup dialog box in PageMaker (the area of the actual printed publication within the crop marks).

• The paper size is the actual size of the paper on which the publication is set up to print, as specified in the Print dialog box in PageMaker.

If you create publications for printing on office printers, the page size of your publication may be identical to the paper size. If you create publications that will be printed on commercial presses or otherwise require the use of crop marks, the page size is always smaller than the paper size to allow for cropping and bleeds. Decide which document area you want to set as the page size in the PDF document, and change the option accordingly. (Think of the PDF page size as PageMaker's paper size.)

To specify the document area:

1 In the Export Adobe PDF dialog box, choose options from the Paper Size pop-up menu, as follows:

• Choose Same as Page Size to set the PDF document paper size to the page size specified in the Document Setup dialog box in PageMaker.

• Choose Apply Settings of Each Publication when you are converting a book of publications to PDF and not all publications use the same page size in File > Document Setup.

• Choose Apply Printer Style's Setting to use the paper size specified in the printer style you chose in the Export Adobe PDF dialog box.

2 Click Export in the Export Adobe PDF dialog box.

Saving and loading settings in the Export Adobe PDF dialog box and subdialog boxes

You can save a collection of settings you specify when exporting as PDF, so that you can quickly reuse them for similar projects.

To save settings:

1 Choose File > Export > Adobe PDF.

2 Define the settings you want using the buttons and options available.

3 When you've completed all appropriate settings, click Save Settings. These settings replace any previous settings you've saved.

To reuse previously-saved settings:

1 Choose File > Export > Adobe PDF.

2 Click Load Settings.

The Export Adobe PDF dialog box and its subdialog boxes take on the settings you loaded.

Changing Distiller options in PageMaker

You can set Distiller options in the Export Adobe PDF dialog box so that you can override Distiller default options without having to open Distiller.

General options specify which version of the Distiller to be compatible with, and tell the Distiller how to compress text and graphics, whether to save as an ASCII file, or embed fonts or a subset of a font in the PDF.

Acrobat Distiller 3.0 offers you two choices for compatibility, Acrobat 2.1 and Acrobat 3.0. PDF files created with Acrobat 3.0 compatibility using compressed text and line art or embedded Type 1 fonts cannot be opened in Acrobat 2.1 or earlier viewers. Therefore, use Acrobat 2.1 compatibility to ensure file access if recipients of your PDF documents use Acrobat 2.1. If all of the recipients of your PDF documents have a 3.0 viewer, choose Acrobat 3.0 compatibility to take advantage of possibly smaller, more efficient PDF files that can also contain better font and image compression, high-end printing information, and other new features.

Choosing a compression method

The compression options for type, line art, and various bitmap formats tell Acrobat Distiller how to downsample and compress objects in the publication.

JPEG compression, best for continous-tone images such as photographs, can vary from low to high. Low specifies the least compression with minimal loss of image quality and the least reduction in file size. High specifies the most compression with the greatest reduction in file size and the greatest loss of image quality.

LZW is best for images with large areas of single colors, such as computer screen shots, simple images created with paint programs, and scanned line drawings. LZW is usually not the best compression method for continuous-tone images. With some 24-bit continuous-tone images, in fact, LZW compression increases the amount of storage required for the image.

Monochrome images include most black-and-white illustrations made by paint programs and images scanned with an image depth of 1 bit. Each pixel of a monochrome image is represented by a single bit. For these images, Acrobat Distiller provides manual compression options only, none of which results in loss of data.

To change Distiller options:

1 In the Export Adobe PDF dialog box, select Override Distiller's Options, and then click Edit.

2 In the General section of the Override Distiller Job Options dialog box, change options as follows:

• For Compatibility, choose the version of Distiller to optimize for: Acrobat 2.1 or Acrobat 3.0.

• Select the ASCII Format option to maintain compatibility with most text-file formats.

• Select the Embed All Fonts option to include fonts in the PDF file. If the fonts are not available on the computer running Distiller, you must also select the Include Downloadable Fonts option in the Export Adobe PDF dialog box before you click Export. Only the fonts used in the publication will be embedded.

• The Subset Fonts Below _ option lets you minimize PDF file size by embedding only those characters of a font that are used in a document—that is, a subset of the font. Type the character threshold that determines when a font subset is created. If the percentage of characters used in the document you are exporting exceeds the character threshold setting, then the entire font is embedded in the file rather than a subset of it. The default is 25%.

Using downsampling and subsampling to reduce file size • Downsampling and subsampling—sometimes referred to as resampling—are techniques whereby information represented by several pixels in a bitmap are combined to make a single larger pixel. You can choose either downsampling or subsampling to reduce the file size, but note that resampling may result in some loss of detail in your images. The default settings downsample color and grayscale images to 72 dots-per-inch (dpi) and monochrome images to 300 dpi.

• Downsampling reduces the resolution of the image to the specifed dpi setting by averaging the pixel color of a sample area and replacing that area with a pixel of the averaged color.

• Subsampling reduces the resolution of the image to the specifed dpi setting by choosing a pixel in the center of the sample area and replacing that area with the pixel chosen. Subsampling signifcantly reduces the processing time compared to downsampling.

For example, a 300 dpi image normally contains more information than is necessary in a PDF file designed for on-screen display, so you can reduce the file size of the PDF by resampling it to 72dpi. You may specify a number higher than 72dpi to preserve detail when the image is magnified.

3 Select the Compress Text and Line Art option to save disk space by using file compression.

4 In the Color and Grayscale Bitmap Images section of the dialog box, select options to control compression and resampling, as follows:

• Select the Downsample To or Subsample To option, and type the number of dots per inch (dpi). For more information, see "Using Downsampling and Subsampling to Reduce File Size" on page 448.

• Select Automatic or Manual compression. With either method, you can control the amount of JPEG compression.

5 In the Monochrome Bitmap Images section of the dialog box, select options to control compression and resampling for 1-bit images, as follows:

• Select the Downsample To or Subsample To option, and type the number of dots per inch (dpi). For more information, see "Using Downsampling and Subsampling to Reduce File Size" on page 448.

• Select Manual compression and choose from the following options:

CCITT Group 3 used by most fax machines, compresses monochrome bitmaps one row at a time.

CCITT Group 4 is a general-purpose method that produces good compression for most types of monochrome images.

LZW produces the best compression for images that contain repeating patterns.

Run Length produces the best results for images that contain large areas of solid white or black.

6 Click OK.

Changing PDF options for hyperlinks, bookmarks, and articles

PDF options control how the content of a publication will be converted into a PDF file and let you add functions to your publication that are specific to electronic publishing, such as document information that can be used as part of a search.

To change PDF options:

1 In the Export Adobe PDF dialog box, click PDF Options.

2 If you have created a table of contents, an index, or hyperlinks in your PageMaker document, you can set options in the Hyperlinks section as follows:

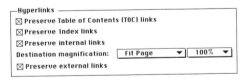

• Select Preserve Table of Contents links to add a hypertext link between each entry in the table of contents and the page to which the entry refers.

• Select Preserve Index Links to add a hypertext link between each entry in the index and the page to which the entry refers.

• Select Preserve Internal Links to include the hyperlinks you specified to anchors within the publication or booked publications. This option is unavailable if you did not define this kind of hyperlink in the current publication or booked publication.

• For the Destination Magnification option, select an option from each pop-up menu to tell Acrobat at which magnification and position it should show a page when opened by a hypertext link from a table of contents, index entry, or internal hyperlink.

Fit Page: Fits the page to the window

Fit Page Contents: Fits the bounding box of the page contents to the window.

Fit Top Left of Page: Fits the top left of the page to the top left of the window, at the desired zoom factor.

Fit Top Left: Fits the top left of the destination point to the top left of the window, at the desired zoom factor.

Fit Context: Fits the width of the bounding box of the page contents to the window, then positions the destination point at the top left of the window.

• Select Preserve External Links to include the hyperlinks you specified to external URLs—that is, to destinations outside the current publication or booked publications. This option is unavailable if you did not define this kind of hyperlink in the current publication or booked publication.

3 If you have created a TOC or index in your PageMaker document, you can set options in the Bookmarks section as follows:

• The Create TOC Bookmarks option creates Acrobat bookmarks based on the table of contents. Select this option to create one bookmark for each entry in the table of contents. For more information, see "Editing Bookmark Names" on page 451.

• The Create Index Bookmarks option creates Acrobat bookmarks based on the index. Select this option to create one bookmark for each entry in the index.

• The Destination Magnification option tells Acrobat at which magnification it should show a page when opened by a link from a TOC or index bookmark. Select a magnification from the pop-up menu, and choose a Fit To option. The Fit To options are described in step 2 of this procedure.

4 Set other options as follows:

• The Create Articles option converts threaded PageMaker stories into threaded Acrobat articles. Select this option to convert PageMaker stories. You can specify how the conversion occurs and which stories to convert. For more information see "Creating Acrobat Articles" on page 452.

• The Add Document Information option lets you enter information that will appear in the File > Document Info > General dialog box in an Acrobat viewer, such as Reader. Select this option, click Edit Info, enter the information, and then click OK.

• The Add Note To First Page option lets you create an Acrobat note that will appear on the first page of the PDF file. This is useful as a way to introduce the reader to the document or to provide instructions. To add a note, select this option, click Define, and then type the note. Click Opened to present the note as an open note window or click Closed to present the note as a note icon in Acrobat. Accept the default name or type a new name, and then click OK.

5 Click OK.

Editing bookmark names

Normally, Acrobat bookmarks are displayed in a narrow window. Bookmarks created from table-of-contents entries may be too long to be easily read in the window. You can shorten the bookmark name before you create the PDF document, or prevent a table-of-contents entry from being added as a bookmark.

To edit bookmark names:

1 In the PDF Options dialog box, click Edit Names.

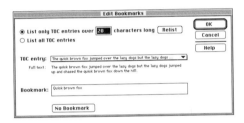

2 Editable entries appear in the TOC Entry pop-up menu. You can constrain the list of entries to edit by their length, as follows:

• To view only entries longer than a certain length, click List Only TOC Entries Over _ Characters Long, enter a number of characters, and then click Relist.

• To view all entries, click List All TOC Entries.

3 Choose a table-of-contents entry from the TOC Entry pop-up menu.

4 Enter a new Bookmark name.

5 If there is a specific TOC entry for which you do not want to have a bookmark, select it and then click No Bookmark.

6 Click OK.

Creating Acrobat articles

An Acrobat article consists of various text "beads," similar to the way a PageMaker story consists of various text objects. You can create Acrobat articles based on PageMaker stories, and you can have one or more stories per article.

You can use the Export Adobe PDF command to create articles automatically, or you can define them yourself, manually.

To create articles automatically:

1 Choose File > Export > Adobe PDF.

2 Click PDF Options.

3 In the PDF Options dialog box, click Create Articles, and then click Define.

4 Select the One Per Story Over _Text Objects option stating that only stories containing more than the specified number of text objects should be converted to articles.

5 Click Relist. The stories will automatically appear as articles.

6 Click OK to close the Define Articles dialog box.

To create articles manually:

1 Choose File > Export > Adobe PDF.

2 Click PDF Options.

3 In the PDF Options dialog box, click Create Articles, and then click Define.

4 Click New to display the PageMaker Stories dialog box.

5 Choose from the following options:

• The List Stories In option controls how you view stories when the publication contains a book list. To view all stories in all publications in the book, click Entire Book. Otherwise, click Current Publication Only.

Note: *The Entire Book option is only available when the publication contains a book list and you have chosen to print the entire book by either selecting the Always Print All Publications in Book option in the Control dialog box or when prompted after having selected the Export Adobe PDF command.*

• The List Only Stories Over_Characters Long option lets you view only those stories that are longer than a certain length. Enter the number of characters you want, and then click Relist.

6 Select one or more stories from the Stories in the Publication/Book list, and then click Add to include them in the Stories in Current Article list.

Each story shows the first few dozen characters, but if you want to see more of a selected story, click Preview.

7 Click OK. The Article Properties dialog box appears. Type a title, a subject, an author, and keywords, and then click OK. (A title is required; PageMaker supplies one by default, which you may change.)

Preserving data for high-end printing options

If you are using the PDF format as a way to deliver a publication to another site for high-end printing, you'll want to control the more advanced Distiller options which preserve or omit certain high-end printing information in the PDF.

To preserve or omit data for high-end printing:

1 Choose File > Export > Adobe PDF.

2 Select Override Distiller Options, and then click Edit.

3 In the Distiller PDF Job Options dialog box, click Advanced.

4 Set options as follows:

• Preserve OPI Comments. This option retains the information needed to replace a For Placement Only (FPO) image with the high-resolution image located on an Open PrePress Interface (OPI) server. The default is to preserve OPI comments.

• Preserve Overprint Settings retains the overprint setting used when printing color separations. The default is to preserve overprint settings.

• Preserve Halftone Screen Information retains halftone screen information, such as frequency, angle, and spot functions, used when outputting to a device that uses halftones. The default is to preserve halftone information.

• Preserve/Apply/Remove Transfer Functions. Preserving transfer functions retains the information so that it is included in the PostScript output at print time. Applying the transfer function affects the display of the PDF file on-screen as well as output. Removing the transfer settings means that they will not be used when printed or displayed. The original PostScript file may have been created for a specific device that uses the transfer function, but this file may go out for general distribution, with no specific output device in mind, in which case it would be best to remove the transfer settings.

• Preserve/Remove Under Color Removal / Black Generation. UCR/BG information is used in the conversion from RGB to CMYK. Remove this information if you do not want device-specific settings in the file. The default is to preserve the information.

5 Click OK.

Setting options in the Control dialog box

If you frequently use PageMaker to create PDF files, you may want to modify the behavior of options available in the Control dialog box. For example, the File > Export > Adobe PDF command alerts you to certain operations which significantly change how a publication is converted to a PDF document. When you become familiar with the details of conversion you may want to turn off the alert messages.

To set Control dialog box options:

1 In the Export Adobe PDF dialog box, click Control.

2 Set options as follows:

• Select the Always Print All Publications in Book option to turn off an alert message that prompts you to decide between converting the current publication or all publications in the book list. Deselect this option to see the alert message every time you convert.

• Select the Always Save Publication Before Exporting PDF option to turn off an alert message that asks you if you want to save a publication before converting it into a PDF document. Deselect this option to turn on the alert message.

• Select the Confirm Folder Location and File Name option to turn on an alert message that asks you to confirm the folder or disk where you want to save the PDF document, and the file-name of the PDF document. If you deselect this option, the PDF document is created in one of three ways: 1) If you selected Distill Now in the Export Adobe PDF dialog box, the PDF and PostScript files are created using the same location and filename as the publication, but with a .pdf extension; 2) If you selected Prepare PostScript File for Distilling Separately, and a watched folder is selected, the PostScript file is created in that watched folder using the same filename as the publication, but with a .ps extension; 3) If a watched folder is not selected, the PostScript file is created using the same filename and location as the publication, but with a .ps extension.

• Select Quit Distiller After Use if you have Distill Now selected in the Export PDF dialog box and you want Distiller to close down once the distillation process is complete.

• Select Check for PageMaker Printer Style Conflicts if you want to determine whether any print settings (defined in the selected printer style) will cause problems in the PDF file.

• Select an option for Output Color Model. The RGB option is useful if the document contains CMYK bitmap images and the PDF document is primarily for on-screen viewing. If the PDF document will primarily be printed to a CMYK printer, select CMYK. If you want to keep the document color consistent from one printer or monitor to any other printer or monitor, select CIE. (The CIE option requires you to turn Color Management on in PageMaker.)

If you choose RGB or CIE, and want the PDF to represent colors in EPS graphics as they are represented on-screen within PageMaker, select Use EPS Screen Preview.

3 Click OK to return to the Export Adobe PDF dialog box.

PREPARING A PAGEMAKER PUBLICATION FOR HTML

The World Wide Web displays information in units called pages, which are built using a standard called the hypertext markup language (HTML). In PageMaker, you can use the HTML export feature to create HTML pages that you can publish on the World Wide Web.

Exporting to HTML: An overview

PageMaker creates HTML pages that conform to the 3.2 version of the HTML specification.

The following points describe, in very general terms, how important aspects of your publication are exported; see subsequent sections of this chapter for details and alternatives:

Type: HTML uses a limited set of named text formats which are conceptually similar to paragraph styles. For example, there are HTML styles for headings, body text, and indented paragraphs. You can specify how to map paragraph styles applied on exported pages to HTML formats. Because HTML does not let you control typeface, leading, tracking, kerning, tab positions, and other type specifications, the line endings and depth of text columns on a PageMaker page are not preserved in HTML. The character-level attributes Bold, Italic, Underline, and Reverse as well as the color of your type, *are* preserved on export.

PageMaker, HTML, and page layout • PageMaker can export pages to HTML in two different ways, depending on whether you select the Preserve Approximate Layout option in the Export HTML Options dialog box. The illustrations below show the differing results. Regardless of the export method you use, remember that imported graphics in PageMaker are converted to GIF or JPEG formats; hyperlinks and text color are preserved; PageMaker-drawn elements and PageMaker typographic controls are not supported in HTML.

Original layout

If you choose not to preserve layout, columns and page layout set up in PageMaker are ignored: text and graphics are exported in a continuous stream. The size of the browser window determines how lines of text wrap.

If you choose to preserve layout, PageMaker approximates the layout as closely as possible using HTML tables. Resizing the browser window does not alter the layout. Multiple pages, if exported to one HTML file, are stacked vertically and separated by horizontal rules.

Graphics: HTML supports the GIF and JPEG image formats. PageMaker automatically converts copies of imported graphics (whether inline or independent) to GIF or JPEG. Shapes drawn with PageMaker drawing tools are not exported, with the exception of horizontal lines which become horizontal rules in HTML.

Page Layout: Using HTML tables, PageMaker can approximate multi-column page design, including elements outside margins, text and graphics that span columns, and text wrapping around graphics. As illustrated on the previous page, you can also choose not to approximate page layout; the result is one column of contiguous text, with graphics occupying separate paragraphs and flowing along with the text.

Learning more about HTML

Some browsers provide built-in links to information about creating HTML pages, late-breaking developments in Web publishing, and other related materials . The exact locations of these resources may vary over time and depend on which browser you use, so see your browser's documentation for details.

Typographical design limitations

Remember that type settings that affect typographical density (such as line breaks, letter spacing, and word spacing) are completely determined by the fonts used by a particular

browser. Other type attributes that are completely controlled by World Wide Web browsers, and won't be preserved if you specify them in PageMaker, include:

- Font, type size, and leading

- Horizontal scale

- Tracking and kerning

- Outline and Shadow type styles

- Paragraph alignment (unless Preserve Approximate Page Layout is selected)

- Indent and tab positions

The simplest way to create a page for the Web is to use PageMaker paragraph styles that correspond to the HTML markup tags that you want to use. This ensures that you are using styles supported by the HTML export feature. You can add the styles to your Styles palette directly, or import them along with the content of an HTML file, for example by using File > Place and selecting an HTML file to import. See "Importing HTML Files and Other Information from the World Wide Web" on page 347.

To import paragraph styles that correspond to HTML formats:

1 Choose Window > Show Styles.

2 Choose Add HTML Styles from the Styles palette menu.

You don't have to add HTML styles; you can use any style names you want, just remap them in the Export HTML Options dialog box. For example, use the PageMaker style named Heading 1 for the HTML style named <H1>. When you export the file, the HTML style names are mapped correctly.

Page layout limitations

If you design a multi-column layout and want to preserve the layout in HTML, remember that the Export to HTML feature can only approximate your page layout. The limitations are due to the HTML language itself; for example, since most typographical characteristics are not preserved in HTML, the length of text columns is not preserved. The following are unsupported features in HTML and might require page layout changes in PageMaker to produce acceptable HTML:

- Objects transformed (rotated, skewed, or flipped) in PageMaker are untransformed in HTML. You can transform the object in an illustration or image-editing application and reimport into PageMaker if you want the object to remain transformed in HTML.
- Overlapping objects in PageMaker are separated in the exported HTML, with results that may not be satisfactory. Before exporting, revise your design so that objects do not overlap.
- Non-rectangular text wrap shapes are not approximated in HTML, and results in objects being moved. Be sure to apply the standard rectangular text wrap shape, or revise the design to avoid non-rectangular text wrap.
- The content of a frame is exported, but not the surrounding frame itself. Non-rectangular frames become rectangular. Images that extend beyond the visible frame area are cropped in the exported file to approximate the original layout. (If you export without preserving layout, the image in the frame is uncropped.)
- PageMaker-drawn graphics are not exported, with the exception of horizontal strokes, which are exported as HTML horizontal rules.
- A masked object is unmasked. Before exporting, unmask the elements and, if you masked an image, crop it with the cropping tool. If you masked text, recreate the effect in an illustration program and import it as a graphic.

Setting HTML export options for graphics, type, and layout

Several options for HTML export can be set at any time and apply to every publication you export until you change the settings.

To set HTML export preferences:

1 Choose File > Export > HTML.

2 Click Options.

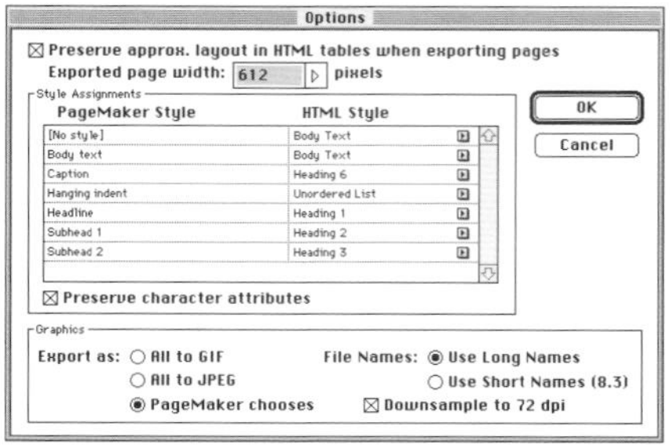

Approximating page layout in HTML • The illustration below shows the kinds of adjustments you might make to your page layout to work within the design limitations of HTML. If you export as HTML and want to approximate your page layout, we suggest you use the built-in View HTML feature in the Export HTML dialog box to confirm that the exported pages meet your needs; you can then make any necessary corrections in PageMaker and quickly export the updated page. Or, for best results, fine-tune the exported pages with an HTML editor that supports tables, such as Adobe PageMill 2.0.

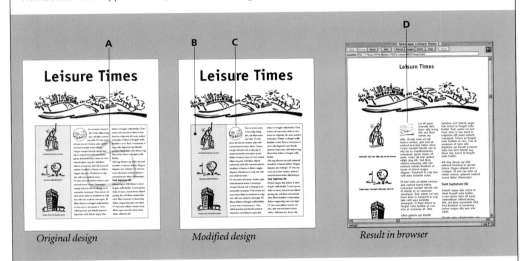

Original design   *Modified design*   *Result in browser*

A Since overlapping objects are not supported in HTML, PageMaker repositions them so the objects are separated in HTML. The results can be undesirable, so we deleted the background graphic in the modified page design.

B PageMaker-drawn graphics, which are not supported in HTML, are deleted from the exported file. We left them in the modified design (the printed version of the newsletter) since their deletion has no effect on other design elements.

C We changed from non-rectangular text wrap to rectangular text wrap. Non-rectangular text wrap is not supported in HTML, and can force objects to be moved in the exported file.

D The image cropped in the circular frame appears in HTML with a rectangular crop shape. If we wanted the circular image in HTML, we could have edited the image in an image-editing package and reimported it. (Note that the frame border does not export to HTML.)

3 Make sure Preserve Approximate Page Layout is selected if you want the HTML documents to approximate multi-column page designs.

Although the result may not look like a table, PageMaker uses the HTML table tags to arrange the exported text and graphics in a way that matches the placement of the original elements. When the option is not selected, the HTML document is essentially a one-column stream of text with graphics that flow with text.

4 For Exported Page Width, type or choose the width (in pixels) of the HTML document. The default value is the page width of the current publication (expressed in pixels).

When creating the exported document, PageMaker proportionally scales page elements (images, column widths, and so on) to approximate the PageMaker page in the new HTML page size.

5 From the HTML Style pop-up menus (to the right of the HTML style names), select the format you want to be applied for the PageMaker style listed to its left. Repeat this step for each style you want to change.

For example, if you use a style called Bullet List you probably want to map it to the OL Ordered List HTML format.

The table on page 461 provides an overview of the HTML formats available.

6 Make sure the Preserve Character Attributes setting is selected if you want the color and type style of your paragraph style definitions to be applied in your HTML documents.

Note: *Color values are converted into hexidecimal values as required by HTML, so a color in the HTML file may not match the color as it appears in PageMaker. To avoid color shifts, use the Online Colors color library available from the Libraries menu in the Color Options dialog box. For more information see "Getting Consistent Color Online" on page 442.*

7 In the Graphics section of the dialog box, set the following options:

• Select whether you want images converted to GIF or JPEG. Or select Let PageMaker Choose to default to whichever of those two formats works best, based on the file type and color data of each image on the pages being exported. Full sample images (RGB, CMYK, LAB, and grayscale) convert to JPEG and indexed images to GIF. (Images already in the GIF or JPEG format are exported without conversion to a different format if Let PageMaker Choose is selected.)

Note: When non-GIF images are copied and coverted into GIF images during HTML export, PageMaker applies the Netscape color palette to the GIFs, and sets the images to interlace (for faster downloading over the Web). When converting images to JPEG images during HTML export, the Image Quality setting is Medium. To convert an image with another palette or image quality setting, first select the image, and then choose File > Export > Graphic. You can use the same command to set image transparency for GIFs. See "Exporting a Graphic in a Different Format" on page 378 for more information.

HTML styles available in HTML Export Options dialog box

HTML heading style	What it does in a browser
H1, H2, H3, H4, H5, H6	Six levels of subheads. H1 has the largest type size, H6 the smallest.
ADDRESS	Sets an address or other short text apart from the body text.
BLOCKQUOTE	Sets one or more paragraphs of text apart from the body text.
BODY Text	Normal paragraphs of body text.
Definition List	List format. The browser automatically indents each paragraph with this format.
Directory List	List format. Usually, the browser automatically indents and adds a bullet before each paragraph with this format.
MENU List	Similar to an ordered list, but more compact.
OL List	Ordered list. Use for a numbered list. Usually, the browser automatically adds the correct number before each item.
PREFORMATTED	Prevents text from being reformatted when changes are made to a browser's style definitions.
UL List	Unordered bullet list. Usually, the browser automatically adds a bullet before each item.

• Select Downsample to 72 dpi if you want to minimize file sizes, for a Web page that downloads most efficiently.

• For File Names, select Use Long Names unless your Web server runs on a Novell network which requires the shorter naming convention.

8 Click OK to close the Options dialog box.

Beginning an HTML project

After you have created a PageMaker publication, the best way to begin setting it up for export as a set of HTML pages is to define which pages or stories will be exported as HTML documents, the document title, and the location to which you want to export them.

To assign a page as an HTML page:

1 Choose File > Export > HTML.

2 In the Export HTML dialog box, click New.

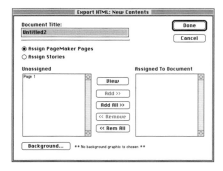

3 Enter a document title (the title will display at the top of the browser window when the document is viewed).

4 Select Assign PageMaker Pages if you want to define a page or range of pages to be exported as HTML or select Assign Stories to define a story or set of stories to be exported as HTML.

5 Select an unassigned page or story to be exported into the HTML document you are defining, and click Add. The order in which you add pages or stories is the order in which they will be exported.

You can click View with a page number selected if you want to display the page (you might need to move the dialog box to see it).

6 If you want to apply a tiled background image for the document, click Background and then double-click the GIF or JPEG image you want to use as a page background.

To export pages with a page background color rather than an image, return to the PageMaker window, and edit the PageMaker color [Paper] to the background color you want to appear in the HTML page.

7 Click Done to save the changes made so far and return to the Export HTML dialog box.

8 Click Document, and do the following:

• Navigate to the location where you want the HTML document to be stored.

• Name the document, following the naming conventions for the platform of the Web server you'll be using to publish the HTML document.

• Select Save Images into This Folder if you want your HTML document to include images from the publication and you want to store them in the same folder as the HTML document. (To store the graphics elsewhere, click OK and then click the Graphics button in the Export HTML dialog box and navigate to the folder you want.)

9 Click OK.

At this point you are only defining a target location, not actually saving the HTML document.

10 If you want to open the HTML document (once the export process is complete) in a Web browser or HTML editing application such as Adobe PageMill, click View HTML. Then click the Application icon to open a dialog box in which you can specify which browser or HTML editor you want to use to open the exported HTML file.

The application you select will open automatically when the export process is complete.

11 To generate the HTML, click Export HTML; otherwise, click Done to save settings made so far.

After you have defined how the publication is to be exported as HTML, the HTML Export dialog box displays a list of all defined HTML documents, their titles, and contents.

The next step in the process is to make sure that the PageMaker publication is HTML compatible. The first time you export a publication as HTML, PageMaker checks it for HTML compatibility. If the publication contains an element or layout attribute that is not supported by HTML, PageMaker presents a dialog box informing you of the parts of the publication that need to be changed. If there are incompatible elements in the publication, correct them, and then export the pages or stories again using the HTML export feature.

Modifying the title, location, or contents

After you have initially defined how your PageMaker publication should be translated to HTML, you may need to change the title of the HTML document, its location, or which PageMaker elements (pages or stories) should be included in the HTML document.

Changing the title

A Web browser displays the title in the title bar of the window, which represents one HTML document. Unlike a heading, you can only have one title per HTML document.

To change a document title:

1 Choose File > Export > HTML.

2 In the Export HTML dialog box, double-click the HTML document you want to edit and then change the title in the Edit Contents dialog box.

Changing the location

The HTML export feature allows you to set a location for each HTML document you create. This allows you to mirror the structure of a Web server if you wish, making it easier to update HTML documents as they change.

To change the location where an HTML document is exported:

1 Choose File > Export > HTML.

2 In the Export HTML dialog box, select the HTML document you want to edit.

3 Click Document.

4 Specify a new location for the HTML document and click OK.

Note: *If you define a location that is not in the same volume (for example, a hard drive or network server volume) as any imported graphics you will receive an error warning you that the graphics are not in the same volume as the HTML file. Since the HTML export feature defines the location of graphics in relative terms, the graphics and HTML documents must be in the same volume.*

Changing the contents of an HTML document

You can alter which pages or stories are included in a given HTML document. You cannot, however, mix stories and pages or switch from a page-based contents definition to a story-based contents definition (or vice versa).

To change the contents of an HTML document:

1 Choose File > Export > HTML.

2 In the Export HTML dialog box, double-click the HTML document you want to edit.

3 Add or remove pages or stories, remove the background image or specify a new one, and then click Done.

Chapter

14

USING SCRIPTS

CHAPTER 14: USING SCRIPTS

S cripts contain simple commands and queries that automate PageMaker tasks, such as setting up pages or importing a standard set of elements.Using scripts is the ideal way to automate repetitive tasks. For detailed information on writing scripts, see the online Script Language Help file.

PageMaker 6.5 includes a number of scripts in a Scripts folder. You can use the Scripts palette to run these scripts as they are, customize them for your specific needs, create your own scripts, and trace scripts command by command.

The Scripts palette displays the contents of the PageMaker Scripts folder, including any subfolders.When you add a script to the Scripts folder, it automatically appears on the Scripts palette. The Scripts folder is located in the PageMaker 6.5 folder as follows:

Macintosh: PageMaker 6.5:RSRC:Plugins
Windows: PM65\RSRC\<language>\Plugins.

RUNNING SCRIPTS

Scripts that you want to run from the Scripts palette must be stored in the Scripts folder. The Scripts palette can automatically copy scripts to this folder.

To run a script:

1 Choose Window > Plug-in Palettes > Show Scripts to display the Scripts palette.

2 Double-click a script to run it.

ADDING AND REMOVING SCRIPTS

You can add scripts to the Scripts palette by either using the Add Script command on the Scripts palette menu or by copying scripts to the Scripts folder. In Windows, you can also add scripts by dragging and dropping files to the palette.

You can also remove scripts from the Scripts palette. When you remove a script, you merely prevent it from being displayed on the palette; the script file itself is not deleted. Scripts you remove from the palette are moved into the Scripts-Disabled (Macintosh) or ScriptsD (Windows) folder. To redisplay a script you've removed from the palette, use the Restore command.

To add a script using the Scripts palette:

1 Choose Add Script from the Scripts palette menu.

2 In the Add a Script dialog box, select a script, and then click Open.

The script you choose is automatically copied to the Scripts folder and appears in the Scripts palette.

To add a script by dragging and dropping files (Windows only):

1 Select a file from the desktop or from Windows Explorer, drag the file over a folder in the Scripts palette, and then release the mouse button.

To remove a script from the Scripts palette:

1 Select a script in the Scripts palette. You can remove only one script at a time.

2 Choose Remove Script from the Scripts palette menu.

To restore a script that has been removed from the Scripts palette:

1 Choose Restore Script from the Scripts palette menu.

2 From the list of removed scripts, select a script and click the Restore button.

CREATING AND EDITING SCRIPTS

You can use the New Script command to create new scripts and then edit them using the Edit Script command.

To create a new script:

1 Choose New Script from the Scripts palette menu.

2 Name the script, specify a location in the Scripts folder, and then click OK.

3 Write the new script in the Edit Script dialog box, and then click OK.

To edit a script:

1 Press Command (Macintosh) or Ctrl (Windows), and click the script. Or select the script in the Scripts palette, and choose Edit Script from the Scripts palette menu.

2 Modify the script, and then click OK.

TRACING SCRIPTS

You can use the Trace Script command to run your script command by command, so that you can see where any problems might be occurring.

To trace a script:

1 Select a script in the Scripts palette.

2 Choose Trace Script from the Scripts palette menu.

3 In the Trace Script window, choose one of the following from the Run menu:

• Run runs the entire script.

• Step runs the script one line at a time.

• Step Out runs a series of command subroutines at one time.

• Reset stops the script from running without closing the Trace window.

• Quit stops the script from running and closes the Trace window.

APPENDIX A: SPECIAL CHARACTERS

The following tables—one each for Windows and the Macintosh—list the key combinations you can use to create special characters. You can type these special characters in story editor or in layout view. You can also type them—using different key combinations—in dialog boxes to find, change, or insert special characters.

PageMaker also supports font-specific extended characters. A PageMaker file, CHARSET.T65, shows the extended characters in your available fonts and the keystrokes that create them. Print the template to see the printed characters and to ensure you have the right printer fonts. For more information, open the CHARSET.T65 template in the Extras folder in the PageMaker 6.5 folder.

Special characters (Windows)

Example	Description	Enter in text	Enter in dialog box
•	bullet	Alt + 8	^8
^	caret	Shift + 6	^^
-	computer hyphen*	n/a (PageMaker inserts it)	^5
©	copyright symbol	Alt + g	^2
-	discretionary (soft) hyphen	Ctrl + Shift + -	^-
…	ellipsis	Alt + 0133	Alt + 0133
—	em dash	Alt + Shift + -	^_
	em space	Ctrl + Shift + m	^m
–	en dash	Alt + -	^=
	en space (.5 em)	Ctrl + Shift + n	^>
	end of paragraph	Enter	^p
	forced line break	Shift + Enter	^n
▲	TOC or Index hyperlink/bookmark token*	n/a (PageMaker inserts it)	^:
▣	index-entry marker	n/a	^;
▨	inline-graphic marker*	n/a	^g
-	nonbreaking hyphen	Ctrl + Alt + -	^~

* You cannot type this character in the Change To edit box in the Change dialog box.

continued on next page

Special characters (Windows) continued from previous page

Example	Description	Enter in text	Enter in dialog box
/	nonbreaking slash	Ctrl + Alt + /	^/
	nonbreaking space	Ctrl + Alt + space	^s
⬛, LM, RM	page-number marker	Ctrl + Alt + P	^3
¶	paragraph symbol	Alt + 7	^7
®	registered trademark symbol	Alt + r	^r
§	section symbol	Alt + 6	^6
	tab	Tab	^t
	thin space (.25 em)	Ctrl + Shift + t	^<
™	trademark symbol	Alt + 0153	Alt + 0153
"	typographer's open quotation marks	Alt + Shift + [	^{
"	typographer's close quotation marks	Alt + Shift +]	^}
'	typographer's single open quotation mark	Alt + [	^[
'	typographer's single close quotation mark	Alt +]	^]
	wildcard (single character)*		^?
	wildcard (white space)*		^w

* You cannot type this character in the Change To edit box in the Change dialog box.

Special characters (Macintosh)

Example	Description	Enter in text	Enter in dialog box
•	bullet	Opt + 8	Opt + 8
^	caret	Shift + 6	^^
-	computer hyphen*	na (PageMaker inserts it)	^c
©	copyright symbol	Opt + g	Opt + g
-	discretionary (soft) hyphen	Cmd + Shift + -	^-
…	ellipsis	Opt + ;	Opt + ;
—	em dash	Opt + Shift + -	^ _
	em space	Cmd + Shift + m	^m
–	en dash	Opt + -	^=
	en space (.5 em)	Cmd + Shift + n	^>
	end of paragraph	Return	^p
	forced line break	Shift + Return	^n
	TOC and index hyperlink/bookmark token*	n/a (PageMaker inserts it)	^:
⬧	index entry marker	n/a	^;
▓	inline graphic marker*	n/a	^g

* You cannot type this character in the Change To edit box in the Change dialog box.

continued on next page

Special characters (Macintosh) continued from previous page

Example	Description	Enter in text	Enter in dialog box
-	nonbreaking hyphen	Cmd + Opt + -	^~
/	nonbreaking slash	Cmd + Opt + /	^/
	nonbreaking space	Opt + spacebar	^s
#, LM, RM	page-number marker	Cmd + Opt + p	^3
¶	paragraph symbol	Opt + 7	Opt + 7
®	registered trademark symbol	Opt + r	Opt + r
§	section symbol	Opt + 6	Opt + 6
	tab	Tab	^t
	thin space (.25 em)	Cmd + Shift + t	^<
™	trademark symbol	Opt + 2	Opt + 2
"	typographer's open quotation marks	Opt + [	Opt + [
"	typographer's close quotation marks	Opt + Shift + [	Opt + Shift +]
'	typographer's single open quotation mark	Opt +]	Opt + [
'	typographer's single close quotation mark	Opt + Shift +]	Opt + Shift +]
	wildcard (single character)*		^?
	wildcard (white space)*		^w

* You cannot type this character in the Change To edit box in the Change dialog box.

APPENDIX B: FONT SUBSTITUTION

PageMaker can warn you if a font used in the active publication is missing from your system, take steps to substitute another font, and then let you approve the results. Font substitution is most likely to occur when you open a publication created on a different computer or on a different platform, or when you import text containing fonts that are unavailable on your system. (PageMaker does not perform font substitution for text within imported graphics.)

If a font is missing, PageMaker uses the PANOSE typeface matching system—a numeric classification of fonts according to visual characteristics—to substitute fonts of comparable appearance. When a font substitution is made using PANOSE, the missing font name is followed by the substitute font name in brackets on PageMaker's Font submenu on the Type menu.

On the Macintosh, PageMaker also supports Adobe Type Manager (ATM), which can simulate fonts—rather than find substitutes for them—for display and for printing. (When a missing font has been simulated using ATM, a diamond appears beside the missing font name on the Font submenu.) To simulate fonts in this way, you must have ATM running on your system, and have fonts that ATM can simulate. If you are using ATM 4.0 Deluxe, PageMaker is able to open any deactivated font sets managed by ATM that contain fonts required for the publication. For details on using ATM, refer to the product documentation.

Matching fonts

Step 1: Responding to font-matching results

When PageMaker detects a missing font, it determines the best match for the missing font, and opens a dialog box in which you can accept, cancel, or change substitutions for the active publication (temporarily or permanently). Select a font change in the list box to specify a substitute font other than the one proposed.

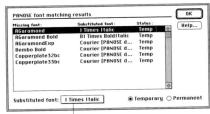

Choose a font to substitute for the missing font selected in the list box

Select Temporary if you want to reconsider the selected font substitution the next time the font is found missing, otherwise select Permanent.

Step 2: Managing the font-matching exception table

If you make font substitution changes in the Font-Matching Results dialog box, PageMaker will ask if you want to update the font-matching exceptions file. This file keeps track of how you have decided to override PANOSE's proposed font substitutions. If you want your preferred font substitutions to apply to the current publication only, click No. If you want PageMaker to make the same substitutions for all publications, click Yes.

Customizing font-matching options

By default, PANOSE font substitution is turned on and is set to display its font-matching results. But you can use the File > Preferences > General command to turn on or off both PANOSE and ATM (Macintosh only), and to specify other font-matching preferences.

To customize font matching:

1 Choose File > Preferences > General.

2 Click Map Fonts.

3 Specify whether you want PANOSE font substitution on or off.

On the Macintosh, click the ATM button and PANOSE buttons to set the status of each method. A black diamond next to the font-matching preference indicates "on," a white diamond indicates "off," and a gray diamond indicates "on" but secondary to the other preference marked with a black diamond. When both font-matching preferences are off, PageMaker uses the default font specified in the Default menu within the dialog box.

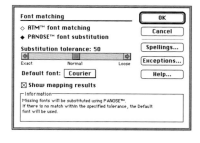

4 Adjust the settings you want, as follows:

• Select the Show Mapping Results option if you want to see which fonts are missing and which fonts PANOSE proposes to substitute whenever fonts are found to be missing.

• Adjust the tolerance level to specify how closely you want the substitute font to visually match the original. If the closest substitute falls outside the allowed tolerance, PANOSE substitutes the font set for Default.

• For Default Font, choose a font to substitute for cases when a suitable substitute for a missing font is unavailable, or when font matching is turned off.

5 Click OK.

To create or edit a list of preferred font substitutions:

1 Choose File > Preferences > General.

2 Click Map Fonts.

3 Click Exceptions.

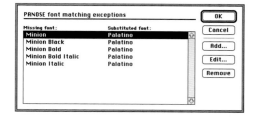

4 Make changes as follows:

• To add a new exception, click the Add button, and type in the exact screen font name for a missing font in the Missing Font field. Then, select the font to substitute for the missing font in the Substituted Font pop-up menu, and click OK.

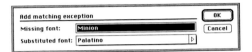

• To edit a font substitution, select it from the list and click Edit. Then, change either the screen-font name for the missing font or select a different substitute font in the Substituted Font pop-up menu, and click OK.

• To remove a font substitution, select it from the list, and then click Remove.

To edit a list of fonts that are different in spelling only and should always be matched:

1 Choose File > Preferences > General.

2 Click Map Fonts.

3 Click Spellings.

4 Make changes as follows:

• To add a new spelling difference, click Add and type or select the exact screen-font name for a missing font. Then, type the exact name of the equivalent font on the other platform in the Substituted Font field, and click OK.

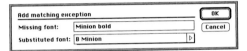

• To edit a spelling difference, select it from the list, and then click Edit. Then, change the spelling information and click OK.

• To remove a spelling difference, select it from the list, and then click Remove.

APPENDIX C: CROSS-PLATFORM COMPATIBILITY

This appendix describes procedures and tips for transferring publications from Windows to Macintosh and vice versa. (You can open Macintosh PageMaker publications on the Power Macintosh and vice versa; likewise, you can open Windows 95 PageMaker publication on Windows NT and vice versa.)

You cannot transfer a publication between PageMaker versions and across platforms at the same time. Therefore, to convert a publication created in PageMaker 6.0 for the Macintosh to PageMaker 6.5 for Windows, you must first open the publication with PageMaker 6.0 for Windows. For more information on converting publications between different versions of PageMaker, see the *Adobe PageMaker 6.5 Getting Started* book.

Note: *A Macintosh PageMaker publication must have the .P65 or .T65 filename extension before you move the publication to the Windows platform.*

When you first open the publication on the destination platform, PageMaker displays a dialog box in which you specify transfer options for graphic file formats that are platform-specific (Metafile and PICT) and for filenames in links (since the two platforms handle filename conventions differently). There may be other platform differences that change the publication and which you can control manually. See "Tips for Transferring Publications" on page 482.

To open a PageMaker publication created on a different platform:

1 Transfer the publication file to the destination platform environment.

You can do this using a network, a modem at each computer, or with a floppy disk (refer to your operating system documentation for details on reading from and writing to disks formatted for the other platform).

2 Start PageMaker, and choose File > Open.

3 Select the publication, and then click OK.

4 If you are moving a publication to the other platform permanently or for final output, make sure the Translate Filenames in Links option is selected.

This option lets PageMaker automatically link to externally-stored files.

5 Specify whether to translate Metafiles and PICTs, as follows:

• If you are moving the publication to the other platform temporarily, and you don't need to view graphics or print final output, make sure the Translate Metafiles to PICTs (Macintosh) or Translate PICT to Metafile (Windows) option is not selected. (When you go back to the original platform, the graphics print normally.)

• If you are moving the publication to the other platform temporarily and you need to view the graphics in the publication, select the For Viewing option. PageMaker will convert all Metafile screen representations in the publication to PICTs (and vice versa), for viewing purposes only. Graphics with Metafile or PICT print representations will not print at high resolution.

• If you are moving a publication to the other platform permanently or for final output, select the For Printing and Viewing option. PageMaker will convert all Metafile and PICT representations (both for screen and for printing) stored within the publication so that they print at high resolution.

Note: Only Metafiles and PICTs stored within the publication are translated for printing. If a graphic's print representation is a Metafile or PICT that is stored in an external file, the graphic will not print correctly at high resolution.

6 Click OK.

The publication opens as an untitled document.

Tips for transferring publications

The following aspects of your publications may require special attention when transferred.

• **Text:** You will probably have to substitute fonts when you first open the publication on the new platform. See Appendix B for more information on font substitution. Always check your publication carefully for changes in line breaks, overset text, and other undesirable results of text recomposition. Also check special characters (such as diacritical marks) to make sure the characters transferred correctly from one platform's character set to another. The characters listed in Appendix A of this guide transfer correctly.

• **Placed graphics:** Graphics stored in the publication in their entirety transfer completely. If you import only a link to a graphic, you must transfer the original linked files with the publication, and then relink the files.

• **OLE objects:** OLE-embedded objects transfer completely with the file, but for OLE-linked objects, you must transfer the original source files with the publication. Relinking is necessary only if you want to edit the object, and the source application is available on the new platform. You can relink OLE objects only if an OLE server application is available on the new platform.

- **Subscribers:** Macintosh subscriber links are broken when you transfer a publication to Windows. The publication will print correctly, but you can't update the subscriber unless you transfer the publication back to the Macintosh. (PageMaker preserves subscriber link information.)

- **Photo CD:** Photo CD images are not stored in your publication, so you'll need to relink to the image after you've transferred the publication to the other platform. Be sure the computer you are moving to has access to a network where the image can be stored, or is equipped with a CD-ROM drive.

- **Tables:** Tables created in Adobe Table and then placed or OLE-embedded in your publication will transfer. However, differences in fonts on the two platforms may cause font substitution problems when printing. We recommend that you transfer the Table file to Adobe Table on the destination platform, reassign fonts, and re-import the table into the transferred publication.

- **Libraries:** You cannot open an object library on a platform other than the one on which it was created.

APPENDIX D: PAGEMAKER TAGS

PageMaker Tags let you import and export both character- and paragraph-level attributes with text-only files. Codes—called PageMaker Tags—are embedded in the text-only file to indicate the type specifications you want to apply to the text.

This appendix lists each PageMaker Tag and offers procedures and guidelines for using tags efficiently. You must have the PageMaker Tags import and export filters installed to use tags. Refer to the *Adobe PageMaker 6.5 Getting Started* manual for more information on installing import and export filters.

When you import a tagged file, PageMaker converts the tag codes and applies the attributes automatically. When you export formatted text, you can have PageMaker generate the tag codes so that you can later import the information with formatting intact.

Only PageMaker can read PageMaker Tags. However, PageMaker 6.5 can read files formatted with Xpress Tags, a similar feature available for Quark Xpress® 3.0 and later.

Note: You must type the following text at the top of a text file you want PageMaker to treat as tagged: <PMTags1.0 Mac> (for files created on the Macintosh platform) or <PMTags1.0 Win> (for files created on the Windows platform.)

TAGGING BASICS

All PageMaker Tag codes begin with the less-than character (<) and end with the greater-than character (>). Type the tag immediately before the text you want to format. For paragraph-level attributes, type the tag at the start of the paragraph. For character-level attributes, type the tag at the start of the text you want to change.

```
<ga1> <fMinion SB> <s54pt>
<cl12pt> T <ga1> <gt <stop2p7>
<align1>) <fMinion> <s9.5pt>
<cl12pt> his appendix lists each
Tag available and offers guidelines
for using the Tags feature efficiently.
You must have the Tags Import and
Export filters installed to use the
Tags in PageMaker. Refer to
<i> Getting Started <i> for more
information on installing import
and export filters.
```

Tagged text in text-editing program

This appendix lists each Tag available and offers procedures and guidelines for using the Tags feature efficiently. You must have the Tags Import and Export filters installed to use the Tags in PageMaker. Refer to *Getting Started* for more information on installing import and export filters.

Imported version automatically formatted by PageMaker

```
<galignment 1>
```

When you import a tagged file, PageMaker converts the tag codes and applies the attributes automatically.

Paragraph-level tag: align left

```
<b>
```

When you import a tagged file, **PageMaker** converts the tag codes and applies the attributes automatically.

Character-level tag: bold

The type attributes you specify remain in effect until you use codes to cancel them or until you apply other attributes. For example, to apply bold text to one word in a paragraph, you type the tag <b> before the word and immediately after it to cancel the bold attribute.

To import tagged text:

1 Choose File > Place.

2 Find and select the text-only tagged file.

3 Make sure the Read Tags option is *not* selected, and then specify whether to import the text as a new story, or to replace the current story, or replace selected text.

4 Click OK.

One of the best ways to learn about using the tag codes is to export text with tags from a formatted PageMaker publication. When you view the exported text, you can see how PageMaker transforms type attributes into tag codes (and vice versa).

To export PageMaker text as tagged text:

1 Select the text tool.

2 Click an insertion point in the story you want to export.

3 Choose File > Export > Text.

4 Select Tagged Text as the Export option.

5 Specify a name and location in which to save the file.

6 Click OK.

Tags for formatting characters and paragraphs

The tables in this section list each text attribute you can set in PageMaker, its corresponding Tag, and notes and shortcuts, if any, for each Tag.

In the "Tag" column for the following tables, the pound character (#) denotes a placeholder for information you provide. The information you enter might be a numeric value, such as the type size or leading you want to specify; a code such as "t" for True; or text, such as the name of a color you want to apply. When the information is text, the case of the characters does not matter unless you are typing a specific color or paragraph style name; also, the text must be enclosed in quotes if the text contains two or more words.

Note the following tips for specifying numeric values or text within a PageMaker Tag:

• By default, numeric values are expressed as points. To use a different measurement system, type the value you want and then type a character to denote the measurement system, as follows: double quotes (") for inches, **m** or **mm** for millimeters, **p** for picas, and **c** for ciceros.

• For tags that use multiple value or text fields to define two or more aspects of a character or paragraph attribute (for example, when formatting a tab you specify its position, alignment, and leader), you can type the placeholders () or "" to indicate that you want to use the defaults currently in effect. This lets you omit details you might not know, or focus only on the specific settings you want to vary from the current formatting.

• For numeric values, you can also use mathematical expressions, if applicable. In these cases, type ^ to denote the current value of the attribute you are specifying. For example, when specifying the Space Before Paragraph attribute,

you can type ^ + **4** to increase the space before by 4 points from that of the current setting.

• You can type **$** for a field to apply the currently defined paragraph style attribute for that setting. If no style is assigned to the paragraph, the PageMaker default is applied. For example, <font$> applies the typeface specified in the currently applied style.

• To include comments within a tag file, type <# immediately before the comment text and #> immediately after. To include a comment within a tag, enclose the comment between pound signs (#). The comments are not imported with the tagged file, but remain in the tagged file for reference.

PageMaker Tags for character-level formatting

Character attribute	Tag	Tag abbreviation
Font	<font "font name">	<f"fontname">
	Optionally, you can type in the character set to use—for example, if you are typing ASCII values to indicate special characters. Between the closing bracket and the closing quote after the font name, type **Win** or **Mac**, depending on the platform you are on. If editing a tagged text file in a DOS editor, type **OEM** (for Original Equipment Manufacturer).	
Type size	<size ###>	<s###>
Horizontal scale	<horizontal ###>	<h###>
Manual pair kerning	<kern ###>	<k###>
Range kerning	<letterspace ###>	<l###>
Plain text	<p>	

continued on next page

PageMaker Tags for character-level formatting continued from previous page

Character attribute	Tag	Tag abbreviation
Bold	`<b>`	
Italic	`<i>`	
Outline	`<o>`	
Shadow	`<~>`	
Underline	`<u>`	
Strikethru	`<x>`	
Superscript	`<+>`	
Subscript	`<->`	
All caps	`<call>`	`<ca>`
Small caps	`<csmall>`	`<cs>`
Reverse	`<creverse>`	`<cr>`
Baseline shift	`<cbaseline ###>`	`<cb###>`
Leading	`<cleading ###>`	`<cl###>`
Linebreaks	`<cnobreak #>` For #, type **t** (or true) if you want lines to break; type **f** (or false) if you do not want the lines to break.	
Small caps size	`<cssize ###>`	`<css###>`
Superscript/subscript size	`<c+size ###>`	`<c+s###>`

continued on next page

PageMaker Tags for character-level formatting continued from previous page

Character attribute	Tag	Tag abbreviation
Superscript position	<c+position ###>	<c+p###>
Subscript position	<c-position ###>	<c-p###>
Tracking	<ctrack ###>	<ct###>

For ###, type the name of a track, or type any of the following abbreviated forms:
none for No Track
-2 or **vt** for Very Tight
-1 or **t** for Tight
0 or **n** for Normal
1 or **loose** for Loose
2 or **vl** for Very Loose

Color (custom)	<c-colortable ("name" # ####)>	<c-c...>

This tag lets you define custom colors which you can then apply with the <ccolor...> tag. Enclose information for each color you want to define between parentheses. For "name" type the name of the color between quotes. The # field specifies the color model. Type **0** for CMYK, and **1** for RGB.
The #### field specifes percentages of R, G, and B, or C, M, Y, and K colors.

Color (existing)	<ccolor "name">	<cc"color name">

For "name" type the name of the color between quotes. The color can be one you have defined with the <c-colortable...> tag, or a color already defined in the publication. You can use the following abbreviations for predefined colors:
p or **none** for paper
k for black
b for blue
g for green
r for red

PageMaker Tags for paragraph-level formatting

Paragraph attribute	Tag	Tag abbreviation
Left indent	\<gleft ###>	\<gl###>
Right indent	\<gright ###>	\<gr###>
First line indent	\<gfirst ###>	\<gf###>
Tabs	\<gtab(\<###>\<align#>\<"leader ">)> \<gt(\<###>\<align#>\<"leader ">)>	
	Each set of parentheses define a tab in the paragraph. \<###> specifies tab position (distance from the left edge of the text block) and is the only required information for each tab. \<align#> sets tab alignment; type **1** for Left, **2** for Right, **3** for Center, **4** for Decimal. \<"leader "> is a string of characters (such as periods, hyphens, or underscores) you want to use as a tab leader.	
Alignment	\<galignment #>	\<ga#>
	For #, type **0** for Left, **1** for Right, **2** for Center, **3** for Justify, **4** Force Justify	
Leading grid	\<ggrid ###>	\<gg###>
Language	\<g& "dictionary name">	
Space before	\<g+before ###>	\<g+b###>
Space after	\<g+after ###>	\<g+a###>
Autoleading percentage	\<g% ###>	
Leading method	\<gmethod #>	\<gm#>
	Type **1** for proportional leading; **2** for top of caps leading; **3** for baseline leading.	

continued on next page

PageMaker Tags for paragraph-level formatting   continued from previous page

Paragraph attribute	Tag	Tag abbreviation
Word spacing	`<gwordspace ### ### ###>`	`<gw### ### ###>`
	The three fields specify Minimum, Desired, and Maximum spacing.	
Letter spacing	`<gspace ### ### ###>`	`<gs### ### ###>`
	The three fields specify Minimum, Desired, and Maximum spacing.	
Pair kerning above	`<gpairs ###>`	`<gp###>`
Hyphenation	`<ghyphenation # ### #>`	
	The three fields specify the following: # sets the prefered hyphenation method (type **0** for Off; **1** for Manual Only; **2** for Manual Plus Dictionary; **3** for Manual Plus Alogrithm). Alternatively, you can specify a new hyphenation method with the tags `<g0>`, `<g1>`, `<g2>`, and `<g3>`.	
	### specifies Hyphenation Zone.	
	# specifies the Limit Consecutive Hyphens To setting.	
Keep together	`<gktogether>`	`<gkt>`
Keep begin	`<gkbegin>`	`<gkb>`
	In conjuction with `<gkend>`, this tag lets you mark a range of paragraphs to keep together within the same page or column.	
Keep end	`<gkend>`	`<gke>`
	In conjunction with `<gkbegin>`, this tag lets you mark a range of paragraphs to keep together within the same page or column.	
Keep with next	`<gknext ###>`	`<gkn###>`
Widow control	`<gkwidow ###>`	`<gkw###>`
Orphan control	`<gkorphan ###>`	`<gko###>`
Page break	`<g+page>`	`<g+p>`

continued on next page

PageMaker Tags for paragraph-level formatting continued from previous page

Paragraph attribute	Tag	Tag abbreviation
Column break	<g+column>	<g+c>
Include in TOC	<gcontents>	<gc>
Rule Above	<gbabove ### # ### ### ### "Color" ### #>	

For the first field, type **Col** for width of column, or **Text** for width of text.

Next, type **T** for a transparent stroke, **F** for an opaque stroke

The next three fields specify left indent, right indent, and distance from baseline.

For "Color" type the rule color.

Next, type the line weight (for example, 12 for a 12-point stroke).

Finally , specify the kind of stroke: **1** for solid, **2** for dashed, **3** for squared, **4** for dotted.

| Rule Below | <gbbelow> [follow instructions for Rule Above] | |
| Define paragraph style | <@###=definition> | |

For ###, type the name of the style you are creating. (Do not use the characters "@," "-," or "=" in a paragraph style name.)

After the equal sign, type the tags that define the formatting you want the style to have; separate the tags with the vertical bar character (|) rather than the characters "<" and ">."

PageMaker will apply default values for all attributes you do not specify. Unlike other tags, a tag that names a paragraph style must be followed by a paragraph return.

| Set Next style | <@-next "###"> | <@-n "###"> |

For ###, type the name of the Next Style. (This tag must be part of a style you are defining with the "<@###=...>" tag.)

continued on next page

PageMaker Tags for paragraph-level formatting continued from previous page

Paragraph attribute	Tag	Tag abbreviation
Apply paragraph style	<@###:>	
	For ###, type the name of the style you want to apply. If you insert this tag within a paragraph, only the character-level attributes of the style are applied, as overrides to the existing paragraph style. Unlike other tags, a tag that names a paragraph style must be followed by a paragraph return.	
	You can apply a paragraph style anywhere within a paragraph: the character-level attributes of the embedded paragraph style are then applied to the specified range of characters as overrides to the initial paragraph style.	
Set Based On style	<@-parent "###">	<@-p "###">
	For ###, type the name of the Based On style. (This tag must be part of a style you are defining with the "<@###=...>" tag.	

PageMaker Tags for special characters and other information

Special Character	PageMaker Tag
Em space	<m>
En space	<n>
Thin space	<t>
Word space	<w>
Non-breaking space	<!w>
Em dash	<\—>

continued on next page

PageMaker Tags for special characters and other information   continued from previous page

Special Character	PageMaker Tag
En dash	<\–>
Soft return	<r>
Page number	<\d>
Discretionary hyphen	<d>
Non-breaking hyphen	<\!->
Non-breaking slash	<\!/>
Any ASCII character	<\#[type the ASCII number]>

Note: Type an exclamation point (**!**) immediately before any space character to make it non-breaking. For example, type <!t> to define a non-breaking thin space. Type a backslash (\ ) immediately before the characters @, <, and > when you want those characters to appear in your text. Otherwise, the characters are read as codes in the Tag language.

Using macros

The PageMaker Tags feature lets you use a macro-like technique for specifying long tags (or combinations of tags) by typing a short abbreviation. The PageMaker Tags import filter transforms every instance of the abbreviation into the full Tag codes.

For example, the following tag <#define_MT_="<i><s12>MyText<i><s$>"> would find every instance of the text "MT," and turn it into the text "MyText," formatted in italic, 12-point type. (The code <s$> tells the Tags filter to change from 12 point type to the default type size for the current paragraph.)

Importing inline graphics

PageMaker can import inline graphics if the tagged text file you are importing specifies the graphic's exact location and filename. The tag is <&### ### ### "pathname and filename">. Be sure to include a space between the last pound sign (#) and the opening quotation mark.

The ### fields (which are optional) specify the width, the height, and the baseline offset of the graphic. Use a colon (Macintosh) or a backslash (Windows) to separate the names of folders (e.g., Hard drive:Graphics:PostScript:Page1.eps, or c:\Graphics\PostScript\Page1.eps).

APPENDIX E: TROUBLESHOOTING

This appendix contains some tips for using PageMaker efficiently and offers information to help you solve problems on your own. For last-minute information not included in the printed documentation, see the Read Me file installed in the Adobe PageMaker 6.5 folder.

Other ways to access technical information include:

• Visiting the Adobe Systems Home Page (http://www.adobe.com) on the World Wide Web.

• Logging on to Adobe's own bulletin board system. To use the Adobe bulletin board, dial 1-206-623-6984.

• Using forums on CompuServe (GO ADOBEAPP) and America Online (keyword: Adobe). Forums and availability may vary by country.

• Calling Adobe FaxYI, a free fax-on-demand system that can fax you any of over 1,000 technical and customer service documents on PageMaker and other Adobe products. Call 1-206-628-5737 from a touch-tone phone and follow the recorded instructions.

• Requesting technical documents from Adobe by e-mail. All documents available through Adobe FaxYI are also available via e-mail. To receive an index of documents, send e-mail to techdocs@adobe.com with a subject line of 100099.

Also note that the Adobe PageMaker 6.5 CD-ROM includes a folder called Adobe Technical Info which contains helpful materials on a number of topics.

AVOIDING PROBLEMS

This section lists several safe practices you can adopt in order to avoid some of the most commonly-reported difficulties with PageMaker.

• Begin a new project by creating a brand new publication or by opening an untitled copy of a template. If necessary, you can then import paragraph styles or colors from existing publications. Avoid starting a new project by opening an older publication and then renaming it or replacing its content with new material.

• It's safest to divide one large publication into smaller publication files. This practice reduces the likelihood of encountering memory limitations, and helps ensure that PageMaker performs efficiently.

• To minimize file size, regularly use PageMaker's File > Save As command to save files smaller. This technique and related techniques are described on pages 26-27.

• Always save a publication directly to your hard drive. If you need to store the publication on removable media (such as a floppy or Zip disk, or a Syquest or Bernoulli drive), copy or move the file from your hard drive onto the external device rather than saving directly onto removable media. Doing so allows the system to verify the file on the removable media.

• Make back-up copies of your publications regularly. A serious hardware or software problem can force you to recreate work that is not backed up in a safe place.

• Consult with your service provider. They'll recommend appropriate graphic formats, print settings, and other requirements to help your project go smoothly.

• Work with high-quality Type 1 PostScript or TrueType fonts from reputable vendors. Low-quality fonts can lead to printing problems.

TROUBLESHOOTING TIPS

The following tips help to narrow down the cause of a problem so that you can solve the problem on your own, or at least work most efficiently with an Adobe technical support technician if a call is still necessary.

About problems with printing

Since many printing problems are due to imported graphics, try selecting the Proof option in the Print dialog box (this option omits imported graphics). If you can print proofs successfully, then most likely one or more imported graphics are causing the problem. To identify the problem graphic or graphics, try printing specific page ranges until you encounter the printing problem once more. If you determine which graphic causes printing problems, reimport the graphic and print again. If it still doesn't work, see if the graphic prints from its original application. If not, revise the graphic until it prints successfully.

If the PageMaker printing problem is still present after doing a Proof print, then it is possible that a font or text element rather than an imported graphic is causing the disruption.

First, try printing without downloading fonts. To do this, choose File > Print, click Options, and then choose None from the Download Fonts pop-up menu. If you can print successfully, you know that a font on your system is causing the printing problem. Reinstall the font to correct the situation.

If the problem persists, try this procedure:

1 On the first page or two-page spread of the publication, select all text objects, and then choose Element > Non-Printing.

2 Select one text object and again choose Element > Non-printing so that the selected object is the one object to print on the current page or spread.

3 Print the current page or spread to see if the text object prints successfully.

Repeat steps 1-3 with subsequent pages until you find the text object that does not print.

4 If you find a text object that doesn't print, recreate it, and then try printing the page again.

Isolating a problem

Determine whether the problem is specific to a certain computer, a certain application, or a certain publication.

• Can you reproduce the problem on a different computer performing the same task? If not, the problem probably has to do with your computer—the software currently running or memory configuration. It's possible that recently installed software or hardware is conflicting with PageMaker.

• Can you reproduce the problem in a different application doing the same task? If so, the problem isn't specific to any one application.

In either of these two cases, a system conflict might be the problem. Try running Windows 95 in Safe Mode.

• Can you reproduce the problem in a different PageMaker publication doing the same task? If not, the problem is specific to the publication.

A good way to troubleshoot a publication is to recreate it step by step:

1 Choose File > New and create a new publication with the same parameters (margins, columns, pages) as the suspect publication.

2 Copy/paste or drag-and-drop elements from the first page or spread in the suspect publication to the first page or spread in the new publication.

3 As you recreate each page or spread in the new publication, try to reproduce the problem.

4 If you can create all the pages without reproducing the problem, recreate the suspect publication's master pages in the new publication and apply them to pages.

With this method it's often possible to track down the problem in the publication.

Solving problems by running diagnostics on publications

PageMaker includes a built-in diagnostics feature for detecting and correcting inconsistencies in a publication's file structure; the same feature simultaneously recomposes all text in the publication. The corrections PageMaker performs on a publication can solve some problems that interfere with linking, indexing, text formatting, printing, and other tasks.

To run diagnostics on a publication:

1 In a copy of the publication, click the pointer tool.

2 Press Shift + Option (Macintosh) or Shift + Ctrl (Windows) and choose Type > Hyphenation.

3 Listen for the computer system to beep:

• One beep indicates that recomposition was successful and PageMaker found no repairs to make.

• Two beeps indicate that PageMaker repaired one or more minor problems.

• Three beeps indicate that PageMaker found a problem it could not correct, or could not complete the diagnostics due to insufficient memory.

4 Choose File > Save As to rewrite the publication. This ensures that the corrections are stored in the publication.

Before you call technical support

There are several steps you can take before calling technical support to report a problem or to discuss technical issues. Performing these steps can solve many problems and often eliminate the need for telephone assistance.

• Delete the file "PM65.CNF" in the language folder within the PageMaker 6.5 RSRC folder, and restart PageMaker. This starts PageMaker with a fresh set of defaults.

• Use the most current video card and printer driver for your operating system. Your video card and printer manufacturer can provide you with updated drivers.

• Browse the technical documents on the Adobe PageMaker 6.5 CD-ROM. They are stored in the Adobe Technical Info folder.

• Reinstall PageMaker into a new folder.

• Record exact error messages, details, frequency, and note what action was taken immediately before the error message appeared. And note the history of the publication—for example, whether it was converted from a previous version of PageMaker, or translated from the Macintosh platform.

• Call Technical Support from your computer so you can quickly answer questions about the computer and the problem you are having, and so you can try solutions proposed by the Adobe technician.

INDEX